MAKING AMERICANS

MAKING MERICANS

Children's Literature from 1930 to 1960

GARY D. SCHMIDT

UNIVERSITY OF IOWA PRESS *Iowa City*

University of Iowa Press, Iowa City 52242
Copyright © 2013 by the University of Iowa Press
www.uiowapress.org
Printed in the United States of America

Design by Omega Clay

The University of Iowa Press is a member of Green Press Initiative
and is committed to preserving natural resources.

Printed on acid-free paper

Library of Congress Cataloging-in-Publication Data
Schmidt, Gary D.
Making Americans: children's literature from 1930 to 1960 /
by Gary D. Schmidt.
    pages cm
Includes bibliographical references and index.
ISBN 978-1-60938-192-9; 1-60938-192-0 (pbk.)
ISBN 978-1-60938-221-6; 1-60938-221-8 (ebook)
1. Children's literature, American—History and criticism.
2. National characteristics, American, in literature. 3. Democ-
racy in literature. 4. Children's literature—Publishing—United
States—History—20th century. 5. Children—Books and
reading—United States—History—20th century. I. Title.
PS490.S36 2013
810.9'9282—dc23   2013010352

For Conrad and Delores Bult

With gratitude for all you have contributed to this book, and with gratitude for all you have contributed to the college we cherish.

CONTENTS

In the mid-1920s, Olive Beaupré Miller founded a private publishing company called the Book House for Children; it produced, among other items, My Bookhouse—six volumes—and My Travelship—three volumes —ingeniously packaged together in a little wooden house, painted orange and gray, with blue windows and two chimneys. My Travelship collected *Little Pictures of Japan* (1925), *Nursery Friends from France* (1925), and *Tales Told in Holland* (1926); My Bookhouse collected, in order of increasing reading level, *In the Nursery* (1920); *Up One Pair of Stairs* (1920); *Through Fairy Halls* (1920); *The Treasure Chest* (1920); *The Tower Window* (1921); and *The Latch Key* (1921). Sold door to door, the latter set in particular was enormously popular, running through several different editions and eventually dividing into a dozen-volume set in the mid-1930s.

The volumes of My Bookhouse were beautiful, large anthologies of poetry, folklore, myth, history, biography, and story. They were profusely illustrated by some major—as well as minor—contemporary illustrators: Maud and Miska Petersham, who also illustrated *Tales Told in Holland* and *Nursery Friends from France*; Maginel Wright Enright, sister of Frank Lloyd Wright and an illustrator for L. Frank Baum; Donn P. Crane, one of the first American fantasy illustrators, known for his copperplate engravings; Johnny Gruelle, who created Raggedy Ann and Raggedy Andy; Hazel Frazee, known for her illustrations of fairies; Glen Ketchum, a fresco painter; Willy Pogány, whose lush Art Nouveau illustrations graced collections of myths retold by Padraic Colum; Milo Winter, who would be an important illustrator for the lavish editions of Rand McNally's Windermere series; and N. C. Wyeth, whose full-color plate appears on the cover of volume 4 of the My Bookhouse series, *The Treasure Chest*. The plate is of an American frontier trapper.

Wyeth's image is a harbinger of a time when American children's literature would speak of its own national experience. But in the 1920s, American children's literature had yet to leave its European moorings and identify a distinctively American subject matter. Those moorings show in all of the My Bookhouse volumes. *Up One Pair of Stairs* is astonishingly diverse in its stories; it includes tales from or about the Middle East, England, Switzerland, the Philippines, Greece, Finland, Norway, Holland, Brazil, Sweden, Mexico, Portugal, Italy, Germany, East India, China, Japan, Belgium, Romania, Canada, and Russia. But only a handful of tales are American in matter: "Betsy Ross and the First American Flag" (293–97), a mythic tale of Lincoln and a fallen bird (298–99), a selection from Henry Wadsworth Longfellow's *Hiawatha* (431–33), a narrative about Johnny Appleseed (352–56), and a Chippewa tale (355–60) among them. *Through Fairy Halls*—predictably, given its title—has even fewer distinctly American works: Carl Sandburg's "The Fog" (251) and "How Brer Rabbit Met Brer Tar-Baby" (237–41). *The Treasure Chest*—that volume with the N. C. Wyeth cover—has childhood biographies of Robert Fulton (396–401) and David Farragut (354–62), a logging story by Stewart Edward White, and a piece by Theodore Roosevelt on George Rogers Clark (390–95) with an inset identifying Clark as the frontiersman of the cover. In *The Tower Window*, "An Address to New-Made Citizens" by Woodrow Wilson (217) is almost the shortest selection in the volume; it accompanies Israel Zangwill's "The Melting Pot: A Story of True Americanism" (173–216), Washington Irving's "Wolfert Webber, or Golden Dreams" (107–51), and a short extract from John Greenleaf Whittier's "Snowbound" (253–54). But these are dominated by histories of King Alfred (80–89), Robert Bruce (281–89), and Joan of Arc (306–15); extracts from *El Cid* (316–25), *Don Quixote* (90–106), Edmund Spenser's *The Faerie Queene* (12–48), and "The Merrie Doinges of Robin Hood" (49–74); and selections from epics like *Beowulf* (413–22), *The Odyssey* (423–35), the Finnish *Kalevala* (359–72), *Le Chanson de Roland* (300–305), the Norse saga of Frithjof (338–58), and *Le Morte d'Arthur* (327–37).

American children's literature as played out in the My Bookhouse set was still mostly British in nature and, where not British, foreign—defined as exotic and quaint and curious. Of the twenty-four hundred pages of My Bookhouse, perhaps only the two texts by Theodore Roosevelt and Israel Zangwill—neither known as a writer for children—pointed in the direction that children's literature in America would take.

❊ ❊ ❊

In June 1919, Macmillan Publishing—the largest publisher in the United States—appointed Louise Seaman to head its Department of Books for Boys and Girls, established the previous year. Seaman thus became the first children's book editor in the United States to head her own department.

It was a propitious moment. David I. Macleod notes in his *Age of the Child* that even in the late nineteenth century, the notion of a separate literature for children was still judged to be odd. "To an extent unimagined today," Macleod writes, "adults read novels about children. *The Adventures of Huckleberry Finn* (1884), *Little Lord Fauntleroy* (1886), *Rebecca of Sunnybrook Farm* (1903), and *Penrod* (1914) were all best sellers. Conversely, children read or heard books written mainly for adults" (127–30)—say, novels by Dickens, Scott, or Thackeray. But between 1900 and 1920, children's literature was separating from adult literature and expanding its offerings, spurred on by post–World War I wealth: serials, adventure stories, school stories, simplified classics, stories that examined the tensions of growing up—such as *Anne of Green Gables* (1908)—all came into the market. And libraries were recognizing the needs of these young readers: where libraries once banned children below the age of twelve, by 1920 libraries had created children's book rooms. Librarians began to publish lists of books denoting suitability by age; Clara Hunt at the Brooklyn Public Library was writing the popular list *What Shall We Read to Children?*, and that concept of reviewing and listing books was repeated in pamphlets such as *The Book Shelf for Boys and Girls*—published by R. R. Bowker Company—and, later, *Children's Books for General Reading* —published by the American Library Association. Anne Carroll Moore was writing reviews of children's books in the *Bookman*. The year in which Seaman began her editorial career saw the first National Children's Book Week. With what George P. Brett, the president of Macmillan Publishing, noted as "the growing interest in America in children's reading," more publishers were thinking of similarly adding children's book departments to their firms.

Upon taking her position, Louise Seaman immediately noted that half of Macmillan's available backlist was "European": Lewis Carroll, Mrs. Molesworth, Reverend A. J. Church's simplified *The Story of the Iliad* and *The Story of the Odyssey*, Arthur Rackham, Charles Kingsley, Charlotte Yonge, Joseph Jacobs's *Aesop*, Lucy and Walter Crane's *Household Stories by the Brothers Grimm*. A decade later, Bertha E. Mahony, the founder and first editor of the review journal *Horn Book*, lamented that before 1920, "the height of our expectations lay with the coming of an attractive new edition of a favorite or classic book, usually an importation from England. . . . Our pitifully small list of picture books remained the same year after year with no addition to the masters' group occupied by Crane,

Caldecott, Kate Greenaway and Leslie Brooke." Seaman did not disdain this list, but she determined that the books on her list "should reflect both the past and the world of today in new ways." Seaman set out to develop an American children's literature not to supplant but to go along with her European "classics"; she would do this by acquiring American authors.[1] In her fifteen-year tenure at Macmillan she published over five hundred children's books, increasing the size of the children's catalog from thirty to eighty pages. But it was her American authors who shone: she would publish three of the first Newbery Honor books named at the inception of the award—*The Old Tobacco Shop: A True Account of What Befell a Little Boy in Search of Adventure* by William Bowen (1921), *The Golden Fleece and the Heroes Who Lived before Achilles* by Padraic Colum (1921), and *Windy Hill* by Cornelia Meigs (1921)—and enjoy a run of consecutive Newbery Award–winning novels: *The Trumpeter of Krakow* by Eric P. Kelly (1928), *Hitty: Her First Hundred Years* by Rachel Field (1929), and *The Cat Who Went to Heaven* by Elizabeth Coatsworth (1930). She would also publish the first photographic documentary for children—Lewis W. Hine's *Men at Work* (1932)—and *Popo and Fifina* by Arna Bontemps and Langston Hughes (1932), the first children's book written and illustrated by African Americans published by a major house.

Though a change in management would eventually force her out of this position, Seaman was a model for the editors who would follow her: May Massee, hired in 1922 as the editor of the newly formed children's book department at Doubleday and a decade later the first children's editor at Viking Press; Marion Fiery, hired in 1925 at E. P. Dutton's new children's department; Bertha Gunterman, hired at Longmans, Green in 1925; Helen Dean Fish, hired at Frederick Stokes in 1922; Virginia Kirkus, hired in 1926 at Harper's; Lucile Gulliver, hired in May 1927 at Little, Brown; Katharine Ulrich, hired at the formation of Coward, McCann and publishing her first books in the fall of 1928; and Alice Dagliesh at Scribner's, who would announce that the contemporary world "is full of interesting, real things, and there is no time for sugary little fairy tales of the type that used to be published by the dozen." Meanwhile Seaman would go on to become the associate editor of *Horn Book* (from 1939 through 1957) and also editor of the column Books for Young People at the *New York Herald Tribune* (from 1948 through 1956), signaling several of the positions that would be occupied by what Leonard Marcus has called the "minders" in his *Minders of Make-Believe: Idealists, Entrepreneurs, and the Shaping of American Children's Literature* (2008) and that Jacalyn Eddy has called "bookwomen" in the most thorough study of the women who developed the professional field of children's literature: *Bookwomen: Cre-*

ating an Empire in Children's Book Publishing, 1919–1939 (2006). These minders and bookwomen and the education, library, bookselling, and publishing establishments with whom they worked would be critically important for the future direction of children's books in America.[2]

Indeed, Seaman's hiring was the beginning of a boom decade for American children's books; the publishing establishment, teachers, administrators, trained librarians, expert editors, reviewers with prominent pulpits, professional societies and awards, national book promotions—all contributed. And it wasn't long before Dagliesh's desire for new subject matter for children's books was commonly accepted. In the spring of 1930, for example, H. D. Roberts, the assistant editor of the *English Journal*, declared confidently that truly progressive schools would free children to read "the literature of today": "The ghosts of the older classics still move among us, but the sturdy push of the contemporary reduces their pale ranks in every anthology and course of study that issues from the presses. Soon only those ancients 'stuck fast in yesterday' and the ever present Philistines will prescribe forced reading in a dead culture." Roberts was naive; the classics would not disappear in the face of the contemporary. But the tonality of his argument suggests a gleeful belief that young American readers were about to enter a world that would banish "the ghosts of the older classics" in favor of new texts that spoke to the experience, needs, and interests of the modern American child.

The unity of the publishing establishment with education and library and bookselling establishments suggests a coherency of purpose, and indeed, the members of these establishments worked together with remarkable consistency, particularly in their sense of what was both appropriate and essential for a child audience. Anne Carroll Moore, librarian, literary critic, director of the New York Public Library's Office of Work with Children, and a powerful determiner of the fate of any children's book published in America, believed that educators and librarians had the authority and obligation to speak to issues of appropriateness—and so she expressed herself forcefully in her *Bookman* column, her Three Owls column in the *New York Herald Tribune*, and her *Roads to Childhood* (1920). The publishing establishment, teachers, reviewers, librarians, and parents all had a stake in a children's literature that formed the young mind, she argued; for Moore, writes Jacalyn Eddy, children's books "represented a code for discussing an entire constellation of behaviors and institutions, the litmus test of responsibility and intelligence, reliable barometers of both public *and* private matters. By them, the nation would be prevented from sinking into selfish materialism, thus preserving family and civic life" (90). And how were they to do this? Anne Scott Mac-

Leod writes that though the bookwomen like Moore rejected the open didacticism of moral books of the last century, they believed that children's books were to impart moral and social values: "The community of adults engaged in bringing children and literature together endorsed, apparently without much real dissension, an implicit code of values which was observed virtually unbroken in thousands of children's books published between 1900 and 1965" (179). This code of values was generally defined negatively: no serious violence, no incapacitating emotional or mental problems, no sexuality, no divorce, no rape, no prostitution, no suicide, no alcoholism.

But the bookwomen were also asking what that code of values would look like if it was defined positively. And how might they work at defining a distinctively American form of children's literature? If Maria Nikolajeva is right in her claim that a national literature is defined not only through its language but also through its depiction of the nation's "tradition and cultural values" and its "national mentality" (21), what traditions, what values, what aspects of the national mentality would be foregrounded in America's children's books?

Twenty years after the My Bookhouse volumes, Maud and Miska Petersham, who had done many of the illustrations for Olive Beaupré Miller, wrote and illustrated a very different volume: *An American ABC* (1941), published three months before the American entrance into World War II. A confident, self-assured text, it begins with an illustration of the Western Hemisphere, with the sun, moon, and stars watching over all; the text for this cosmic image reads inclusively, "This is America." Confident, indeed.

In the opening illustration, the Petershams wished to set both tone and matter: "A is for AMERICA / The land I love," they write. Over a sleeping boy, a huge bald eagle stares fiercely off the page, his wings spread high in front of red and white stripes. The eagle's protective position over the boy affirms that all the might of America stands ready to protect and nurture this young child. The final illustration—"Z is for Zeal / An American trait"—reprises the eagle and the boy, though this time he is awake and, hand in hand with a young girl, walking eagerly forward. Above them the eagle flies, its wings now fully outstretched, still protecting the boy, who marches off zealously to take up his own role as an American. "It was zeal which made navigators of old voyage over dangerous seas and find this New World," the Petershams write. And "it is this same zeal that will keep America a great land and a land of liberty and freedom."

There is nothing like these illustrations in My Bookhouse, nothing like this intense patriotism, this sense of children participating eagerly in American citizenship, this image of American power and dominance enacted as a promise for the protection of the American child. And this bravado is played out on every page of *An American ABC*. "P is for PLEDGE OF ALLEGIANCE / The salute to our flag," and the Petershams note that this pledge "is the promise of loyalty to our country which is in the heart of every true American." The illustration shows three young boys, each from a different period in American history, holding a flag overhead. "F is for FREEDOM / That precious thing for which America stands," and the Petershams conclude that "today it is the will of every American to keep our country the Land of the Free." "B is for BELL / Our Liberty Bell," and the Petershams write that even today, the Liberty Bell is "honored and loved" and "reminds us of our good fortune." Each entry bears the confident sense both of America's foundation in principles of freedom and liberty and of the continuing necessity for each citizen—including each child—to be loyal and to work diligently for the preservation of the nation's freedom.

There are, as well, the expected models, who are almost always denoted by a distinctive courage that enabled them to settle and build America. "D is for DANIEL BOONE," who is among "the bravest and strongest of the white men" to enter the American wilderness and who is to be honored because he "helped to make this country grow." "G is for GEORGE WASHINGTON," who is "one of the greatest of the men who worked for America's freedom." The Pilgrims faced incredible hardship, but "their spirit was never broken, and the courage and faith of those Pilgrims helped to build our country." The men at Valley Forge "had great courage and valor" as they fought for independence, and "it was the valor of men like these at Valley Forge that won freedom for America." The illustration includes a young boy who is participating in the suffering and commitment of the adult soldiers.

This confident vision of America and of the child's stake in that vision might be expected in a work coming just before America's entrance into World War II, but the book also complicates the narrative of America. "E is for Emigrants," write the Petershams. "Many were unhappy in their own countries and came here to escape ways of living which had been forced upon them. They left their homes in the Old World and came to find homes in the New. They came to America because this country stood for Freedom." In fact, the Petershams assert, "our great-great-grandfa-thers, our grandfathers, even perhaps our fathers, were all emigrants to America." And, they note, this wave of emigrants has not ended: "People from all over the world are still coming to our shores. Good emigrants make true Americans"—though the Petershams leave undefined what a "good" emigrant would be, as they have left undefined what a "true American" would be. It is assumed that the reader would know instinc-tively. But at the beginning of the war, a time when ethnic loyalties were suspect, the Petershams were arguing that America is in its essence a land of diverse immigrants.

The place of the Other within American society was, of course, not a tame topic, and aside from the progressive position on immigrants, *An American ABC* seems unaware of larger issues of civil rights. In her *Sus-pended Animation: Children's Picture Books and the Fairy Tale of Modernity* (2010), Nathalie op de Beeck complains that the Petershams go about "erasing or essentializing people of color," and certainly it does seem that this is true (204). The book includes only one African American figure, who is stereotyped. In the illustration for George Washington, a thick-lipped boy watches in exaggerated astonishment as young George gleefully rides a stallion bareback; the boy—presumably Washington's slave—sits on a rail fence, holding the horse's unused halter and guarding Washington's rich clothing. Native Americans too are stereotyped and designated as "Other" through the fact of their nudity. And as with the depiction of Washington's slave, there seems to be a blithe acceptance of this designation. There is no suggestion in any of the entries of con-cern for the survival of the Native American culture. Native Americans are always pictured in friendly relations with Europeans or in innocuous relationships with white children—an adult Native American handing an eel to a white boy (linked to the Native American adult through his similar nudity), or two white children handing a bowl of food to a (once again, almost nude) adolescent Native American boy. But—and this is critical—the Petershams do take up the question of Otherness: although Native Americans enter the book under "R is for REDSKIN," the second line of the heading suggests the Petershams' wider vision: "The first real Americans." They write that "long before the coming of the white men, tribes of redskins with their families were living in America. Their land was taken from them as more and more white men settled here. Many of the tribes were hostile, but there were friendly Indians too." If the text is ambiguously toned (and it is), and if, as op de Beeck claims, the illustra-tions of Native Americans represent a "superficially inclusive story [that] verbally and visually marginalizes Native Americans in [America's] national origin myth" (and they do), at least the Petershams are suggesting overtly to a child audience that dealing with "Otherness" in America is neither simple nor easy—something that Olive Beaupré Miller would never have suggested. And in this, their work is representative of American children's literature at midcentury.

An American ABC celebrates American origin myths, but it also asks complex questions about America. Who is the "true" American? Who is the "real" American? Is it the descendant of the white settlers who fought for freedom? Is it the "good" emigrant who comes in search of freedom? Is it the Native American whose land has been taken and resettled? What role does the African American play in this? And what does it mean to say that every American wants to keep America free? Or to say that loyalty to America lies "in the heart of every true American"? How does that fight for freedom, that loyalty of the heart, look in the real world? How does it look to those who need to be defined from outside as "good" before they can "make true Americans"? And especially, how does American freedom and loyalty look to a child?

In the twenty years that separate My Bookhouse from *An American ABC*, children's literature in America had finally begun to do what Emerson had called upon American letters to do almost exactly a century earlier: "Perhaps the time is already come, when [American letters] ought to be, and will be something else; when the sluggard intellect of this continent will look from under its iron lids and fill the postponed expectation of the world with something better than the exertions of mechanical skill. Our day of dependence, our long apprenticeship to the learning of other lands, draws to a close." And thus begins the American Renaissance. But children's books had remained in their long apprenticeship, though, as Anne Scott MacLeod has chronicled, there was a desire for a distinctly American children's literature at the same time that Emerson made his call. She notes, for example, the nineteenth-century children's book writer William Cardell's claim that "foreign books . . . are not to be proscribed, but it is absurd that they should be made, among our children, the main standard of feeling and thought." But Cardell was not as radical as Emerson; he was not calling for distinctive American meanings; in fact, he still affirmed what was held true in both Europe and America: that, as MacLeod notes, the purpose of children's literature was the creation of texts whose abstract moral qualities—kindness, decency, obedience, temperance, spiritual piety—would function as models for the young citizen of the republic, models that would propel that child toward an adulthood defined by a sense of public morality. And Cardell was not calling for American books for children to be anchored in the physical landscape of the country or to evoke a particular vision of the culture or mentality of America. MacLeod notes that early American children's books had few details to connect the stories to an American setting and concludes that "most stories were played out against backgrounds almost abstract in their generality." Instead, Cardell was simply calling for children's books written by Americans. As Louise Seaman would.[3]

Despite *The Adventures of Tom Sawyer* and *Little Women*, that anchoring would still not be in place when Louise Seaman sat down to her desk at Macmillan. Children's literature in its form and matter had remained principally British and Continental. It had yet to become, as Seaman hoped, in any way distinctly American. And though the field of American children's literature would quickly complicate and outpace what Seaman meant by a distinctly American children's literature, for Seaman, an American children's literature was defined by two things—though those two seem in conflict. First, it meant a strengthening of her stable of American writers. In her list of books to be published in the fall of 1928, she included Vachel Lindsay's *Johnny Appleseed and Other Poems*; Cornelia Meigs's *The Wonderful Locomotive*, with illustrations by Berta and Elmer Hader; and Holling Clancy Holling's *Rocky Billy*. Her second, seemingly contradictory meaning was a globalizing of American children's book publishing through the incorporation of international authors and illustrators. This globalizing would enable American children's books to compete internationally, a thrust that came out of her belief that European publishers (particularly German and French publishers) were printing finer books for children than anything being done in America. Thus, the same catalog cites *East of the Sun and West of the Moon*, illustrated by Hedvig Collin, a Danish artist; René Bazin's *Juniper Farm* and Odette Larrieu's *The Story of Reynard the Fox*, both French artists; Einar Nerman's version of Hans Christian Andersen's *Thumbelina*, Nerman being a popular Swedish artist; and two books set in ancient Egypt, Alice Woodbury Howard's *Sokar and the Crocodile* and Winthrop Palmer's *Abdul: The Story of an Egyptian Boy*, the catalog noting that Palmer had been living in Egypt. The notion of an Americanized children's literature that was distinctly American in its forms and matter and even geography was beginning to be noised in places such as *Horn Book*, but Seaman was more attuned to creating an American children's literature by focusing on her stable of artists and their international credentials, not necessarily on the matter of the books.

Seaman was supported in this global interest by Anne Carroll Moore, who believed that American children's books should take their place in a global tradition not only to compete with the higher quality of European picture books but also to impart an international awareness to children. In fact, Moore chided publishers who safely printed "remnants of history and poorly drawn portraits of very dead heroes and heroines, and then have wondered why so few children or grown people seem to be interested in other countries or races" (*Roads to Childhood*, 74). In this, both Seaman and Moore were rejecting the intense isolationist nationalism the country embraced after World War I; this side of their vision for an American children's literature would grow stronger and stronger over the next thirty years.

But that other thrust—that American children's literature would become American by adding more American writers to a publisher's list—was soon seen as an inadequate way of understanding the Americanness of a book. There needed to be something more, and between 1919 and 1960, defining the nature of American children's literature would become a major project among the "minders" and artists of the field. To that end, publishers of American children's literature would shift its subject matter away from Europe and to the physical landscape of America, and they would refine its emphasis on a spiritual morality leading to public virtue into a personal response to the contemporary social culture of America. Thus a large purpose of children's literature in the mid-twentieth century would be to define what America meant, what democracy in America meant, and what being an American meant for a child of the twentieth century. The question was, How might a coherent set of social values set in the physical terrain of the nation look as it came into works for children?

In 1932—three years into a depression that gave good reason to wonder about the success of the American experiment—the Children's Book Council selected a poster by Walter Cole that pointed in the directions that children's literature in America would take over the next three decades. The poster was to highlight National Children's Book Week, and while most of the posters since the 1919 inception of the Book Week celebration had simply pictured children reading books—the first two posters, both by Jessie Wilcox Smith, had each incorporated a young boy and girl engrossed in books, with open volumes spread around them—Cole decided to make a statement not just about reading but about American children's reading. He entitled his poster "Young America's Book Parade" and set out to stir patriotism with what the *Wilson Library Bulletin* called the poster's "American Theme."[4]

Once again, a boy and a girl sit with open volumes; however, here the background is not a set of shelves carrying still more volumes, as in earlier posters. Instead, the background shows the viewer what has captured the imagination of these young readers. A parade of American figures walks toward them: pioneers heading west in front of a Conestoga wagon, New England fishermen, Puritan settlers, a dignified Native American chieftain, a buckskin-clad explorer, a lumberjack with an axe over his shoulder, a welder representing American industry, a deep-sea diver representing exploration, a pilot. And as these American figures approach the two children, they dissolve as if their stories of industry and fortitude are being inculcated into the young readers. Reading, the poster suggests, is a way of coming into an awareness of and participating in the life of America; it is a means of taking in what is strong and good about the country. And what is strong and good about the country is suggested in the poster: its pioneering spirit—manifested both in the earliest days of settlement and now in reaching toward new frontiers of discovery—and its sense of democratic equality, in which all figures—regardless of race, ethnicity, social status, or religion—march side by side toward the children whose lives they will impact.

Four years after Cole's poster, in the summer of 1936, Bertha Mahony wrote a reflective article on the relationship between children's books, values, and America for *Horn Book* titled "Children's Books in America Today." She noted that "human affairs are bewildering" and that "everywhere we look in vain for a true sense of values." But, she wrote, that true sense of values might be found in children's books, a stream "unique in this country," and—reaching for the hyperbolic metaphor—"because of its genius and sound values, this stream is like a crystal-clear mountain brook." She attributed the brook's clarity first to "the nature of America itself," which is best seen in the country's pioneer heritage as represented in both the movement westward and the flow of immigrants, each contributing to "the rich, multi-colored strand which is the atmosphere and life of America," and second to the democratic ideals of the nation, inculcated in such institutions as the children's book room of the public library, where "one finds respect for an appreciation of all races; genuine tolerance of varying points of view, unfailing and deeply imaginative kindness; all the sensitive appreciation of genius, what it means, how it works and how often it grows out of hardship, loneliness, and suffering." Mahony was remarkably close to Walter Cole's National Children's Book Week poster. She was invoking two huge elements: the history of the pioneer and the immigrant in forming American culture and providing a mythic understanding of a national spirit that has infused, among other things, the arts; and the democratic quality of a tolerant, understanding American society that showed itself through the arts—specifically, art for the child audience made available through the civilizing and educational agency of the public library. Seth Lerer argues—with Mahony—that public libraries of the first quarter of the twentieth century socialized children into democracy: "Libraries made *citizens*. They offered amenities designed to teach children how to read and how to behave: to be quiet, respectful, thoughtful, and literate." Even the system of overdue fines was "designed not merely to pay for library upkeep, but to instill a sense of discipline and economic responsibility in the young citizen" (276). In children's books and the institutions that housed them, Mahony and Cole saw an understanding of the ways in which children's literature in the mid-twentieth century could picture and even inform the American experience, teaching and reinforcing social qualities rather than narrowly moral or religious qualities of earlier children's books.[5]

As H. D. Roberts looked for "the literature of today" for contemporary American children, he might have seen clues to its nature in these two works by Cole and Mahony. Midcentury children's literature would simultaneously posit America as pioneer nation and America as democratic experiment, the first a story of rugged independence and self-reliance, the second a story of interdependencies, social tolerance, and cooperation. America would be envisioned as a dangerous but exciting wilderness and as the place of a newly settled life; as a nation of individual freedom and as a nation of democracy; as a myriad of regional cultures and as a country marked by tolerance and acceptance. And unlike Seaman's original vision, by midcentury a distinctly American children's literature was often the story of America itself, and often the story into which child readers were engrafted, usually through an assumed identification with a national culture. It was as if the child reader needed to recognize that an American narrative was a story that involved the reader as a citizen and that citizenship mattered, and was intimate and powerful, and needed to be perceived if the reader could hope to understand the power and impact and even the tonalities of the narrative. One read, much of children's literature insisted during the midcentury, as an American.

✳ ✳ ✳

But how a children's book represents its culture is a fraught question. It is certainly tempting to see a literary text as a mirror that accurately reflects the temper of the cultural moment in which it was produced; as Nathalie op de Beeck argues, children's books are not "timeless" nor "outside time in their representation of the past and anticipation of the future" (xv). Frances Henne, of the School of Library Service at Columbia University, in an essay titled "American Society as Reflected in Children's Literature," agrees that a book for a young reader reflects immediate societal issues that involve children and young adults: "Moralistic, ethical, and behavioral values . . . in children's literature give evidence of many aspects of society and the changes that have occurred over the years: existing social problems; dangers and temptations facing youth; developmental values for youth; prevailing attitudes toward other countries and toward minority or ethnic groups." Gail Schmunk Murray, in her *American Children's Literature and the Construction of Childhood* (1998), is also willing to travel down this road a ways: "Children's literature provides insights into the social milieu in which the work was developed and uncovers the values that society hopes to transmit to its children." And Dennis Butts narrows this observation, arguing that "the interests, concerns and values of [a] society's dominant class pervaded its literature, including its children's books" (x–xi), and that even specific genres can be viewed as a response to specific societal issues, the English "adventure story," he claims, thus being a response to issues of British imperialism.

But—and here lies the fraughtness—Murray also observes that "children's books often tell us much more about the image of the ideal child that society would like to produce than they do about real children" (xv). That is, if children's books are mirrors meant to reflect society and its understandings of the child, then those mirrors are trained very purposefully and intentionally and perhaps are distorted just as purposefully and intentionally; children's literature is not simple mimesis. In her essay "Children's Books and Social History," Gillian Avery affirms and complicates Murray's claim: she warns that meanings in works of children's literature are tied closely to the ways in which adults perceive their own childhoods, their own sense of what children need, and their own social contexts: "The heroes of the children's story of any given time show the qualities that elders have considered desirable, attractive, or interesting in the young. Sometimes they have wanted the obedient, diligent miniature adult, sometimes the evangelical child, or perhaps they have had a penchant for sprightly mischief, or sought to inculcate self-knowledge and independence." In terms of this kind of complex reflection, Karín Lesnik-Oberstein distinguishes between the essentialist and constructivist points of view, the first suggesting that children may be defined "as trans-historically and trans-culturally consistent beings, shaped primarily in a deterministic way by biology and brain-development," while the second suggests that each culture creates its own sense of the identity of the child, leading to children's books that reflect what the adult artists and publishing establishment would want to say about a child. This second is most famously championed in Jacqueline Rose's *The Case of Peter Pan, or the Impossibility of Children's Fiction* (1984), where Rose argues that the notion of the child is a social construction that varies with cultural and historical contexts. "Most likely, the idea of speaking to all children serves to close off a set of cultural divisions," she writes, "divisions in which not only children, but we ourselves, are necessarily caught . . . class, culture, and literacy—divisions which undermine any generalized concept of the child" (7). Anne Scott MacLeod sums up the fraughtness: "Writing for children, adults bring to bear their own experience of childhood, their ideas of what childhood is or ought to be, their commitment to the conventions of their own time, and their concerns for their own society's problems and progress. . . . [Writers for children] often tell children the truth, but it is seldom the whole truth" (*American Childhood*, vii–viii).[6]

If any writer can indeed tell the whole truth, it is certainly true that a writer for children will bring to bear his or her own sense of what is appropriate for a child audience in terms of the writer's beliefs about what a child may comprehend, what is appropriate to a given age, and even what is needed in the cultural setting of the child reader. In *The Hidden Adult: Defining Children's Literature* (2008), Perry Nodelman goes so far as to argue that children's books "possess a shadow, an unconscious—a more complex and more complete understanding of the world and people that remains unspoken beyond the simple surface but provides that simple surface with its comprehensibility." In that shadow, Nodelman asserts, is the hidden adult with his or her own meanings: "What texts of children's literature might be understood to sublimate or keep present but leave unsaid is a variety of forms of knowledge—sexual, cultural, historical—theoretically only available to and only understandable by adults. . . . [S]o children's literature can be understood as simple literature that communicates by means of reference to a complex repertoire of unspoken but implied adult knowledge" (206). Joseph Zornado problematizes this relationship between children's text and adult authority even further: "Children's literature is a part of a montage of adult cultural practices that [reproduce] unconscious relational practices bent on exercising and justifying adult power over the child" (xviii). So. But for the writers of mid-century, this balance between a simple text for children and the adult consciousness with its authority and power and large contextual knowledge would hardly have been an issue at all. While these complications may be seen as challenges even to the possibility of children's literature in recent decades, before 1960 they were strongly in place, an affirmed, even axiomatic, part of the definition of children's literature.

What the history of children's books of midcentury America shows again and again is that children's books reflected the socially progressive nature of their writers, publishers, editors, reviewers, and librarians and that this reflection was deliberate and virtually unchallenged. MacLeod argues that children's books are not histories meant to document social changes and developments, but the "shifts in cultural attitudes are there, recorded in the indirect way in which children's literature always documents its time and expressed in the values the books held out to young readers" (*American Childhood*, 157). But in midcentury America, many books for children were hardly "indirect"; they were clear and unsubtle expressions about the meaning of America and the role of the child as a citizen. These books did not want to reflect a culture only; they wanted to inculcate a complex vision of culture. Thus they would show an America that was to be extolled and an America that was deeply flawed, and in doing so, the artists and "minders" created a literature that showed a concern about society's problems, that accepted the old American assumption that the child did have a responsibility to the republic, that argued that artists and those who supported and disseminated their work to children had a responsibility to young citizens to depict America as it was and to challenge their young readers to engage in their country's progress. Thus much of American children's literature at the middle of the twentieth century was more John Steinbeck than Horatio Alger, and more Dorothea Lange than Pollyanna, and more Lynd Ward than the Five Little Peppers—all mediated through a sensibility of appropriateness and purpose within the larger social context of America.

In *Original Subjects: The Child, the Novel, and the Nation* (2001), Ala A. Alryyes recounts the anecdote of the newcomer who arrives in Washington, D.C., for the first time and marvels at the monuments that evoke a powerful golden past of American goodness, strength, wisdom, and fortitude. "This persuasion of civic freedom as an inheritance, emphasizing the continuity of old and new liberty," Alryyes writes, "resonates with a strong current of American national identity, which identifies being American with being free, linking this very liberty to an ahistorical mythologizing of the Founding Fathers' inaugural acts" (24). The response of more sophisticated, knowing viewers of the city to the newcomer is mixed: there is scorn and derision for such simple naïveté, but there is also a less conscious yearning for a time when the more sophisticated viewer could herself still believe in a golden America of the past, when the "inaugural acts" of the Founding Fathers did indeed codify the right to natural liberty among a democratic citizenry. In the mid-twentieth century, those fashioning books for children steered a middle course between these responses to America. America would indeed be presented mythically, with a golden history that glowed with words like "freedom," "liberty," and "democracy"; this would be particularly apparent in those books that spoke of America's pioneer heritage. But in addition, children's books would speak of a movement away from a naive belief in America as a utopia; there would not be the disdain of which Alryyes writes, but there would be a conscious desire to realistically present an America that had significant and urgent problems with which its citizenry—even its child citizenry—had to wrestle.

Thus it would be a complex America that was depicted. Julia Mickenberg has shown in her study of children's books of the 1950s—*Learning from the Left: Children's Literature, the Cold War, and Radical Politics in the United States* (2006)—and in her edited work with Philip Nel—*Tales for Little Rebels: A Collection of Radical Children's Literature* (2008)— that many radically leftist writers and illustrators came into the field at midcentury and had to negotiate the publishing and education and librarian establishments as they addressed social issues in a progressive manner. In *Learning from the Left* she notes, however, that the audience seemed ready: "As children who 'ducked and covered' became increasingly mistrustful of adults who said this activity would make them safe, they found in children's books further evidence that authority was often arbitrary and unjust and that critical, independent thought and activism were fundamental to good citizenship" (144).

But in fact, these radical writers and illustrators of midcentury had little to negotiate, finding a body of educators, librarians, and publishers in the field of children's books who were overwhelmingly socially progressive. These were the "bookwomen" who had been breaking down employment barriers in publishing (ten years after Seaman's hiring, thirty publishers had children's book departments run by women), who had been opening children's book rooms to the poorest citizens, who used story hours to train children in social behaviors, who brought books to hospitals and schools and Boy Scout meetings, who were participating in the Women's Educational and Industrial Union (the union that founded Boston's Bookshop for Boys and Girls in 1924, the store that led to the establishment of *Horn Book*), who were arguing for books that showcased tolerance and diversity and racial understanding, who were (like Anne Carroll Moore and Bertha Mahony) arguing that books provided global awareness and worked toward establishing a "unified conscience and unified consciousness."[7] The concerns that American writers and illustrators of children's literature began to raise as early as the 1930s—concerns about the treatment of the immigrant, the place of the "Other" in society, issues of racism, issues of pacifism and violence, issues of the just war, issues of progress and modernization—would be handled implicitly and explicitly not only in the radical presses that Mickenberg documents so fully but also in mainstream presses publishing for children. Here would be played out attempts to define the nature of the American experiment in democracy. Here would be debated the strategies of "tolerance" versus "acceptance." Here would be imagined the role of the common citizen in shaping national affairs. Here would be examined the desperate need for civil rights. Here would be vocalized America's role in global affairs. All here, as American children's literature found its voice and matter and as its "minders" asserted that if society was to evolve toward a larger understanding of how American democracy should look at home and abroad, then what better place to implant and nurture such ideas in the younger generation than in the books they took up?

Cultural critics of midcentury American children's literature have argued that though many of these books dealt with disturbing realities in American culture, they handled those realities in ways that affirmed, if not an ideal world, a world of certainty and security. In "Children's Literature in America, 1870–1945," Gillian Avery writes that "American children's books, and their counterparts in Britain, responded only obliquely to the social and political events of a period that saw the Great Depression, the Wall Street crash, the 'Roaring 20s,' the New Deal, and Sinclair Lewis' attack on Middle American values in *Main Street* (1920)" (241–42). Nathalie op de Beeck concurs: early twentieth-century books for children "acknowledge cultural anxieties by buttressing ideals, and their superficial sunniness belies socioeconomic events." These books, she writes, preserve a past "first by making it available in commodity form, and next by ensconcing a culturally approved version of history in children's collective memories" (*Suspended Animation*, 10). This was certainly often the case. Boys in midcentury children's books like Robert McCloskey's Homer Price or Oliver Butterworth's Nate Twitchell live in small towns or on farms and aren't concerned about World War II or Cold War perils. But it is the contention of this study that one large purpose of children's literature at midcentury was to "acknowledge cultural anxieties" quite directly and to posit a vision of America that was meant as a corrective to those anxieties.

In the foreword to his *Minders of Make-Believe*, Leonard Marcus notes his fascination with "children's books as messages passed down between generations—messages forged at the crossroads of commerce and culture" (xi). He goes on to take up the road of commerce, as Mickenberg takes up the road of culture. This study takes up the receptivity of the "messages passed down between generations" from 1919 through 1960—though of course all three works must speak to all three elements. Our interest here lies in the messages that described America and the responsibilities of citizenship to the children of the generation that would live with the atomic bomb, that would be divided by the Berlin Wall and the Iron Curtain, that would grow up to usher in civil rights, to work toward women's rights, to protest wars in Vietnam and Cambodia, to lose a naive trust in government, to perceive the limitations of the "melting pot" metaphor, to explore the boundaries of freedom, and to raise a new generation that would ask harder questions about America's global influences than had ever been imagined. But these are conceptions and questions nonetheless seeded by earlier debates around tables in the quiet libraries and publishing offices of midcentury America—debates that began with questions about what America itself was.

The story of American children's literature at midcentury is the story of its growing depiction of the meaning of democracy; it is this growth that the present study charts. Louise Seaman's dual thrust—the use of more American authors as well as more international authors—would change a great deal from 1919 to 1960; the "minders" of children's literature would shift those thrusts to an emphasis on America itself and, later, to a commitment to what would be called "One World." In other words, the field would define "American democracy" more and more largely; its definition of democracy as a fair and just social condition in which every participant has a voice and a stake would expand in its sense of inclusiveness. Over the decades of the mid-twentieth century that expansion would begin by pairing the Emersonian self-reliance of the pioneers with an understanding of that experience as one of social cooperation and community. In the 1930s that expansion would be enlarged by the inclusion of immigrants and then, during the war years, a growing inclusion of minorities and their roles within America's democracy. In the 1950s the expansion would lead to an understanding of the country as one player in a large global community. And in each of these expansions, a case would be made that the child reader had a stake in this democratic experience; the expansion included the child, too.

Thus children's books at midcentury used America itself as a complex metaphor for the progressive notion of social inclusion. It was a conscious and decided position on the part of the artists and the "minders," informing the largest purposes of children's books published between 1919 and 1960.

PART ONE

Defining America as the Pioneer Nation

1930 — 1940

1   Imagining the American Democracy

Self-Reliance and Social Cooperation

In his study *Huck's Raft: A History of American Childhood* (2004), Steven Mintz describes the effects of the Great Depression on American families, which faced an unprecedented collapse. By the end of the Depression, 14 percent unemployment was common; in some cities, unemployment was over 50 percent. Average income was halved as jobs disappeared or became part-time. Homes that had seemed absolutely secure fell to banks as savings accounts disappeared and mortgages went unpaid. The accompanying stress brought family disintegration; as desertion increased, children were placed in custodial institutions or took to the rails—a quarter million children became drifters. Economic failure led to the diminished stature of fathers, and though mothers entered the workforce for some income, their hours were long and their pay was low. Jobs traditionally belonging to older children disappeared as adults took them up; the result was increasing high school enrollment and a new class that would eventually be called "teenagers." Yet still, in 1938 half of high school graduates could find no work. Lacking funds, many schools closed or shortened their school years, while the movement of children whose families were seeking a job disrupted educational opportunities. Mintz concludes: "For many children, the Depression meant a declining standard of living, heightened family tension, inconsistent parental discipline, and an unemployed father. Many children experienced severe psychological stress, insecurity, deprivation, and intense feelings of shame. Parents became more irritable, marital conflict increased, and parents disciplined their children more arbitrarily. The impact of family conflict may have been worst for young children, since they were not insulated by the buffer of peers or jobs outside the home" (237). How should America respond? The commercial culture, Mintz argues, decided to entertain the young. Thus were born the comic book, the child-centered film revolving around the Little Rascals or the Dead End Kids, and the teenage star—Mickey Rooney, Judy Garland.[1]

But this was not the direction children's book publishers would take. Sally Allen McNall has called the children's literature of this time "a democratization of experience," a realism focused on the stuff of immediate life. Alfred Habegger suggests that American realism of the period depicts democratic action, "the primacy of what ordinary people, living under recognizable pressures, try to do" (111). Children's artists of the period and the "minders" affirmed this approach, but the gritty realism of the contemporary American experience would often—not always—be considerably tempered by the romantic vision of the American pioneer experience. The pioneer books offered a heightened vision of that experience, suggesting to families in despair an alternate way of life that was part of their own heritage. These books showed the young reader an America defined by both individual resourcefulness and communal awareness and connectivity.

During the 1930s American children's literature linked the pioneer experience and the democratic experiment together again and again. That same 1936 issue of *Horn Book* in which Bertha Mahony had written "Children's Books in America Today" carried the Newbery Award acceptance speech of Carol Ryrie Brink for *Caddie Woodlawn* (1935), in which Brink identified the pioneer experience as a particularly American event whose potency and meanings needed to be passed on to later generations who were not themselves pioneers but who, through the arts, could participate in the experience vicariously. "The blood of these pioneers still flows in the veins of our children," Brink argued, and although the problems children of the Great Depression faced were distinct from those the pioneers faced, still, "the pioneer qualities of courage, willingness to go to meet the unknown, and steadfastness under difficulties are the things most needed today, as they were then." Here again is Bertha Mahony's sense of values flowing within the clear mountain brook; in children's books, America could produce value-laden stories about its own heritage so that the stories of the American experience—particularly the pioneering experience—could pass on the qualities necessary for young Americans to grow into the kind of citizens who might face the difficulties of the contemporary world.

The linking of the pioneer spirit and American democracy took this form: On the one hand, the pioneer experience expressed self-reliance and independence. The virtues are those of resolution, hard work, close connection to the spacious land, an established home and family, individual resourcefulness, and the independence which that resourcefulness makes possible. On the other hand, the pioneer stories also valued and celebrated the virtues of democracy and the community which that democracy makes possible. It is the common citizen who is celebrated, and to that citizen's independence is added social cooperation; to individual resourcefulness is added a dependence on community and its larger resources and skills; to valuing the family is added the valuing of the Other outside the family. Thus while the myth of the American pioneer certainly used an Emersonian sense of self-reliance as one of its stalwart elements—a quality strongly celebrated in the novels of Laura Ingalls Wilder, which use stocks of food as the concrete exemplification of self-reliance—the notion of living within a democracy did carry with it a social contract that was also part of the narrative of American pioneer life. From time to time, even Pa Ingalls negotiates with neighbors, suggesting a community that is built around mutual dependence and need, even as the virtue of self-reliance is preached.

Anne Thaxton Eaton, who five years earlier had begun to edit a biweekly page-long review of children's books for the *New York Times Book Review*, wrote in that magazine that *Caddie Woodlawn* was a testament to the American experience because the novel was marked by a "sense of the stirring qualities of frontier life"; she suggested as well that Kate Seredy's illustrations themselves offered "the space and freedom of a new country." Much of the novel is, indeed, a celebration of the space and freedom that the frontier offered in early Wisconsin, and one detects here the pleasure in space that Laura Ingalls Wilder also would celebrate in the 1930s in Pa's yearnings. But in *Caddie Woodlawn*, the pioneer experience is complicated in that the family could easily opt out of it. Buried in the first half of the novel is a mystery about Caddie's father, disinherited by Lord Woodlawn when he supposedly married beneath his station. Caddie's father defines America by opposing its democratic ideal to the Old World's social stratification: "You have grown up in a free country, children.... Whatever happens I want you to think of yourselves as young Americans, and I want you to be proud of that. It is difficult to tell you about England, because there all men are not free to pursue their own lives in their own ways" (88–89). While Caddie's mother laments the loss of her husband's aristocratic heritage and inherited wealth, the independent Mr. Woodlawn has no such qualms: "It was a hard struggle, but what I have in life I have earned with my own hands.... I want no lands and honors which I have not won by my own good sense and industry" (95). As she learns of her father's history, Caddie rejects the Old World out of familial loyalty—"because they were unkind to father in England" (106)—but she also uses this separation to define herself as an American. This definition is tested when the lordship is indeed offered to Caddie's father and the family must decide if they will abandon American citizenship and the hardships and equalities of the pioneer life and head to England to live in ease and wealth. Mr. Woodlawn suggests that the decision should be made in a very American way: they will vote democratically as a family, rejecting an aristocratic society even in their decision process. And though at first some of the family members are attracted to the prestige of the new life, they all vote to remain. "I never knew how much I loved it here until I had to choose" (262), notes Caddie's mother. The frontier and a life lived with democratic principles—with the possibility of choice—are here united.

"Good sense and industry" might be the central phrase of this novel, as the Woodlawns define what these are through what they do with their pioneer experience and American democratic idealism. Caddie, who leaves Boston to move to the frontier prairies of Wisconsin, is first given freedom from gendered expectations: she is permitted to grow up like a tomboy so that she will not be too sheltered; the frontier itself almost demands this latitude. But this particular freedom has boundaries defined by age and communal expectations. So when Caddie uses the skills acquired because of this latitude to humiliate her cousin Annabelle, Caddie's father, in a chapter called "Father Speaks," gives her a new alternative based on her crossing the boundaries of childhood:

> A woman's work is something fine and noble to grow up to, and it is just as important as a man's. But no man could ever do it so well. I don't want you to be the silly, affected person with fine clothes and manners whom folks sometimes call a lady. No, that is not what I want for you, my little girl. I want you to be a woman with a wise and understanding heart, healthy in body and honest in mind. Do you think you would like to be growing up into that woman now? How about it, Caddie. Have we run with the colts long enough? (244–45)

Brinks has been severely criticized by later critics for this passage. Gail Schmunk Murray calls this a "lecture," a severe "reprimand" that "reifies the dying Victorian sentiment that supported such dichotomized gender distinctions and has Caddie acquiesce to her father's dictum" (151). Much as this speech may offend twenty-first-century sensibilities, these charges are distortions of the narrative; in the text, Caddie's father delivers this speech quietly and in darkness. He is distressed himself, and this is not a lecture or a reprimand. He is giving her a choice and hoping that she will choose to live as a mature and wise woman whose pioneer experience has given her the strength and independence that she will need to negotiate the gendered social expectations and tensions of a woman living in community. Caddie responds to this: she takes on a larger, firmer identity, one that is no longer afraid of growing up, and one that is affirmed by a telling and powerful image: "Her face was turned to the west. It was always to be turned westward now, for Caddie Woodlawn was a pioneer and an American" (270)—the very last words of the novel. For Caddie—and for Brinks—America is defined by the pioneer quest within which industry and good sense, embedded in the fairness of a democracy, can fuse to lead to prosperity and happiness and selfhood. *Caddie Woodlawn* is Brink's conscious statement of those qualities that she saw embedded in the pioneer experience and democratic sensibility.[2]

The distinction between the Old and New Worlds is also at the center of Roger Duvoisin's *And There Was America* (1938), which he both authored and illustrated. The year marked his taking the oath of allegiance to the United States, and as if in celebration, Duvoisin's new citizenship was advertised on the book's dust jacket. The cover expresses Duvoisin's sense of the national story to which he had been grafted: half a dozen explorers—Portuguese, French, Spanish, English—stand anachronistically together on a new shore behind the bold figure of Columbus, whose left hand holds a flag and whose right hand holds a drawn sword. Behind the European conquerors stands the subdued, almost unobtrusive figure of a Pilgrim—whom Duvoisin will soon elevate. In the distance, made diminutive by the perspective, stand two Native Americans, dwarfed and ignored by their powerful conquerors.

The cover suggests Duvoisin's sense of America as a pioneer narrative that begins with greedy conquest and moves toward the establishment of a home: the story of a people displaced, the story of one conqueror after another who comes to exploit, the story of a people who finally come to settle. Duvoisin chronicles the coming of European influence beginning with the Vikings, then the Spanish and Portuguese with Christopher Columbus, the English with John Cabot, the French with Jacques Cartier, the Dutch with Henry Hudson, and finally the English again with Sir Walter Raleigh and the Pilgrims. Up until the English influence, Duvoisin's narrative depicts greedy conquerors eager only for wealth, as in this fabricated exchange:

"Oh! Really," the King of France was saying to his admiral. "Really, the King of Spain thinks the whole world is his. He is setting up his flag all over these new lands which Columbus had found."

"True," his admiral answered. "Soon there won't be a big enough space left for you to put up the flag of France. Why don't you send Jacques Cartier over there? He is a fine French captain. He knows the sea near these new lands. He has been fishing for cod there."

"That is a good idea, Admiral! Tell him to find these mysterious cities of China. And tell him to bring back gold, too." (25)

But Duvoisin makes clear in his stories that people searching only for money have little chance to fully appropriate a land they only wish to exploit. That is not America's true story. America's story is one about settling deeply into a land and about grasping for freedom through democracy.

Thus when Duvoisin writes of the Pilgrims, he takes an utterly different tone: "Their faces looked serious as they sailed away. They were not crossing the sea for gold, as the Spanish had done. They were not going for furs or fish, as the Dutch and French had done. They were going to build homes and to be free" (60). Nothing could be more opposed to the former European policies, Duvoisin suggests. There is the drive for wealth, and the drive for a home; there is the drive for exploitation, and the drive for freedom. And it is these latter drives that enable settlers to survive and to endure the first winter, the loss of half their number, and the dreadful situation of being fixed between an endless ocean and a wilderness. "We came here to be free," Miles Standish exclaims. "Let's stay" (62). And thus, Duvoisin concludes, "Englishmen gained the most, for they came to build their homes and in this way they kept the land" (75). This final line of the narrative is illustrated by a small image of a rough-hewn house, its domestic tranquility represented by a cow, a clothesline, a woodpile, children, and a returning hunter; a field of stumps suggests the new dominance over the land by the pioneer family.

In Duvoisin's work, the story of America is a narrative of the drive for home and land, the drive toward freedom, the drive from dominance derived from inherited power and wealth toward a democracy that fulfilled and satisfied the citizen. As with Mahony, America—the land itself—was both the story and the setting that made all other stories possible, the clear mountain brook in which one saw reflected an entirely new vision of life where a people, free and equal, governed themselves. They had endured as pioneers and homesteaders and learned to see themselves as interdependent, and so they defined their nation as a democracy and earned their way to the country's large and fulsome rewards.

And the pioneer books for children often showed America's physical landscape as formative. In books that celebrated self-reliance, the nature of the land itself often insisted upon a narrative that extolled the common man and woman, that spoke to the equalizing effects of the pioneer life, that valued cooperation as well as self-reliance—all elements of a democratic ideal, and all elements linked to the land. Thus Hendrik Willem van Loon and Grace Castagnetta's *The Songs America Sings* (1939) celebrated America's pioneer experience by carrying implicitly in its illustrations a sense of the equalizing effects of the country's vastness. The illustrations for the twenty-one folksongs of *The Songs America Sings* stress the spaciousness of the country that is being settled, re-creating, the *New York Times Book Review* noted, "our American scene in arresting and suggestive pictures. . . . Here is the New England that the author of 'America' knew, the West that moved Katherine Lee Bates to the writing of 'America, the Beautiful.' The broad Mississippi, the Kentucky cabin, the proud clipper ship, the lighthouse above the waves, the frigates at war. The mesa rises against a yellow sky, and the red shell-burst is over Fort McHenry."

The reviewer—who begins with the songs but moves quickly to the wide American landscape—correctly notes that the illustrations are dominated by large spaces. But what is equally important are the signs of settlers, who are dwarfed by the magnitude of the natural features that dominate the landscape. Yet they all stubbornly hold on: the New England farm huddles beneath high mountains that dwarf the skaters on the pond; the illustration for "Massa's in de Cold, Cold Ground" pictures a huge starry sky with a bent horizon of flat mountains and, again, a tiny figure below; "Dixie" is accompanied by a vast image of the Mississippi River, whose water and sky dominate the small steamboat; and the illustration for "Darling Nelly Gray" is two-thirds blank sky, with a tiny cottage almost hidden in the high grass beneath it. Here is America as a huge and vast land, ready to be settled and remade by anonymous Americans bound together by their pioneer experience.

Rosemary and Stephen Vincent Benét's *A Book of Americans* (1933) captured the twin themes of America as a pioneer nation requiring self-reliance and America as a democracy requiring social cooperation, and if *And There Was America* and *Caddie Woodlawn* stress the first, *A Book of Americans* stresses the second. In the frontispiece, Walter Cole's National Children's Book Week poster has become a collection of Americans outlining the country. Here, in a great dance, is the farmer with his hoe and the professor with his book, a sailor and a cowboy, an Indian and a frontiersman, the immigrant merchant and the pirate, the sportswoman and the belle, the African American servant and the buccaneer. All elements of society are gathered and put together in this dance—and thus the Benéts create an America for the young reader that is represented by community.[3]

In *A Book of Americans*, the Benéts consistently elevate the common man of the democratic nation. Thomas Jefferson affirms:

> I liked the people,
> The sweat and crowd of them,
> Trusted them always
> And spoke aloud of them. ("Thomas Jefferson," 39–41)

In "Nancy Hanks," Abraham Lincoln's mother comes back as a ghost and recounts her son's frontier birth. "Do you know his name?" she asks as she inquires for information. "Did he get on?" (65). The humor of the question depends entirely on the reader's knowledge of his rise out of humble circumstances. And when the Benéts write of George Washington, they note that Washington did not become an admiral or an emperor. Instead, he became "our George Washington," rejecting power in favor of the democratic experiment ("George Washington," 28–29).

The Benéts complicate the pioneer experience of the common man by evoking its tensions. They affirm the strong pioneer spirit of the Puritan settlers:

> When we face a bitter task
> With resolute defiance,
> And cope with it, and never ask
> To fight with less than giants. ("Pilgrims and Puritans," 14–16)

That same Puritan spirit, the Benéts suggest, leads to the westward movement: "We shall starve and freeze and suffer. We shall die, and tame the lands" ("Western Wagons," 72–73). But the Benéts decry an intolerance that is by its nature undemocratic. The Puritans

> fought and suffered, starved and died
> For their own way of thinking.
> But people who had different views
> They popped, as quick as winking,
> Within the roomy local jail. ("Puritans and Pilgrims," 14–16)

It is an intolerance the Benéts lament, and so they remind child readers not only of the injustice of intolerance but of the loss it engenders as they turn to the pioneer experience in "Crazy Horse":

It was his land. They were his men.
He cheered and led them on.
—The hunting ground is pasture, now.
The buffalo are gone. (79)

Here, the dance of social cooperation has been defeated by a too-strong focus on individual responses.

Doris Gates's novel *Blue Willow* (1940) shifts away from the pioneer experience as it was commonly evoked and focuses on American democracy as it was playing out in the contemporary world, turning once again to issues of social cooperation. Set in the San Joaquin Valley, the story of the Larkin family was a familiar story to child readers in 1940: a journey from prosperity in northern Texas to a desperate search for a job in the cotton fields of California. This is still a story of pioneer adventure, but here Janey Larkin and her parents seek to survive unemployment, homelessness, sickness, and ill will, all of which are very much in evidence at the end of the Depression. It is a pioneer adventure where the qualities extolled by Carol Ryrie Brink are, as she said, still needed. As Janey's father tells her:

> Some day, Janey, perhaps when you're grown up, you'll realize that every day you've been living these last five years has been an adventure. You know, an adventure is just something that comes along that's unexpected and you don't know for sure how it will turn out. Sometimes there may be danger mixed up in it. And it doesn't matter whether it happened a thousand years ago or right this minute. It's still an adventure. Every day that comes along is an adventure to us, and may be dangerous because we don't know for sure what it's going to bring. (98)

Janey does indeed come to understand this, particularly when she becomes the one who courageously exposes the schemes of Bounce Reyburn.

This is a picture of America very different from that of *Caddie Woodlawn*. In this contemporary America, families are left homeless, exposed, and helpless not because they have chosen the dangers of the pioneer life but because forces beyond them have pushed them to this place. The Blue Willow plate that Janey keeps safe shows a loving and secure domestic scene, the goal of so many westward-moving pioneers, but now such a scene seems almost mythic, unreachable. The family's arrival at such a goal—even its survival—depends on three things. First, there is self-reliant hard work and industry. Mr. Larkin is a champion cotton picker whose perseverance pays off with handsome prize money, firewood, and food for his family. Second and more importantly, survival depends on the community of neighbors, defined by democratic tolerance and equality. Racial bias makes no sense to families who are all in the same desperate straits, and Janey quickly befriends Lupe Romero, her first friend in five years. Lupe is so accepting, so glad to be a friend, that Janey's suspicion of her otherness is completely overwhelmed. In fact, when Janey goes to the county fair, the narrator notes that "only the staunch presence of the Romeros prevented her from being afraid of this strangeness all around her" (53); the Mexican family mediates Janey's American experience. And in the end, it is a Mexican house that is built for the Larkins, built by Mexican friends. Third, survival depends on the sheer kindness of others within the community; the novel's plot is built around this notion. Lupe's kindness to Janey is mirrored by Mr. Romero's kindness to Mr. Larkin, as he helps him to win the cotton-picking contest. Dr. Peirce comes out to see Mrs. Larkin during her illness, though he knows that there is no money to pay for his services. And largest of all, Mr. Anderson—who is himself apparently secure from need because of his great wealth—hires Mr. Larkin, returns the money stolen by Bounce Reyburn, and provides the resources for their new home, in which they can stay "as long as we want to" (172).

Though hopeful elements appear in the narrative, this is a much darker vision of America. Without the hard work in which everyone engages, without tolerance for the Other, without large kindness, the Larkin family would not survive. Here, America is a land of potential dread and disaster only barely staved off. But it is also a land whose democratic instincts and responses are necessary for mutual survival.

When all is solved and the Larkins are healthy and thriving, they go to town and there dance around the new Maypole: the flagpole. Despite the difficulties of the family's life, the notion of America is so large, so powerful, that Janey cannot really define it.

> It didn't matter in the least, she thought, as with eyes glued to [the flagpole] she reached for the high notes in the national anthem; it didn't matter in the least whether it floated from the unpainted pole at Camp Miller or here above the tall gables of Weston Union High School. It was simply the flag; nothing could add to its splendor or dim its glory. She could feel that it stood for something important and big. But what that something was, she couldn't have said if anyone had asked her. It would take a grown-up to do that. For to Janey and to the other boys and girls standing there, the flag stood for their trust in the present and their hope in the future. (166–67)

It is a remarkably optimistic vision of the country, given the difficulties the Larkin family has experienced. And yet, they should be optimistic, for hard work, tolerance, and kindness have won out, and they have food, income, and a house. Democracy has worked. It was a dream for which millions were yearning, and it has been provided. In this sense, *Blue Willow* as a novel held out the same mythic hope for young readers in a democratic nation during the Depression that the blue plate in the narrative held out for Janey.

Yet the success of democracy in this novel was not universally affirmed by the publishing establishment, though the novel would be frequently cited on lists of suggested books for children for the next decade. Some argued that the harsh realities of the failed American Dream needed to be safely portrayed to a child audience, as in this novel. Writing in the *Library Journal*, Julia Sauer argued in "Making the World Safe for the Janey Larkins" that children, in confronting the social and economic problems of *Blue Willow*, were confronting the reality of the world around them; books for children, Sauer argued, needed to do this, and to do less—to provide mere imaginative escape—was to harm children in the long run. "When children in other parts of the world are sacrificing their lives, their health, their security, is it asking too much that America's children should sacrifice some of their carefree childhood?" The point was particularly cogent when what Sauer was asking children to sacrifice was ignorance. But others argued that *Blue Willow* avoided true engagement with the issues facing the Larkins by handing them a fairy-tale ending: it all comes right for them, as the bad foreman is punished and the Larkins are given a house and job. Julia Mickenberg cites a 1942 *New Masses* review by Harry Taylor where a child reader is quoted: "She thought its author, Doris Gates, should have been honest to the last page, and not blamed the suffering of the Larkins on a farm foreman" (312). Despite the bias of the journal, the point is a valid one: for most children of the American democracy suffering during the Depression, the fairy-tale ending was hugely desirable—but hugely inaccessible.

Brink in her historical novel, Duvoisin in his narrative history, van Loon in his illustrations, the Benéts in their poems, and Gates in her contemporary novel were each arguing that the pioneer experience and the democratic ideal were inevitably linked—what Bertha Mahony was suggesting when she called the pioneer experience a particularly

American myth. The pioneer experience, fused with the democratic landscape of America, was the experience of mostly nameless settlers who beat westward to establish new homes and communities in wide spaces, their resourcefulness a testament to their pioneer spirit, their anonymity and cooperation a testament to the democratic equality that marked their resolute journeying. It was this vision of the American heritage that American literature for children in the 1930s affirmed—and nowhere more forcefully than in the pioneer stories of Laura Ingalls Wilder.

In books such as *Little House in the Big Woods* (1932), *Little House on the Prairie* (1935), *On the Banks of Plum Creek* (1937), *By the Shores of Silver Lake* (1939), *The Long Winter* (1940), and *Little Town on the Prairie* (1941), Wilder plays the complementary roles of protagonist, principal point of view, and author. This merger reinforces her authority as the witness of and participant in the myth of the American frontier. Wilder believed that her books represented the "frontier spirit," a spirit that "shines through all the volumes of my children's novels." She did not feel it necessary to define what that frontier spirit was, though in a speech titled "My Work" written during the drafting of *On the Banks of Plum Creek* (1937), she defined this spirit in terms of self-reliance. Following the Civil War, her parents, she wrote, "suffered cold and heat, hard work and privation as did others of their time. When possible they turned the bad into good. If not possible, they endured it. Neither they nor their neighbors begged for help. No other person, nor the government, owed them a living. They owed that to themselves and in some way they paid the debt. And they found their own way." It is hard not to hear in this Wilder's rejection of Franklin Roosevelt's New Deal principles in favor of an uncompromising dependence on the self, modeled on the American pioneer experience, though critics have suggested that Wilder is consciously or unconsciously rewriting her past to conform to an ideal. Gail Schmunk Murray has argued, for example, that "Wilder's construction of frontier life [is] skewed to conform to the 'frontier myth' that historian Frederick Jackson Turner used to hypothesize the American spirit of conquest, adventure, and individualism" (147–48).

Laying aside the question of how closely Wilder's life conformed to the pioneer heritage of self-sufficiency, certainly it is the case that the frontier myth as Wilder constructs it is one element of the books' early acclaim. Murray argues that the books' appeal during the Depression lay in their reversion to "simpler and happier times" as they celebrated a frontier past that was as much nostalgia as history (147). But Leonard

Marcus in *Minders of Make-Believe* is probably closer when he locates their popularity in the ways in which the books "held up the struggles for survival of an earlier generation of pioneers as implicit proof that Americans possessed the moral strength and determination to weather any adversity" (116). Wilder's frontier myth foregrounded the values of industry, self-reliance, and independence, and it affirmed the westward drive; Marcus cites "the pioneers' bare-knuckled resourcefulness and adaptability but also their capacity for joy even under the most trying circumstances." These are the same values of frontier mythology that Wilder depicted in her family living on the cusp of a wilderness.

But even as Wilder presents those virtues, she complicates them. She balances the drive to move westward with the need for civilization as defined by Ma. Independence must be balanced with community. Self-reliance must be balanced with the relationship to the Other. Even hard work and industry must be balanced with song, play, and the imagination. For Wilder, the frontier is a world being domesticated; hers are domestic tales. Here the heroes of the frontier are Pa and Ma, and their pioneer focus is not to conquer a land and make it suitable for further expansion but to forge a home on the edge of the wilderness, which is a place, admittedly, where there are dangers but also potential abundance and prosperity. The familiar name of the series—Little House—suggests the domestic quality, and the focus of the first two books in the series—*Little House in the Big Woods* and *Little House on the Prairie*—is indeed on the literal house: the domestic sphere defined by Ma and Pa. In the first, the house protects against the big woods that lie all around, the woods where bears dwell and where there is darkness and stillness once night falls. In the second, the house is the focus of action, as Wilder takes a great many pages describing the building of the walls, then the building of the barn for the horses, then the building of the chimney and fireplace, and then the raising of the roof—which is to say, she describes the work of Pa. This site, when finished, is domesticated by the homey touches of Ma, whose province is the interior world. While Pa is inclined to pursue the retreating line of the frontier, in Wilder's construction of the frontier myth his role has been domesticated: his work is to support and protect his family. His wanderlust is muted by Ma, whose calm, competent, reasonable, and sometimes firm voice reminds Charles of his responsibilities to the domestic sphere. The strong walls (within which most of the books' action occurs), the warmth of the fireplace, the good meals, the sense of propriety, and even the playing of Pa's fiddle are all signs that Pa and Ma have done their mutual domestic work well.[4]

Wilder does assert the same wonder at the vastness of the American landscape that marks van Loon's illustrations. *Little House in the Big Woods* opens with a sense of the huge proportions of the frontier in Wisconsin, rendered in very simple language—only one out of seven words in this opening have more than a single syllable: "The great, dark trees of the Big Woods stood all around the house, and beyond them were other trees and beyond them were more trees. As far as a man could go to the north in a day, or a week, or a whole month, there was nothing but woods. There were no houses. There were no roads. There were no people. There were only trees and the wild animals who had their homes among them" (1–2). When the family leaves the Big Woods for Kansas, this sense of proportion is noted in similar words: "Kansas was an endless flat land covered with tall grass blowing in the wind. Day after day they traveled in Kansas, and saw nothing but the rippling grass and the enormous sky. In a perfect circle the sky curved down to the level land, and the wagon was in the circle's exact middle" (13). In *By the Shores of Silver Lake*, the family's travel across the prairie is almost overwhelming for Laura, as she considers the scale of the place and its complete unknowing of their presence: "All morning Pa drove steadily along the dim wagon track, and nothing changed. The farther they went into the west, the smaller they seemed, and the less they seemed to be going anywhere. . . . Laura thought they might go on forever, yet always be in this same changeless place, that would not even know they were there" (59). Juliet Dusinberre, in *Alice to the Lighthouse: Children's Books and Radical Experiments in Art* (1987), argues that Pa and Laura are, in these yearnings, linked by immaturity: "Wilder knew that the drive which impels the pioneer comes from the child's eagerness for what lies ahead, whether or not the pioneer is, in physical terms, still a child." But Laura's musings, here in the fifth book in the series, are almost melancholy and are clearly those of an older imagination and mind that can complicate simple wonder at size and vastness—here, in the American landscape.

Even when the frontier does represent danger to Laura, that danger is deliberately muted by Pa's dominance and resourcefulness. Over and over in *Little House in the Big Woods*, Pa's mere presence reassures Laura: "Laura stood at the window and watched Pa, big and swift and strong, walking away over the snow. His gun was on his shoulder, his hatchet and powder horn hung at his side, and his tall boots made great tracks in the soft snow. Laura watched him till he was out of sight in the woods" (119–20). One night after Pa has started the house in *Little House on the Prairie*—and before he has finished the roof or the door—the family is surrounded by a pack of wolves. Pa himself is so confident in the family's security that he raises Laura to the window so that she can see the surrounding pack as they bay at the moon, repeating a scene from *Little House in the Big Woods*. Even when Laura realizes that "wolves eat little girls" (3), she is calmed by her father's symbols: his gun hanging over the door and his faithful bulldog. These images of strength, combined with his playfulness and music, make Pa's presence reassuring even when Wilder does show real danger beyond the walls of their house.

Ma also mitigates danger in the novels. When winter comes on in *Little House in the Big Woods*, Wilder writes that though they were all alone in the Big Woods, "the little log house was warm and snug and cosy. Pa and Ma and Mary and Laura and Baby Carrie were comfortable and happy there, especially at night" (37–38). On the day when Pa and Ma decide upon the place where they will settle in *Little House on the Prairie*, the girls wake up and smell bacon and coffee and pancakes. Their immediate concerns are remarkable, given that they are all alone, with miles of prairie all around them, and nothing at all but the wagon nearby: "Mary could dress herself, all but the middle button. Laura buttoned that one for her, then Mary buttoned Laura all the way up the back. They washed their hands and faces in the tin washbasin on the wagon-step. Ma combed every snarl out of their hair, while Pa brought fresh water from the creek" (39). That Pa and Ma are cooking pancakes and combing snarls out of the girls' hair suggests much about the response of Laura and her family to the blank wilderness around them. There is no sense of fear or panic, no sense that the isolation is overwhelming. Ma's calm composure in extraordinary circumstances establishes the response to the vastness of the country; she is just as reassuring as Pa but through the steady strength of her determined and disciplined character. This is reinforced when later Ma irons the girls' dresses on the back of the wagon. The reader feels again that this is the proper response to the vast country: the routines of the family are not to be disturbed, even though, "all around them, to the very edge of the world, there was nothing but grasses waving in the wind" (48).

Pa's resourcefulness and self-reliance are nowhere exhibited more fully than in his ability to support his family; thus, much of the narration is about food. The opening chapter of *Little House in the Big Woods* is given over to showing the ways in which the land provides for those who know how to use it well. Wilder recounts the butchering of a deer, the smoking of its meat, and the storing of the venison in the attic of the Little House. This is immediately followed by the story of

Pa catching a wagonload of fish in Lake Pepin with his net. "They all feasted on the good, fresh fish. All they did not eat fresh was salted down in barrels for the winter" (10). Then the garden is harvested: "Now the potatoes and carrots, the beets and turnips and cabbages were gathered and stored in the cellar, for freezing nights had come" (12). The imagery is that of abundance: "Onions were made into long ropes, braided together by their tops, and then were hung in the attic beside wreaths of red peppers strung on threads. The pumpkins and the squashes were piled in orange and yellow and green heaps in the attic's corners" (12). Meanwhile, "yellow cheeses were stacked on the pantry shelves" (12). After this abundance is chronicled, the pig is butchered, and the meat is salted and pickled and smoked. "There were hams and shoulders, side meat and spare-ribs and belly. There was the heart and the liver and the tongue, and the head to be made into headcheese, and the dish-pan full of bits to be made into sausage" (14). Wilder concludes this chronicle of abundance with this summary: "The little house was fairly bursting with good food stored away for the long winter. The pantry and the shed were full, and so was the attic" (18). The illustration drawn by Garth Williams for the 1953 uniform edition of the Wilder books shows Mary and Laura in the attic with their dolls, sitting on pumpkins and surrounded by the stores that Pa and Ma have put away.

But a fertile and rich country must still be worked, and none of the novels go by without some evidence of Pa's effort—or without the insistence on the American notion that if one simply works hard enough and is resourceful enough, then one will succeed. This is the central notion of *The Long Winter*, the novel that puts the Ingalls family in its most difficult circumstances and even questions Pa's decisions about moving out from the safe settlement at Plum Creek to an isolated community that, when cut off from the supplies brought by the railroad, seems defenseless. Nonetheless, here is where Wilder shows the value of resourcefulness and hard work. Despite the unceasing blizzards and cold and lack of supplies—the family actually begins to starve—Pa and Ma always seem to have some new strategy out of the dire circumstances, either through a clever way to make a button lamp, or through almost magically producing a fish, or through keeping warm by folding hay together—hay that has to be brought in by Pa from the claim miles away through pathless tracks of deep snow. Pa, in this novel, defines himself through the responsibility that comes with freedom: "We're humans, and like it says in the Declaration of Independence, God created us free. That means we got to take care of ourselves" (13). When

Laura suggests that God takes care of them, Pa almost rebukes her. That is true, he argues, as far as the moral sphere of action. But that moral sphere is different from working to provide what is needed to live. Ma observes later, "The Lord helps them that help themselves" (118), a cliché that is powerful for her and that suggests the unity of working in the physical and spiritual worlds simultaneously.

But *The Long Winter* complicates this sense of individual resourcefulness and begins to explore the other side of the pioneer experience: communal interdependence. When a blizzard hits, Pa can say with ease: "We're snug and warm, as we've been before without even the people and the stores [and the railroad]" (119). Laura laments being separated from neighbors by the snow, but Ma affirms Pa's individualism: "I hope you don't expect to depend on anybody else, Laura. . . . A body can't do that" (127). More largely, Pa insists that they shouldn't even depend on the government, for, being so far away, the government could not understand the practical realities of life on the prairie, and "none of the rules worked as they were intended to" (99). But what Pa never acknowledges is that self-reliance and independence and individual resourcefulness must be balanced with community activity and interdependence—familiar themes. In *The Long Winter*, the Ingalls family survives because the Wilder brothers have an ample store of grain, which Pa forces them to share. The town survives because Almanzo Wilder and Cap Garland travel through the snowy landscape on a hunch that there might be grain to buy—grain that the buyer at first refuses to sell, blaming them (as Pa might have) for not providing for themselves. Even the train tracks cannot be cleared through individual resources; the men of the town go as a team to do this—unsuccessfully, as it turns out. Though they are similarly unsuccessful in the antelope hunt, once again the men must organize themselves together in order to have any hope of gaining meat for each other. In fact, even the family unit functions as a small community that is utterly dependent upon mutual skills and work: Pa acknowledges, for example, that without Laura's help in twisting the hay to keep them warm, they would not have survived the winter. Resourcefulness and independence are important qualities in this country, especially on the frontier; but they do not negate the equally important quality of communal interaction and mutual dependence. On the American frontier, those qualities must be balanced.

In his *Consumerism and American Girls' Literature, 1860–1940*, Peter Stoneley finds in Wilder's work a response to what Wilder perceived as a society that had lost its regard for self-reliance; he argues that Wilder saw in the progressive New Deal a loss of the rugged individualism and independence that had characterized the American frontier. Instead of the "resourceful vigor of the past," Wilder saw "the artificiality of the modern age," by which Stoneley means an inability to create for oneself a home, a living, a sufficiency of any sort. Stoneley traces this to her belief that the contemporary age of capitalism, in which society's workings depended upon the smooth and productive workings of its large economy, had removed "constructive resources" from America's citizens. Pa and Ma always have something to do; the Depression removes anything to do, for who can fight back against large economic forces? "How could the modern child or adult respond constructively to a problem that was both pandemic and invisible; real, but also only numbers and percentage points?" Stoneley admits that Wilder "did romanticize the energetic simplicity of the past, even as she dared to show how unremittingly difficult life had been"; nonetheless, the implied comparison is between the present generation, made weak through a lack of individual resourcefulness, and the generation of Wilder's childhood, where fire, drought, waves of grasshoppers, long winters, wolves, Indians, and soldiers worked against the settler, but there was always a way to make the house cozy and bright, full of food and music.[5]

Certainly ingenuity, resourcefulness, discipline, and industry are the virtues that Wilder extols to her contemporary readers. In *On the Banks of Plum Creek*, it may seem that Pa has no options as he struggles to feed his family; there is little game and no money, and the crops are not in yet. So Pa builds an ingenious fish trap. "You always think of something, Charles," Ma tells him. "Just when I'm wondering where our living is to come from, now it's spring" (139). This is a recurrent theme: Pa will always think of something. It is his ingenuity that consistently saves them. This is not necessarily a direct criticism of her contemporary readers; it is Wilder's affirmation of a lifestyle that enables a family to survive hard times—until, if Stoneley is correct in his claims, capitalism and dependence on others take it away.

Nowhere is this clearer than in *Farmer Boy* (1933), where the options of hard work and self-reliance are pitted against the ease and wealth of a mercantile position—in other words, a choice between industry and its resultant self-sufficiency or wealth with its dependence upon a consumerist market. At the end of the novel, Royal Wilder decides to become a storekeeper to lead an easier life—he hates the drudgery of the farm. When Almanzo is offered a similar choice, his mother—in his hearing, but speaking to his father—reveals for the first time to the reader what she thinks about Royal's choice: "Oh, it's bad enough to see Royal come down to being nothing but a storekeeper! Maybe he'll make money, but he'll never be the man you are" (367). Both parents acknowledge that Royal is likely to have an easier life, but to each, money and ease are irrelevant to the quality of one's life—and quality depends upon self-reliance, not "trucking to other people." Apparently one's very soul depends upon this independence. And though this might sound cavalier to a Depression-era audience, Wilder sees life lived in dependence upon others as less than a life lived depending on oneself.

This is exactly the way that Almanzo's father poses the situation to his second son. He begins, over his wife's objections, to lay out the benefits of being apprenticed to Mr. Paddock: "With Paddock, you'd have an easy life, in some ways. You wouldn't be out in all kinds of weather. Cold winter nights, you could lie snug in bed and not worry about young stock freezing. Rain or shine, wind or snow, you'd be under shelter. You'd be shut up, inside walls. Likely you'd always have plenty to eat and wear and money in the bank" (370). These elements stand in strong contrast to what Almanzo has seen in a novel that shows the family out in dreadful weather, sometimes in the middle of freezing nights, running the cattle around until they get warm or desperately working to save the corn from a frost by watering the stalks before dawn—no part of which Wilder has romanticized. But then his father chronicles the other side of the Paddock apprenticeship: Almanzo will be dependent on other folks, whereas a "farmer depends on himself, and the land and the weather. If you're a farmer, you raise what you eat, you raise what you wear, and you keep warm with wood out of your own timber. You work hard, but you work as you please, and no man can tell you to go or come. You'll be free and independent, son, on a farm" (370–71). The final line is the principle that Wilder wants to assert: life must be free and independent rather than dependent. And if the weather or land works against you, then you have Pa's resourcefulness to fall back on.

Almanzo has been giving his response to this choice throughout the novel: he will be a farmer and not "live inside walls and please people he didn't like, and never have horses and cows and fields" (371). Throughout the novel he has shadowed his father, and here, he steps into the very roles that his father has followed. It will be an independence different from that which James Daugherty asserts, different from that of an individual living on the frontier. But it is an independence that, Wilder suggests, is certainly possible and desirable in an America that has seen its dependence on capitalism collapse.

Farmer Boy was written immediately after *Little House in the Big Woods*, so although it is marketed today as the third in the *Little House* sequence, it is actually the second in Wilder's understanding and shows many of the same impulses and themes that the first showed. Its early chapters, for example, mirror the emphasis of the early chapters of *Little House in the Big Woods* on food and provision. The house and extensive barns of the Wilder family suggest a wealth and resultant security well beyond that of the Ingalls family, but in both novels, there is the sense that hard work diligently done leads to the ability to secure one's needs—and not just physical needs. Wilder uses sensory experience to suggest Almanzo's loving response to this hard work: "Almanzo could hear the crunching of all the animals eating. The haymows were warm with the warmth of all the stock below, and the hay smelled dusty-sweet. There was a smell, too, of the horses and cows, and a wooly smell of sheep. And before the boys finished filling the mangers there was the good smell of warm milk foaming into Father's milk-pail" (19–20).

Wilder connects this virtue of hard work explicitly to the settlement of America. When Almanzo's father claims that muskets won the Revolution, but axes and ploughs made the country, Almanzo—and perhaps the young reader—does not understand the claim. So Wilder has his father explain it: "All the land our forefathers had was a little strip of country, here between the mountains and the ocean. All the way from here west was Indian country, and Spanish and French and English country. It was farmers that took all that country and made it into America" (189). When Almanzo still does not understand, his father explains again and repeats his favorite line:

> "Well, son, the Spaniards were soldiers, and high-and-mighty gentlemen that only wanted gold. And the French were fur-traders, wanting to make quick money. And England was busy fighting wars. But we were farmers, son; we wanted the land. It was farmers that went over the mountains, and cleared the land, and settled it, and farmed it, and hung on to their farms.
> "This country goes three thousand miles west, now. It goes 'way out beyond Kansas, and beyond the Great American Desert, over mountains bigger than these mountains, and down to the Pacific Ocean. It's the biggest country in the world, and it was farmers who took all that country and made it America, son. Don't you ever forget that." (189)

Farmers took what Almanzo's father sees as empty wilderness and created farms and settlements and America itself. And though his claims to the country's size are exaggerated, he is speaking of America's largeness in terms of its energy and power and fertility—all of which grow and emerge out of the hard work of farmers. He spurns the pretensions and goals of the Europeans as ephemeral and vain; he praises what seems to him to be most lasting and meaningful—the acquisition and disciplined use of land. This is what has made America.

But Wilder complicates the emphasis on self-reliance. The title for *Little Town on the Prairie* suggests a significant shift, one away from the singular "house" to the communal "town," where Pa and Laura become wage earners as they participate in the settlement of a community. The shift is not an easy one; Laura's work as a seamstress is numbing, and her later work as a teacher is one that she does not embrace happily. But in fulfilling community needs, she takes her place in a larger social order that is quite different from that of the earlier novels. And in *These Happy Golden Years*, Laura shifts from a focus on her own family to, in her maturation, a focus on the larger community of the other young adults in town; in fact, even when she marries and begins her own new home, she has something that her parents did not have in her young years: "She knew she need never be homesick for the old home. It was so near that she could go to it whenever she wished, while she and Al-manzo made the new home in their own little house" (289). America is the land of the pioneer, suggests Wilder, with all of the pioneer's need for self-sufficiency. But America is also the land of the community of neighbors, whose presence defies even the powers of nature because of the established community's interdependencies and supports and whose mutualities contribute to a tightly knit social order on the edge of the frontier.

Wilder offers to her Depression-era readers a country that cele-brates its pioneer heritage by affirming self-sufficiency, bounty, strong family ties, union with the land—but also union within social groups. Her explicit message is that America still offers possibilities that do not need to be mediated through the largess of governmental agen-cies, of which Wilder was quite skeptical. One only needs the industry and resourcefulness and goodwill to reach out toward those possibili-ties, she asserts, even in the face of huge contrary forces, whether those forces are natural—like the snows and grasshoppers and drought of the Little House books—or the huge and faceless economic forces of the 1930s. "We need today courage, self reliance and integrity," she wrote sometime around 1936. "When we remember that our hardest times would have been easy times for our forefathers it should help us to be of good courage, as they were, even if things are not all as we would like them to be." She wrote this as the text for her essay "My Work," describ-ing her purposes in writing for a child audience. And at midcentury, this connection between the past and present defined the ways that the books were perceived, as Irene Smith noted in her 1943 *Horn Book* assessment:

> [The novels remind] a needy world today of the canniness of the pioneer, the strength and joy of the builder, and the dreams of free individuals working toward a better future. Your present-day readers can learn from Mrs. Wilder that vicissitudes must be faced, and that real happiness is not measured by material possessions. She enlarges and deepens their understanding of their native land when she tells them how it felt to live in the big woods, and on a raw new prairie homestead when frontiers were moving west. The wavy fields of wheat and the summer blackberry thickets are the plentiful realization of good American earth. The carpenter's saw and the new muddy streets are proof of the frontier community built by families like the Ingallses. Where stores and houses sprang, the church and school rose with them, bringing personal responsibilities of citizenship.

At midcentury, at midwar, the novels were perceived to be calls to an enlargement and appreciation of a frontier vision of America—an appreciation that encourages the responsibilities of citizenship and the optimism of individuals born into freedom who are at liberty to work toward a stronger future for themselves, bravely shouldering trials and tribulations.[6]

The emphasis on self-reliance and communal work, on citizenship and democracy that was so much a part of the pioneer works of the 1930s thrived in the context of a larger emphasis on the importance of teaching the precepts of democracy to American children. In her study *Cradle of Liberty: Race, the Child, and National Belonging from Thomas Jefferson to W. E. B. Du Bois* (2006), Caroline F. Levander has documented the twentieth-century American belief in "the child as a benchmark of the democratic process," noting, for example, the 1940 White House Conference on Children in Democracy, which argued that "society could be perfected through the socialization of the child" (2). The professional literature in the fields of education, library science, publishing, and children's books during the 1930s was overt in its expression of this same belief, consistently asserting the need for teachers and librarians to educate children in the experience of the pioneers and in the ways of American democracy. "Precisely at this juncture the teacher enters the current scene," wrote Robert Baldwin of the College of Education, West Virginia University. "If our American tradition of pioneering is to persist . . . our schools must drive deep the social claim-stakes of truth, justice, freedom, and clear-visioned patriotism.

. . . [W]ithin the framework of American traditions for blazing new trails, [teachers] can help youth of today to see American social and economic life more clearly than we appear now to see it." Baldwin called for teachers to educate in tolerance and open-mindedness, to encourage interdependence in both individuals and societal groups, and to affirm all effort that contributes to the democratic good of the whole. Other writers heightened the stakes, laying on teachers the burden of preserving American society itself. In October 1933 Harold L. Ickes, secretary of the interior, argued before the National Education Association for the powerful leavening presence of an education in democracy: "Every child should have an education not only for his own sake but for the good of the whole. . . . No nation in these times can hope to survive, to say nothing of progressing in the arts and the sciences, in commerce, in trade, or in industry, unless it is composed of a well educated citizenry." Specifically, Ickes claimed, an educated citizenry is the foundation of democracy: "The individual American must be educated not only that he may be able to enjoy a happier and fuller life; he must be educated in order that, in cooperation with other educated Americans, he may do his part toward sustaining and upbuilding an intelligent and beneficent and capable government."[7] In the spring of 1940 John E. Anderson defined the teacher's role in *Childhood Education* as one in which the child is taught—and this will sound familiar—the principle of "self-reliance and democratic cooperation": "Whether or not a democratic society can continue to exist, whether or not the ills of our society can be met, depend in no small degree upon the ability of each teacher to envisage her relations with children in terms of this principle."

But how to do such education? The first impulse in the professional education literature was not immediately to turn to the arts but to model democratic principles in the classroom. S. A. Courtis's November 1937 *Childhood Education* article, "Of the Children, by the Children, for the Children," for example, argued that children needed to be taught democratic ideals through embodiment. "Today the country desperately needs creative teachers with inventive minds who will band together with other like-minded teachers and give their best in solving the many problems that must be solved in shifting school procedure whether administrative, supervisory, or instructional, from the autocratic to the democratic basis," he suggested. It was a sweeping call, and it echoed again and again. Of school administrators, William H. Kilpatrick complained in the October 1937 issue of *Childhood Education* that "school room and school system are but too often benevolent autocracies. . . . Only as [democracy] is lived can it be learned."

Of teachers, in the spring of 1938, Frank E. Baker encouraged the embodiment of democratic principles to "create those positive conditions that insure the opportunity to grow in the capacities for democracy by experiencing democracy." More specifically, James S. Tippett, in his "Toward a More Democratic Citizenship," argued for embodying democracy through exercises in group work that encouraged shared responsibility and communal growth: "Democracy demands that the individuals who compose it should be helped to find themselves as surely as possible and that each individual's abilities be turned not only to his own advancement but to the advancement of the social order." And all of these writers would have affirmed Kilpatrick's observation: "As for the schools, we must find in them ways of enthroning democracy in all their works."

Democracy as it was affirmed in these pieces was not merely a political choice but an ethical position that needed to be taught. George W. Hartmann, writing in *Childhood Education*, argued that education about democracy was a value-laden process: the teacher should "aid in the enlargement of the culture so that new values become incorporated into the lives of the young." Speaking out of the context of the Depression, Hartmann argued that teachers needed to ask questions of social and cultural justice, about widespread American poverty, about free speech, and about civic loyalty, and Hartmann warned that "without a virile educational program managed by courageous and competent teachers social catastrophe will soon be upon us." Childhood education, he argued, should combat the possibility of such social catastrophe. Thus, for example, R. H. Markham, an editor with the *Christian Science Monitor*, wrote in the fall of 1941 that America's teachers "must inspire our young with a wholesome, dynamic, triumphant ideal. It is they who must arouse more faith and less skepticism, more devotion and less cynicism. It is they, too, who must help society plan for its youth so that they can have something in which to believe, something to which they belong and to which they can make their contribution." It was a heightened, exciting, and somewhat fearful call—to entrust the defense of democracy to the country's teachers.

But librarians who during the 1930s had seen the rise of totalitarian regimes in Europe that controlled their citizens through controlling media also recognized librarians' own crucial role in educating for democracy—particularly as they discerned that some sorts of totalitarian control would not necessarily be met with sharp rebuff in America. (It was in 1938—and not with the McCarthy hearings in the 1950s—that the House Committee on Un-American Activities was established.)

Desiring to embody democracy, the American Library Association developed "The Library's Bill of Rights" in June 1939. In the face of "growing intolerance, suppression of free speech, and censorship affecting the rights of minorities and individuals," the ALA asserted:

1. Books and other reading matter selected for purchase from the public funds should be chosen because of value and interest to people of the community, and in no case should the selection be influenced by the race or nationality or the political or religious views of the writers.
2. As far as available material permits, all sides of questions on which differences of opinions exist should be represented fairly and adequately in the books and other reading matter purchased for public use.
3. The library as an institution to educate for democratic living should especially welcome the use of its meeting rooms for socially useful and cultural activities and the discussion of current public questions. Library meeting rooms should be available on equal terms to all groups in the community regardless of their beliefs or affiliations.

Buried in the dependent clause of the third "right"—a right that deals with access to meeting rooms and not books at all—is an axiomatic assumption: that a library is "an institution to educate for democratic living." It would perform this function in the use of its physical spaces, in the access it provided, in its book selection. And at midcentury, this would be a task appointed for its children's collection as well as its adult collection.[8]

Democracy could also be taught through embodiment in the school's curriculum, and here, reading in democracy as a political concept was judged to be potent—perhaps even more potent than reading about democracy as part of the pioneer experience. In the spring of 1939, Eric Estorick of New York University was arguing in his article "Literature and Democracy" that American letters have a tradition of authors assuming an active role in democracy by taking "a public stand on social issues in the interests of a more effective and genuine realization of democratic ideals." Particularly since the onset of the Depression, he argued, American literature has been forward-looking, and it is a literature of protest insofar as it arises from issues of social conscience and identity. Further, American literature is linked to democracy by its very existence, since democracy is made dynamic by such voices of protest, even as such voices are made possible and nourished by democracy. Speaking of the effects of reading on children, writers about children's books were no less passionate in their connections between reading, democracy, and American citizenship. One way in which writers and publishers responded to the calls to educate for democracy was through producing books for children that addressed the definitions and questions of democracy directly—even apart from pioneer connections. One such book for the very young child was Munro Leaf's *Fair Play* (1939). Leaf—already known for his *Story of Ferdinand the Bull* (1936)—merged simple, childlike line drawings with an understanding but strong-willed adult narrator to define the nature of democracy through exploring relationships that a child reader would recognize easily.

Fair Play begins by affirming the interdependencies within a nation: "If there were only one person in the whole United States, and that one person were YOU or YOU there would not be any . . ." This statement is followed by a list of fourteen professions upon which everyone depends as well as a list of eighteen necessities, such as houses and trains and churches and hospitals (3–9). Given these interdependencies, "we can't do everything just the way we would if we were alone" (14). Thus, Leaf points out, we have rules—as players have rules in games.

> If, when they finished playing, they all wanted a drink of water at the drinking fountain, there would be two ways for them to get a drink. One way would be the way Justme would try—with every body shoving and pushing to be first and nobody getting a good drink for a long time and maybe somebody getting hurt. Or they could make a rule that they form a line and take turns quickly. That way everyone would get a good drink and it wouldn't take one half as long as the crazy way and nobody would get hurt. (20–21)

The contrast to democracy, as Leaf defines it, is selfishness. And the selfishness of others, Leaf argues, is what laws protect us from: "We have [laws] so that everyone gets a fair chance and no one selfish person can make the rest of us sick or unhappy, or hurt us" (39). Leaf points out that these rules come about through a mutual consensus: "When you are twenty-one years old, whether you are a man or a woman, you have just as much right as anyone else in the whole country to help make the laws by which we rule ourselves" (42). Everybody participates through choosing our government, and here again, Leaf affirms the principle of cooperation: "And what *most* of us choose is what *all* of us must follow. That is the only fair way" (44). He concludes, "Our country is not perfect and the way we run it is not perfect, but most of us think it is still the country in which we want to live and we can all make it still better" (79).

The "all" in that conclusion is especially telling, for Leaf wants to stress the inclusiveness of democracy. In fact, though throughout the text he has simplified the precepts of democracy into terms that children will recognize, inclusiveness is inculcated in all of those principles: the rule of the majority is inculcated in the principle of fairness; the significance of interdependency and cooperation is inculcated in the principle of rules. And the stance of Leaf's narrator, who throughout the text speaks in the second person, directly to the reader, suggests mutuality, with the feeling that you too, reader, must see the reasonableness of fair play; and you too must see the destructive quality of selfishness within a community; and you too must see not only that you are participating in the democratic experiment but that, as an adult, you will help to define it.

For slightly older readers, Ryllis Alexander Goslin and Omar Pancoast Goslin wrote *Democracy* (1940). In a series of quick chapters, the Goslins define elements of democracy through connections with the familiar. Thus, the adage "Democracy means freedom" (10) is illustrated in both text and photographs by the difference between a wild bird and a chained parrot in a cage. "Democracy means accepting responsibility" (18) is illustrated by the collaborations of an orchestra; "Democracy means differences of opinion" (34) is compared to a family discussion over where to go for a vacation; "Democracy means tolerance" (42) is illustrated by stories of good and bad sportsmanship. The notion was that democracy was already deeply embedded in the experience of the American child, and books such as *Democracy* clarify what is already implicit experientially.

For older readers still, narrative histories about America often suggested that the American story was about the drive toward democracy and freedom for the common citizen. Marion Florence Lansing's *Great Moments in Freedom* (1930), for example, ranges widely to chronicle stories about the urge toward freedom in classical Rome; in leaders and reformers and scientists such as Saint Francis, Copernicus, and Martin Luther; and in the work of national heroes such as Robert Bruce in Scotland and Gustava Vasa in Sweden. But the book ends in a final section with what Lansing suggests is the culmination of humanity's drive toward freedom, and here she sounds much like Bertha Mahony in her comments on the public library. For Lansing, freedom's highest expression appears in the democratic qualities of America's polling stations, schoolrooms, and courts. "For each age," she wrote, "there is a new and wider vision of freedom. It is our business to be watching for it in the events of every day and to be furthering it by our own interest, understanding, and activity" (ix). At times these texts, familiarly, use the language of the pioneer experience, even though the narratives do not evoke that experience particularly. Marie A. Lawson's *Hail Columbia* (1931) argues that Americans who understand and affirm their pioneer heritage are Americans who are striving to be "better citizens" (367) by using the values of the pioneer heritage to craft a distinctly American culture in the present.

Gertrude Hartman, in her social and economic history *These United States and How They Came to Be* (1932), pointed also to the American pioneer heritage but added more emphatically the role of the immigrant in shaping the political landscape of America.

> These people were free to form a nation and devise a government—not a nation which they inherited from their forefathers, but a new nation which they themselves created in their effort to make their dream of a good life a living reality. It was natural that such people should work out a government founded upon the ideals of freedom, justice, and equality of opportunity to all. So a new order of society was developed, and government "of the people, by the people, for the people" began in the world. (330)

"These people" whom Hartman describes are, in her words, workers who came to America to support "the swift development of our great industries" (329), who "cleared the forest, cultivated the vast prairies, developed our mines and our other great resources, built our great network of railroads and our mighty cities" (329–30). "From these people we have inherited our ideals and our institutions" (330)—and here she speaks specifically to the ideals of individual freedom and contribution to the larger social and cultural needs. Thus the narrative movement behind Hartman's history—and each of these books—was to identify the history of America as a progression toward an ever fuller and more inclusive definition of democracy.

That same historical narrative was affirmed by leftist writers who claimed the pioneer heritage and democratic elevation of the common man as matching a progressive paradigm—and indeed, Hartman's language of the "worker" is strikingly progressive. In 1931, for example, Lucy Sprague Mitchell, the progressive educator and founder of the school that became the Bank Street College of Education, published her *North America: The Land They Live in for the Children Who Live There* (1931), a geographical study illustrated by Kurt Wiese and based on Mitchell's beliefs that children are fascinated by the real environment that lies around them. Her suspicion of capitalism and interest in Marxism is suggested by the concluding section of her study. When

Mitchell asks rhetorically who sustains the people of North America, her answer could be a Whitman poem:

> It is the workers of North America—the thousands and millions who toil in the open with plants and tame animals, working on the stone-walled farms of hilly New England, on the wheat fields and dairy farms of the great valley country of the Middle West, on the cotton and rice plantations of the South, on the big open ranches of the West; or who toil through the days (and some through the nights) in the big mills or factories taking what animals and plants give and making clothes or food to be used; or the thousands and thousands who stand in the heat of stoves so that the one hundred and sixty millions of hungry men, women and children of North America can be fed and clothed. (369)

The central image here is, of course, the worker, particularly the common and anonymous worker who is the real sustainer of society, reflecting Hartman's language of the previous year.

Similarly, the Socialist writer Leo Huberman—still two decades away from his interrogation for un-American activities by McCarthy's legislative committee—published *We, the People* (1932), which specifically defined the American worker in Marxist terms. Here the story of America is the story of the worker as farmer, as pioneer, as frontiersman, as industrial employee in an unceasing battle between those who control wealth and capital and those who are controlled by it, though that line is blurry: "Many capitalists would have done more for their laborers if they could, but they felt they were in the grip of a system which dictated each for himself and the devil take the hindmost" (346). Huberman was emphatic in his vision of an America that was founded as a democracy but was now facing economic forces that threatened the subsistence of the people that democracy was to serve; his last chapters speak of the conflict between "The Have-nots vs. The Haves" (335). Here was the most pointedly leftist of the books for children that focused on democracy, but it is a testament to the progressive questions being raised in children's literature during the 1930s that the concerns of the Left found an easy home in the arena of mainstream children's books given the assumption that children's literature could be one tool in the instruction of democracy.[9]

When Jessie Campbell Evans reviewed Gertrude Hartman's *These United States and How They Came to Be* and Leo Huberman's *We, the People* together in *Horn Book*, she demonstrated the willingness of children's literature to be honest and realistic in its assessment of America, noting that in dealing with the seamier side of the American story, Huberman revealed "things which are usually hidden from children."

She found in the two books a balance. "Both [narratives] are vivid and interesting and dramatic, but they are entirely different. Miss Hartman has given us a tale, beautiful, romantic, heroic and thrilling. Mr. Huberman has given us another, ugly, sordid, strong, dramatic and realistic. Both pictures are true." Children's literature, in short, could affirm a lovely, powerful, exciting vision of a pioneer history, and, at the same time, it could point to a democracy that was powerful yet fragile, a history and heritage that needed constant supervision and wide-eyed observation even as it was celebrated.

✳ ✳ ✳

Writing of novels such as the pioneer stories of the 1930s, Sara L. Schwebel argues that historical fiction can help young readers "to understand the nation as a means of organizing society and an entity that engages in political action, including telling stories about itself. When students and teachers interact with historical fiction in this way, the books they read can become catalysts to cultivating thoughtful, engaged citizens" (9). Though Schwebel is writing about later children's novels, her point would have been affirmed by the "minders" and by the artists of children's literature during the Great Depression. America was, in children's literature, a nation whose pioneer history was to be embraced and celebrated, but that pioneer heritage was also active, to be used to confront the real problems that Americans were facing in the contemporary culture. These would be the new frontiers that Americans had to face and to which children's literature would speak.

James Daugherty

The Democracy of the American Pioneer

When the English illustrator Leslie Brooke died in early 1941, James Daugherty wrote an open letter of farewell to him that was published in the May–June issue of *Horn Book*. He spoke of Brooke's "rich and gentle spirit," the "whimsy" and "cavortings" of his illustrations, and the "shy and subtle essence of the English spirit" out of which he drew. Daugherty wrote the letter in the context of the London Blitz and only six months away from America's own entrance into World War II. But he did not find it incongruent to link Brooke's gentle, whimsical, and cavorting illustrations to what England was experiencing: "Under the bright valour and quiet courage of your people in their ordeal by fire is a vast and enduring humanity that is the steadfast and peculiar characteristic of the English genius and its faith.... It is this persistent humor and unfailing courage which are so magnificent in England's darkest and finest hour."

In this letter, Daugherty was asserting unabashedly that a work of children's literature such as Brooke's *Johnny Crow's Garden* (1903), or his *The Story of the Three Bears* (1904), or his *The Story of the Three Little Pigs* (1904) could reflect a national identity. Daugherty believed this could be true in America as well. And he believed that children's books could not only reflect but shape a national identity and spirit toward the future. Though he would not follow the path of Leslie Brooke in doing so—whimsy would never be a part of Daugherty's art—Daugherty set himself precisely this task at the beginning of the second quarter of the century. For Daugherty, America was a teeming, energetic, productive, vibrant world whose exuberant art and story reflected the exuberance of a people nourished by the vivid heritage of the pioneer trails and the rich traditions of freedom and democracy. He set out to paint that world for a child audience.

✳ ✳ ✳

When Daugherty went to London at the age of sixteen—his father had been appointed the European representative of the U.S. Department of Agriculture—he enrolled in the London School of Art. One of his instructors was Frank Brangwyn, whom Daugherty later praised as "the most virile painter in England." Brangwyn was a muralist, etcher, and illustrator, and his work was characterized by a remarkable freedom and activity; Daugherty described Brangwyn's palette as "opulent."[1] In London's museums Daugherty studied the characterizations of James McNeill Whistler and the landscapes of J. M. W. Turner, and he began to roam Europe to develop what the artist Norman Kent would later call a "first-hand acquaintance with the masters": Michelangelo, Rubens, El Greco.

Yet though those influences would impact Daugherty's work, the foremost influence of those years was a literary one. Another American student at the London School of Art introduced him to Walt Whitman's *Leaves of Grass*, and Daugherty immediately recognized its vigor, intensity, and uniquely American voice at about the same time that Carl Sandburg was discovering those same qualities in Whitman. It was in America—not Europe—that Daugherty believed he would find his true subject; it was in American energy and purpose that he would find the context for both his matter and his form. "Was this really my America, this splendor of democracy, this new world of affirmation and fraternity and hope?" he wondered after reading Whitman. He resolved to return home immediately. "Farewell Europe, the museums, good-bye King Arthur! Good-bye dear London friends and all you genial hospitable Londoners. I shall always love you!" (*Walt Whitman's America*, 13). His imagined farewell, written more than fifty years after the event, was a powerful memory of a powerful artistic decision.[2]

He returned to America. "We passed under the great green Lady with the Lamp, silent, subdued by thoughts and feelings beyond words. Suddenly we were ashore on American soil, each on his own, an individual American person, a drop in the vast rushing torrents of American life—of Walt Whitman's America, our America" (13). Daugherty set up a studio in Brooklyn Heights, where he balanced commercial art—"a waste of years too well known to many American artists" (14)—with experiments in abstract art and cubism. During World War I he camouflaged ships in Baltimore, perhaps preparing him for his own mural work, which he set to immediately after the war under the sponsorship of the Loew Movie Theaters. And like many American artists, he turned his hand to magazine illustration, drawing for *Forum*, *Golden Book*, the *New Yorker*, *Collier's*, *Harper's Weekly*, and the *New*

York Sunday Herald. But he had not yet found the venue that would allow him to re-create Walt Whitman's version of America in his own texts and illustrations, though he was convinced that American exuberance could be captured in art: "The pageant of today is fascinating," he wrote in the *Horn Book* in November 1928. "Our America—its engines, machines, steel mills, modern factories all in roaring action. A world of new designs, forms and colors awaiting its Micael Angelos." In this, he was echoing the American Scene artists practicing in the 1930s—artists like Grant Wood, John Steuart Curry, and Thomas Hart Benton—who were painting American landscapes and arguing that it was not provincial to find inspiration in America but personal. Lynd Ward in "The Book Artist" described these artists as "concerned with seeing the world about them clearly and rendering it literally and honestly"; Daugherty would agree up to a point: in his work, the American scene would be rendered honestly—but not necessarily literally.[3]

In the early 1920s Daugherty moved out of New York and into the countryside of Connecticut; at almost the same time he met May Massee, then at Doubleday-Page. She had seen his work and felt it was well suited to a new edition of Stewart Edward White's *Daniel Boone: Wilderness Scout.* She offered him the book without any restrictions. As Norman Kent recalled, "There was no niggling about medium, number of illustrations or anything else. Just the green light to go ahead and do it." Daugherty began immediately; the pictures, he later said, "had been boiling in his creative kettle since childhood and now they fairly leapt from his brush onto the canvas and paper." They would represent Daugherty's first formulation of his Whitmanesque vision of the American democracy—an honest formulation, if not a literal one.[4]

Stewart Edward White's book was aimed at a young male audience, specifically the Boy Scouts, which participated in the book's copyright and stamped it with the organization's approval. Throughout the text White spoke directly to that audience to celebrate the pioneer qualities that marked Daniel Boone and that the Boy Scouts recited in their Scout Law:

> Daniel Boone was reverent in the belief that he was ordained by God
> to open the wilderness. He was brave with a courage remarkable for its
> calmness and serenity. . . . He was trustworthy, so that when wilderness
> missions of great responsibility were undertaken, he was almost invariably the one called. He was loyal to the last drop of his blood, as you shall
> see in this narrative. He was ready ever to help others. These are simple,
> fundamental qualities, but they are never anywhere too common; they are
> rarely anywhere combined in one man: and in those rough times of primi-

tive men they sufficed, when added to his wilderness skill and determination, to make him the leading and most romantic figure. If the Boy Scouts
would know a man who in his attitude toward the life to which he was
called most nearly embodied the precepts of their laws let them look on
Daniel Boone. (2–3)

White links Boone's independent and resourceful childhood to the
kind of childhood that a Scout would envy, for "any normal and healthy
boy would have reveled in a youth similar to that of Daniel Boone" (4).
Boone trained in working the land for food, in woodcraft to survive Indian attacks, in forest lore for tracking, in sport and work for physical
hardship. "These things were not sufferings, were not so very terrible,"
White writes. "I do not doubt that a certain number of my readers in
the rural districts may be a good deal in the same boat themselves"
(12). Altogether, White was evoking the ethos of the pioneer world:
this "was an age of individualism, wherein every man was supposed to
take care of himself" (96).[5]

In the face of such a strong authorial presence, Daugherty shaped
his own voice as the book's illustrator in two ways. First, he decided
to use his drawings to point the reader toward American ingenuity.
If this is a book celebrating the self-reliance of the American pioneer
and its antecedents in the Boy Scout movement, then Daugherty intended to show how that self-reliance worked itself out in practical
ways. So although Stewart's text makes no mention of these pioneering skills, Daugherty's pen-and-ink drawings depict soap making (35),
sheep shearing (130), the boiling of sap into maple sugar (144), and
loom weaving (246)—all of these contributing to a strong sense of resourcefulness and harvest developed through American ingenuity. In
fact, the weaving illustration is set against a full-page illustration entitled *Abundance* (247), in which a farmer, hoe in hand, stands beside a
hunter, rifle in hand, and between them both a huge cornstalk sprouts,
twelve feet tall, with fat ears. This is the true end of self-reliance: abundance and fruition, whose reaping, Daugherty suggests, is the story of
the American pioneer spirit.

Daugherty's second strategy for his own voice as illustrator was to
define the qualities of that American pioneer spirit through illustrations that lean toward allegory. This approach is suggested by the four
color plates Daugherty drew for the book: *The Wilderness Road*, which
acted as the frontispiece for the first edition; *Vision* (66); *Struggle* (112),
which was also cropped and used for the cover of the book; and *Escape* (186). Of these, only the last illustrated a narrative scene from the

book: three Native American warriors, carrying savage weapons, look over a cliff for the fleeing Boone, not realizing that he is blended into the woods nearby in the lower right corner of the illustration, his knife half-drawn from its sheath.

The *Vision* plate depicts Boone half-kneeling on rocks and looking out past a river toward the wilderness. He holds his rifle determinedly. The ground beneath him glows redly, and arching above his head is a rainbow, as though God himself were establishing a covenant with Boone. The plate follows a passage in which Boone has scouted out the Kentucky territory and now senses that he is ordained to settle the country; he will reprise the role of the spies sent into the promised land to bring back stories of wealth and store. In the 1926 edition of *Daniel Boone: Wilderness Scout*, this plate was brought to the beginning of the book to function as a summation of Boone's pioneering aspirations and to suggest the presence of a divine hand in the settling of the American frontier.[6]

The plate entitled *Struggle* counterpoises the *Vision* plate, suggesting the difficulties of making that vision come to pass—again, mirroring the difficulties of settling the promised land. In this illustration, Boone has already dispatched one Native attacker—the axe used earlier to clear the forests now shows a bloodied blade. He battles with another enemy, their bodies geometrically angled to suggest their equality. Almost unseen, a pioneer woman holding a child rushes away, her face turned back toward the combatants. She represents what Boone is fighting for and what the Native American warrior is struggling against: settlement, the ensuing domestication of the land, and a national citizenship that does not include the Native American.[7]

The Wilderness Road plate—the only two-page spread in the book—sets the larger purposes of Boone's explorations in context: Boone is a forerunner for the fulfillment of America's Manifest Destiny. In the illustration, pioneer figures travel toward the wilderness, a community of the common citizen. In the center, a Madonna figure is surrounded not by a halo but by the billowing tent flaps of the Conestoga wagon in which she sits. The largest figure in the spread is the weary pioneer who has laid out this road; he props a foot on a stump as he recognizes that what he has done has made possible this westward movement. Around the Madonna and the pioneer are gathered the old and young—a young Revolutionary War soldier holding his hand out to the future, the brooding face of John Brown in the lower left corner, an allegorical female figure holding the scriptures to suggest the expansion of Christianity into the wilderness, an Abraham Lincoln–looking figure with an axe over his left shoulder. There is a general air of exhilaration, of determination, a fleshing out of the ideals of *Vision* and *Struggle*.

Anne Carroll Moore, writing in the spring of 1947, almost twenty years after the publication of Daugherty's edition of *Daniel Boone: Wilderness Scout*, recalled her first sight of the original drawings for the book:

> I well remember the spirited comment and the sharp disagreement aroused by an exhibition of the originals held in the Children's Room of the New York Public Library that year. The right of young American artists to put an Italian Madonna in a covered wagon on the Wilderness Road and the face and figure of the young Abraham Lincoln upon the same road was hotly contested. James Daugherty had caught sight of the pioneers laughing and shouting and singing as they worked, and had dared to set down, as he saw it, the bold romantic life of the frontier, dared to picture the beauty and joy which belong to youth in every age.

Moore's suggestion of Daugherty's boldness is correct: Daugherty does not pit the Old World against the New World; that contest he assumes is already over. His illustrations instead unapologetically take images of the Old World—here the image of the Madonna—and baptize them in the youth, freshness, and vigor of the New World. It is a young Abraham Lincoln beside the Madonna. The beauty and joy Daugherty pictures are those of youth, not European agedness. Moore's interpretation of those images certainly suggests that what Daugherty is about here is to develop the mythos of an America that had, because of its vigor and youth, taken over spiritually from the tired Old World.

The challenge that Daugherty wanted to set for the young reader, however, was to continue to maintain that energy and passion of the pioneer spirit into the coming years. Daugherty suggests this challenge early on, during White's digression on the youthful education of Daniel Boone. He illustrates this section with a full-page black-and-white drawing entitled *Effort* (10), in which a powerful pioneer farmer, straining mightily, pushes a plow behind a team of yoked oxen who seem to follow the curve of the earth. A sun rises behind them as if to spread its blessing. The power and dignity of this effort leads to the head illustration for the book's final chapter (269). In that drawing, a pioneer with flintlock, sheathed knife, and coonskin hat points toward the "New Frontier," which is a city rising magnificently under the sun. Beneath his outstretched arm sits a Boy Scout, his hand resting on his chin, thoughtful, poised, ready to take up the next challenge, as the pioneer had been ready to take up his challenge. Though the frontier may have changed, Daugherty is arguing, the qualities that marked Daniel Boone's life and that are part of the pioneer inheritance of Americans are still to be embraced as new pioneers head out to new frontiers. That sense of the pioneer spirit—and the necessity of its recognition and adoption by young Americans—would become the hallmark of James Daugherty's work in illustration.

But no artistic career moves in a perfectly linear trajectory. In the next few years, Daugherty would illustrate some very un-American titles: A. Conan Doyle's *The White Company* (1928), Arthur Quiller-Couch's *The Splendid Spur* (1927), Andrew Lang's *The Conquest of Montezuma's Empire* (1928), Herbert Escott-Inman's *Wulnoth the Wanderer* (1928), Cameron Rogers's *Drake's Quest* (1927), and *Three Comedies by Shakespeare* (1929). These are hardly the stuff of Whitman's America, and Daugherty's illustrations for books such as *The Splendid Spur* looked backward, closely recalling in their activity and palette the work of Frank Brangwyn.

Still, by the late 1920s Daugherty was being spoken of as a particularly American illustrator. In 1929 Josiah Titzell entitled his *Publishers Weekly* article about Daugherty and his work "James Daugherty, American."

> His inspiration, his stimulation is the same as the Greek's, but he has combined with them a quality that is entirely American. This is true both of his line, that is impelled by a native robustness, impetuosity and extravagance, and his color, which shows (perhaps more in his later work) the influence of our early Indian art, both in its original exuberance and in the tamed form in which it was adopted by the pioneers. It is a plastic manifestation of Americanism, and the spirit that is responsible for it is as thoroughly American as Faneuil Hall. . . . [Daugherty] is thoroughly, undeviatingly American in background, appearance, attitude and in his art.

Titzell concluded his piece with something of a plea. He recognized that Daugherty had plans to work in murals and etchings. "Hurrah and banzai, we say, but don't let it interfere with his contributions to American book illustration."

Daugherty listened. Soon he was crafting his own *Daniel Boone*, articulating his vision of what a robust Whitmanesque America was all about in a familiar way. The pioneering spirit, he wrote, "this is the real American processional." When in 1939 his *Daniel Boone* was published, Daugherty must have been pleased by the *Horn Book* review, which was an affirmation of Titzell's analysis: "The power and exuberance of the writing well fits the spirit of the mighty hunter and trail breaker which calls the generations that come after him to far horizons and freedom."

It was as if the reviewer was recalling the final chapter head illustration of *Daniel Boone: Wilderness Scout*. Anne Carroll Moore was even more exuberant: "It has pioneer flavor and authenticity. Only a pioneer at heart who has seen freedom at a crossroads could have reached back over a hundred years with so warm a handclasp for the Pioneer of the Wilderness." With *Daniel Boone*, Daugherty had indeed found his true subject and purpose, that which he had come to find when he returned to America from England.[8]

Writing of *Daniel Boone*, Norman Kent suggested that Daugherty's goal in his art was to "take up his brush to exploit his own native land" and that his work "smells of the earth and has about it that homespun character so genuinely American." The artist Lynd Ward agreed. Writing the biographical article that followed the publication of Daugherty's Newbery acceptance speech for *Daniel Boone*, Ward argued that Daugherty was "rendering in visual terms the roots of American life." Ward spoke of that effort with an almost missionary zeal: "The real juices of American life have been captured [in *Daniel Boone*] and held fast for our own and other generations to cherish and make use of." Daugherty, he wrote, is like Whitman, "singing a song of America." So far so good. But Daugherty had more in mind than capturing a homespun American mythos, and Lynd Ward came closer to it at the end of his article. James Daugherty, he wrote, "now stands in a kind of symbolic relation to our culture, his talent firmly rooted in American experience, his creative motivation well attuned to the techniques of our age, his voice well able to speak out for the values of democratic life." Daugherty, in Ward's mind, speaks about the American experience because he comes out of the American experience; he is a part of his context and a voice for his context. And for Daugherty, that experience from which he emerged could be summed up in the notion of a vital, vigorous democracy, the enabler as well as the fruit of the American pioneer experience.

Daugherty had found his matter and form as well as his purpose. To present these, he developed two strands in his illustrative and textual work, both of which find their roots in Walt Whitman. First, he would write about the pioneers—about their bravery and struggle and fortitude. He would write about them as those who personified the destiny of the American people to move ever westward, beginning (as he would later define it) with William Bradford's movement westward over the Atlantic. And he would couple that dramatic sense of movement with a corresponding sense of settlement and permanence, as those pioneers either created communities that they inhabited or paved the way for settlers to come in their paths. In other words, he represented in his work the twin themes of independence and self-reliance, and interdependence and community. Second, Daugherty would write about the glory of the average, common person whose abilities and hopes and very life are given the opportunity to rise to greatness through the freedom that democracy provides. In terms familiar to both Whitman and Vachel Lindsay, who also wrote of the American democracy, Daugherty sings of America as the land of the glorious commonality.

In *Daniel Boone*, Daugherty was explicitly representing the virtues of American democracy to a young American audience during a time in history when, he felt, the vices of the Old World were readily apparent. His prologue to the book is a letter ostensibly addressed to Daniel Boone, but actually he is addressing his young readers on the eve of World War II:

> Rise up, you lanky sons of democracy
> . . . .
> Pray to the God of your Fathers that their spirit be upon you.
> That you may have the enduring courage to cut a clean straight path for a
> Free people through the wilderness against oppression and aggression,
> For generations marching to higher freedoms
> Riding toward the sun
> Singing in the canebrakes
> Singing in the tough spots
> Chanting: Democracy, here we come. (7)

The passage reads like a liturgy, setting democracy in a religious context, with a prayer invoking the "God of your Fathers," a chant to focus meaning and emotion, and a concluding triumphant affirmation of faith and confidence.

The religious quality of democracy as enacted in America is a dominant motif in *Daniel Boone*; Daugherty frequently employs biblical echoes to suggest the meaning of the democratic urge and to unite that urge with the American pioneering spirit. Daniel Boone first encounters the West as "a world almost as new as Genesis" (15). Later, he receives an epiphany: "Next day the clear-shining sun rose over the vast land like high-calling trumpets of glory. The splendor and the brightness came upon his spirit like the rushing of mighty wings, and the voice of mighty thunderings: 'Enter into a promised land such as no man has known, a new born creation all your own; drink deep, O Daniel, of the mysterious wine of the wilderness'" (34). This epiphany blends God's promise of a new land with American rugged individualism—it is a creation "all your own." That Promised Land is labeled as Kentucky (26), and Daugherty defines it as a "land of plenty," a "garden of Eden unknown to man, teeming with a fabulous abundance of fat land, of fish and game" (27). It is both the Promised Land for a people who have been in exile and the garden from which we were exiled, a linking of that which was lost and that which was promised, the link made by the richness and abundance of that world. But it is even more than that. That new Promised Land "might be the gateway to a new America, a fabulous western world with a destiny of glory like the towering storm clouds in a fiery sunset" (27). It is this sense, writes Daugherty, that "had pulled the feet westward since the first white man beached a boat on American shores" (28). Democracy and the land the pioneers will settle both are hallowed.

✳ ✳ ✳

In terms of the text of *Daniel Boone*, Daugherty's biography of Boone is much more succinct and direct than that of Stewart Edward White, because their intentions are so different. Daugherty is not working at completeness of detail; he crafts the life impressionistically, creating images of Boone's wanderings and explorations. Daugherty's succinctness emerges out of his focus: having used his prologue to establish the notion of democracy as the overriding thematic concern of his biography, he wanted to show Boone as the embodiment of both the American pioneer spirit and its democratic urgings. Thus Boone's youth is depicted as a time of preparation for his westward movement: "Boys learned the easy way to swing an ax all day long, hold an ox-drawn plow on a straight furrow, mend a harness, and hitch a horse, all with a sure swift skill and easy grace" (12), Daugherty writes, while girls made their own world, "busy with making and mending or caring for the gentle or rambunctious farm animals that were almost members of the household. They provided in wise ways for the needs of tomorrow" (12). The illustration accompanying this text is one of Daugherty's allegorical ones. A man, children climbing about him, stands easy with an axe; beside him, a woman sits by a spinning wheel, one hand on an open book, the other in an occupied cradle. He looks into the present; she gazes into the future (13).

From this point on, everything that Boone does becomes an enactment of the pioneering spirit, that vigorous spirit Daugherty defines as so American. When Boone is old and takes one last trip beyond the Mississippi, Daugherty speaks of that spirit in familiar terms: "He was going west again, floating down the ample river in the beautiful Ohio spring, following the American dream" (85). The movement west, the pioneering spirit, destiny of glory, the American Dream—these are the synonymous terms that Daugherty uses to reflect the spirit of a people "Singing in the canebrakes / Singing in the tough spots / Chanting: Democracy, here we come." In this sense, democracy is both the means enabling the journey and the journey's goal.

There is still, however, the issue of the "Other" in a democracy, the minority that does not find an easy place in the pioneer expansionism. Here Daugherty is ambivalent. The Native American figure in *Daniel Boone*—in fact, in all of Daugherty's renderings—is almost always naked and savage, though at times noble. One two-tone illustration in *Daniel Boone* depicts a warrior striding over the prostrate body of a British soldier. He is almost demonic in his fierce expression, in his wielding of a knife overhead, in the angular musculature of his body (20). In an illustration of one of the episodes in which Boone is captured, Boone stands surrounded by four Indian captors. Though they are large—even larger than he is—yet the clothed, muscular figure of Boone is clearly superior to four captors, who wield all sorts of horrid instruments; Boone's hand is still clutching his pioneer flintlock, suggesting that his superiority comes from his connection to the pioneering enterprise (33). That image sets up the next full-page illustration, in which Boone has escaped and is jauntily leaving his captors well behind him as he leaps from a cliff into a treetop—a jump his captors fear to make (35).

In the face of the Other, Boone is clearly dominant, as Daugherty suggests in a passage describing Boone's stay in Kentucky.

> A new sense of freedom and power possessed him as he ranged over the long hills and followed shrewdly the secret waterways. He was the only freeman in all the western world, like Man himself in the Beginning of Things. Hunter and hunted, he measured his woodcraft against the forest prowlers. Chased to the edge of a high cliff and cornered by Indians, he leaped into a tree-top and so away like the wild rabbit. He hid under waterfalls and swung across streams on wild grapevines. He lay in the canebrake and sang to himself an old Virginia ballad with a rousing refrain. He loved to think of himself as a jack rabbit dodging the Shawnees in the laurel bushes, a red fox of the canebrakes with a fat partridge in his teeth, a lean young wolf of the wilderness trotting over the long hills sniffing the four winds of Kentucky or nosing down the valleys, finding the ways to the salt licks and the sweet waters flowing under the stars. (34–36)

The images are telling. The land is a fertile one, and he is part of it, even heir to it. He receives it as Adam received the entire Creation, and so he becomes the only true freeman. Those here earlier are mere obstacles to be defeated through his superior and arrogant cunning.

But precisely here is where Daugherty's ambivalence emerges. In an illustration set beside poignant passages from a Native American point of view, Daugherty pictures another fierce warrior; his body takes up the entire page. But now he does not bestride a defeated British soldier; he stands over a Native American woman who is clutching the dead body of her very young son. While the warrior raises his arms in defiance, allegorical hands emerge from the side, one offering a whiskey bottle, another a Bible, another a musket (41). Each offers extinction for the Native American, who rejects them all and opts instead for his own hopeless fight. "Amid their burning villages and the awful butcheries and sickening betrayals of friends and foe, they met the personal tragedy of violent death with a serene indifference" (39), Daugherty writes—and he means this to be admiring.

Daugherty is caught in a bind. He wants to depict the absolute rightness of the American movement westward, the necessity of following the robust democratic urge to conquer the continent. The Native American is the most dramatic danger standing in the way of that urging. And yet, the Native American also represents the rugged strength and independence so essential to living in the wilderness. The same woodcraft and resourcefulness that allow Boone to survive in the wilderness of Kentucky mark the Native Americans already there. Hence Boone's respect for the Other, though it is not a respect that allows him to perceive truly the world through the Other's perspective; the urgings of the pioneer spirit and, ironically, the democracy that fuels it are too strong for that. And though by the end of the text it is clear that the wiles of the white man are as damaging to Boone as they are to the Native American people (even as he contributes to their being dispossessed, he too will be dispossessed through the connivance of lawyers back home), still, one closes the book with vivid images of the dangers not of lawyers but of the muscular savages who appear out of the woods.

Though Daugherty's focus is on Boone, the underlying question of the book is one of purpose. To what does this pioneering spirit, this movement against the frontier, this democratic urge lead? Here Daugherty is not ambivalent: the answer is settlement and community, which for Daugherty represent a state of plenty, of peace, of prosperity. In *Daniel Boone: Wilderness Scout*, Stewart Edward White pictures settlements as a subversion of the rugged individual life; Daugherty sees them as the interdependent experience toward which the pioneer life works. Again and again, Daugherty makes this equation. Once the pioneers have built the fort of Boonesborough, he describes the development of the town in joyful tones: "Parties were arriving with their flocks and herds, cows and pigs, innumerable children and shirt-tail boys. Plows were cutting the forest loam in fresh-made clearings. Spinning wheels hummed and cradle songs drifted across the drowsing river. Girls brought water from the spring and the young men shaved and washed behind their ears" (47). He accompanies this with the illustration of a young farmer chopping down part of the forest while doffing his hat to a young woman who has brought water out to him. A chicken, a pig, and an ear of corn stand by, while a fence forms the background (47). These settlers are, writes Daugherty, "a barefooted rail-splitting, haranguing, horse-racing democracy" who are "raising up green armies of tall corn in the valley bottoms" (46). Daugherty is here depicting the larger social fabric that this rugged pioneering has made possible, and it is no less muscular or joyous or raucous than the pioneer vision. Later, in two images set side by side, Daugherty depicts a rugged pioneer leaping into the air when Boonesborough is saved from a siege; he holds his flintlock above his head, and his knife and powder horn are by his side. His arms held high, he seems to embrace the whole of the walled town (66). But across the page, that energy of celebration is metamorphosed into the strength of the farmer, as the flintlock is replaced by the plow, and the raised head is replaced by the head bent in work, a head that once again suggests Abraham Lincoln (67). The combination of these two illustrations presages the concluding image of the book, which is that of settled and cultivated fields and split-rail fences. Boone is thus a trailbreaker to advance the destiny of free people marching on; the fulfillment of the pioneer life is the settlement of the farm and the abundant yield it produces.

That concluding image is, in fact, a repetition of the same image that comes about midway through the text. There, it is used to illustrate the confident and optimistic collective voice of the American democracy, with its own distant identity and purpose: "We are the nation of the valley, the tall corn-fed, hog-fed sons of the West. We make our own destiny and we like it. We make our own glories and shames and we've just begun. Our songs and our dreams are made of the new moon over the dry corn shocks, of the wind in the maple groves, of the silver-weathered rails in the fence along a prairie road" (52). At the book's conclusion, the illustration is used to mark the description of Boone as a "trail-breaker for destiny for a free people marching on" (95). For Daugherty, there is not substantive distinction between the two ways of life, the pioneer and the settler. They are a single union.

And when that peace and plenty and prosperity are threatened? Daugherty wishes to speak to the present generation even as he had spoken at the end of *Daniel Boone: Wilderness Scout*, and he places his sentiments in a passage describing the settlers of Boonesborough as they reject an offer for surrender from a French and Native American army about to besiege the town: "But the tough cantankerous spirit of the frontier urged: 'Go ahead or bust.' They would not have been where they were if they had not been stubborn survivors of a rough, tough, restless race who lived and died in their own independent way by the rifle, the ax, the Bible and the plow. So they sent back the eagle's answer: 'No surrender,' the answer of the sassy two-year-old baby democracy, the answer of Man the Unconquerable to the hosts of darkness— 'No surrender'" (59). It is hard not to hear in this passage the sense of imminent war in Europe.

James Daugherty's acceptance speech for the Newbery Medal that honored *Daniel Boone* articulates his presentation of American democracy for a child audience. Entitled "Children's Books in a Democracy" and published just sixteen months before America's entrance into World War II, the article begins by asking, "What, if any, is the function and value of children's books in a democracy? Can these books help children to live more richly?" The second question he poses suggests his answer to the first: yes, children's books, particularly those of "good nature, affection, and regard," will help a child to live a richer life. But Daugherty has not, in that answer, meant to answer the first question fully. It is possible, certainly, to imagine children's books of "good nature, affection, and regard" under the auspices of, say, a monarchy, though it is more difficult to imagine these qualities under a totalitarian agency. So what is distinct about the workings of children's books and democracy? Particularly the American democracy?[9]

Daugherty's answer probes the same ground as that explored by Anne Carroll Moore: the writer must be free to write about "the American scene," and in describing that exuberant scene, Daugherty sounds much like his cherished Walt Whitman:

> Certainly the vast and fantastic epic of America is a rich storehouse of true stories that make the legends of Greece and old Europe seem trivial and tame. Instead of a handful of bad-tempered legendary national heroes, we have a vast lore of very actual saints, desperadoes, romantics, inventors, robber barons, Indian chiefs and rail-splitters roaring across the plains and mountains in a cavalcade so fierce and gaudy, so splendid and ragged, so near and so real that a whole race of writers and artists is needed to sing and to image it, make books, and plays and symphonies, sculpt friezes and

murals in libraries—celebrating the nation composed of all nations marching on the very long rough road to freedom.

For this reason, Daugherty asserts, American artists have "'chucked' their Paris imitating" as well as the "silly goddesses and allegories of the Boston and Washington libraries" in order to paint "the life of today in our America—the true art of democracy." He continues with a ringing call.

> Let us look more realistically and idealistically at the present in our own land—these teeming grade and high schools, with their dynamic young Americans stepping out to the great adventure of living, call for fresh and candid thinking. "Junior" writing needs more air and room, exposure to the weather, more of a look around America today—going up the side streets of industrial towns, working on a cattle ranch in the dry West, the wheat and cotton and corn harvesting; needs to take a hand in the epic struggle for survival of any American family under the economic and social pressures and crises of the time. Living in America today is more heroic and desperate than in the old frontier, the visual scene infinitely more swift and stirring than Buffalo Bill's Wild West.

Here is the American Scene painter working for a child audience. And Daugherty concludes with this assessment of what a writer of children's literature in America might do: "If those of us who spend years among children's books—publishers, librarians, authors, illustrators—doubt sometimes of what avail this shrill piping may be among the crashing of the nations, let us remember that we have this privilege above all others—that we strive to serve the hope of a better world, the children of democracy." Daugherty's answer to the question of what role a children's book may serve in the American democracy is to argue that it is a venue for depicting a real, vital, energized, youthful life of the nation that, through telling the stories of that people, will embolden and ennoble them and so help the children of democracy strive to create a better world. This is the natural extension of the final illustration in *Daniel Boone: Wilderness Scout*, pointing to the new frontier and the responsibility of the American democracy to prepare young Americans to enter into it. In short, he was arguing with Leslie Brooke that children's literature could embody a national spirit, one that challenged "the Nazi Primer, the brutality and dullness of dictator propaganda," and instead "help[ed] to realize the fullness and goodness of living that is the American faith."

✳ ✳ ✳

In *Poor Richard* (1941), written two years after *Daniel Boone*, Daugherty took up more particularly the celebration of the average person in the American democracy, the kind of person he saw as essential to the success and onward movement of that democracy. In this book, he pictured Benjamin Franklin, not a rambunctious pioneer moving westward but instead a model of the virtues of industry and frugality, which, Daugherty insists, are also necessary to encourage the march of democracy. He dedicated the book to "Young Americans of courage and imagination to build a strong destiny for these States" and connected Franklin to them by illustrating the dedication with a full-page depiction of Franklin surrounded by books and a smaller illustration directly below in which a contemporary boy reads as he bites at an apple; the virtues of the past and the present are the same, he suggests. So when Daugherty writes of the young Franklin, "It would be fine, he thought, to conquer the world and rout the armies of darkness by writing and printing words" (20), there is a real sense that he is not writing only of Franklin's time.

Throughout the biography, Daugherty focuses on what Franklin *does*. Beginning with his "tireless Yankee stride" (28) as he walks toward Philadelphia and ending with the writing of his *Autobiography*, Daugherty pictures Franklin as the man of action, not in terms of physical action but in terms of the practical know-how that Daugherty sees as a distinctly American trait, as he had years before in *Daniel Boone: Wilderness Scout*. "His inventive mind and the experience of the years worked to find practical ways to get a thousand things done that America might be strong and ready for her ordeal by fire" (114), Daugherty writes of Franklin just before the American Revolution— an assessment he had set up earlier when he had noted Franklin's persistence as an apprentice "in putting right-thinking into practical action" (42). Thus, while other printers fail around him, Franklin succeeds, because "'Industry and Frugality' was Ben's motto" (58). His later successes as a diplomat would emerge, Daugherty insists, from that same persistence.

And in all of this drive, there is nothing of the industrialist, nothing of the tycoon. Daugherty sees Franklin as a representative of democracy, so he pictures him as a lover of humanity: Franklin decides, for example, not to patent his Franklin stove, a "Yankee contraption . . . to help mankind" (60). Daugherty pictures him as a man who is willing to speak his mind truly and freely: his writing for his brother's paper, Daugherty asserts, had a "breezy feeling of free speech and democracy in their remarks about the way things were" (22). And perhaps most importantly, Daugherty pictures him as a person who rejected status and pomposity as valid forms of power and prestige: "With his curious crab-tree walking-stick, he was Democracy in person among the powdered wigs and silk coats and gilt swords of the court aristocrats" (126). The stress is always on Franklin as an active representative and product of democracy—and, in this sense, the common man.

Both *Daniel Boone* and *Poor Richard* had been published shortly before America's entrance into the war. Their connection to it did not go unnoticed, nor did Daugherty's intention to speak of courage and determination to his young audience with words centered on freedom as it is represented in the American democracy. Of *Daniel Boone*, Anne Carroll Moore wrote in the fall of 1939: "The courage to face reality without bitterness in any place or time, the feeling for beauty and the search for truth and justice are all here for boys and girls to feed upon." Two years later, in 1941, Moore identified books such as *Poor Richard* as "on the side of defense" during wartime. In that same year, Elizabeth Janet Gray—herself only two years away from becoming a Newbery Medal winner for *Adam of the Road* (1942)—opened her article "Young People and Books" with this question: "At the outset of the third winter of a world in flames and the flames spreading, what are we saying to our young people? . . . What resources do we wish to give them which will help to prepare them to meet it and—we pray—some day to better it?" Her answer: books, which teach the conviction that freedom must be earned, that life is worth living, that people respond to love and trust. Thus, her selection of books represents those texts that "leave that imponderable residue that makes for 'courage and gaiety and the quiet mind.'" One of the few published images from the books she selects comes from *Poor Richard*; it is that of Franklin, the great writer and thinker and diplomat and patriot, sitting in a chair surrounded by four children and a playful cat—courage, gaiety, and the quiet mind (97).

❊ ❊ ❊

Daugherty published his next biography in November 1943: *Abraham Lincoln*, focusing on a great man leading a country during wartime. Dedicated to Daugherty's son Charles and to "his comrades in arms throughout the world," the book celebrates democracy through the combination of the two strands that Daugherty had pursued in *Daniel Boone* and *Poor Richard*. From *Daniel Boone* he took the pioneering spirit of America and its drive toward settlement, beginning *Abraham Lincoln* in fact with Daniel Boone's trailblazing in Kentucky. But in terms of his depiction of Lincoln as a representative of American democracy, Daugherty turned to the forms he had used in *Poor Rich-ard*. Here he had been careful to depict Franklin as the citizen whose own industry allowed him to rise in his service to his country and who therefore stood against those who had merely inherited power, prestige, and wealth. This is the major thrust of *Abraham Lincoln*: that Abraham Lincoln rose out of a people, a rising that occurred only because of the freedom that American democracy produced. Daugherty sets the theme in his introduction, drafted as a prose poem:

> It was certain that out of the womb of American Democracy
> A man should come to the nineteenth century,
> The common normal type in full stature....
> He did not hail from the smug colonial strip, the eastern slopes
> He had no credentials from the tide-water plantations
> He was not a son of the New England Dynasty
> He came as an axeman from the cabins ...
> And now the drawling voice of the all-inclusive tolerant average man
> Weighing the reasons in balance, speaking out as the voice of Truth ...
> And the land and the people of the land saying,
> This is he for whom we have waited
> A man to be lifted up
> By the choice and faith of the people....
> Abraham Lincoln—he who happened to be a little more than another
> The average all inclusive type of tolerant democratic man. (7–8)

Writing in the middle of the war, Daugherty was clearly not talking about the patrician Franklin Roosevelt (though politically Daugherty was a supporter of Roosevelt); he was talking about the genius of American democracy. In Daugherty's definition, the American experiment had created a world of inclusion, of tolerance, of equality that allowed for the extraordinary qualities of any individual—not just one born to privilege—to be recognized and elevated through the choice and faith of an entire people. This is the reiterated theme of the biography.[10]

Though Daugherty is careful not to make this book a hagiography, and though he often allows Lincoln to speak for himself (long passages are cited from his speeches), and though he adds contextual material about the Civil War, Daugherty still provides a mythic vision of Lincoln. He is a man who emerges from the land itself, working alone in the tall timber, becoming acquainted with the forest animals and recognizing their autobiographies, as Daugherty writes, written through their tracks. In the illustration accompanying this description (21), Lincoln stands thoughtfully; he is tall and lean, his own vertical line matched by the trees beside him. He is surrounded by the abundance of the American forest, and the dove brooding over his head (accompanied by a hawk) seems a spiritual sign. In fact, Lincoln is connected to Christ not infrequently. When he resolves to fight against slavery, Daugherty cites John 18:37, Christ's words to Pilate in explanation of his purpose: "To this end I was born, and for this cause I came into the world, that I should bear witness to the truth" (71). As Lincoln prepares to head to Washington to assume the presidency of a nation dividing, Daugherty reflects on the crown of thorns waiting for the president to wear and notes that this trip was his Gethsemane (102). Later, as Lincoln waits for news from the front, Daugherty evokes this same garden as Lincoln waits with "the sweat of agony to his brow" (152). In fact, democracy itself is given ecclesiastical overtones. The box in which the ballots are cast is the "Ark of the Covenant of Democracy" (100). A presidential election is the "high sacrament of Democracy" (178).

But the voice of the book that undergirds Daugherty's own is that of his beloved poet, Walt Whitman; Daugherty cites him six times. He quotes from Whitman's *Democratic Vistas*, on democracy as "the highest form of interaction between men" (196) and as "a training-school for making first-class men" (127); it is that ground that provides for "fair play" (148). Daugherty quotes, too, from *Specimen Days*, suggesting that the war "was no quadrille in a ball-room" but was fought out among private soldiers—the essence of a democracy. And Daugherty cites—in fact, concludes the book with—Whitman's lament for the dead president, "When Lilacs Last in the Dooryard Bloom'd" (209). In each case, Daugherty chooses passages that attest to the image of a vibrant democracy that is not the product of prestige but "the boisterous hurly-burly of a frontier democracy" (44) and peopled by the "normal" who have been elevated by their community's choice.

This equalizing frontier democracy is captured most effectively in Daugherty's illustration for Lincoln's delivery of the Gettysburg Address, an image that prepared Daugherty for his full-color illustrated edition of that text four years later. Lincoln stands in the center, head bowed, hands out; there is no triumphalism here. On one corner are the soldiers from both white and Negro battalions. On the other corner is Daugherty's Madonna figure, gazing up at Lincoln. Beyond Lincoln are the crowds of people, old, young, a mother with her hands to her face, anonymous heads. Beyond them are the graves upon which the sunlight slants down. A decorative eagle behind Lincoln seems to light on his shoulders; it is not honorific; it is a burden (164). Lincoln has risen because of his own merit and because of the democracy that these figures represent. That rising, however, does not lead to prestige and glory but to burden and responsibility, which are themselves the rewards and glories of democracy, suggests Daugherty. The implication is that these are the responsibilities that the new generation will take up in a new time of war.[11]

In *Suspended Animation*, Nathalie op de Beeck comments unfairly that "Daugherty's all-American reputation was carefully stage-managed, at least in the publishing industry"; there is no evidence of the kind of inauthenticity suggested in this comment. But op de Beeck does note fairly that "Daugherty's political ideals always were part of his narrative style" (195). To this might be added, "part of his illustrative style." With *Daniel Boone*, *Poor Richard*, and *Abraham Lincoln*, James Daugherty established the matter and form of his work. Though the forms would change somewhat, and though the matter would later change slightly in emphasis, they would remain virtually intact in terms of Daugherty's presentation to young readers of the nature of the American democracy as he saw it and in his understanding of the American democracy's pioneer origins, in his stress that democracy was about the elevation of the common citizen, and in his belief that he was passing on the glories of that democracy to his child readers. In these early years of his career, questions about how that democracy was being worked out in American culture were, for Daugherty, of less importance than sheer exuberant celebration.

But that was to change after World War II, when the antagonists of the war were antagonists no longer. New antagonists had risen to challenge that democracy, and not all of them were external. Writing in this period, Daugherty could have drawn the 1922 illustration of Daniel Boone and the Boy Scout looking toward the future frontier once again. But perhaps he would not have drawn that image with the same unquestioning confidence. In his postwar work, he hinted of cracks in the democracy; now, as he looked about at the Cold War, the McCarthyist responses, the racial divisions separating communities, the rise into dominance of moneyed interests, the numbing quality of the suburban commuter lifestyle, the looming dangers of the atomic age, the virtues he celebrated did not change, but the tone of their presentation did. Daugherty allowed more urgency, even more stridency, into his proclamation of those virtues, and stridency colors optimism.

❊ ❊ ❊

At the end of the war, Irwin Shapiro published his *John Henry and the Double-Jointed Steam Drill* (1945), recounting the contest of John Henry and the steam drill driving through a mountain. In this version,

John Henry does not die at the end; much of the book is instead taken up with Shapiro's account of what happened after the steam drill contest, in which John Henry repeatedly battles and outwits John Hardy, a cotton merchant, finds his wife, drives steel in every state of the union, and finally turns to a steam drill to finish the Big Bend Tunnel. Since Shapiro seems aware of the oddity of John Henry using a steam drill, he has the steam drill give in before John Henry once again.

The repeated phrase that Daugherty chose to evoke in his illustrations for the book is that John Henry is "a natural man." This seems a misnomer. When John Henry is first linked to this phrase, what follows in the text suggests the opposite: he was "the greatest steel driver that ever was. He was almost as tall as a box car is long. His arms were thicker than the cross-ties on the railroad." So "natural" does not mean ordinary—at least physically ordinary. Nor does it mean innocent—though there is a kind of innocent quality about John in his remarkable confidence in his own supposedly limitless self. In Daugherty's evocation, "the natural man" is the one who is born to aspiration, the one born to dare and perform greatly, to reach in strength and confidence toward a destiny that he, because he is a natural human being, must have. Both the destiny and the ability to attain it are "natural" to him. Daugherty uses the illustrations here to assert the theme of the common man in America—who has a destiny beyond being a commuter—and to use it to point to the experience of African Americans.[12]

And this is what makes the opening illustration of the book so gripping in terms of what Daugherty wants to say about John Henry. In the illustration, John Henry poses as we might expect: he strides across a rock, a hammer propped upon his bare shoulders. His centrality and strong vertical stance enhance his dominance and power. But beneath him are a series of portraits that we might not expect: a gathering of prominent African American statesmen, artists, and intellectuals; they include George Washington Carver, Marian Anderson, Paul Robeson, and Booker T. Washington. Here too, Daugherty suggests, are natural ones who have aspired and dared greatly—and who have succeeded greatly. But Daugherty does not want to highlight only the well-known success stories. Standing by the rock, above the representations and just to John Henry's left, is an African American mother and child; she is teaching her child to read. On John Henry's right is an African American World War II soldier; the grave behind him recalls the sacrifices he has made. There are no names listed by these two figures. Nor do they play any part in the narrative text. But Daugherty is suggesting that here, too, are the common extraordinary ones of the American democracy. And the seriousness of this image—more serious than any other illustration in *John Henry and the Double-Jointed Steam Drill*—suggests the intensity of his message, drawn at the very end of World War II and looking forward to the beginnings of the civil rights movement.[13]

This sensitivity prepared Daugherty for his illustrations for Earl Schenck Miers's *The Rainbow Book of American History* (1955), whose preface, entitled "A Call to Adventure," epitomized the progress of American history: "So the story unfolded—a story of war, of incredible bravery and courage, of hardship and endurance, of invention and industry and an unending struggle for social justice, until on the new frontier of science, it now stands at its most challenging moment" (9). This is real confidence, a sense that the American spirit can overcome all difficulties. But it is not exuberant. There is a struggle for social justice that is unending. And at the beginning of the Cold War, science has brought America not to new heights but to "its most challenging moment." It is an adventure that has brought the country to a precarious point. If this is confidence, it is a sober confidence.

Daugherty does not begin with this soberness. His title-page illustration depicts a jovial Uncle Sam sitting happily on a stump. Beside him, a Boy Scout and Girl Scout salute smartly while smiling across the page to the eagle, whose wings are spread and who is also smiling. The bird is perched on the shoulders of a trail scout (also smiling), who leads a Conestoga wagon and dog (also smiling). In the distance, the sun is rising, and there is a real sense of an adventure filled with characters who are supremely confident—no hint of challenging moments here.

In fact, this is the tenor of most of the illustrations for the book, where Daugherty uses the exaggerated muscularity of his characters to suggest a kind of physical omnipotence. A huge Leif Ericson lifting his arm in greeting and striding like a colossus onto the shores of "Vineland" (11), the casual power of the whalers (165), the indomitable strength of the D-day invaders (298)—all are suggested by sheer physical prowess. At times Daugherty suggests this omnipotence in posture, as in Columbus's aggressive leaning over his ship as he sights land for the first time (20–21), or in the rigid uprightness of George Washington in any of the several illustrations in which he appears (67, 106, 109, 115)—even for that of Valley Forge, where, though his head is inclined in sorrow, the rest of his body is a straight Greek column (94–95).

But in the latter half of the book, the illustrations change: the adventure has shifted, and the postures are not so confident. Even the powerful muscularity is gone. Daugherty's depiction of the tale of Leif Ericson shows two powerful Vikings carrying a huge, weighty load of grapes on a staff between them, suggesting that America is much like the promised land from which the ancient Hebrew spies brought back grapes and tales of a land of milk and honey (12). The illustration is brightly colored in reds, yellows, and blues. But at the end of the work, the illustrations have shifted to sober blues and reds and browns. Now, amid eagles that are no longer smiling, there are the tales of a different kind of American adventure, one that is not confined to national borders but that suggests a global presence. A fierce eagle matching an array of cannons on the other side of a spread watches over the Spanish-American War (258–59). Troops, watched over literally by President Wilson, rush out of the trenches of World War I (278–79). A second fierce eagle watches over Franklin Roosevelt, Churchill, and Stalin as the Allied forces are fused (296–97), and two-toned grim illustrations in army green depict the D-day invasions (302–3), dominated by cannons firing from the sea. Interspersed among these images are those of America's advancing sciences: tales of Thomas Edison (274), of the radio (283), and of television (275), of Lindbergh's first flight (287), and finally of the "birth of the atomic age" (304).

The strong suggestion on the part of the text is that America's position as a world leader is supported and even encouraged by America's position as a leader in the sciences. But here is where Daugherty affirms the soberness that Miers has suggested in his preface. The two-tone green of the illustrations is sober and serious, suggesting the kind of new challenges that America needs to take up, and the images themselves are, for the first time, harsh, even frightening. The smoke rising from the atomic bomb, whose detonation announces the birth of the atomic age, bears a skull embedded in its billows (306).

Miers concludes with optimism: "So came America to the middle years of the 20th century. War never had been made more fearful or peace more beautiful. A great new source of power had been created. Men have not yet fully conceived what unimaginable riches can flow from this source of energy. But to men of good will the future is bright with hope" (309). Daugherty is more sanguine. The layout of his final spread matches almost precisely the layout of the title page, which had been so joyful and colorful and exuberant (308–9). On the left, the Statue of Liberty holds her torch with her powerful right arm; her face is set and determined. On the right, two peaceful doves descend toward two hands reaching out and about to clasp. Where the sun was rising in the first spread, here a rainbow (all greens) arches across both pages. For Daugherty, this is grim, serious stuff, this time in the middle of the century. Here is his pictorial statement of the new atomic challenge that America must face—a challenge that comes out of American power and ingenuity and that has, paradoxically, placed America in an entirely new kind of adventure where physical prowess and courage may no longer be enough. In fact, they are almost certainly not enough.

That concern continued the next year in what seems at first blush to be a lighthearted and sunny book—*West of Boston: Yankee Rhymes and Doggerel* (1956)—as Daugherty returned to these same issues in a series of poetic musings on American history. In *West of Boston*, Daugherty's optimism and confidence are no longer intact. Thus, for example, he questions the influence of economics on contemporary culture. In "Astoria," writing of the very man who had initiated the westward movement that Daugherty himself had written of in *Trappers and Traders of the Far West* (1952), Daugherty shows less patience for John Jacob Astor, the merchant:

> John Jacob Astor in his pride
> Hankered after the hair and hide
> Of beavers and bears and buffalos.
>
> . . . .
> Mr. Astor covered his sins
> With bison and bear and beaver skins. (36–37)

This is followed by poems about pioneers hurt by American capitalism: "Jim Bridger" ("I owe the Company for powder and ball, / Been clawed by a grizzly, and that ain't all" [46–47]) and "John Coulter" ("I've done with commissions and real-estate deals, / With time-clock serving and grinding wheels. . . . / I'm riding west footloose and free / To a lonely camp by a cottonwood tree" [48]). Here, Daugherty has pitted business or economic restrictions against the rugged individualism of earlier history. The only easterner of wealth and means he praises is Francis Parkman, but only because in Daugherty's hands, Parkman escapes the trap of his economic situation by becoming an American pioneer: "He proved a Boston Brahmin was not afraid to follow / The dragging travois of the Crow and the painted Ogallala" (52–53).

Perhaps for the first time in Daugherty's work there is an unhappy cynicism that sometimes appears as he considers the current generation of Americans and their response to the challenges of democracy. Against the willingness of the pioneers to embrace the difficulties of the trail ("Wheel Ruts," 46) or to celebrate the kinds of communities that developed with shared hardship ("Missouri Rhapsody," 59), or to build cities out of plowed plains and cities "out of prairie dust and sin" ("The Forty-Niners," 66–67), Daugherty pits the contemporary American desire for a complacent ease. In "Thomas Hooker and the Dinosaur Tracks and How Connecticut Got the Way It Is," Daugherty gives a quick history of the state, noting the Yankee farmers picking up glacial rocks for two hundred years and the independence of the early settlers but concluding with real estate agents who buy the played-out farms and sell them "to furriners from the Park Avenue penthouses who air-conditioned them and remodeled the hen houses into studios." These agents are so removed from the pioneer experience that, even though they are from New York City, they are called foreigners. And Daugherty concludes with the insurance agents who insured everything in the U.S.A.: "They've fixed it so, come the atom bomb, we the survivors can collect / our insurance and doze on the green benches in St. Petersburg / Florida, till kingdom come" (24–27).

The cynicism is heavy, though Daugherty uses it not simply to despair but to warn. With the loss of the pioneer spirit, he argues that Americans have opened themselves to a dangerous potentiality, one that dominated the 1950s:

> Pack train, stage coach, pony express, climb over the mountain passes;
> The Iron Horse roars west, spouting smoke and cinders,
> The continental express streaks on, faster, faster, faster.
> On the six-lane highways the sleek speedsters are streaming west;
> The airliner drones across the sky, six hours from coast to coast.
> The jet plane, the supersonic rocket, trail a white line across the blue.
> The mushroom blast of the H bomb announces
> the terror and the splendor of the
> Atomic Age. (56–58)

This poem is revised from its appearance in *Trappers and Traders of the Far West*, where it ended with a hopeful note about the fulfilling of the American westward movement. Here, that optimistic stanza does not appear, and the poem depicts a westward movement that has been distorted by increasing speed and ease, an ease that makes it difficult to face fully the possibilities of the H-bomb. The accompanying picture is the skull in the mushroom cloud—an image repeated from the *Rainbow Book of American History*, but one that seems out of place in a book of doggerel.

So in such a situation, how, then, should Americans respond to the outward threats of the Cold War and the inward threats of complacency brought on by economic ease? Daugherty's answer is the expected one: return to those virtues fostered by American democracy. These are the virtues he had written of in his earlier biographies. In the first three poems of *West of Boston* he presents portraits of Franklin, Jefferson, and Paine; their repeated theme is the wisdom of the common man. There is a call for a kind of purity of dream and vision as Daugherty excoriates Francis Drake (17) and Coronado (15) as mere opportunists. And there is, of course, the celebration of Liberty, seen in the poems about William Penn (18–19) and Roger Williams (20–23) and most particularly in "Boston Common" (30–33), where Daugherty pictures the ghosts of the past walking around the Common, the more familiar ghosts superseded by those who reflect liberty of conscience and thought: Anne Hutchinson, Mary Dyer, Roger Williams. Here are those who are not afraid to think differently from others and who are therefore oppressed. The final two lines are aimed at the McCarthyism of the period: "You won't find much about them in the story books / and perhaps you'd better not try to make inquiries of the FBI."

Daugherty does not conclude *West of Boston* with optimism. His final poem turns to questions of change and progress, to a world of ranch houses covered in aluminum siding, a world in which the pioneers are ignored and their old homesteads legally stolen. The poem is ironically entitled "Progress" and is illustrated with a policeman motioning Jim Bridger along.

> Where the wildcats clawed at the buffalo-shooters
> Rolls the five-o'clock trainload of daily commuters.
> Where the deer browsed down a forest aisle
> Stands a ten-room house in the ranch-house style.
> . . . .
> Where the red men listened to the meadowlark's song
> They're raising up billboards forty feet long,
> Reading "This little girl likes her beer dry,"
> And "Red Horse gasoline makes you fly." (94–95)

West of Boston is a collection of rhyme and doggerel, and the cover illustration of a Yankee fiddler and three dancing dogs suggests a work whose tone is light and sunny. But in the mid-1950s, Daugherty's message had shifted. He wanted to see America as he had seen the country in *Daniel Boone: Wilderness Scout*, but he was no longer convinced that his vision was universally held as the war experience faded away. *West of Boston* became, in the end, a book filled with prophetic urgency, and the hope for a democracy was proving more fragile than he had anticipated.

PART TWO

Otherness within a Democracy

1930 — 1955

3   Defining American Democracy

Normalizing Inclusion

The pioneer America of James Daugherty and Laura Ingalls Wilder is an abundant and vast and free America, but it is not an America in which liberty and resources are allotted with equity—a fact to which Wilder and Daugherty alluded to with ambivalence. They struggled with depicting stories outside the majority story, and their struggles are illustrative of the period's desire to define a democracy that was inclusive of all of America's citizens. Neither would succeed in this depiction, but others would come up with stronger answers to the problem.

The issue of Wilder's depiction of Native Americans has drawn the most censorious criticism of her Little House books. S. Elizabeth Bird has argued that shifting representations of Native Americans follow a distinct pattern: "Indians are the quintessential Other, whose role is to be the object of the White, colonialist gaze. Once Indians were no longer a threat, they became colorful and quaint." This certainly seems to be a pattern in the Little House series, where the Indians are at first seen as holding on to land that Pa wants and to which he believes he has a right as a settler bringing the country from a wild into a civilized state. On Laura's side, the wildness of the Indian is in early books a threat, but Laura also participates in what Louis Owens has called "a strange dance of repulsion and desire that has given rise to one of the longest sustained histories of genocide and ethnocide in the world as well as a fascinating drama in which the colonizer attempts to empty out and reoccupy not merely the geographical terrain but the constructed space of the indigenous Other." Laura imagines herself as being an Indian. Still later in the Little House books, when the Indians are gone, the memory of them shifts—though not necessarily to Bird's idea of quaintness or to what Shari M. Huhndorf has called in *Going Native: Indians in the American Cultural Imagination* (2001) "nostalgia," in which a vanished culture contributes "symbols and myths upon which white Americans created a sense of historical authenticity" (22), but to what Cari M. Carpenter, in *Seeing Red: Anger, Sentimentality, and American Indians* (2008), calls sentimentality, in which "the boundaries between the sufferer and the observer are at least momentarily obscured; the reader is not only taught to feel as another does but to (mis)take that feeling as her own" (4). This sentiment is most closely associated with Laura—though it also touches Pa and Ma.

✳ ✳ ✳

The series' first reference to Native Americans comes in *Little House in the Big Woods*, in which Pa tells a story from his own childhood: "I began to play I was a mighty hunter, stalking the wild animals and the Indians, until the woods seemed full of wild men" (54). Robert F. Berkhofer, Jr., in *The White Man's Indian: Images of the American Indian from Columbus to the Present* (1978), identifies this description— "wild men"—as one of the oldest stereotypes of Native Americans and notes that "wild" came to connect both a people, a country, and undomesticated animals. The adjective "wild"—used twice in Wilder's sentence—similarly places the Indians apart from the world of "civilized folks" and links them to the animals—and though this is told in the form of a story from the past, it suggests an attitude that heightens the imaginative adventure of young Pa while diminishing the Other: Indians are wild, just like wild animals, and Pa is able to subdue them because he is a "mighty hunter."[1]

But in *Little House on the Prairie*, that easy and dismissive envisioning of the Indian as "wild" is made much more complex. Laura, the young girl, has absorbed the vision of the wild Indian from Pa's story, and yet she is eager to see Indians—especially because the family is in Indian territory and because she is aware that "Pa knew all about wild animals, so he must know about wild men, too. Laura thought he would show her a papoose some day, just as he had shown her fawns, and little bears, and wolves" (56). Ma, on the other hand, is clear in her dislike, as in *The Long Winter*: "She looked as if she were smelling the smell of an Indian whenever she said the word. Ma despised Indians. She was afraid of them, too" (64). Because of this perspective, the first contact between the two cultures that comes in *Little House on the Prairie* is full of tension. Pa has left to go hunting, and Jack the dog is tied to the corner of the house—not to keep him nearby but to keep him from attacking an Indian and so causing trouble that Pa might not be able to contain. Mary and Laura are playing outside when Jack growls, and when Laura looks up, she sees two Indians, whom she describes in the very terms that Pa has used in his story in *Little House in the Big Woods*: "Then she looked over her shoulder, where Jack was looking, and she saw two naked, wild men coming, one behind the other, on the Indian trail" (134). The narrator's description of them—again, from Laura's point of view—affirms what is to Laura their wildness: "They were tall, thin, fierce-looking men. Their skin was brownish-red. Their heads seemed to go up to a peak, and the peak was a tuft of hair that stood straight up and ended with feathers. Their eyes were black and still and glittering, like snake's eyes" (134). Since they are still some distance away, it seems that Laura is herself contributing the details about the eyes, especially the simile. But to her mind, the details are appropriate, because these are "wild" men, and she, like Pa before her, resorts to comparisons with animals.

After the Indians enter the house, Laura rushes inside, and there Wilder posits a strange mix of the civilized and the uncivilized. Ma is bending over the fire to prepare a meal for the two men—she is doing what "civilized folks" would do for a visitor. But the two standing men are still described as the "naked wild men" (137), because the narrative point of view remains Laura's. In addition, the two Indians give off "a horribly bad smell" (137)—fresh skunk skins hang from the leather thongs around their waists. Then again, Wilder uses description from the point of view of Laura: "Their faces were bold and fierce and terrible. Their black eyes glittered. High on their foreheads and above their ears where hair grows, these wild men had no hair" (139). But this description in the house is quite different from the earlier description. Laura is afraid, hence the words "fierce and terrible." But she gives no details to develop this—and "bold" is not a particularly negative adjective. Again, she focuses on their black eyes, but there is no animal simile to make them "wild." And even the description of their hair suggests Laura's sense of their otherness rather than a belief in their wildness. A few lines later, the narrator notes that though Laura is afraid, she is still fascinated and watches the Indians until "two black eyes glittered down into her eyes. The Indian did not move, not one muscle of his face moved. Only his eyes shone and sparkled at her. Laura didn't move either" (140). Now the description is significantly different. Once again, the narrator uses the word "glitter," and nothing negative is suggested—particularly when "glittered" is followed by the verbs "shone" and "sparkled," which are positive in their connotations.

After they leave, Ma sits on the bed, trembling, and Laura believes she must be ill. But instead, Ma gets up and tells Laura that they must get dinner ready for Pa, thus reestablishing the order of "civilized folks."

When Pa returns, he sees it all as one of his stories; he imagines that the girls will share that perspective, and he is eager to defuse their fear. "'What's all this? What's all this?' he said, rumpling their hair. 'Indians? So you've seen Indians at last, have you, Laura? I noticed they have a camp in a little valley west of here'" (143). Ma's response is to affirm their status as wild men. She tells Pa that they have stolen his tobacco and eaten much of their cornmeal—narrative information left out when the visit was told from Laura's point of view. But Pa does not affirm the rightness of Ma's fear—though he does affirm the otherness of the Indians. "'We don't want to make enemies of any Indians.' Then he said, 'Whew! what a smell'" (143). Both lines acknowledge that the Indian is not part of "civilized folks"; the conversation begins with Pa affirming Laura's curiosity about Indians, but it ends with a return to the story of the wild men.

Though Pa can be friendly with Indians and even respect their claims, he will not respect those claims so far as to recognize his own impertinence in moving into treated land. In *Little House on the Prairie*, when Pa first hears that the government might evict them due to Native American complaints, his response is one of denial: "They always have let settlers keep the land. They'll make the Indians move on again" (273). In his mind, the very act of settling establishes rights to the land. When he is indeed about to be moved off, he leaves abruptly and angrily, before the soldiers arrive to notify him, because he believes those rights have been violated; he cannot equate the experience of his family and the Native American families, who are also being driven from the land. When Laura asks him about this, his response shows his inability to rationalize his position. "When white settlers come into a country, the Indians have to move on. The government is going to move these Indians farther west, any time now. That's why we're here, Laura. White people are going to settle all this country, and we get the best land because we get here first and take our pick. Now do you understand?" (236). But Laura does not understand; she asks again about their presence: "Won't it make the Indians mad to have to—" But Pa cuts her off and will not allow more questions. He realizes he has no just response to taking someone else's land. In *The Long Winter*, he will try again when Mr. Scott argues that the "only good Indian is a dead Indian" (284); still, Pa's response shows his back-and-forth reasoning: "Pa said he didn't know about that. He figured that Indians would be as peaceable as anybody else if they were let alone. On the other hand, they had been moved west so many times that naturally they hated white folks. But an Indian ought to have sense enough to know when he was licked" (284). Pa simply cannot articulate his own position, because it is so very muddled. Pa's mixed attitudes come out of his own concern about his family and the land he wishes to settle, which are pitted against his understanding of the injustice being perpetrated. He has no way of resolving the conflicting attitudes.

But Pa is not the only character with mixed attitudes. Wilder gives over a lengthy passage in *Little House on the Prairie* to the leave-taking of the Native Americans—a passage that shows real growth in both Laura and Ma. One morning, one of the great chiefs rides past the house, ignoring the Ingalls family entirely; he is followed by other ponies and warriors. "Brown face after brown face went by. Ponies' manes and tails blew in the wind, beads glittered, fringe flapped, eagle feathers were waving on all the naked heads. Rifles lying on the ponies' shoulders bristled all along the line" (306). Their passing is threatening on one level: the presence of the rifles ensures that. But it is also fascinating, and soon the entire family watches. When the women and children ride by next, Laura remarks on their eyes again, and she uses familiar terms: "Their straight black hair blew in the wind and their black eyes sparkled with joy" (307). The earlier warrior's eyes had "sparkled" too, but there was no narrative language to indicate how Laura was to understand that sparkling; now Wilder has made it clear: "with joy." Later, when she sees an Indian papoose, Laura is first attracted because "its eyes are so black," and then, trying to comprehend her desire herself, she sobs, because "she could not say what she meant" (309). Laura's fullest response is a mix of her mother and father: "She had a naughty wish to be a little Indian girl" (307), the latter half of the line connecting her to Pa's identification with Indians, the former half connecting her to Ma's sense of propriety for "civilized folks." Her inability to negotiate between these two impulses leads to her frustrated sobs.

For the entire day, the Indians process past the Ingalls cabin, heading west; the family watches them from horizon to horizon, and the leave-taking saddens them all in a very deep way: "Then the very last pony went by. But Pa and Ma and Laura and Mary still stayed in the doorway, looking, till that long line of Indians slowly pulled itself over the western edge of the world. And nothing was left but silence and emptiness. All the world seemed very quiet and lonely" (311). Ma's response is the first one given, and the most startling: "Ma said she didn't feel like doing anything, she was so let down" (311). She realizes, tied to the land as she is herself, that something profound has just happened. Though she had gotten a desire that she never specifically articulates but that she clearly wishes—she will no longer have to confront Indians—she is moved by their dispossession and their dignity in adversity. Pa's response is to affirm his status as a settler, but he realizes that he is, in part, responsible for what he has just seen: "He went soberly to hitch up Pet and Patty, and he began again to break the tough sod with the plough" (311)—this despite the fact that it is already evening. And Laura knows that the people who were most connected with this land are gone; they will exist now only in her imagination, and she realizes the terrible loss: "She sat a long time on the doorstep, looking into the empty west where the Indians had gone. She seemed still to see waving feathers and black eyes and to hear the sound of ponies' feet" (311).

✳ ✳ ✳

While James Daugherty and Laura Ingalls Wilder struggled with the question of representing the Native American within a dominant culture's story, even sidestepping any kind of definitive answer as to how this might be done, other writers were taking up the question in ways that would deliberately widen the depictions of societal inclusion that children's books would offer and that would define that inclusion as central to America's democracy. In 1940 Eleanor Weakley Nolen published *A Job for Jeremiah*, an eighty-page illustrated story about young Jeremiah living as a slave on George Washington's Mount Vernon plantation immediately after the Revolution. A librarian with the Cincinnati Public Library, Nolen saw children's literature as "an integral part of national life and development" and her own work as depictions of "certain periods, places and problems which seem to me to be significant in the development of our nation as a democracy." *A Job for Jeremiah* was to be such a depiction; specifically, she would look at the development of the national life and American democracy through the lens of racial inclusion.[2]

But *A Job for Jeremiah* illustrated the problems that those in the children's book world at midcentury faced as they crafted books about the roles of ethnic and racial minorities in the national life. Was it appropriate to speak frankly to a child audience about the histories of racial minorities in America? Was it feasible to address the issues of racial disharmony in plotlines? Was it possible to craft a minority protagonist or character without stereotyping or patronizing condescension? Could an author write authentically about a character whose ethnicity he or she did not share? Was it possible to affirm cultural distinctiveness without assuming a perspective of cultural dominance? Was it possible to affirm cultural distinctiveness within a democracy whose dominant metaphor was a melting pot? Would a work for young readers in which the protagonist was a minority character be publishable?

Not all of these questions would be answered, but Nolen's book answered at least the last: *A Job for Jeremiah* proved that a book with a protagonist of minority ethnicity could be successfully published and marketed: it was the third in a series that began with *Shipment for Susannah* (1938)—also set at Mount Vernon—and its sequel, *Cherry Street House* (1939). And as to the question of a depiction that was not condescending, here, again, Nolen shows some success. Jeremiah is a young boy filled with curiosity and interests. He rides Washington's horse for the thrill of it and gets into trouble when he disobeys rules. He is easy around adults and interacts freely with those around him, both black and white. He wonders what his future life will be like and dreams of travel, of vocation, of a life doing something he loves. He is outspoken, charming, ready to try anything even if it risks failure. He struggles with an adult world that is busy and may not think his problems are as immediately important as he thinks they are. In short, Nolen creates an African American character who successfully avoids playing out expected stereotypes—other than those of any boy.

But as to the question of representing racial history in America, *A Job for Jeremiah* blinks at every turn. Jeremiah is a slave at Mount Vernon, but that word is not used even once in the text. The map on the endpapers identifies the slave quarters as the "Quarters" and identifies the house where Jeremiah lives as "Jeremiah's House," as if he and his family owned it. Throughout the book, young Jeremiah "spent a lot of time wondering what he'd like best to do as soon as he *was* big enough" (9), but he is a slave; he has no personal choice. Though for a time he imagines he would like to travel, he is consistently dissuaded from this by the other slaves, such as Uncle Dorsey, who reminds Jeremiah, "You belongs right here 'n' here you'll stay for the rest o' your days, 'n' you better be mighty thankful you *don't* have to go round working for other folks that more'n likely'd treat you like dirt" (26). Later, Uncle 'Lijah affirms this: "You just be glad you belongs to Mount Vernon" (62), attaching Jeremiah not to a person but to an estate—the closest any speaker comes to identifying Jeremiah's status as a slave. There is no irony in any of this on Nolen's part, as there is none when Jeremiah boasts of wool coming from "our own sheep" (43), as if he owned Mount Vernon; or when Jeremiah listens to the visiting owner of a sugarcane plantation in Barbados talk of the beauties of his land and decides that he would like to visit it—without any notice given of the brutality of slave conditions in those plantations. When Jeremiah finally decides to tell Washington that he has decided to be a gardener—Jeremiah now linking *himself* to the estate—Washington tells him, "We're going to need all the hands we have, to make things grow now, in this country" (80), speaking metaphorically, as if Jeremiah's announcement brings him into a place where he can choose to contribute to the building of the new country. Jeremiah seems to be entering into the American Dream. In fact, he isn't. He is a slave. His is a literal pronouncement. Washington's metaphor does not extend to him—a problem that Nolen elides.

This is not to say that Nolen was unconscious of the problem. Two years later, she observed in *Horn Book* that realistic depictions of Americans of all races and ethnicities showed "a very wholesome and growing concern over the quality of American life. . . . Race prejudice has no place in a democracy, and the place to combat race prejudice is with the child's first books and first social relationships." The sentiment is a fine one; the problem lay in the ellipses that permeated her realism. She could show Jeremiah as a real boy; she could not show him as a real boy who was a slave.

✳ ✳ ✳

In 1942 Eleanor Frances Lattimore published *Storm on the Island*, a novel set on the coastal islands off the Carolinas. Lattimore was a prolific author—almost sixty books written and illustrated—and perhaps her childhood in China gave her a particular interest in interracial relationships, a narrative that dominates her books. In this novel, Rose Ann's white family struggles with a terrible storm that wipes out much of the island community's housing. Rose Ann's family is safe; the house is relatively undamaged, and her father is able to keep them in supplies. Others are more destitute.

As her family takes stock of the damage and helps the neighbors, a small cast of African American characters hovers in the background. There is Marcy, "the colored servant" (8), who is brought in to take care of Rose Ann's baby brother and who sleeps in a little cabin with her daughter and son-in-law before she comes in the morning "to do the work" (12). Marcy survives the storm but is frightened by it: "I thought the Lord had sent for me, sure enough" (58). And there is Dan, "the colored man who worked for Father" (63), whose speech is always presented in slight dialect: "Yes, boss . . . I've took good care of your mule" (75). When they come upon Dan after the storm, Father instructs Dan to leave his home—which presumably is damaged, too—and come to theirs, where he will help replant the chinaberry tree, find the missing boat, and start the car: "I'll need you to help me with some work" (76), Father tells him. Later, when they go to find the Smiths, Dan is the rower in the rowboat and the one who stays behind to watch over it while they go on up to the house. When Father and Rose Ann come back to the boat later, they find Dan still waiting, but "he had probably been asleep" (172)—a criticism. And there is Isaac, who "caught fish for most of the white people on the island" (71). And Sweet Marie, who loses her kitten in the storm and collapses in unhappiness, helpless. And a "little boy child" (151) who finds the kitten. And other nameless "colored people" whom Father allows to farm that part of the island he owns but does not farm himself. When Rose Ann worries about her friend Sally Smith, Father reassures her that Tom Smith knows what to do; it's people like Dan who are in trouble: "The colored people are the worst off, always. We've got to look after them" (77). Apparently the colored people do not know what to do.

The work of Nolen and Lattimore illustrates the routes that some writers of children's books took to deal with the task of writing about a democracy that included various ethnicities and races. Avoiding easy stereotyping, Nolen created a vivid character in Jeremiah. Yet she simultaneously missed any opportunity of speaking forthrightly about what slavery meant or about continuing questions of racial injustice. She did not offer any ways to contextualize those issues or to even think about them beyond Washington's banal offer; in fact, she affirmed a world where those issues are nonissues: Jeremiah should be grateful he is living at Mount Vernon, since he has no other place; he must fit into the cultural world of Mount Vernon. Lattimore's novel was meant to be a coming-of-age story for Rose Ann, who after the storm and her rescue work around the island "did not think that she would ever care about playing with dolls any more" (181). But as Lattimore represented Rose Ann's growth as learning how to take care of the "colored people" on the island, she defined all of the African American characters only in relationship to the white families, and that relationship is always related to work: Dan rows the boat, Marcy tends the baby, Isaac catches the fish—each contributes to the needs of the white families, and, in turn, Father looks after them. The stereotyping is not purposefully vicious, but it does speak of superiority and inferiority, of power versus want, of competence versus inability, of full human development versus a state of perpetual childlike need. Neither Nolen nor Lattimore crafted a work that attempted to seriously engage, or affirm, or even describe the cultural distinctions that marked their characters other than to affirm stereotypes and Otherness.

And yet, these writers were trying to ask the right questions, even as they emerged from a history of writing for children about minority characters that, in comparison, made their work remarkable. Before 1930—and well into the 1930s—depictions of African American characters fell into one of two modes. The plantation mode depicted characters content with their plantation lot, happy in their security, and blissful under the paternal eyes of benevolent masters. "The master and mistress were very busy too, for they must see that the work went on; that the slaves were well-fed and clothed and cared for when sick. . . . [A] plantation was a very happy place too, with plenty of fun and much company coming and going, and good times for black folk and white folk alike," writes Rose B. Knox in her introduction to *Miss Jimmy Deane* (1931) (xi–xiii). And Maud McKnight Lindsay's *Little Missy* (1922) assures young readers of the kindliness of the relationships between masters and slaves: "All that 'Little Missy' tells of child-life in the old South is true. Never were there happier or more care-free children than those who grew up on the great plantations in the midst of the kindly black folks who were their guardians and their friends. . . . The trust that the masters and mistresses put in the negroes is almost beyond belief; yet comparatively few of the slaves failed to justify their trust" (7–8).[3]

The humorous mode depicts African Americans in exaggerated stereotypes; they are the comic relief, the dumb sidekick, the butt of the minstrel show jokes and burlesques—and happy to serve in that guise. Here are books like Lucy Fitch Perkins's *The Pickaninny Twins* (1931) and Inez Hogan's *Nicodemus and the Little Black Pig* (1932) and *Nicodemus and the Goose* (1945)—the character whom Charlemae Rollins, a children's librarian at the Chicago Public Library, called in her *We Build Together* (1942) "the most exaggerated of all the stereotypes in children's books" (7). Elizabeth Coatsworth's *The Cat and the Captain* (1927) burlesques Susannah the cook, who is fat, thick-lipped, and foolishly superstitious. Beneath her red bandanna, she rolls her eyes to indicate excitement and fear; most of her language is heavy dialect. The stereotyped cook was not uncommon, appearing in Anne Parrish's *Floating Island* (1931) in coal-black Dinah and in Ruth Sawyer's *Roller Skates* (1937) in "Black Sarah" the cook—the first a Newbery Honor book, the second a Newbery Award book. In *Narcissus an' de Chillun*

(1938)—one of her many novels set in early 1900s Tennessee—Christine Noble Govan lamented that "like the simple good times we had outdoors, the freedom of field and road that we enjoyed, the kindly old darkies are dying out. Their patience and service will never be forgotten by those who knew them, and I wanted my own children to see them as we did" (xii); apparently this meant they were to be remembered as horn-footed, turtle-like, ridiculously named, ludicrous in their actions, credulous in their superstitions.[4]

* * *

At midcentury, the American children's book world was looking for radically better modes of representing minorities in children's books. Could minority groups be represented not through stereotypes but through authentic encounters in children's books? Might it be possible for children's books to offer real solutions to cultural problems, disseminating those solutions to a new generation who might learn something other than the old prejudices through their reading? Could childhood reading offer ways of defining democracy so that prejudice itself would fall away in the face of the ideas of cultural equality and mutuality? And if this was possible, how might it be done? What, even, were the options?

By the 1930s the old modes of representing minority figures were clearly seen as problematic, but what was not clear was how to address the problem, or even how to articulate it. Marjorie Hill Allee, for example, struggled with representation in her 1938 *Horn Book* article, "Books Negro Children Like." African American children, she wrote, liked the same stories that white children liked, but especially they liked stories that included African American characters. They did not like the inclusion of words such as "nigger," "pickaninny," and "darky." These words, she wrote, are "likely to be scratched out of the book by an indignant child." But though Allee recognizes the issue of offensive diction, she does not think that stereotyped images are much of a problem at all: "Illustrations are a sore point with teachers and librarians who want good books about Negroes . . . but truth compels us to admit that the Negro children who read the books seldom object to the pictures, however grotesque they may be"—a remarkable claim. Allee eventually comes to her unintentionally belittling conclusion: "A book on an American topic, clearly written in a vocabulary not beyond that of a fourth grade child, and exhibiting ordinary courtesy when and if it treats of Negroes, is as likely to please a colored child as a white one. A Negro child will not be fooled by shoddiness of characterization, nor will he be tolerant of muddled action, any more than the white child; perhaps less, for his mind seems to work with a more direct simplicity." If she is starting to ask the right questions, Allee is still groping for answers amid old patterns.

By the time of *A Job for Jeremiah* and *Storm on the Island*, questions had been raised for over a decade about the ways in which children's books depicted minority children. In *Horn Book* reviews of the 1930s, these concerns emerged again and again. One option for appropriate depiction was a genial, heartfelt inclusiveness—an inclusiveness that proved to be, in reality, unreflective. When Alice Jordan reviewed Rachel Field's *Calico Bush* (1931), Cornelia Meigs's *The Willow Whistle* (1931), Caroline Dale Snedeker's *The Town of the Fearless* (1931), and Elinor Whitney's *Try All Ports* (1931) in a composite review, she spoke of their "American settings" and the connection of inclusiveness to American democracy, but she struggled with how to assess that inclusiveness. In writing about *The Willow Whistle*, she argued that Cornelia Meigs had given her readers "a realization that races learn to understand each other only through good will and kindness," but Jordan ignored Meigs's characterization of Native Americans as "wild creatures" (3), Meigs described them as having "strange ways" that make them "more like children than grown people" who could be "turned aside from their purpose by any white man who would stand his ground" (19, 133), as foolishly superstitious (65, 132), as speaking a "guttural" language (128). Apparently, all that was necessary to be appropriately inclusive was "good will and kindness"—a happy if naive assumption.

The same assumption lay behind Nellie Page Carter's 1935 *Horn Book* review of several books with African American characters; she, too, suggested that children's books might encourage readers toward a larger democratic conception of the country: "The all-inclusive friendship of the book world admits no racial or geographical barriers, and particularly is this true in the scope of children's affections. Since there are racial and geographical problems to be grappled with in our own great country, might there not be a leaven of understanding through the medium of children's literature, an entering wedge of affection that could mature into largeness of heart in our dealings with the races within our boundaries?" Again, kindness and goodwill. Yet the review itself is rife with unreflective stereotyping, referring to "pickaninnies" and "darkies" and to Negro stories being incomplete without "hants" or "Negro types."

✳ ✳ ✳

In October 1943 Charlemae Rollins published an article in the *Elementary English Review* speaking specifically of books such as *A Job for Jeremiah* and *Storm on the Island*. She argued for an entirely new presentation of American minorities in books for children, a presentation more in tune with the democratic principles that should define America, a presentation that offered not the false and easy cultural assumptions of the past, and not the naive assumption that kindness and goodwill would prevail if children's books pictured all races playing together, but more realistic, honest, hardheaded portrayals of specifically African American culture.

> Some authors seem to feel a nostalgic yearning for a "glorious past" of slavery time when the Negro knew his place. They regret that the old "darkey" types are disappearing and feel that they should preserve them in books for children today. Yet books of this type do nothing to help create democratic attitudes; they are more apt to destroy the child's concept of the Negro who sits beside him at school or plays with him on the playground, by substituting a false picture of his background or actual life. . . . It is gratifying to find this type of book being superseded by books of more varied phases of Negro life, illustrated with lifelike pictures of Negro children that are appealing and neither barefoot, ragged, nor unkempt.

Three years later, in November 1946, Rollins would make the same point in a speech before the National Council of Teachers of English (NCTE), using almost the same language to affirm a new vision: "We need excellent books, written by authors and illustrated by artists who are sincerely interested in bringing a true picture of the many different kinds of Negroes who make up America." There are two important prongs here. The first deals with authorial *ethos*: the writers are "sincerely interested" in raising cultural awareness. Here may fit the kindness and goodwill. But kindness and goodwill are not enough without the second prong, which comes out of the writer's *logos*: the writer needs to bring "a true picture" of African American culture, "lifelike" images, "true" pictures of a culture, where authenticity trumps stereotype.[5]

Charlemae Rollins's argument represents a midcentury understanding that children's books could play a role in creating a democracy by envisioning all members of that society as parts of a single whole whose diverse composite groups were to be treated with equality and represented fairly. Her words were echoed. Two teachers in the Detroit public schools, Helen J. Hanlon and Stanley Dimond, wrote in the *English Journal* in January 1945 that "the democratic ideal is debased daily—by the inequalities and hatreds fostered by discrimination against classes, races, or religious groups. The democratic way of life is endangered daily by such senseless behavior because in a democracy we stand together and share alike of good or of ill, or we fall." Rollins agreed and connected this problem to books: children's books should contribute but were not contributing to a fostering of the democratic ideal; they were simply resorting to stereotypes, yielding false pictures—even those books of goodwill. And in doing so, children's books were dividing the American citizenry when they could, in fact, work toward true democracy. In a November 1946 *Elementary English Review* article, Rollins was even more direct: "Teachers, librarians, parents, and all those interested in intergroup relations, must continue to demand the right kinds of books about Negroes, the ones that give a true picture of the race and its contributions to American life. We must talk about them in our religious and political meetings as well as in our school and church libraries as well as in our homes. We must continue to write letters to publishers, editors, and authors, commending them for so courageously giving us the tools with which to combat racial and class discrimination in America."

John J. DeBoer, the editor of the *Elementary English Review*, affirmed this call. In a short editorial entitled "The Time for the Offensive Is Here!"—published in March 1944 but not referring to the war effort—DeBoer argued for what today would be called multiculturalism in education and particularly in language arts studies.

> Two basic principles in intercultural education require emphasis today. The first recognizes all racial and religious discrimination as essentially a single disease, whether it affects Jews, Negroes, or any other minority. . . . An attack upon any cultural minority is an attack upon the people of the United States. On the other hand, our children cannot fully understand the meaning of civil rights unless they see their application to specific groups of people, especially to often despised minorities.

The study of language arts, he argued, is to encourage understanding, "because America cannot speak with one voice and one language, in peace or war, until it has broken down the barriers that exist within the hearts of the people, barriers that shut out brotherhood and comradeship and understanding." Ten years later, DeBoer would not have been able to use words like "comradeship," but here, in the spring of 1944, DeBoer was arguing passionately for a single society marked by the removal of barriers and the building of community, and the possibility that this could be achieved through an "intercultural education."

✳ ✳ ✳

What were the books to do this? In her NCTE speech, Charlemae Rollins cited a list of "books which show likenesses rather than differences and which show Negro children in familiar experiences with other children—showing them as being accepted in groups," not simply being included as Others drawn in by the goodwill of a white culture. The first book that Rollins cited was Lorraine and Jerrold Beim's *Two Is a Team* (1945).

It is a slim and unassuming book, its endpapers illustrated with children riding scooters, flying kites, jumping ropes—all playing innocently, even those with toy guns and paper hats who march in formation off the lower right corner. What is remarkable about the grouping of scenes is its easy and unassuming diversity—African American and white children play side by side—an easy diversity shown also on the title page, where the faces of the two protagonists, Ted and Paul, are pictured beneath the book's title: Ted is African American; Paul is white. Nowhere in the text of the book is there any mention of their races.

The story is quiet and undramatic. The text opens without any apparent surprise: "Ted and Paul were friends. They played together every day after school. 'We're just the same age!' they told Ted's mother when they played at his house." The spread for this text shows Ted and Paul sitting side by side with a ship model; Ted's mother, who is African American, talks on the phone behind them. "'And we're just the same size,' they showed Paul's mother when they played at his house." Paul's mother watches the two boys as they stand back to back. The point, of course, *is* to show no surprise; the book argues with Rollins and DeBoer that here lies the real democracy, an absolute sense that this kind of relationship is normal. The children are not defined by otherness but by equality and acceptance.

This is not to say that the Beims create a world in which there is no conflict. Seeing some children with coasters, Ted and Paul run home to find the materials to build a coaster of their own. But the building quickly becomes unhappy as both boys assert their own way of doing things: "Paul took the hammer and started to nail the box to the piece of wood. 'You're not doing it right,' Ted said. 'I am too!' Paul answered, and he wouldn't let Ted help him." Eventually their anger leads each to take what he has brought and go home, where each makes his own coaster "the way he wanted to." When they meet again, their relationship is one of competition: "'My coaster's better than yours,' Paul said. 'Mine's better than yours,' Ted said." The exchanges lead to a challenge, and the Beims give no tag to alert the reader to the identity of the next speaker: "Let's have a race and see!"

The race suggests the damage done when competition enters a relationship. During their careening downhill run, they knock a woman's bundles from her arms, tumble a doll from a young girl's carriage, and almost hit a man whose dog then escapes. After a wordless spread that shows the boys tumbling into a wreck together—now ironically together—they are confronted by the three, who demand compensation: "Poor Ted and Paul! They didn't know how they were going to pay for all they'd done. They started home together, looking sad and worried, carrying the parts of their coasters with them." The accompanying illustration shows them walking together again, but the text has already made this connection: the pronouns are "they" and "them" and "their"; the passage opens with a union: "Poor Ted and Paul!" When they see, on the next page, a job opening for "a boy," their union solves the problem, as they take the job for an individual and convert it into a job for a team. Their need for a delivery wagon leads them to convert their two coasters into a single wagon, and using the money they earn, they pay for the damage they have caused. "And they learned how to drive their wagon down a hill—zig-zagging around anyone with bundles, carriages, or dogs. That was the most fun of all." The text bleeds into the illustration here, as the two boys fly down the road together in the mutually owned wagon. The brightly colored landscape of the last spread is suggestive of their newfound understanding and pleasure in each other. Both boys, having crafted the wagon together, ride together, heading in the same direction, working toward the same purpose.

This is, on the one hand, a story about friendship. Two boys begin the tale as friends; they have an argument and are separated. The separation leads to a weakening of their abilities, and their anger leads to damage in the larger community. Recognizing both of those problems, the boys find ways to come together and to build something stronger, something that will repair damage and work to strengthen their friendship—and so the book comes full circle. The community itself is racially diverse, but the boys' friendship has no place for racial identification; their play and their work come in a context of mutual interests and respect; they are, as the book asserts in its first line, "friends." No one reading this book in 1945 could fail to recognize the message of racial acceptance and democratic union. For the Beims, the larger message is a pointed one: even as the two boys assert their friendship and become stronger through their mutual work and play, so too must America move toward mutuality in the relationships of its own races so that the country can become stronger as each contributes what it may bring to the larger culture. It is an overt book that veers very close to political allegory, though it never yields its narrative energy to simple allegorical meaning.

Here, in DeBoer's words, is brotherhood and comradeship and understanding. Here, in Rollins's words, is a book for the creation of a united democracy. In 1948 Evelyn Wenzel reflected in *Elementary English* on the effect of children's books on the development of a child's personality and noted that in *Two Is a Team* "Negro and white children can be viewed against the same cultural background." Further, the two boys learn that "they can accomplish more by working together," which Wenzel argued is a distinctly democratic value. In 1951 Ethel R. Taylor would report on favorite books among her second graders in the journal *American Childhood*; she chose *Two Is a Team* particularly because it was "written especially to develop better human relationships among children."

Two Is a Team emerged from a context in which librarians, teachers, and educators argued vehemently that American children's books must address the issue of racism if children's books were to play their part in developing the minds of a new generation to take up the tasks of a democracy. In fact, children's books were essential for this task, it was suggested. Malcolm S. MacLean, writing in *Childhood Education* in 1942, argued that "to build democracy in this nation and the world we must recognize all the forces of unification of culture, [and] admit the debt we owe to all minorities, the chief among which is our Negro minority." "Of course books alone cannot prevent or overcome prejudice," noted Mary Alice Jones in a speech before the New York Library Association Conference in Syracuse in 1949. "But they can help. If the boys and girls find from their reading that persons who are 'different' yet share many of their own joys and sorrows and values, and are often interesting and attractive persons, they may begin to understand that differences are not necessarily unpleasant and that persons who are different do not have to be either inferior or superior to one another." And in 1943 Margaret Thomsen Raymond rejected easy inclusiveness through a presentation of happy scenes by linking "good will" with a reflective "understanding." She argued in the *English Elementary Review* that children, particularly during a war year, needed books that celebrated the virtues of democracy—the very thing for which their country was fighting. Such books, she argued, must celebrate the historical development of the country and its growth out of many cultures, the cooperation so essential in developing a national and international culture, and the nature of the rights and responsibilities that the American democracy conferred on its citizenry. "All children of the so-called white race," she wrote, "must be given a wider knowledge of children of other races who are also citizens of America; not of 'tolerance'—God forgive us for the insufferable word—but of understanding and good will toward our native minorities, the Indian, whose heritage antedates ours, and the Negro, whose people came by our will and not by their own." The common thread in these arguments is the insistence that children's books can play a strong role in developing democratic values.

Part of the understanding for which Raymond argued involved honest discernment of American failures in racial relationships. When, for example, Elizabeth Johnson, a sixth-grade teacher at the Campus School of Western Michigan College in Kalamazoo, wrote "A Letter to Parents" in *Childhood Education* in which she sought to articulate those books that children should read to learn about democracy, she used "democracy" as a synonym for "racial justice." She offered, for example, Eleanor Estes's *The Hundred Dresses* (1944), Jesse Jackson's *Call Me Charley* (1945), and Hildegarde Swift's *North Star Shining: A Pictorial History of the American Negro* (1947). There could be no democracy, she suggested, without racial justice—and the place to begin that work was in children's books.

And certainly these books were trying to find their way toward that goal. Jackson's *Call Me Charley*, for example, shows two boys (older than those in *Two Is a Team*) who seem almost blind to racial issues; they see each other as friends who like building electrical gadgets, who want a newspaper route, who enjoy swimming, and who attend the same school, though Charley is the only African American in the school. When Tom Hamilton's friend George calls Charley "Sambo" and "nigger"—this within the first few pages of the book—Tom doesn't even respond. He is so innocent of racism himself that he hardly seems to recognize it. In fact, this is the point of the book: that prejudice is a learned hatred. Tom simply cannot understand, for example, how his friend can speak the words of the Pledge of Allegiance and not want Charley in their club: "That kind of stuff ain't what we say in school," he says (59).

Certainly the book is an attempt to use children's literature as a means of describing democracy, and it does this principally by creating a realistic character in Charley. His character is given almost as much play as Tom's, the white boy. But the two boys—both twelve—are almost absurdly naive. Both are shocked when Charley is not given a part in the school play, and both are shocked again when he is not allowed to join the town swimming club. It is as if they had never encountered racism at all. And the education that both undergo is problematic. For a time, Tom gives up on Charley when his friend won't assert himself: when he won't go through the school initiation, when he won't demand a part in the play, when he won't complain about his treatment at the pool. The book's final message is encapsulated in what Tom learns: that an African American boy may not assert himself because he has been so routinely beaten down, and that it is the duty of white boys to grow up to be those who befriend the helpless in society. "As long as you work hard and try to do right . . . you will always find some good people like Doc Cunningham or Tom and his folks marching along with you in the right path" (183), Charley's mother promises him. It is a patronizing promise. Still, the book was a breakthrough in its use of a realistic—sort of—African American character who shares the stage without being the sidekick or the butt of the joke or regional color.[6]

John Tunis's earlier *All-American* (1942), a story of racial conflict and resolution, responded directly to the question of how a book could develop democratic values: it showed overtly that democracy grew out of the union of diverse cultures. Its title seems to suggest a protagonist's athletic prowess, but its meaning comes to radiate more widely than that. In the opening of the novel, Ronald, playing football for the elite Academy, helps to tackle viciously Meyer Goldman, who plays for the town high school, almost paralyzing him. Ronald's guilt over this tackle, which he recognizes as motivated in large part by his prejudice against Goldman, combined with his disgust over the easy acceptance by the other boys at his school of their own racial and class superiority, leads Ronald to leave the Academy—presided over by the "Duke"—and enroll at the public high school. There, the principal and students offer Ronald his first lessons in democracy. He comes to understand from Meyer Goldman, for example, that Ned LeRoy, who is African American, however skilled an athlete he might be, would never be allowed to play in the major leagues (74)—a seemingly obvious truth that Ronald had never considered. He questions, "If there was all this unfairness, all this injustice, why did older folks like teachers and the principal and the Duke talk about America? A democracy. And all that sort of thing?" (78). Unlike the Duke, the high school principal links democracy to individual maturity and communal responsibility: "In a democracy each citizen is on his own. It's up to him. . . . You're old enough now to be on your own. You're a citizen of a democracy. You have responsibilities. See you live up to them" (151, 155). Eventually Ronald does, and Tunis depicts his maturation through Ronald's growing commitments to boys of other ethnicities. Meyer Goldman and Jim Stacey, who are

Jewish and Irish, become his closest friends, and when the football team is invited to participate in an interscholastic event in Florida, it is Ronald, despite enormous pressure from the town, who leads the crusade to reject the invitation because Ned LeRoy will not be allowed to play in a southern stadium. Tunis fails to resolve this conflict in the narrative when another invitation is offered from a school in Chicago, removing (too easily) the plot problem.[7]

At the center of this school story is a set piece that occurs outside of the major plot concerns and that becomes an epiphany for Ronald. At the train platform, he sees the townspeople—few of whom had ever entered the Academy grounds—grouped around men who are hardly older than Ronald and who are headed for basic training and so to war. Ronald stops next to Meyer Goldman, whose cousin is among the men leaving.

> They stood watching the crowd. At one side was Ed Swift with his dad, the president of the Trust Company, and Doc Rheinstein, standing with an arm around a boy's neck. Beyond was a black-haired Italian in a leather windbreaker whom Ronny sort of remembered having seen before. He was an island in a sea of emotional relatives. His father, old, bent, needing a shave, his mother, short, fat, with a shawl over her head, and two girls, evidently his sisters, stood beside him. In the center of the room was a bunch of Negroes with their girls, all laughing and joking. They called across the packed room, shouting and kidding. Nearly everyone else, especially the older people, was solemn and quiet. (178)

Though stereotyped by twenty-first-century standards, this is a wartime scene that tries to capture a vision of the democratic experience in America. In this experience, all are united—rich and poor, young and old, the recent immigrant, the African American. There is Tom LeRoy, Ned's brother, and Ray Kelley, Mr. Crispi's son, "that Polish kid who used to deliver the *Courier*" (183), and as the national anthem is played and the train pulls out, Ronald finds himself weeping and glad that he is not with the other boys from the Academy. "It brought everything close to Ronny, made him feel a participant and not a spectator of what was taking place. The platform of noisy jostling people became real to him" (180). And that is the moment of maturation: when Ronald discovers that he is a part of the tapestry of America, a tapestry of lives woven together from diverse backgrounds to fight for the democracy of which they are all a part, when all of those people become defined not as "other" but as "real." They are all American.

* * *

Other writers looked for a more radical approach. *Two Is a Team* resists distinctions in any of the racial representations. In that book's best construction, inclusiveness is defined as the flattening of cultural differences, so that the two boys seem to have absolutely no cultural distinctions at all; each is completely at home in the other's world because it is, essentially, the same world. But it is not hard to come to a construction of that book's meaning that suggests that "tolerance" and "acceptance" could mean accepting the "Other" by placing him or her safely in one's own culture. This is what Margaret Thomsen Raymond had meant when she recoiled at the "insufferable word": "tolerance." Was there another option, one that perhaps could enhance cultural distinctions and picture American culture as marked by heterogeneity? Or, as Shaobo Xie constructs this dichotomy, a book might "homogenize differential otherness" and in focusing on "cultural commonality" may "subsume cultural marginalities into the imperialism of the same." A book might even establish "radicalized difference as the identity of otherness . . . to realize cultural multiplicity and tolerance." Was it possible to craft a book of "radicalized difference" that might be marketable?

In the same year in which Margaret Thomsen Raymond had written her warning, Barbara Biber, a psychologist at the Bank Street School in New York, argued more directly that democracy is not about tolerance; it is much more radical: "It flourishes successfully where there is a warm, wholehearted acceptance of differences as the primary resource for creative human living." Raymond and Biber were both proposing a model that went beyond Charlemae Rollins's desire that writers "show Negro children in familiar experiences with other children—showing them as being accepted in groups," or Evelyn Wenzel's later claim in "Children's Literature and Personality Development" that "Negro and white children can be viewed against the same cultural background." They were suggesting that books could show minority protagonists not set within a dominant culture, and not taken outside their own culture into a kind of nebulous Every-Culture, but instead set within their own cultures, which were defined not as Other, not as alternate, but as normative.

In fact, this more radical way had already been suggested. In 1936 Evelyn Egbert pointed out in *Childhood Education* that though children study other races and cultures, they did not study Negro culture, though it was a part of the American experience. "Might not the study of the Negro race be made a basis for our appreciation of other races? Why should we wait until we are adult to know that there is such a thing as Negro culture and that there are 'all sorts' of Negroes just as there are 'all sorts' of white people—that the difference in color of face is not a final criterion as to the interests and thoughts of the mind within?" Even in these questions, Egbert was still defining the white culture as normative and the study of the Negro as equivalent to the study of the Other. Yet as she struggled with what studying another culture might entail, Egbert did suggest the crucial importance of not leveling the distinctions of a culture but learning about the culture's distinctiveness *and* seeing it as a part of the larger whole: "All the wealth and richness of their culture lie immediately at hand and is so inextricably woven into ours that in order to understand our own we must know about theirs." How to do this?

In "Reading for Democracy," a piece published in the *Wilson Library Quarterly*, the well-known African American librarian Augusta Baker reported on the development of the James Weldon Johnson Memorial Collection in the New York Public Library. Its purpose was to celebrate African American life and to educate without stereotypical representations, thus cultivating and encouraging democratic ideals in children: "In order to give children more democratic attitudes towards all the racial groups that make America the great nation it is, we must use literature that will strengthen the growth of democracy," Baker wrote. To do this, one did not read to tolerate another but to learn about and affirm the rich qualities of all cultures. Books for children would encourage the growth of democracy when they encouraged the growth of awareness of all races within American culture. This indeed was something more radical. It was an urge to eliminate racial bias by insisting upon the importance of cultural distinctions to the health of the American democracy itself.

By the end of World War II, a number of children's books were published that included African American characters living within an African American culture as opposed to being the only minority kid at a school. The goal was to present stories in which the presence of African American characters was as normative as the presence of white characters. Thus, a book like Margaret Taylor's *Jasper the Drummin' Boy* (1947), a story of a young boy whose mother forces him to learn to play the piano, though all he wishes to do is be a drummer—a desire that gets him into trouble with his mother and his neighbors until they are all able to perceive his talent. Ellen Tarry and Marie Hall Ets's *My Dog Rinty* (1946) follows the story of David and his dog, Rinty, who is always, always getting loose and causing mischief, until David's father demands that the dog be sold. The day is saved only when it is discovered that Rinty is escaping in order to chase mice, and so the dog and David become the neighborhood mousers. Both books are set in an African American neighborhood (*My Dog Rinty* is illustrated with photographs from Harlem of the mid-1940s), and both assert that they are stories about American boys.

This was also the approach of Georgene Faulkner and John Becker in their novel for young readers, *Melindy's Medal* (1945). The frame story of the novel deals with young Melindy, who is a smart, conscientious, talented, and quick-witted African American girl who lives with her grandmother and father in their new apartment in the Projects in Boston. Much of the novel consists of the stories Melindy's grandmother tells of three generations of Melindy's male relatives, all of whom won medals in battle—one with Colonel Shaw in the Civil War, another in the Spanish-American War, another in World War I. Melindy, who seems to go to a largely African American school, believes that she will never win such a medal (a belief that her grandmother oddly reinforces again and again), yet she does win one when she notices a fire in the school basement and saves the other students through her quick-witted action.

This novel deliberately works at portraying an African American family in realistic ethnic and cultural practices (the powerful role of the grandmother, the food that is mentioned, the music that Melindy's father plays), but it does not show those elements as in any way representative of Otherness. In the stories of Melindy's family, the reader discerns the stories of African American repression: her great-grandfather's escape from slavery and his role in Colonel Shaw's battles, the relegation of her grandfather to caring for horses rather than fighting in the Spanish-American War, the relegation of her father to being a cook in World War I. But what comes first in this novel is the sense that this is a family with a history, and that it is a brave history, and that it is a family comfortable in its culture. For the reader, there is never a sense that this family perceives itself to be anything other than American.

Cultural distinctiveness need not be denied, these books insisted— and America could be a democracy that enabled unique cultures to survive and thrive even as they lived side by side.

In *Shuttered Windows* (1938), Florence Crannell Means crafted a novel where cultural distinctiveness was not only affirmed but insisted upon as the characters learn its importance and worth. In the novel, the African American protagonist, the orphaned Harriet Freeman, has lived all of her life in Minneapolis and intends to stay there. But when she learns of a grandmother on the South Carolina sea islands, she goes to visit and is attracted to her own African and African American heritage. She remains in South Carolina, despite the racial prejudice she will face, to go to a school that is, on some level, beneath her in its facilities. At first questioning the decision because it will affect the development of her musical career, then questioning the decision because she is ostracized as a northerner, then questioning the decision because of the lack of opportunity she might find at the end of her education, she eventually embraces her school and her new life on the sea islands because she embraces her ethnic heritage, an embrace that begins in a mythic story of her ancestor, a slave in South Carolina: Black Moses. "With what satisfaction he would have regarded this descendant of his, whose head was unbowed in the land of his captivity!" Harriet comes to understand (6). The embracing of her heritage is depicted as nothing short of noble, and Harriet and her grandmother are repeatedly referred to in noble terms: Harriet is "a bronze maiden, eyes straight-gazing under brows that frowned with thought" (6), Granny "a fit child of Moses" (23) who seems to Harriet to be "like an Ethiopian princess" (23), "as stately and beautiful as an old woman could be" (26).

When Harriet resolves to remain in South Carolina, she understands that racial bias will affect her powerfully; she finds herself face to face with Jim Crow laws she had only heard about in Minneapolis. Nonetheless, she resolves to stay and is particularly moved by her new friend Richie's passionate belief that he will grow up to become a teacher and thus serve his people, whose land is being sold out from under them because they do not know how to make it profitable. He wants, he says, to "lead my people out into a grand new life on their own land" (58)—another noble characterization. Eventually Harriet comes to this same position, recognizing that her own gifts should be used in teaching. Anything less is "like being crushed under a burden too heavy to bear" (136). And so, just as one of her white teachers resolves to go up into the mountains and serve those who have no teachers, Harriet decides to join with Richie in this great resolve, earning her grandmother's designation of her as "de chile of Moses!" (200).

Though Means would earn greater acclaim for her novel about the Japanese American internments during World War II—*The Moved-Outers* (1945)—her characterization here, as well as her union of place with meaning, is more potent and effective. Harriet is a fully fleshed out character, with grace, wit, and ability. Her choices are striking in that they deny much that she understands about herself; certainly they deny her intended musical future. But her growth is real and powerful, and the resolution that she makes to be part of a movement to raise hope for her people even in this South Carolina setting is affecting. Here in 1938 is a set of African American characters who are not stereotyped, who are distinctly individualized, who work toward greater hope for all African Americans in realistic ways, who confront the bigotry and insularity of the world around them, and who come to maturity in the acceptance of their own culture apart from the dominant culture, which will punish them for this acceptance.

During the same period, Lois Lenski was working to do for American regional distinctiveness what was being done for American racial distinctiveness; her regional novels powerfully asserted her belief in an America that saw its regionalism as a central aspect of its democratic nature. Thus, for example, her foreword to her *Blue Ridge Billy* (1946), a novel set in Ashe County, North Carolina, articulates the vision of America that she had embedded into her regional novels.

> Just as recent American painters no longer go to Paris for painting material, but have found here, on our own doorstep, a vivid, dramatic America which they are portraying not romantically and sentimentally, but realistically and truthfully, just so accurate regional books for children should present all the vividness and drama that the American scene holds. We need not manufacture excitement—it is here, inherent in the scene itself. The way that Americans have struggled and fought and mastered their environment, in all its great variety, in an unending American saga. (xiv)

The opening and final sentences of this passage recall almost to the word the sentiments of James Daugherty, but it is the center of this passage that most truly gets at the heart of Lenski's purpose as a writer: to write a vivid, dramatic, realistic, truthful, accurate representation of America as a single country of diverse regions and cultural traditions, each with its own character, each playing a role within the saga of the larger United States. Lenski's regional novels were deliberate calls to America to recognize its multilayered nature and to embrace that nature as its strength. In an age that called for America to be a "melting pot"—a favorite midcentury metaphor for American society—Lenski wrote to deny both the aptness and the desirability of that metaphor, calling instead for larger understandings of the fascinating diversity of American traditions and the recognition that that diversity was necessary, given the way the country had been settled and the distinct environments those settlers had encountered. That diversity was also desirable, in that all traditions could contribute to the American saga in noble and honorable ways.

Her purpose in writing was to help children "see beyond the rim of their own world" (xv) and to do this by sharing vivid stories so that a child reader would be able to share in the experience of another American, though one whose culture might be vastly different from his or her own: "I am trying to say to children that all people are flesh and blood and have feelings like themselves, no matter where they live or how simply they live or how little they have" (xiv). In that essentialist spirit, Lenski writes, her books will teach "something of that tolerance which will make all men brothers" (xiv). Once we learn to accept others, we can understand their lives and conditions and so empathize, Lenski asserts: "We can imagine ourselves in the same situation, and we wonder if we would be different" (xiv).

In a later essay, entitled succinctly "My Purpose," Lenski wrote of herself as an "interpreter and guide" and suggested her own sense of her novels' seriousness: "I believe that a book for the middle-age child (from nine or ten upward) should be more than a pleasant conceit aimed to amuse and entertain and pass the time away. Children of this age are thoughtful children, and a book should broaden their experience, and widen their sympathies to include all kinds and conditions of men." The result of her desire to express this vision is a line of characters embedded in a series of novels designed to explore aspects of the country's regions by vividly depicting that culture and its regional setting and by creating a strong empathetic link between the reader and the experience of an Other. What John Steinbeck was doing with *In Dubious Battle, Of Mice and Men*, and *The Grapes of Wrath*, Lenski wished to do for young readers.

Lenski was strongest when she incarnated her vision of regional America in characters tied closely to their regional situations; she found drama in the stories of figures like Billy Honeycutt in *Blue Ridge Billy*, who wants a banjo. Or Judy Drummond in *Judy's Journey* (1947), a ten-year-old migrant worker who yearns for a home with a picket fence. Or Birdie Boyer in *Strawberry Girl*, who wants the independence that strawberry fields and orange orchards might give. Or Darrell and Delores Wagner of *Prairie School* (1951), who hope to attend school during the long Dakota winter in safety. Or Felix Fong in *San Francisco Boy* (1955), who yearns for the countryside after moving to the city.

Lenski's story of America is of a people whose lives are marked by distinct customs and traditions that have adapted to and been formed by the region in which they live. She embeds these distinctions in the characters, who are shaped by the customs and issues of their regions; thus Billy, in *Blue Ridge Billy*, knows about illegal moonshine whiskey, but he also has tremendous empathy with those who need to find a way to make the excess corn produced in their crops pay. In *Judy's Journey*, Lenski first evokes the difficulties of being a sharecropper—always finding oneself behind, not being permitted to plant even a small vegetable garden because all the land is to be used for the owner's crops, the loss of self-respect—and then tackles the hardship of becoming a migrant worker, symbolized by the gradual yet inexorable loss of the family's possessions until even the beloved sewing machine must be sold. And Lenski details the tension of outside workers coming in to a community; when the Drummonds stop in South Carolina, they are not wanted because, as one woman puts it, "plenty people in this town need work, without outsiders comin' in" (140). It is Judy's noble response to these difficulties that drives the novel.

The evocation of a particular region's issues is strongest in *Strawberry Girl*, where those issues are very closely tied to the plotline. When Mr. Boyer puts a fence around his property to protect his strawberry field, he closes off the pasture and water to which Mr. Slater's hogs have always had access. The result is a battle between the notion of maintaining a free and open range and the possibility of establishing a "Fence Law" and farming profitably. "I warned you before," says Mr. Boyer, "if I catch a cow or a hog of your'n on my place, I'll shoot on sight! Open Range—we'll see! We'll get a Fence Law passed!" (97). This real regional dispute provides much of the antagonism between the two families that drives the action of the narrative.

But behind this issue is yet another: the changing economy of the state of Florida, which will eventually drive the cattle farmers out of business. New companies begin to move in to mine phosphate for fertilizer, leasing most of the open plains upon which the cattlemen had depended. The mining also ruins surrounding farms with its operations. The result is that the cattlemen begin to take jobs with the mining company. Meanwhile, even the fruit growers must adapt, for despite all of their southern disdain for northern Yankees, they find themselves economically dependent upon those same Yankees as a market for their produce. The suggestion here is that even as Lenski is chronicling the lives of their regions, those cultures are being threatened by larger, mostly economic forces at midcentury. But this point is made not through abstraction but by embedding it within the action of the novel.[8]

Contemporary professional writers tended to level Lenski's work to a simplistic celebration of diversity. In November 1953 Dora V. Smith, a professor of education at the University of Minnesota, argued in *Child-*

hood Education that Lenski's work presented "with understanding and integrity the peoples of our country" and that Lenski had "devoted herself to introducing boys and girls of America to each other." That same month, Fannie C. Hunn offered in *American Childhood* that Lenski had "made practically every region of the United States take on new meaning" and that she had "woven into her vivid, absorbing stories hundreds of geography facts children have tried to 'learn' from the geography text." Eloise Rue, in "Children's Reading and the War" in the fall of 1943, suggested that Lenski offered children "a new awareness of our own country and its various regions and aspects as reflected in geographical material, biographical material, historical fiction, and stories of children in different states." Eight years later, Miriam Webb used Lenski's work to affirm the principle of internationalization: "Before we can understand foreign nations, we must know the life of different kinds of people in different sections of our country" who live "off the beaten path." Mildred Harrington, writing in the *Wilson Library Bulletin*, agreed. In her "Regionalism in Books for Children," Harrington argued that regional books "make our young people more understanding of human nature in general, and thus contribute to our one world concept." Each of these articles reduced the purposes of Lenski's stories to an affirmation of political principles—and sometimes to bald didacticism.[9]

More recently, Fred Erisman, in "Regionalism in American Children's Literature," argues that regional books like Lenski's worked to affirm American cultural myths: the nation's soul is embedded in the good, natural, rural world; life is always moving toward the better, though there will be difficulties; life has coherent meaning. He notes that, indeed, regional works are about acquainting readers with cultural sites that may be unfamiliar to them, but he notes too that the cultural assumptions of the characters in these works tend to be those of an older generation. "The result, whether accidental or intended, is to pass on to the members of the next generation a conservative, traditional view of American life"; Erisman cites the novels of Laura Ingalls Wilder as examples.

If Lenski only wanted to evoke regional life for the purpose of exposure, Erisman's sense that these works evoke a "traditional view" would hold true. But Lenski had an additional purpose in her regional novels—again, a purpose not unlike that of John Steinbeck: to suggest that the American scene was more complicated than it might appear, because beneath the image of the shining American city that James Daugherty had espoused, there was ugliness, poverty, and injustice that must be faced. Her books, she argued, were to be realism in the truest sense: they were to be based on real-life events that she herself had witnessed or that she had researched. She would raise awareness and create empathy by vivid and dramatic realism. In doing this, she argued, she ran the risk of portraying life as hard and difficult, perhaps even tragic. But in America, life could be hard, difficult, and tragic. There were children picking cotton, and migrant families trapped in an endless cycle, and violence over moonshine whiskey, and subsistence farming that kept children in poverty by forever barring them from education. Certainly it was these elements that led one British reviewer to write about *Judy's Journey* in 1947: "This is a brave book, splendidly contradicting the false Hollywood picture of the United States by its convincing realism." In 1964 May Hill Arbuthnot referred to Lenski's regional novels as "grimmer realism than anything since *Tom Sawyer*," but it is much grimmer than *Tom Sawyer*. While the realism of Lenski's regional novels seems mild and even tame in comparison to twenty-first-century works, what was remarkable was the willingness to speak to the underside of the American Dream, to call the reader's attention to the migrant children whose work fed happy suburbanites.[10]

Writers such as Langston Hughes and Arna Bontemps—who individually and collaboratively wrote children's books during the Harlem Renaissance—also opposed books that illustrated racial harmony through erasing cultural distinctiveness, but they would go further than Lenski. Was it possible, they wondered, that a child's book could identify, affirm, and celebrate cultural distinctiveness and at the same time work toward a democratic sensitivity by eliminating not signs of a culture but all negative connotations associated with those signs? And—though Lenski was sensitive to this issue too—was it the case that this would best be done by a writer from the culture being portrayed?[11]

Hughes and Bontemps's *Popo and Fifina: Children of Haiti* (1932) was such an attempt. It is a slight story in terms of its narrative: Popo and Fifina move with their family from their grandmother's home in the country to Cape Haiti, a seaside village where their father will hire on to become a fisherman. Once there, Popo begins to explore—he finds the docks, the market square, the public fountain, the place where the women wash the clothes—and he begins to dream of the day when his father will have his own boat and Popo will go out with him to catch fish. The family enjoys their new home, but both Popo and Fifina are glad to go back with their mother to visit their grandmother in the country, where, one night, they follow the beating drums through the darkness to a dance. But back in the village, Popo's time of play must give way to work for his family. At first he washes milk cans in the market, but soon his father finds a place for him in his uncle's cabinet shop, and he gains real skill. The story concludes with a celebratory trip out to the lighthouse and the promise that Popo, because of his diligence and hard work, may go out fishing with his father the next summer.[12]

Though the culture through which Popo and Fifina move is marked by real poverty, the book's tone is happy and joyful. There is no sense that Popo is ground down by that poverty, no sense that his choices are limited. When Popo's father is first described, the narrator notes that Papa Jean was "a big powerful black man with the back torn out of his shirt" (2). The detail suggesting poverty—the back is torn from his shirt—is not a mark of poverty at all but a way of suggesting Papa Jean's strength: his skin is three times described as metallic in the narrative, and he walks with his family "proudly, and there was a happy bounce in his step" (2). Popo himself is usually naked or wearing only a slight shirt. Again, the suggestion might be of poverty, but the authors reject that connotation: "And Sunday clothes for black peasant boys in Haiti usually consist of nothing more than the single shirt Popo was wearing to town" (3). The conjunction "And" rejects the notion that the reader should even consider this a sign of poverty; the conjunction is not "But," which would affirm such a connotation. Similarly, the next sentence suggests how Popo sees himself: "Like all dressed-up people, Popo was proud of himself this afternoon" (3). There is no irony here at all; in his world, he is dressed up, and there is no sense that he may be looked down upon by anyone—including the reader.

This is the tone for the entire narrative: a celebration of Popo's world and its cultural distinctions, with no sense of cultural inferiority at all—in fact, with no room for a reader's criticism. When they visit their grandmother's home, they sit on the ground outside the hot house, and there is a celebration as Popo and several of the other children climb the mango tree and shake mangoes to those waiting below, and Fifina eventually goes to the well to fetch water so that the old people can wash their sticky hands. There is a sense here of joy and ease: Popo's "heart was light and happy, but he was beginning to feel sleepy" (38). The succeeding chapter, "Drums at Night," suggests in its title and opening narrative that there is something ominous afoot and that there is about to be a turn in the narrative. But the reader's assumption here would be wrong; the drums call neighbors to a dance, and when Popo heads back to bed afterward, "all the way up the hill under the banana trees, and across the gurgling brook, they could hear the drums beating happily in the valley below" (46). Even the storm that thunders rain down upon them ends with a light note: "In a little while the storm passed, the sky lightened, and there came a rainbow over the ocean. The world brightened. Fifina puts all their wet clothes outside to dry, Papa Jean went off down the street, and Mamma Anna began cooking supper" (80). The single cultural criticism that appears in the narrative is a criticism of America, whose demanding work patterns are contrasted with the less time-conscious rhythms of Haitian work. In a pineapple factory in which the fruit is canned and shipped to the United States, "Popo saw many black men working. They did not move about leisurely, like other workers, and Popo thought he wouldn't enjoy working so hurriedly" (35).

Bontemps and Hughes evoke a world other than the American experience. It is not a world that is defined as odd or cute or interestingly exotic, because it is so rigorously placed in the perspective of Popo, who finds happiness and joy in his world and who does not see it as "Other"; he would not understand readers who might see it as "Other." There are no judgments that compare Haitian culture to other cultures other than the reference to the pineapple factory; the reader is simply to see Haitian culture as marked by its own distinctive elements—as is true of any culture.

That same year, Langston Hughes published his *The Dream Keeper and Other Poems* (1932), a selection of sixty of Hughes's poems which he chose "expressly for young people." In "A Cross-Written Harlem Renaissance" Katharine Capshaw Smith argues that the poems were directly meant to situate children within the Harlem Renaissance.[13] The collection begins outside the African American culture, with fairies and nymphs, and lyrical nods to Paris, Ireland, and Mexico. In most of these opening poems, there is no evocation of the African American experience, though the illustrations clearly evoke that culture. But halfway through, things change. The language becomes dialectal; in fact, almost a third of the poems are in slight dialect. And the experience becomes specifically African American, as in "Minstrel Man":

Because my mouth
Is wide with laughter
And my throat
Is deep with song,
You do not think
I suffer after

I have held my pain
So long? (38, lines 1–8)

The rhythms shift to the blues:

Goin' down de road, Lawd,
Goin' down de road.
Down de road, Lawd,
Way, way down de road.
Got to find somebody
To help me carry dis load. ("Bound No'th Blues," 40, lines 1–6)

And the poems evoke African American spirituality:

Ma Lord ain't no stuck-up man.
Ma Lord, he ain't proud.
When he goes walkin'
He gives me his hand.
"You ma friend," he 'lowed. ("Ma Lord," 55, lines 1–5)

But it is in the final section, marked by an illustration of two figures whose stances, though not their forms, evoke the confidence of James Daugherty figures, that Hughes celebrates the African American culture in the way that he and Bontemps had set out to do. In "Sun Song" he speaks to the hard experience of the "dark ones of Africa" to whom he brings his songs "to sing on the Georgia roads" (70, lines 5, 7). His "African Dance" recalls the drums of *Popo and Fifina*:

The low beating of the tom-toms,
The slow beating of the tom-toms,
Low . . . slow
Slow . . . low—
Stirs your blood. (64, lines 1–5)

"Aunt Sue's Stories" evokes the ways that slavery times are remembered through story and through song:

And black slaves
Singing sorrow songs on the banks of a mighty river
Mingle themselves softly
In the flow of old Aunt Sue's voice. (65, lines 10–13)

In "The Negro" he rhythmically chants the roles Africans and African Americans have played: slaves for Caesar and Washington, workers for the pyramids and the Woolworth Building, singers, victims. He concludes as he begins: "I am a Negro: / Black as the night is black. / Black like the depths of my Africa" (72, lines 1–3).

Like Daugherty, Hughes concludes the collection by encouraging his young readers to look forward, and in "I, Too" he directly addresses the role of his African American readers in America, evoking Walt Whitman—another echo of James Daugherty: "I, too, sing America" (76, line 1). In this powerful poem Hughes rejects the notion that racism will win the day:

Tomorrow,
I'll sit at the table
When company comes.
Nobody'll dare
Say to me,
"Eat in the kichen,"
Then. (76, lines 8–14)

In fact, he affirms, "They'll see how beautiful I am / And be ashamed" (76, lines 16–17). He concludes by varying his opening line and affirming what so many writers of children's literature were affirming in other ways: "I, too, am America" (76, line 18). The claim is not that the African American is a minority culture within the larger culture or that the African culture needs to be defined in terms of its place within the white culture. The claim is one of equality, and the claim affirms that culture's distinctive beauty.

Though this more radical vision of inclusiveness—this celebration of cultural distinctiveness—was not immediately embraced after the publication of *Popo and Fifina*, the vision did enter into the professional literature in the late 1940s and 1950s, and not just regarding African American culture. In 1954 Ethel Newell in *Elementary English* declared optimistically in "The Indian Stereotype Passes" that "the Indian in new books is the Indian of reality who is psychologically valid for our boys and girls today." Newell, a teacher in Mesa, Arizona, praised the focus on the "particular Indian" rather than on the stereotype and lauded the examination of real problems: "The serious reader may find with satisfaction that these books do, in addition to telling a good story with good style, clarify the Indian's problems, do portray him as an understandable human being, do make significant his importance in history and his contribution to the world, do bring the particular Indian and his culture into focus, and do help a young reader gain understanding, sympathy, and friendship for the Indian." Along a similar line, though using a negative example, Maria J. Escuerdo, professor of foreign languages at Arizona State College, argued in an aptly entitled article, "Exotic but Unfair," in *Childhood Education*, that the curriculum for children dealing with modern Mexico represented that country as a nation of peasants who wore sombreros and walked beside two oxen pulling a cart. She suggested that in presenting these images as "authentic," one might as well take pictures of the slums of New York and bring those to Mexico, posing these as authentic pictures of America. "The curriculum in the elementary level is the cornerstone of democracy," she argued. "The teacher is entrusted with the country's greatest and most precious treasure—the citizens of tomorrow. It is his duty to be well informed so that he in turn can impart knowledge in its essence rather than distorted data." In December 1954 Brenda Lansdown complained in the *Reading Teacher* that many of the reading difficulties that her minority students faced grew out of a lack of identification with the characters, situations, and language of their books; they could not recognize their own experience. "Where is the *experience* of a Negro or Puerto Rican six-year-old in the background of Judy or Dick?" Newell, Escuerdo, and Lansdown were each arguing for representation that educated and enlarged their readers by abandoning stereotypes.

✳ ✳ ✳

In November 1954 Edwin H. Cady, a professor of English at Syracuse University, spoke to a meeting of the NCTE in Detroit; his speech was titled "The Role of Literature for Young People Today."

> Ours is a culture of cultures, the heritage of an infinitely varied ancestry. . . . It is our proud boast to the world that America is in this way, as in others, a new experiment in human living in which successful unity can be found without obliterating the diversity in the unity; and we are, thank God, making progress toward solving the problems this experiment presents us with. All hope of solving these problems rests on understanding from one group toward another and on widening understanding being communicated to our young people as they grow up to citizenship.

To effect this communication, Cady insisted, we must turn to artists. "The artist has the advantage of being able to command the whole imagination, powerfully rousing the emotions, reaching down into some of the unconscious depths of the mind, for instance, in ways not often available to the statistician, the lawyer, or the social scientist." Literature for children and young adults, he argued, is the hope for the successful outworking of the American experiment.[14]

He was echoing twenty years of voices in the children's book world who had been calling for exactly that.

4 The Bobbs-Merrill Childhood of Famous Americans Series

Quiet Challenges to the Mythic Narrative
of the American Dream

In November 1952 Douglass Adair wrote a piece for the *New York Times Book Review* in praise of "a new literary genre that captures the interest of even my children, who don't particularly like books." The genre Adair found so compelling was "the fictionalized biography, wherein imaginary episodes reveal the character of a historic person"—a genre that, he claimed, had its roots in Parson Weems, who had connected the famous cherry tree incident with George Washington. In the article, Adair cited the Signature Book series by Grosset and Dunlap, the American Heritage series by Aladdin, the American Landmark series by Random House, and one other—though he could have listed a number of others, because he was writing during a period when series biographies were enormously popular. He might have looked as well to the Real Books series published by Franklin Watts; the Real People series by Row, Peterson; the American Adventures series by Wheeler; the Shelf of Biographies for Young People by Julian Messner; the Land of the Free series by John C. Winston; or the Makers of America series by Abington. None of these, however, were as strongly marked by a purposefully fictive nature as the Childhood of Famous Americans series published by the Indiana publisher Bobbs-Merrill—the other series that Adair cited and whose technique and purpose he accurately discerned: "to tell fictional episodes as if they had actually occurred during the childhood of famous men and women [in order] to dramatize and establish characteristics which these leaders actually did exhibit in later life." Thus, he suggested, Parson Weems has been "modernized for twentieth-century readers."[1]

Adair—the editor of the *William and Mary Quarterly: A Magazine of Early American History*—is careful to assert that this new genre is not, strictly speaking, biography. But he does not examine the question of whether a young reader would be able to distinguish between biography and fictional biography, since there is no clear distinction in the texts between entirely fictional episodes, episodes based loosely on actual events, and authentic episodes. And these are not necessarily easy distinctions to make, particularly for a child reader. But Adair muddied the waters further. He noted that the books "show a much greater concern for historical accuracy than did Weems," arguing that "the imagined event is based on evidence of the sort that a scholar uses to achieve historical truthfulness." The books, Adair argued, "keep the fictionalized material psychologically true to life"—by which Adair meant that the characters act like real children, not like the flat figures of didactic children's tales, such as Washington and his too-good response about the cherry tree. Here, Adair seems to affirm a quality of truthfulness in the books apart from their factuality.

But many critics would not accept Adair's assessment. In a 1952 article published in *Social Studies*, Ralph Brown and Marian Brown, with the State University Teachers College at Cortland, New York, argued that the books were falsely advertised: "Some publishers apparently feel that if a book contains a smattering of 'true' happenings and others that seem plausible, it is excusable to title the results 'biography.' On their dust jackets they frequently speak of such books as 'true stories.' Young people, however, lack both the background and the judgment to evaluate such books." They argued that biographies for children needed to be based on scholarly work and should invent neither actions nor motivations; that kind of writing, they suggested, should simply be labeled as fiction, and their dismissal of fictionalized biographies as "imaginative dreams" suggests their disdain. More recent critics have affirmed their view. Stuart Hannabuss and Rita Marcella, in their *Biography and Children* (1993), condemn series biographies for their practice of condensing and simplifying lives, for the distortion of subjects into characters who have no flaws at all, for the inanities of fictional dialogue, for the stylistic straightjackets imposed on the writers, for their timidity in the choice of figures, and for their questionable relationship between fact and fiction—all charges that might be leveled against the Bobbs-Merrill series.[2]

Adair was much more tolerant of the fictional constructions of the Bobbs-Merrill series. His single warning about the books is of their scope: the books are limited introductions, he wrote, presenting only superficial characters whose lives can be "too neat." "Here Washington, Wild Bill Hickok, Grant, Boone, Franklin, Lincoln and Lee all appear as 'normal' happy boys, with good average parents, playing the right kind of pranks and dreaming only respectable adolescent dreams. And inevitably they all look very much alike." But for Bobbs-Merrill, presenting their subjects as normal, typical American children was a deliberate strategy: the notion was to depict children who are as recognizable as the kid around the suburban block, demonstrating all the good and normal impulses that living in America can bring out in a child. In fact, the advertisement for the books published on the inside of the 1950s book jackets noted that these works "make the child of today the friend and playmate of great Americans of the past," linking reader and subject tightly together in mutual American normalcy.

So carefully did the biographies attempt to create a child figure immediately recognizable to an American reader that three years after the end of World War II, the US army incorporated Augusta Stevenson's *Buffalo Bill: Boy of the Plains* (1948) into its program of weaning German children away from Nazi tenets and toward an American definition of normalcy. In this book, young Bill Cody is the archetypal American boy—a figure that James Daugherty would have affirmed. He is obedient and resourceful: "He knew how to do things, too, and he did them without being told" (15). He is trustworthy, able to tend his father's camp alone. He is independent and brave, not afraid to live alone on the frontier or to jump into the river to save a young Indian boy from raging water. He loves the outdoors and can hardly imagine himself locked into a schoolroom—until he recognizes the necessity of learning to write. He works hard, traveling with wagon trains and protecting their herds—despite dangers from Indian raids, rustlers, and blizzards; he also sends the money he earns home to his widowed mother. He is strong and able but subdued and straightforward: "There's nothing foolish about that boy," observe employers for the Pony Express. "He's quiet and doesn't try to show off" (175). He is also, like James Daugherty's Daniel Boone, tolerant: "We're all alike under the skin. It's a pity we can't be better friends" (141), he says of the white settlers and Native American tribes. And he is patriotic: "Bill looked up and took off his hat. His heart thrilled when he saw the Stars and Stripes floating gently in the desert breeze" (133). Here is the all-American boy, a Scout before there were Boy Scouts, playing his part in the great American scene.[3]

The biographies adhered to familiar themes, finding qualities in their subjects that were easily recognizable to an American reader. It was a cliché to say that George Washington was a great general, or that Ben Franklin was intelligent and inventive, or that Daniel Boone was a great frontiersman, but Bobbs-Merrill set out to flesh out those clichés in childhood stories to show these traits in incipient form developing in an American landscape. "George was the leader" (58), the narrator and young boys at his school affirm, and when a company of boys is formed, "they chose him for their captain" (62). "Ben was different," the narrator notes of the Franklin children. "Ben was interested in animals, stones, plants, clouds, and everything he saw" (23–24). And Daniel Boone may not be particularly good at his studies, but "we know he'll come out of the forest alive" (45).[4] In showing these expected qualities of familiar figures, the books validated the mythic narratives that represented these figures' roles in the development of America. But they also affirmed the notion that these figures were marked by American qualities that could flourish in an independent nation and that could therefore be found in any American neighborhood or schoolyard or home. And that last possibility is where the Childhood of Famous Americans series began to move past the expected vision of America and approach something more radical as it took its place in mainstream children's books that were defining American democracy more and more inclusively—though in this series, this movement would often be subdued, more implicit than explicit.

❋ ❋ ❋

The biographical series that were being published at midcentury were phenomenally successful, despite warnings from some reviewers that a series book "often smells of fabrication. In some cases it reeks of the assembly line." (When Grace Miller Heriot, a professor of education at the University of South Carolina, listed fifty current biographies for children in the late 1940s, none were from the Childhood of Famous Americans series.) Nonetheless, the Julian Messner series had sold more than a million copies of its ninety titles by 1953; Random House sold 700,000 copies of the first thirty titles in the Landmark series; Grosset and Dunlap printed 600,000 copies of its first twelve titles. But it was Bobbs-Merrill that led the other series, paving the way by proving the potentiality for a market, even during the Depression years. By 1953 Bobbs-Merrill had sold 100,000 copies of its first title, Augusta Stevenson's *Abe Lincoln: Frontier Boy* (1932); it added another seventy volumes to its series in the next twenty years, bringing in sales amounting to over two million dollars. The series would eventually extend over two hundred volumes, thirty of which were written by the local Indianapolis teacher Augusta Stevenson, whose work by the 1960s represented the largest hardcover circulation of any juvenile books by a single author anywhere in the world.[5]

In the fall of 1952 *Publishers Weekly* affirmed the extraordinary success of the series biography, citing, for example, booksellers in Indiana —"*The Childhood of Famous Americans, Landmark Books,* and *Real Books* literally walk out of our store"—as well as Elsie Stokes of a prominent Nashville bookstore, who believed that the books were popular because they were so very American: "When [Augusta Stevenson] wrote the first book in the *Childhood of Famous Americans* series, she did it because there were no interesting books which a child could read for himself where he might learn in an entertaining way about his American heritage and the great men who have helped America's destiny. She planted the seed, because she earnestly believed American children had a right to know about these riches." *Horn Book* seemed to agree with the significance of this American emphasis when it examined the Landmark series: "They are not stock people with set virtues. Many of them are rough, some are intelligent and thoughtful, some clever and ingenious. But they are all alike Americans, with American roads to travel, American problems to face."[6]

Yet despite this American centering, what was remarkable about the Childhood of Famous Americans series, particularly during the war years and beyond, was its challenge to the American scene. Yes, America was a free land whose liberty ensured the possibility that anyone could rise, given natural talent and gifts and the will to use them fully. This was true if one came from privilege—like George Washington—or from poverty—like Benjamin Franklin. It was true if one were physically strong and adept—like Buffalo Bill or Davy Crockett—or if one were more studious and scholarly—like Robert Fulton or John Quincy Adams. The assumption is that the American Dream was intact and manifest in the lives of the subjects of these biographies, even though at times it sounded like a Cinderella story that had come true for some American children, but perhaps it could come true even for the reader.

But by the war years, the biographies in the Childhood of Famous Americans series were questioning the universal quality of the American Dream. Though the volumes suggest the reality of the American Dream for all the subjects—particularly in the final summary chapter, which shows the rise of the subject to importance—the Bobbs-Merrill writers were also interrogating that Dream. Did it extend to women? If so, in what shape? How were Native Americans to be regarded? Did the Dream extend to them, or were they obstacles to the fulfillment of the American Dream? Did the Dream extend to African Americans? To immigrants? Though none of the biographies suggested that the American Dream was false, some implicitly questioned the naive belief that the Dream extended to all. The answers they tendered belie any sense that the Bobbs-Merrill series easily affirmed the dominant American narrative. It did not. The series quietly challenged that narrative.

✳ ✳ ✳

The opening chapter of that first title in the Childhood of Famous Americans series—Augusta Stevenson's *Abe Lincoln: Frontier Boy*—reads very much like a fairy tale, with its emphasis on an oral-sounding voice, the repetitive structures of folklore, and a Cinderella plot: "There was once a little boy in a little cabin on a little farm in a little clearing on a little creek. Now this little creek had a little name—*Knob*. But the boy had a big name—*Abraham*" (11). Stevenson continues this fairy-tale mode by recounting the poverty of the family, as well as its cultural isolation: "He saw nothing but the forest and the rough road that passed the cabin where the family lived" (12–13). And having established this scenario, Stevenson asks the question that will drive the narrative of the book: "And so, shut off from the world of cities and people and books and pictures, could Abe ever get out of the forest? Would the outside world ever hear of him?" (13). Stevenson, who is not one to dwell on suspense, assures the reader that "something wonderful was to happen to this poor little boy someday" (14), and, having established this close connection between narrator and reader, she ends the first chapter with an affirmation of the assumptions of the Childhood of Famous Americans series:

> *And the kind of man he became was the kind of boy he was.*
> *And the kind of boy he was* will be told in these stories. Read them, boys and girls, and you will understand why Abe Lincoln became a great man and why everyone loved and trusted him. (14)

The clear suggestion is that this is biography—or hagiography—and that the reader may perceive the greatness in the adult by understanding the greatness suggested by Lincoln's early activities in his American frontier home.

There is a sense here of the author working backward. Having recognized the qualities that the figure shows in his or her adulthood—qualities that lead to that figure's place in history—the biographer then moves into the figure's past—though little might be known about it—and those qualities are used to craft a series of short vignettes that reflect those same qualities. The reader, however, is asked to move in a different direction; for the reader, those youthful qualities are meant to be predictive, speaking to the future. The pattern is encapsulated most perfectly in Augusta Stevenson's *U. S. Grant: Young Horseman* (1947), in which the young boy is examined by a phrenologist who tells him that the bumps on his head show clearly that one day he will be president of the United States. Though the incident is intended to be a joke upon the young boy, and though it leads Grant to declare that he did not want to be president and did not want "to be a great man" (111), the reader is intended to be in on the larger joke—that he will one day become both, because everything in his life seems to predict it.

These premonitions in childhood of future greatness form the stage upon which the action of the Bobbs-Merrill series is performed. Thus, for example, in *Ernie Pyle: Boy from Back Home* (1955, 1962), young Ernie is given a composition assignment, asking him to write about a proud moment in history; all of his classmates choose episodes from significant historical figures. But Ernie decides that he will write about the first time he caught a fish—a proud moment for him. When his classmates read their assignments aloud, Ernie is shamed by his own insignificance. However, his composition is lauded among all the others, leading him to recognize that "it's all right, after all, to write about an ordinary person . . . instead of always writing about generals and such" (125)—which is exactly what Pyle does during his years as a war correspondent. In *John F. Kennedy: Young Statesman* (1964), written and published only a year after Kennedy's assassination, Lucy Post Frisbee foreshadows Kennedy's career even more explicitly. When he and his brother Joseph talk about the next election, they worry whether it would be possible in America for a Roman Catholic to be elected president. "I think this religious thing can be bad," suggests Joseph. But Kennedy's reply presages his later claims: "'By the time you are grown up, Joe, there probably won't be this feeling about religion,' Jack said thoughtfully" (80). Similarly, Kennedy is fascinated by Camelot, so that when he visits West Point, he is reminded "of King Arthur and the Knights of the Round Table. The covenant of the knighthood was even a little like the Boy Scout Code. Perhaps the noble King Arthur had influenced Cadets and Scouts alike!" (85), foreshadowing later comparisons of his own administration to Camelot. And writing back from school, Kennedy reflects that his "swimming coach thinks swimming is very important because it's a sport that can save lives. I never thought of it that way but I guess he is right. Who knows? Someday my being able to swim may save my life. Or better yet, somebody else's!" (104), suggesting his later heroics in saving his PT boat crew.

In Flora Warren Seymour's *Sacagawea: Bird Girl* (1945, 1959), the reader is deluged with premonitions of Sacagawea's journeying life. In the opening chapter, the young girl is drawn to follow the sun, leaving camp and hiking up through hills to see the dawn and so find the sun's home. On one hill she exclaims, "How big the world is! . . . I did not dream that it reached so far" (21). Later, when her mother recounts the journeys of "Old Man," Sacagawea responds, "Mother, will we ever go down to the end of the river? I would like to do that" (61). Her mother assures her that they would never go so far, but when the young girl falls asleep, "in her dream she was a shining fish. She was swimming down the swift stream, past the lands of the Chopunnish, to the lake which people called the stinking water" (62). Similarly, when Sacagawea hears of the "*tabba bone*"—white people—she resolves that someday she would see such people, and "when she went to sleep that night, she dreamed that a whole village of people with pale faces were dancing about her" (79). Toward the end of the narrative, when Sacagawea has been abducted by another tribe, she consoles herself by thinking, "I shall see strange places and new people. Perhaps even the *tabba bone*. And wherever we go, the stars will look down on us. They'll be the same kind stars that shone down on us at home" (145)—a strange and remarkably calm thought for a young girl who has just been kidnapped but in keeping with the narrative's foreshadowings. Sacagawea's decision to stay with the Lewis and Clark expedition at the conclusion of the narrative—"I shall go on to the setting sun with my husband and the party of Americans" (157)—the only decision in this sequence with historical veracity—is made logical and compelling by the way in which Seymour has crafted the young Sacagawea's responses to her world.

In the Bobbs-Merrill series, the difficulty of crafting biographical stories and pegging them to a meaningful structure is not a difficulty at all, because what is central is not the biographical facts but the character of the figure, to which the stories are adapted easily because they are fictional. The stories are like the miracle tales of medieval hagiography, readily transferred in whole or in part from saint to saint; the issue was not the miracle itself but the holy character of the figure who performed it.

So it is only natural that when Stevenson comes to end her book with Abe going on to become the great man he would be, she returns to her fairy-tale opening: "The little boy who lived in a little log cabin on a little farm in a little clearing on a little creek, was now out of the forest and into the world of cities and men" (186). As she has pictured it, it is a Cinderella story indeed, with this one difference: Lincoln needed no glass slipper, for he himself had the character traits that would bring him out of the little cabin and into the city. This is the truth toward which Stevenson aims; she sees it as much more important than biographical fact.

Certainly Abraham Lincoln is one of the figures to be expected in a biographical series published in America at midcentury. But as the series moved toward less expected figures, so too it moved toward the hard questions those figures raised about their place in the American narrative. By the mid-1940s the series was moving toward these questions with its incorporation of female subjects—though it was a slow movement. Jean Brown Wagoner's *Louisa Alcott: Girl of Old Boston* was published in 1943, but the ensuing biographies of female subjects were defined principally by male relationships, and most appeared in a category later defined by the publisher as Noted Wives and Mothers: Wagoner's *Martha Washington: Girl of Old Virginia* (1947) and *Abigail Adams: A Girl of Colonial Days* (1949); Helen Albee Monsell's *Dolly Madison: Quaker Girl* (1961); and Katharine E. Wilkie's *Mary Todd Lincoln: Girl of the Bluegrass* (1954). If this was a tentative beginning in terms of asking hard questions about the place of women in the American scene, later biographies moved further afield for their choice of subjects and found women whose significance did not lie with a connection to a powerful male figure. Thus there would be biographies on political leaders (Shirlee Petkin Newman, *Liliuokalani: Young Hawaiian Queen*); on scientists (Grace Hathaway Melin, *Maria Mitchell: Girl Astronomer*, and Joanne Landers Henry, *Elizabeth Blackwell: Girl Doctor*); on athletes (Lena Young de Grummond and Lynn de Grummond Delaune, *Babe Didrickson: Girl Athlete*); on authors (Mabel Cleland Widdemer, *Harriet Beecher Stowe: Connecticut Girl*, Miriam Evangeline Mason, *Kate Douglas Wiggin: The Little Schoolteacher*, and Miriam Evangeline Mason, *Mary Mapes Dodge: Jolly Girl*); on settlers and explorers (Flora Warren Seymour, *Sacagawea: Bird Girl*, Augusta Stevenson, *Virginia Dare: Mystery Girl*, Jane Moore Howe, *Amelia Earhart: Kansas Girl*, Ann Spence Warner, *Narcissa Whitman: Pioneer Girl*); on entertainers (Ellen Wilson, *Annie Oakley: Little Sure Shot*, and Shirlee Petkin Newman, *Ethel Barrymore: Girl Actress*); on social activists (Augusta Stevenson, *Clara Barton: Girl Nurse*, Grace Hathaway Melin, *Dorothea Dix: Girl Reformer*, Jean Brown Wagoner, *Jane Addams: Little Lame Girl*, Jean Brown Wagoner, *Julia Ward Howe: Girl of Old New York*, Helen Boyd Higgins, *Juliette Low: Girl Scout*, Helen Albee

Monsell, *Susan Anthony: Girl Who Dared*, and Constance Buel Burnett, *Lucretia Mott: Girl of Old Nantucket*). By the mid-1960s biographies of women subjects represented almost 20 percent of the entire Childhood of Famous Americans series.

The early biographies in the series that focused on women subjects presented the characters in traditional roles of midcentury America—starkly different from the active, inventive, physical, outdoors life of the young boys being depicted. In *Martha Washington: Girl of Old Virginia*, Jean Brown Wagoner, who would write several of the biographies of women subjects, pictured Patsy Dandridge's life as moving clearly and inexorably toward the management of a fine plantation; she would become a woman who would be responsible for the good economy of the place, as well as providing its social graces. Young Martha—called Patsy throughout the biography—is particularly adept at sewing; her cousins marvel at the nimbleness of her fingers as well as her ability to sit and persevere at the task. When Aunt Mary sees her work, she declares, "I've never seen prettier, neater, daintier work in my life" (46). Her cousins, meanwhile, beg her to come over every day at sewing time: "Seeing Patsy sewing so busily and so happily had put them all in a good humor. They had forgotten to be bored!" (46). But her mother sees her sewing as an important step toward something larger than Aunt Mary's praise. It is one aspect of Patsy's larger work as a gracious woman. Acknowledging that Patsy has learned to ride a horse well, her mother notes, "But there's a great deal more to managing a plantation than that. You do very well with your stitchery now. You must learn to cook also" (137). Later, she repeats her advice: "There's a great deal more to running a plantation than knowing how to dance and ride and cook and sew. You must know how to manage. . . . You will have to look after your own families and your slaves' families. You have to know how to do just about everything that's done on a plantation" (167–68). In short, all the skills that Patsy is to learn—riding, cooking, sewing, dancing—are directed at making her a proper hostess on a large plantation; this is her vocation. And Patsy accepts this position gladly.

Along with those skills comes the more social skill of managing people—her family, guests, and slaves. And Patsy learns these lessons as well. When an artist comes to paint the three children but brings items for them to hold in the portrait that they do not like, it is Patsy who finds other objects and so saves the business from turning into a rout; the chapter is entitled "Patsy Tries to Please Everybody" (92). When all is settled, Wagoner resorts to metaphor to suggest the adeptness of Patsy's skill at handling her siblings: "The storm was over soon. The sun came out. The air was cool and fresh. The artist got out his paints and brushes and the picture was begun after all" (101). When Patsy admits to her mother that she might be afraid of the night, her mother tells her that she must never show fear, because the slaves are watching her: "You have to be their leader. They learn from watching you" (113). Patsy resolves that she will be just like her mother in this and so manage her slaves well. And later, Patsy practices her manners when a ship sails up the river to the plantation, carrying a new pony for her. Instead of begging Captain George to unload the pony right away, she asks him in: "'Of course you must have breakfast first,' she said, though she didn't see how she was going to wait" (127). She soon becomes the person she was born to be: "She was quiet and well behaved, and her manners were perfect, but she didn't do very well in her studies. She could hardly wait for the dancing lessons" (161). In her role, studies are not necessary. The gracious hostess doesn't need to know very much outside of the sphere of her activity.

In the earlier biographies of female subjects, even those women later known for their challenges to gendered expectations are leveled as the character qualities that led to those challenges are subdued. Jean Brown Wagoner, in her *Louisa Alcott: Girl of Old Boston*, does not focus on Alcott's strong desire to contribute financially to her family nor on her creation of an alter ego—Jo March—who specifically refused to accept her gendered position. Instead, Wagoner focuses on Alcott's attempts to overcome qualities in herself that might have been perceived as unladylike. She is enjoined to act like her mother (who was a remarkably strong and able woman but who appears very little in this biography). "When you're angry and want to pinch someone or throw something, just say to yourself, 'Mother wouldn't do that.' It will help you guide your hands" (20), her father recommends, and Louisa accepts that advice wholeheartedly. The narrative then shows Louisa learning the lessons of patient selflessness: she gives the last cake at her birthday party to a young boy (32–34), she brings her dinner to a poorer family (54–58), she patiently bears her punishment when she comes home late one night because she resolves that "she wanted to be treated like Mother's little girl" (52). When she is tempted from this path, her parents decide to send her to friends in Providence so that she will learn to "play quietly at home with Anna and her little friends. They have such good times with their dolls" (71).

The hints of Louisa's less acquiescent nature are few and subdued. Sometimes she runs from the house and leaves her share of the work to

Anna. "Anna didn't mind. When Louisa came home, she always had exciting adventures to tell" (61)—an unlikely reaction on Anna's part but meant to be a hint at Louisa's storytelling abilities. During the Providence visit, she welcomes young beggars in from the streets and opens her hostess's pantry to them, an act for which she has no regret, though she does regret her angry response to her host's rebuke. The narrator remarks, in fact, that her anger at this rebuke makes her act "like a bad-tempered, naughty little girl" (119); the narrator gives no affirmation of her act of radical kindness in opening the pantry. But even this anger on her part leads to a decision that reflects the leveling of the biography: "If I ever get home again, I'm going to be more like Anna. I'm going to do my work and not run away and play all day," she promises to herself (121). Though she remains unrepentant about the food, she does repent about the anger, and so she "cried all her naughtiness away" (123)—about as unlikely an event in the life of Louisa May Alcott as a writer could contrive. Even when she does become a successful writer, the narrative hints that it comes about because of her father's work in building her a room: "You have been patient and kind, and have worked hard. You have earned this room. You will enjoy it more now that you deserve it" (178).

Little mention is made of Alcott's challenges to gendered expectations, other than her move to Boston to live alone and write and her move to Washington to act as a nurse during the Civil War—both of which are challenged by the townspeople of Concord (in this biography), but both of which quickly receive her parents' approval. The narrative trajectory of the book is for her to conquer unladylike activities and mindsets; but these are, in fact, the very mindsets that allow her the independence to succeed as a writer and that place her in the situation of being the financial head of the Alcott household. But again, this is something not mentioned in the text.

The character of the Quaker activist Lucretia Mott is similarly leveled in Constance Buel Burnett's *Lucretia Mott: Girl of Old Nantucket*. Mott was a leading nineteenth-century voice for the rights of all individuals and so was an aggressive abolitionist, inviting African Americans to her home and church. She also spoke out for the rights of women, challenging white male hegemony in the political sphere and taking an important part in the Quaker tradition of female preachers. And she argued vehemently for the rights of children, urging an acceptance of their value as individuals who, like adults, could hear and respond to the Inner Voice. In other words, this was an individual who powerfully challenged many of the assumptions of her culture.

But the subtitle of this biography is predictive of how Burnett would handle her subject; here, Lucretia's childhood is really a tale of growing up on the island of Nantucket, with all the adventures that a child on an island is likely to have. Though there are brief moments when Lucretia's later beliefs emerge in seed form, they are minor moments, almost asides. When her seafaring father returns after a long voyage, Lucretia listens to the conversation among his friends that night, informing him of all the latest political news, and she imagines that "it would be nice to be a statesman, too, maybe a President. It was queer that no one had mentioned the name of a woman President tonight" (103)—though it is hard to understand why she should find that odd, since there never had been one. But this is a small note; otherwise Lucretia is, like the other female figures of the biographies, firmly in her expected female roles. She understands that "boys knew lots of useful things" (26) and that her angry response when she is told during the sheep shearing to "go back to the tents with the women and girls!" (120) is problematic not because of her response to a gendered slight but because she, like Louisa, had grown angry. When Lucretia does show spirit, she does so out of a sense of gentleness—as in rescuing a tern with a hurt wing (45–47) or a young boy being unfairly punished (173); but in both cases, others must come to aid her. She is praised for being polite, "as Mother had taught her" (101), for "minding her own business" and "holding her tongue" (126)—there is no irony—and for having a "nine-year-old head [that] was full of good sense" (131). When Lucretia asks hard questions about death—her father being presumed dead on a voyage—the female preacher comforts her first by telling her that she should listen to her heart and then by counseling her against being quick-tempered, or having a sharp tongue, or being angry or impatient or unhelpful. When she can avoid those vices, then "thee finds a great joy. No sorrow can keep that kind of happiness from crossing thy path" (149–52), which again levels the fiery character of Lucretia Mott. Even the final summary chapter, which mentions very briefly some of her political positions, is tempered: "Without James [her husband] . . . I could have done little," she humbly confesses (187). The end result is a book that pictures an island childhood, but one that firmly entrenches the accepted gendered positions of the midcentury.

But by the 1960s the biographies about women subjects were changing, incorporating figures who were not merely Noted Wives and Mothers but known for their own contributions. Shirlee Petkin Newman, who would become an associate editor at *Child Life* magazine and develop a career in writing about the children of other countries, drafted *Liliuokalani: Young Hawaiian Queen* in 1960, the year after Hawaii was declared a state. The narrative bears all the marks of the ethnocentrism that contributed to that statehood. There is no hint that the gradual growth of American power in this independent nation, or the intruding importation of American missionaries and culture, or the growing power of American "advisors," or the gradual assumption of American authority is problematic. "Mrs. Cooke, do the Hawaiians still seem strange to you?" asks the young Liliuokalani of her American missionary teacher. "Some of your ways are different from ours, but you are learning quickly" (102), her teacher replies. There is no hint of irony in the narrative at all nor any regret when the measles brought by this infiltration is passed over without any sense of responsibility: "The Hawaiian people were healthy because they spent so much time outdoors, but many could not get over measles" (104). In fact, the depopulation to which this disease contributes is used as an excuse for the necessity of "a peaceful revolution" (187) carried out by the Americans on the island, which removes Liliuokalani from her throne. At the close of the book, Newman suggests that, had she lived, Liliuokalani would have been proud that Hawaii had become a state—an unlikely scenario.

Nonetheless, Newman works hard to present Liliuokalani not as the ladylike hostess so adept at sewing and the social niceties but as a powerful and even aggressive personality whose character fits her for becoming a queen. When the opportunity comes for her to go to school, she is much more taken by the prospect of riding in the king's outrigger canoe (12). When she sees boys diving deep after coins thrown by sailors in the harbor, she resolves that she, too, will do that when she is older (21–22); later, she will surf with the boys (126–27) and ride out as a cowboy (163). When she is to sing in front of a crowd, she is surprised when her sister wonders whether she is nervous. Appearing before others, Liliuokalani says, is "nothing" (44), and only then does she begin to wish that she might have been born to be a queen (there are quite a few people in line to succeed to the throne before she ascends to it); nonetheless, she resolves that "I must serve the King and the people of Hawaii" (45). When her brother—now king—leaves Hawaii for a state visit, "she showed that she was wise, generous, and able to rule well" (181)—this just before the narrative moves to the peaceful American revolution, for which no real reason is given.

The determination of Liliuokalani is precisely the same quality that marks the narrative of *Babe Didrickson: Girl Athlete* (1963), the subject of which, the narrative notes several times, works very hard at whatever she sets her mind to. "Whatever she does, she does with all her might," remarks her father (18). Didrickson is consistently shown as one who uses all of her might in breaking gendered barriers because of her athletic prowess—just as *Jim Thorpe: Indian Athlete* (1956) shows that athlete breaking barriers established by racism. In fact, the two biographies are much alike in their focus on their subjects' astounding ability in multiple sports. When asked which races he enjoyed, Jimmy Thorpe answers, "I like all of them" (121); Didrickson similarly reflects that "there's no hard sport as far as I'm concerned—and that's the truth!" (191). The experiences depicted in the biographies work to bear witness to these claims. But what is remarkable in *Babe Didrickson: Girl Athlete* is that despite the qualification of the adjective in the subtitle, the biography handles Didrickson's athletic prowess quite similarly to that of the Jim Thorpe biography, though the Thorpe biography qualifies that athlete's abilities by noting how small he is physically and so how surprising it is that he can do so well. The Didrickson biography could similarly have qualified her abilities by noting that they were accomplished by a young girl. But the narrator does not do this and in fact—except for the subtitle and concluding line—never hedges the accomplishments of Didrickson by noting that she was a girl.

In the early pages, the narrative puts Didrickson in some tension; there are always chores to do—often chores understood to be the work of a young girl—and yet she is eager to be part of various teams that are always dominated by boys. In the first incident of the book, she threatens a young boy who calls her by her given name—Mildred—and then is immediately chosen first on one of the boys' teams (14–15). She later wins a marble game—though only boys, and older ones at that, had entered, causing her sister to declare that "I've decided I'm not going to waste my time worrying about you in tournaments any more" (34). A little later, when her neighborhood football team is challenged by another team that has not seen Didrickson before, she endures the taunts of the other boys—"Let's see how long that captain of yours is going to last once we get going" (79)—and then shows that she is the best player out there, leading to this exchange:

> He was quiet a moment. "She says she's going to be the world's greatest athlete," he added.
> "Well, I'll tell you," said Al, "if anybody had told me yesterday that a girl had said that, I'd have just about killed myself laughing. Today I'm not even smiling." (84)

Didrickson has resisted the qualified "world's greatest female athlete"; young Al here has also learned a lesson: it may well be that the world's greatest athlete is not male. It is hardly surprising, then, that when Babe goes to high school, the narrative takes pains to show her skill in the female sports in which she is allowed to compete but more fully explores her workouts with the male basketball team, in which she shines.

Early on, Didrickson resolves that she will be like her father, who has sailed around the Horn and survived a shipwreck. "I'm going to have exciting things happen to me," she declares, because "I'll *make* them happen" (24). Her definition of being like her father is living a life of excitement and adventure—and she understands that sport will be the venue in which she can do this. She further understands that sports can level distinctions caused by expected gender roles—distinctions that appear only in brief moments in this biography, as, for example, when she cannot play on the men's basketball team in high school. In fact, it is often hinted that Babe is just as strong as any man against whom she competes; when she plays one of her first rounds of golf—with only male partners—she hits a drive that astounds them: "All the men were amazed" (180). But no reader, by then, is amazed.

But this is still 1963, and the authors—Lena Young de Grummond and Lynn de Grummond Delaune—have no desire to be too radical. At the end of the biography, Babe is brought back to expected gender roles. When she meets the man who will be her husband, "she began to want to look more like a girl. She curled her hair. She wore jewelry and high-heeled shoes. She wore lipstick. It was amazing how different she looked. Her friends started saying, 'Why, Babe, how pretty you look!'" (184). Until this time, she had enjoyed short hair and wearing boys' blue jeans. Similarly, the final line of the biography gives the qualifying hedge that no other part of the biography except the subtitle gives: Didrickson is "the greatest woman athlete of this—or perhaps any—century" (191). It is as if Al's hopeful expectation, and Babe's own, had not quite come to pass. Nonetheless, *Babe Didrickson: Girl Athlete* presents a female subject in ways completely outside the worlds of the Noted Wives and Mothers, a woman who uses physical strength and determination and will do so in ways that had mostly been kept part of the male world of the Childhood of Famous Americans series.

✳ ✳ ✳

For the most part, the Childhood of Famous Americans series deals with figures within the mainstream white experience. But early on, the series began to incorporate subjects from outside that experience, though it would not make this a priority—at least, in terms of the number of subjects chosen. The year after *Louisa Alcott: Girl of Old Bos-*

ton, Bobbs-Merrill published Stevenson's *George Carver: Boy Scientist* (1944); it would wait six years before publishing another biography of an African American subject: Stevenson's *Booker T. Washington: Ambitious Boy* (1950). By the mid-1960s it had published only one more: Dharathula H. Millender's *Crispus Attucks: Boy of Valor* (1965), which Bobbs-Merrill listed under the category Founders of Our Nation. The company was more committed to publishing biographies of Native American figures, perhaps believing that there was a greater school market in that arena. The year after the Carver biography, Bobbs-Merrill published *Sacagawea: Bird Girl* (1945), following that the next year with *Pocahontas: Brave Girl* (1946), both by Flora Warren Seymour. By the mid-1960s there were nine biographies of Native American subjects. All of these biographies would question the majority American narrative, and some would do so radically, though usually implicitly, for challenges to the American narrative would be set in a context that tended to minimize their subjects' sense of "Otherness." In fact, by the end of the narrative, subjects who are minority figures are usually drawn into the mainstream and usually lauded by it—the subject is not, at the end, set directly against the larger American narrative.

Distinctions in the ways in which African American and Native American children move toward the American Dream—or the ways in which that American Dream is or is not available to them—do not take center stage within these biographies. Instead, there is an emphasis on each of these figures attempting to work out—usually for himself or herself—how it is that, given the social restrictions of the culture, he or she can find his or her way to greatness and how that greatness might be defined. That is, these are books that do consciously want to show young readers the problematic effects of prejudice, even while they are themselves not always able to emerge out of a cultural consciousness stained by that prejudice. Thus these particular fictionalized biographies are marked by uneasy tensions.

In *Pocahontas: Brave Girl*, for example, Flora Warren Seymour (who would spend much of her writing career focusing on the Native American experience) is, obviously, aware that Pocahontas comes from a Native American tradition—but the character of Pocahontas herself seems strangely unaware of this. When Seymour wants to introduce an element of the Native American culture, Pocahontas seems to be the outsider who needs the information, taking the place of the reader. When "Aunt Jappy" adopts a young boy caught during a raid, she explains the tradition to Pocahontas: "Our warriors captured him. They would have killed him, too, but I chose to adopt him instead. I will take him in place of my own boy who was killed in fighting with the Mohawks. Now he will learn to call me Mother, and I shall call him son" (51). When Pocahontas is with Arrow Maker, she asks questions that again put her strangely outside the culture's experience. "Do you give the arrowheads to other people?" she asks. Arrow Maker explains that the tribes must trade with others. "They give us things for them . . . [s]kins, perhaps, or feathers to make into the robes we wear when it is cold. They can use the arrows to shoot birds and beasts" (49). At the beginning of the biography, Pocahontas is ten years old. She would certainly have known of these practices; however, she is set in place of the reader outside the Native American world. It is, then, hardly a surprise that she becomes so very pro-European, despite the dangers the Europeans pose to her own people.

Nowhere is this removal of Pocahontas from her Native culture more pronounced than in the lines of dialogue ascribed to her and her people. "I'll run ahead and tell them you are coming," she tells her brother on his return to the camp (16). "All right, come along," she says, agreeing to the request of a young boy of her tribe (37). "No, I suppose not," Pocahontas replies when asked if she hopes to become a warrior (77). "Bother!" says Fisher Girl. "I just know we'll have to carry him all the way," complaining about bringing a young boy along on a trip. "I would never want to hurt any of them. I don't like all this fighting and hurting, anyway. I want you to promise me that you will always be friendly to Captain Smith's people," Pocahontas instructs young Chanco (135–36). "Well, Chanco, there is something I have to tell you. Fierce War Chief has decided it is time for all of us to get together and get rid of these people who have come to our land. We don't want them here," Chanco's brother tells him, setting up a moral quandary for the young boy (181). There is no differentiation made between the Native American speech and the English speech of the new settlers. Seymour includes no Native American words except for the most stereotyped and clichéd, as "paleface." There is no attempt to find authentic speech patterns, diction, or tonalities. In fact, the only differentiated speech pattern is that of the Jamestown minister, who says, "I baptize thee Rebecca" (164) during Pocahontas's religious conversion. This is, after all, the childhood of a famous American, and so in the context of this series, Seymour has made Pocahontas into a very American (not Native American) figure in terms of both her inclinations and actions and her cultural attributes.

Seymour uses the same strategies in *Sacagawea: Bird Girl*. Upon hearing of approaching salmon, Travels Fast proclaims "Hooray! . . .

Plenty to eat!" (45). When Sacagawea rescues "Baby Brother" from a river, her parents' response sounds like something out of a *Dick and Jane* reader: "'My own good girl!' said Mother" (57). After being told that she might never have a horse until she herself has a daughter who receives a dowry, Sacagawea laments, "Oh dear. . . . That sounds too far away. It might almost be forever," sounding like a formal schoolgirl (87). It is the same tone she uses later when she watches the boys go into the medicine tent to prove their manhood: "They're telling about all the horses they have taken and the enemies they've killed and—oh, just everything" (97)—the last phrase betraying a very non–Native American linguistic turn. When Sacagawea asks when the salmon will come back, her mother tells her that "many moons go by" (59), a stereotyped bit of dialogue repeated later to scorn Little Grass (88). There is here, however, at least one attempt at authentic diction in the use of "tabba bone" (69) to indicate Caucasians—those people with whom Sacagawea, like Seymour's Pocahontas, will entirely throw in her lot.

Certainly there are some authentic cultural elements depicted—the "historical truthfulness" that Douglass Adair claimed was moderately central to the books. Sacagawea explains the rite by which boys enter into manhood to Little Grass: "First they'll put up a tall, tall pole in the center. The boys are strapped against it by strips of leather under their skin. They have to look right at the sun. After a while their skin breaks and they fall to the ground" (100). She later sees the rite performed with her friend, Travels Fast (112–13). A few pages later, when the tribe moves on, Seymour has Sacagawea's grandmother remain behind in the abandoned encampment because she is old and hurt, unable to move about. In both cases, though Seymour presents real cultural elements, she blunts what children might find disturbing about them. Sacagawea makes no comment on the rite other than to be proud when she sees that Travels Fast does not flinch when his skin is cut to insert the leather thongs and to wonder whether it is the case that girls need to be brave, and then to resolve that she will herself be brave. When the tribe abandons Sacagawea's grandmother, Seymour does not indicate that she will most certainly die when left alone, and, in fact, the author has Sacagawea run back later to bring her grandmother a basket of berries. In the end, Sacagawea's sensibilities, even in the face of accepted cultural elements, are not far from those of her twentieth-century North American readers.

In dealing particularly with Native American figures, the authors of the Childhood of Famous Americans series were comfortable with leveling cultural distinctions, so that impulses and sensibilities of the Native American culture seem not far distant from those of Anglo-Saxon America. Here, Douglass Adair's observation that all the figures seem remarkably similar is fair. Narrative lines such as the following—all written by Augusta Stevenson—might come from either culture:

> Suddenly he had an idea. He hurried to the brook and looked at the wet sand. Sure enough! Their footprints showed plainly. He got down on his knees and studied the marks a long time. (32)

> He'd like to have a case for his bow . . . He wanted one made of fur, like Tonka's new one. Any fur that was soft and handsome would do, such as mink, marten, or beaver. Tonka's was beaver and it was a beauty. He had told his father how much he liked it. (103)

> His father and friends had gone to the Cheyennes to buy horses. He was a little lonely, but not very. He was working out a plan by himself. He was trying to see how much riding he could stand. Each day he rode farther.
> He boasted about it at home. "I rode halfway to the Missouri River today, Mother. And I don't feel tired." (140)

Any of these texts could easily fit into a narrative line for young boys from either the white or the Native American culture; the first is from *Buffalo Bill: Boy of the Plains* (1948); the second, from *Kit Carson: Boy Trapper* (1945); the third, from *Sitting Bull: Dakota Boy* (1956, 1960). The assumption here is one that Adair pointed out: "All these stories present youthful heroes and heroines that behave like children. The dominant virtues are the same that Weems admired: intelligence, courage, loyalty, generosity, independence, honor; but they always emerge in terms that real children can accept." Here particularly, the assumption is that a boy on the frontier is a boy on the frontier, and he will respond in the same way, regardless of cultural affiliations.

This same leveling is not quite at work in those biographies that deal with the lives of African Americans, however. Here, the sensibilities of the series seem conflicted, even at odds, as the books try to make sense for young readers of the presence of racist attitudes and understandings in American culture. The series acknowledges that making distinctions between cultures has been at the heart of the troubled relationship between races in America and that the biographies need to deal forthrightly and honestly with those distinctions. But how to deal forthrightly and honestly proved to be problematic.[7]

Augusta Stevenson's *Booker T. Washington: Ambitious Boy* (1950, 1960) invented Washington's early life along the assumption that slaves were happy and content in their slavery and that freedom brought with it unwanted responsibilities—"They didn't know what to do out in the world" (119). Though Stevenson uses the word "ambitious" to describe Washington, in fact, his only ambition seems to be a well-liked slave. Early on, he is chosen for the inside chore of being the "fly-boy" (the child who waves a broad fan over the dining room table to chase away the disturbing flies from the diners) because he is clean and precise and dependable, and there is no hint of any problem that this description comes from the point of view of the masters who hold his life in their hands; in the narrative, it is meant to be praise for his eagerness to embrace his duties. Later, Washington celebrates the fact that he was chosen as "fly-boy" and hopes to do as well as his brother, who has been allowed to work out in the field now because he is old enough, stated as if this were a graduation of sorts (14–18).

In fact, the entire plantation world of the novel seems happy and merry, despite the privations of the war. (At one point, the white family has to eat the same food as the slaves, given the privations of the war economy. The reader is supposed to be startled by this.) Because the cabins of the slaves are small, Stevenson writes, "in good weather, everyone was outside. The older people rested and talked. The younger people joked and laughed and sang. The boys and girls ran about and played games" (25). When Booker is made to carry the books of the daughters of the owners, he does so just after having resolved that he himself would one day learn to read. But, Stevenson writes, "it was impossible for the girls to carry so much. They had to carry their parasols" (47). Booker, having resolved to read, carries the girls' books so that they can carry the frivolous signs of their mastery—and there is no irony at all. Later, when Booker is free, he spends a year earning fifteen dollars so that he can travel to the newly opened Negro college. But when he hears that Tom, the son of his former master, is sick and needs fifteen dollars, he sends it to him—and again, there is no sense of irony. This is just what the good, obedient, trustworthy slave—or former slave—should be doing.

Nor does the final chapter—in which Washington's later career as a writer, orator, and college president is summarized—escape from this vision of happy subjugation. Washington's ambition seems to lead him to found a college that is remarkable because it is clean, well kept, and useful. "He is giving our young Negroes a chance to make something of themselves," one character notes, as if Washington were merely continuing the obedient and careful work that had marked his slavery years and instilling those same qualities in his students. In fact, in Washington's final oration—as Stevenson crafts it—those very qualities of loyalty and obedience to masters suggest that Negroes can be trusted even when they are freed from slavery, and now, because they can be trusted, they should be given the chance to become useful citizens. The response of a white southern audience to Washington's appearance is, to modern ears, almost ludicrous: "When the professor had finished, the audience clapped and cheered. Southern white women and men stood waving handkerchiefs and hats. They shouted with delight. All were carried away by the speaker's words. The Governor of Alabama rushed across the platform and took his hand. So many wanted to speak to him he could hardly get out of the building" (188). Here, not only facts but the psychological reality that Adair praised are wildly violated. And a modern reader has to wonder which is more problematic: the vision articulated by Washington in this fictionalized speech, or the inaccurate picture of strong southern support for the needs of the freed slaves. In either case, Stevenson, writing exactly at midcentury, has not leveled the ground here, particularly if the qualities in young boys praised so earnestly in other texts—qualities of independence, imagination, good-hearted mischief, self-reliance—are set next to the meek and earnest obedience of this portrayal of Booker T. Washington. She seems to be almost an apologist.

And this is why the Bobbs-Merrill series seems at times so odd in its orientation to African American figures. The earliest treatment of an African American figure in the Childhood of Famous Americans series comes in Augusta Stevenson's *George Carver: Boy Scientist*. This book, too, begins with the troubling narrative situation of the young slave's loyalty to his owners: in fact, the antagonists in the opening narrative sequences are not the slave owners but the slave stealers, who have come to catch slaves from their rightful owners and resell them farther south. Even after Carver is freed by emancipation, he still considers the home of his former masters to be his home. When thieves vandalize the property, Carver offers to go to work for the family—since there is no longer any money to send him to the colored school—and Mrs. Carver only agrees reluctantly and with the assurance that he will come home if he can't find work to support himself and them: "So it wasn't like going away for good" (85). This from those who have previously owned him.

But despite the stance of this beginning, the biography—written six years earlier than *Booker T. Washington: Ambitious Boy*—does attempt to assert the injustice—and ultimate fatuousness—of racism in America. In this narrative sequence, George's brother Jim tries to explain why he may not go to school:

"Mr. O'Connor said you'd have to learn to read first. And how can you, George? They won't let us go to school."

"Why won't they? They let us go to the church for white folks. They ask us to come."

"I can't understand, never could."

"I want to go to school! I've got to go to school, Jim!"

Jim shook his head. "Looks like learning is only for the white folks."

"I'll ask Marse Mose to talk to the teacher."

"It wouldn't do any good. If you went the white children would leave."

George's voice trembled. "Because I'm black?"

Jim nodded. "You've got to get used to that."

"But the white boys play with me! They come to see us!"

"I know they do, but school is different somehow." (58–59)

The power of this poignant passage comes from the inability of the boys to understand the reasoning behind racism. They cannot figure out why their race demands separation in terms of education, while race seems insignificant in terms of their religious and social experience. For Stevenson, writing in 1944, racism is, at the start, irrational. She makes no attempt to explain to her young reader why education would be perceived to be threatening to a racist white community; she simply leaves the reader with the frustrated and puzzled boys, placing her readers in union with her characters, trying to perceive reason in what is unreasonable.

Carver's response to racism is, at first, a religious one. He goes to the schoolhouse and sits on the steps, listening to what he is barred from. He is still unable to understand the cause of this barring: "Why couldn't he go inside? It wasn't his fault his skin was black. God made him black" (60). At first, since this discrimination seems ultimately to be God's fault, Carver yields to despair: "Young as he was, he understood. He'd never have a chance to be anybody. He'd be shut out of things. He cried a long time that night up in the loft, and Jim didn't try to stop him" (62). But his conclusion is not to stay in despair but to return to the causation: "Dear Lord, please let me go to school! I want to read and write. Dear Lord, please fix it so I can learn! Please, please fix it, dear Lord!" (62–63). He prays this in his garden—which will be his own ultimate schoolhouse, though he does not know this yet. Here, he no longer tries to understand causation or circumstances; he simply recognizes that something has happened that unfairly and unjustly bars him from what he wants. And his only recourse is to turn to prayer.

Much of the remaining narrative is Carver's growth in understanding racism and trying to come to grips with a society that condones it—Stevenson's attempt to portray injustice to her young readers. Once,

Carver is accused of breaking into a cooper's shop, and he is almost lynched, until the cooper—for whom Carver works—shows up and saves him. Nonetheless, Carver is forced to flee the town, recognizing that the man who falsely accused him—and who now seems like a fool to the town—would take vengeance on him: "He'd better go now and keep out of trouble" (113). But in the next town he is accused of stealing a knife, and though he is later proved innocent, he recognizes that the accusation came out of prejudice: "'He accused me because I'm black,' he thought" (120). He rejects his brother's advice to simply accept the way the world is—to grin and bear it: "But George couldn't smile; he couldn't bear it" (120). When he is later given advice about the world— "A lot of things aren't right in this world, my boy. And if you don't know that now, you'll soon learn it" (128)—he rejects simple acceptance as a way to live. Instead, he will use his intelligence and artistry to define himself.

But Carver understands that there is no guarantee that intelligence and artistry will provide for him. In fact, soon after his resolution to define himself through those qualities, he is thrown into a pond and almost drowned by four white boys envious of his art. The same prejudice comes up when Carver is finally about to graduate from high school. At first, two boys refuse to sit on the platform with him, and the principal tells Carver he may not participate. When he has to send money to his stricken brother and cannot get the proper clothes, Carver is almost glad, since he would not be able to sit on the platform now anyway. But Stevenson then moves toward an absurd sentimentalism: when the two boys hear of Carver's gift of money, they are ashamed, and repent, and purchase the clothes for Carver themselves. Carver's response goes back to his earlier prayer: "I thank Thee, dear Lord" (181). Ultimately, in the final chapter, the issue of prejudice resolves itself neatly with a general recognition of Carver's gifts of intelligence and artistry. Well-known science teachers in northern colleges come to hear him speak, and, Stevenson's narrator notes, "it didn't matter to them that his skin was black. They were interested in his mind" (194).

In *George Carver: Boy Scientist*, Stevenson deals with the issue of racism in America through pathos. She presents George Carver as a Horatio Alger figure—the kid with the odds stacked against him who knows the odds are stacked against him but who succeeds ultimately because of his sterling qualities that eventually force those around him to acknowledge his worth. Here, the ending is not particularly different in tone from that of *Booker T. Washington: Ambitious Boy*. But for the most part, Stevenson leaves racism as something that is not to be rationally understood, and not necessarily to be combated, but as something to be endured in the hope that one's real qualities will come to the forefront and lead to acknowledgment.

But by the middle of the 1960s, the Bobbs-Merrill series had seen the inadequacy of that approach, and so Dharathula H. Millender's *Crispus Attucks: Boy of Valor* (1965), dealing with a figure about whom almost nothing is known, took a very different approach. In *Crispus Attucks* there is still the presence of the happy slave, content to be in bondage, but with two distinctions. First, the slaves in that narrative live quietly because they believe that slavery is inevitable, and they want to give their children, as much as possible, a contented life within the confined space of that inevitability. Millender suggests strongly that this is terribly misguided, but at least it is a rationale that can be understood by a reader, if still rejected. Second, and more importantly, however, is Millender's placement of this particular narrative of contentment entirely in the experience of the older generation of the biography; young Crispus himself never accepts this narrative of the content slave. In fact, Millender has him place his understanding of slavery in a very different context.

As the biography begins, it is hard to discern that the relationships involved in the opening action are those between a master and a slave. Colonel Buckminster, the narrative suggests, "owned many acres of land," and so "many workers were needed to keep everything going" (15). Among those workers are the members of the Attucks family, and the "Colonel was very nice to the Attucks family. In fact, he was fair but firm with all his slaves and servants" (15). Aunt Maria, another favored slave, is "well dressed, as were all of the Colonel's slaves" (19), and when the Colonel comes to see her, he speaks "affectionately" (20). When Aunt Maria tells Colonel Buckminster that Cato, her husband, has run away, the Colonel cannot understand why he would do so: "We've been good to him and Aunt Maria. We've taken care of them and given them a good home" (23). The text here sounds much like that of *Booker T. Washington: Ambitious Boy.*

However, early in the biography, there are powerful hints that Millender will not accept this narrative of slavery. First, she uses the same problem of understanding that Stevenson used in *George Carver: Boy Scientist*: young Crispus cannot understand his parents' explanation of their relationship to Colonel Buckminster.

> "We belong to the Colonel and do as he tells us," Prince [Crispus's father] answered. Cris's mother busied herself with her baking.

> For a long time Cris said nothing. Then he asked, "What does 'belong' mean, Father?"
>
> "We are members of Colonel Buckminster's household," his father said. "We live on his land and work for him."
>
> Cris looked out the window again and watched the Colonel and Tom [Buckminster] disappear through the dusk. "I don't quite understand, but I guess it's all right," he said. (18)

Crispus clearly knows the word "belong," but he does not understand it in relationship to himself and another human being. His father gives a pleasant euphemism, suggesting that they are part of a household, but that euphemism indicates nothing of the power and economic relationships between the members of that household. Crispus is left in confusion, and it might well be that he could have stayed with the understanding he gains from his father and settle into a confined contentment—"I guess it's all right." But in the immediately following incident, he goes to bed and resolves that "I must find out more about this belonging" (19), a resolution that escapes even George Washington Carver. Crispus will not accept contentedly what he has been told.

Crispus's parents never resist the narrative of contented belonging, and though Millender will not criticize them severely in a biography stressing the childhood of her subject, she will show them to be desperately mistaken and trapped by their own acceptance of another's definition. His mother later tells Crispus's sister that though slaves can never be free, "they can be just as happy as other people. I chose this kind of life to be with your father, and I am happy. You can be happy, too" (46–47). When Crispus begins to yearn for something else, his father urges him to settle down, learn a trade that would be useful on the Colonel's farm, and grow up enough to understand that he should think for himself and not be talked by complaining slaves into unlikely dreams of freedom. "We hardly know we're slaves here," his father reminds him. "We have our own cottage, our own piece of land, and our own animals. We have plenty of food to eat and good clothing to wear. We can keep on living this way as long as we wish. Why should we want anything else?" (95).

But when Crispus befriends Aunt Maria, Cato's wife, who herself yearns for freedom, he sees that slavery does not necessarily lead to contentedness. When Crispus's father accuses Aunt Maria of inciting Crispus to rebellion, she responds, "I don't teach him to rebel against anybody or anything, . . . but he has strong feelings. He has a mind of his own, and I can't teach him anything he doesn't want to learn" (82–83). What he wants to learn is the distinction between belonging to Colonel Buckminster and the freedom to which Cato ran. He spends more and more time behind the Big House with the slaves "who wanted to be free" (93), despite his father's concern about his association. Finally, Crispus is drawn to a decision. "I don't like the idea of belonging to someone, not even to the Colonel. Father said I should think for myself, and I've been thinking. I just don't like the idea of being a slave all my life" (101). When he is forced, then, to drive his master's carriage rather than become the sailor he had yearned to be, he replies with sullen obedience—which eventually leads to his being sold, the very fear that his parents had held.

Millender is not willing to leave the narrative here, as Stevenson had. She turns to the white owners and explores their understanding of the relationship. When the Colonel learns that Cato has run off and expresses wonder that he would flee such a splendid situation, it is the Colonel's wife who tries to instruct him: "Would you like to be a slave? Would you like to have to wait on others, never really having a life of your own? Would you like to feel that you belonged to someone else and weren't free to lead your own life?" (24). She, too, uses the word "belong," and she is quite clear about its meaning. Cato's motivation is clear to her, and to the reader, and it is this understanding of slavery that will lead Crispus to reject the understanding held by his parents and other contented slaves. Ironically, the Colonel's response to this question of belonging is exactly the opposite of that of Crispus: "The Colonel abruptly changed the subject and started to hang his coat on a peg. 'Let's talk about something else, something more pleasant'" (24). He wishes not to understand but to deflect understanding.

The rest of the narrative develops Crispus's growth toward his own vision. What does it mean to belong? What does it mean to accept the condition of belonging in human relationships? Why should such belonging be thrown off? How should it be done? These are all questions that Crispus must grapple with in his experience. And Millender will craft the book by unifying the answers Crispus comes to and the principles he finds embedded in the call for liberty that leads to the American Revolution. In fact, by the end of the biography, those two journeys are closely united.

In the final, summary chapter, Millender transports the reader to the Boston Massacre, where Crispus becomes a dramatic orator, calling for the freedom of the colonies, urging patriots to take up arms lest anyone enslave them: "The way to be free is to strike out against those who would enslave you! You must stick together! You are in the right and must not be afraid. You must have courage" (171). Though nothing in the narrative has prepared the reader for this public persona, Crispus's unifying of his own situation as a former slave with the injustice afflicting the colonies is established throughout the text, so that Crispus emerges both as a hero of the Revolution and as a hero of those who would defy slavery. Here is a much more nuanced and complete handling of the issue than had ever yet appeared in the Bobbs-Merrill series, one that spoke to an America that had embarked on its civil rights movement.

✳ ✳ ✳

Though libraries removed the covers of these biographies and the publisher was eager to have them recognized as "Little Orange Books," the dust jackets of many of the books in the 1950s bore, on their inside, a message to "Parents, Relatives and Friends of Children." It spoke to the publisher's conception of the series. "Why should you encourage your child to read these books?" it asked. Because they made good readers. Because they had a wide appeal, not limited by age. Because the books competed well with "distracting influences less helpful to your child." But in the very center of these reasons stood an explanation of why these biographies were important to the understanding of the American narrative and what they truly hoped to accomplish in a child reader. Children should read these biographies, the publisher claimed, "because they reflect true Americanism, a love of freedom, equality and fraternity, a strong distaste for racial or religious, economic or social prejudice. They radiate honesty, courage, ambition, kindness. They cover the whole panorama of American life in all periods and regions, showing the way our people lived, their hardships and their triumphs."

True Americanism—though defined here by the absorption of a French motto—involves a sense of equality and a rejection of prejudice on all levels, declared Bobbs-Merrill. If these books were not always able to remove the prejudices and assumptions of the cultural contexts in which they themselves were written, still, they made a conscious attempt at asking radical questions about the majority's exclusive claim to the American narrative.

PART THREE

American Children's Literature and World War II

1940 — 1945

Adapting American Democracy

Responding to the Urgencies of War

In February 1941, ten months before America's entry into World War II, Siddie Joe Johnson wrote an article for the *Library Journal* exploring trends she had observed as a librarian in Texas, watching children choose books during a time of international stress: "Americanization, citizenship, patriotism, democracy. More and more books are being asked for and checked out in these fields; more and more these headings are being stressed in children's room card catalogs." Why? Because children's books, she wrote, are sources of "learning and practicing the lessons of good citizenship"; they can make "distinct and individual contributions to the youngsters' growth in patriotism and Americanism" and can show the goodness of America so vividly that children will "carry the dream and the reality of this early reading through all their later lives."

The books that Johnson chose included some fiction: Peggy Bacon's *Buttons* (1938), for example, whose story of a cat rising from alley cat to gentleman "is no fairy tale to [children], but an understandable reality" because it is "an indirect sort of Americanism." And she included *Caddie Woodlawn* (1935) and the Laura Ingalls Wilder novels—"the lovely fiction saga." But principally she included nonfiction, such as narrative histories: Edgar and Ingri D'Aulaire's *The Conquest of the Atlantic* (1933) and Roger Duvoisin's *And There Was America* (1938). She wrote of those books that celebrated democracy: William Oliver Stevens's *The Patriotic Thing; or, What It Means to Be an American* (1940); Munro Leaf's *Fair Play* (1939); Ryllis Clair Alexander Goslin and Omar Panacoast Goslin's *Democracy* (1940); and *Stand Fast for Freedom* (1940), by the journalist Lowell Thomas. She wrote of books that celebrated American culture: Alice Dalgliesh's *America Builds Homes: The Story of the First Colonies* (1938); Robert P. Tristram Coffin's *Ballads of Square-Toed Americans* (1933); Carl Sandburg's *The American Songbag* (1927); Rosemary and Stephen Vincent Benét's *A Book of Americans* (1933), which "should strike patriotic fire in any reader in the young people's room." And she cited biographies, to which she believed children in times of national stress were drawn naturally: Edgar and Ingri D'Aulaire's *George Washington* (1936) and *Abraham Lincoln* (1939); Robert Lawson's *They Were Strong and Good* (1940). In wartime, she argued, children's books could and should inspire young readers, explain the tensions, extol the country, contribute to patriotism, and define democracy by its broadest meanings. In short, children's books themselves could be a part of the war effort.

And this is exactly what happened over the next five years.

* * *

In the middle of World War II, James G. Dyett published *From Sea to Shining Sea* (1943), an optimistic, exuberant boasting of America's wealth and productivity whose photographs celebrated America's diverse cities and "sleepy villages"; its natural resources of corn, ore, lumber, oil, and water power; its rich forests and tilled fields. "America is many things," Dyett wrote, "and to explain it you would have to tell about all the things and all the people." Dyett's "things" are the natural resources turned to productive uses: "Despite wars, the men and women who were making America went right on building houses, making new farms, taming rivers, building cities and throwing miles of railroad tracks across the country. These are the important things." But "all the people" are Dyett's real focus: "America is not a place, it is people; all kinds of people from all countries. The Indians were here first; then came the English, Spanish, French, Dutch and Swedish. The Germans came, and the Scotch, Negroes, Irish, Russians, Poles, Italians, Hungarians, Czechs. More and more people came—Greeks, Turks, Chinese, Japanese, Philippinos. People came by hundreds, by thousands and even by millions." Here the emphasis is strongly on the diversity of the American people—including Americans from Germany and Japan, America's wartime enemies. (No distinction is made between the waves of immigrants and the "Negroes" who also "came.") In Dyett's description, ethnic distinctions no longer applied: "The Yank," one photo caption reads, "is all races mixed into one—an American." And how does this happen? "Gradually the newcomers get used to America and Americans get used to them. Their children go to public school; they meet other children; and when they grow up and marry they begin to spread out into other parts of the cities or into the country. Slowly everyone becomes part of America and American life." This is dubious sociology but powerful melting pot mythology: that immigrants come to America, abandon ethnic distinctiveness, and so blend into the "Yank" who will join with other Yanks to participate in the great movements of the country.

All this is familiar ground—that democracy is about the creation of unity within a nation. But in the last section of *From Sea to Shining Sea*, Dyett points out that just as Americans have always come together to take on the vast projects of their times, so must America today come together to fight. After textual headings such as "America Is People Working," "America Is People Playing," "Americans Can Go to Any Church," and "America Is People Governing Themselves," Dyett now adds "America Is People Fighting."

> There are times in the life of every country when its people must fight. They must defend their land, their homes, their right to decide their own future. When the United States was attacked by Japan on December 7th, 1941, America was thrown into war. When faced with war, everyone has a job to do.... Our war is a people's war, and everyone in America can help. ... Even children can help by collecting scrap to keep the factories going; by acting as messengers for the air raid wardens; by selling war savings stamps. There is something for everyone to do. America at war means everyone doing something—all he can to make his country strong.

The full argument comes into play here. Americans have come from diverse places. They have formed themselves into one people. As one people they have tackled huge problems. Now, Americans must again come together to face this war, bolstered by the knowledge that every single citizen—every child—is doing his or her best to contribute to the war effort.

Here, Dyett was not atypical. After 1941 American children's literature adapted its progressivism to the new urgency by defining democratic unity not only as a social virtue but as a wartime necessity. Children's books asserted that the war meant that the full integration of all citizens into a single democratic nation, with a resulting banishment of bias and prejudice, was not only just and right but strategically imperative. In short, the achievement of justice at home would benefit the achievement of justice abroad. And children's books urged their readers to recognize their own responsibilities as full citizens: democracy, to survive, must be inclusive across all social lines, all generational lines. In *Huck's Raft: A History of American Childhood*, Steven Mintz points out that the war introduced profound changes into the family; one effect was that "a shared sense of danger and privation instilled a strong sense of patriotism" (255), leading to children participating in the war effort through collecting scrap metal and newspapers, selling bonds, planting Victory Gardens. Mintz cites a 1943 booklet entitled *Your Children in War*, which told children: "You are enlisted for the duration of the war as citizen soldiers. This is a total war, nobody is left out, and that counts you in, of course." Children's books had arrived at this same position earlier, thus Munro Leaf's *A War-Time Handbook for Young Americans* (1942), whose narrator spoke directly to the child reader as a child, with exactly the same message: "Any person who tells us that this war isn't any of our business doesn't know what he's talking about. This war is just as much our job as it is that of any grown-up in the country" (4).[1]

A War-Time Handbook for Young Americans is something of a surprise to those who had read Leaf's earlier *The Story of Ferdinand the Bull* (1936) as a pacifist tract. The thesis of the book—and it is a thesis-driven book—is that every American can, and should, be contributing to the war effort: "Every real American Boy and Girl wants to do his or her share to help win this war and bring it to an end just as soon as we can" (3). Some citizens, Leaf's narrator notes, are clearly contributing; we can see this because they are wearing a uniform. But "there are millions of other people who are dressed just the way they always have been and we can't tell just by looking at them whether they are helping to win the war or not. That's the way it is with most of us" (7). The inclusive pronoun is meant to suggest, again, that children, though they may not wear a uniform, can be active agents in the war effort. "How we are dressed is not important. But WHAT WE ARE DOING is very important," the narrator notes, speaking directly to children and as if *for* children. "And We know it. And our country will know it too. That's what counts" (11).

This is a handbook and not a narrative, so the text is a series of suggestions for contributing to the war effort. There is no sense of children being affected by the war psychologically or emotionally; there is only the sense that the child should be contributing—that is, if he or she is a "real American" (3). Leaf's strategy is to establish responsibility for children in circumstances where they can truly participate, so he organizes the suggested contributions by moving from home to community to nation. "Our first duties to our country start right in our own homes. It is to defend them that our soldiers and sailors are fighting. If we don't help to make those homes pleasant, happy and comfortable places to live in, why should they bother to fight for us?" (12). If the text seems manipulative—and it is—it is also meant to provide real opportunities; children can contribute to the war effort by being cheerful, by happily doing "the work that has to be done and being a *good friend* to everybody in your own house" (15), and by getting the right food, exercise, and sleep (these three words are printed in red [17]) so that we are not cross with each other. "There is a good way to beat [unhappiness in the home], and our government wants us to try it now in war-time when it is so important for every one of us to do a share of the work" (22). What our government wants is for families to divide the work according to ability, thus the militarization and democratization of household chores. The young boy and girl are shown standing beside their neatly made beds and their neatly organized closet, saluting, preparing to organize "REPAIR SQUADS" for the house (27).

There are overt military concerns to recognize, Leaf insists. "Most of our country may never have an air-raid or be shot at, but we can't really be sure. So the very best thing we can do is to be all prepared and ready anyway" (30). Children can contribute by following the advice of those who are encouraging safety. Since "many grown-ups are so busy doing other extra things these days that they don't always remember what they have been told" (32), children can help by reminding them. And children can learn first aid—though the most important thing to know is where to get help. Leaf leaves space on one page for the phone numbers of the local doctor, the nurse, the hospital, the drugstore (39). The narrator wonders if the child reader would be able to direct someone to a "drug store, mailbox, hospital, school garage, church, fire alarm, post office, fire hydrant, library, air raid warden, telegraph office, air raid post, taxicab, policeman, bus stop, railroad station? Could you tell them?" (45–47). Again he leaves a blank spread meant for the helpful map the young reader should draw. And children can grow community gardens; grow flowers for people in hospitals; eliminate caterpillar nests and ragweed; collect paper, tinfoil, metal tubes, scrap metal, rubber, old clothes, toys, "and books for soldiers and sailors to read" (53–57). And they can, of course, buy war stamps and bonds (64).

All of these suggestions emanate from a sense that children must be part of the larger whole if America is to succeed in the war. When Leaf turns to national contributions, this sense is sharpened into the themes of democratic inclusiveness implicit in his earlier material.

We hear and read a lot these days about the United States being a Good Neighbor to other countries. This is fine, but some of us still have to learn what it means to be a good neighbor to the people we see almost every day. There are some of us who seem to think that we are the only kind of Americans who really are Americans and people who are a little bit different from us aren't American at all. That is stupid and a foolish thing to believe or say. (58–59)

All of us who are not Native American, Leaf asserts, come from another place, and that is America's strength: "What has made this country so wonderful and strong is that we have come here from all over the world bringing with us so many great and different ideas, talents and skills" (60). The necessary conclusion, then, is understanding and communality. Heedless that his own narrative defines a "we" and an "us" versus "people who are a little bit different," Leaf's narrator affirms the need to demonstrate the true nature of an inclusive democracy so that the United States can be an exemplar: "Now, in War-time, is certainly no time for us to be quarreling and fighting among ourselves and calling each other names because we aren't exactly alike" (61). Instead, if all kinds of Americans unite, "the whole world will want to be like us and wars may stop for good" (61). From this, the book concludes—after a plea to buy war bonds—with an affirmation of the child's participation in the fuller community of America: "When this war is won with the ships, tanks, planes and guns that our government has bought with the money you helped to lend it, then everyone will know you helped your country and your bonds and stamps will be worth more than ever to help *you* in the better world we are going to make" (64). Here, individual need and fulfillment are balanced with communal needs the child has helped to support, leading to "the better world we are going to make."

The same theme of children participating in the war effort is sounded in the contemporary fiction as well. In Allena Best's *There Is the Land* (1943), written under the pseudonym Erick Berry, the unlikely plotline, riddled with implausibility, sets out a conventional spy drama: A family finds itself in a country home and is quickly beset by attempts to dislodge them—as it turns out, spies are using the backyard as a path to smuggle German saboteurs across Lake George, New York. The children spy on the spies and eventually convince the local authorities of the danger and nab the lot. There are a number of expected war references in this 1943 plot: for example, the family is forced to stay at the country house when someone steals a tire, precious in these days of rationing, as is gas, another commodity that is almost stolen from the family.[2]

What drives the matter of the book, however, is not the spy narrative but the transformation of the family from a city-dwelling, rather useless group of children into a farming family and thus true contributors to the war effort. As they look around their acres, they find all sorts of useful ways of having the land produce, thus preserving the food they would have consumed in their New York City apartment for soldiers on the front. It is, in a sense, the story of the growth of a family toward independence and self-sufficiency, but these qualities are defined specifically as they apply to the war effort and the needs of the country. Thus, when Cloris's city friend Fran comes to visit and tells her of her uniform and her nights spent dancing with soldiers, Cloris is not sure that Fran's contribution is sufficient: "What real use was Fran's rushing around? What was she producing?" (86). On the other hand, Cloris comes to understand that she herself is truly producing:

> It was July now; gas rations were stricter, and more rationing of every kind loomed ahead. But every stick of wood Aunt Hesper burned in the big kitchen stove was grown on The Picket and saved just that much of the nation's tires, gasoline transport and communications that were needed for other things. Every pailful of water brought from the spring saved that much municipal pumping, filtering, metering and accounting. Milk, peas, beans, salads, everything they got from the goats and garden, not only saved the Carr pocketbook, but saved also something of the nation's resources. That was a pleasant thought to carry on with. (93–94)

Thus when Cloris is tired and does not want to finish weeding a row of beans, the thought of her contributions helps her to carry on: "It was *her* bucketful, and *her* efforts. That was all that mattered. She would finish this row before she went indoors to rest" (94). That mindset, naturally enough, leads Cloris to reject the partied life of the city that had once mattered so much: "These people still sailed and danced and dined and went to the movies. But you began to wonder why they worked so hard at doing nothing. All their efforts didn't produce so much as a quart of beans or a pint of milk" (100). The binary that Best here establishes—the useful producers versus the useless entertained—is driven home to the reader by her subtle use of the second person: "you began to wonder." The "you" suggests an entry into Cloris's mind and language, but at the same time it seems to address the reader, inviting the reader to share her position: that each person should be producing for the war effort.

The theme and stance of *A War-Time Handbook for Young Americans* and *There Is the Land* reflect much of what the professional literature in the field was also projecting. The spring after the publication of *A War-Time Handbook for Young Americans*, Marie Nelson Taylor, a librarian at the Woodward Memorial Library of LeRoy, New York, reviewed the book in the *Wilson Library Bulletin* and affirmed its importance as a part of the war effort. "It is significant that authors of children's and young people's literature are meeting the need for books concerning the war. . . . Young Americans are anxious to make their contributions toward victory.... *A War-Time Handbook for Young Americans* ... tell[s] simply, but well, what every boy and girl can do to help win this war." She affirmed as well the role of novels like Berry's *There Is the Land*, with its emphasis on the role of children in the war. Taylor cited also Elizabeth Enright's *The Four-Story Mistake* (1942), in which the children of the Melendy family—the same family of Enright's better-known *The Saturdays* (1941)—raise money for war bonds, plant a Victory Garden, collect paper and metal salvage, and cheerfully substitute an old surrey for their car when a hard-to-replace tire blows, and Jack Bechdolt's *Junior Air Raid Wardens* (1942), a spy novel in which two teenage boys expose an incendiary traitor living in the town of Harmony—a book, Taylor wrote, "devoured by young patriots."

But Taylor wanted to go further, affirming an even larger consciousness: American children might feel greater empathy and understanding, and a greater sense of the importance of their wartime work, if they could understand what children of other nations were facing. "Perhaps most important and meaningful . . . are those stories which concern children living in war-torn countries abroad," she wrote. She cited Elizabeth Foreman Lewis's *When the Typhoon Blows* (1942), about Li's growing nationalism during the Japanese invasion of China; Mirim Isasi and Melcena Burns Denny's *White Stars of Freedom* (1942), about a Basque boy who flees the Spanish Revolution and comes to America; Antoni Gronowicz's *Bolek* (1942), in which a young boy's growing musical genius is set against the Nazi invasion of Poland and his flight to America; and Eleanor Frances Lattimore's *The Questions of Lifu: A Story of China* (1942), which obliquely referenced the Japanese invasion of China in having six-year-old Lifu leave home to search for his father, who is a soldier. The assumption behind each of Taylor's choices is that children's literature becomes part of the war effort through practical suggestions for children's contributions, as in Munro Leaf's book; through inspiration, as in Jack Bechdolt's books; and through the development of a sympathetic reaction, as in the books by Elizabeth Foreman Lewis and Mirim Isasi. All of these were legitimate means by which children's literature could take its proper place in the war.

But it was not always that way.

In the years before the war, teachers, librarians, and publishers of children's books advocated the role of children's books in "peace education." Of these voices, John J. DeBoer, the editor of the *English Journal*, was one of the most vehement. In a series of articles during the 1930s, he urged educators to work toward peace education and to use books for this task. In a 1933 editorial, "The Technique of Teaching for Peace,"

DeBoer rejected nationalism as chauvinistic and argued that education should foster an international vision that would be constructive of peace education: "In the place of the sentimental symbols of nationalism the school must establish a living ritual of internationalism interpreted in terms of a world co-operative society. . . . By directing the creative energies of youth to the fashioning of the co-operative ideal, we shall be appealing to a powerful adolescent impulse while at the same time we turn our thoughts to the essential mechanism for the abolition of war."

DeBoer saw this hope for an international vision fade with the rise of the Nazi regime, but his voice was to become shriller in his insistence that educators must still be about the business of peace education, using every means possible. In November 1935 he used military imagery to highlight the coming danger: "We have no time to lose. War will destroy us, and our Shakespeare and Shelley with us, if we do not abandon our policy of polite disapproval and proceed at once to dig our trenches and drill the new recruits. . . . As the legions of Mars come nearer, let us pledge 'our lives, our fortunes, and our sacred honor' to the determination that 'they shall not pass!'" The next spring, he was even more vivid: "There will be blood on our hands if we do not speak out. Even now the war-makers are plotting against the lives of the young people in whom we are trying to develop the arts and attitudes of civilization. Seeing this, we cannot keep silence without sharing in their dreadful guilt."

In the spring of 1937 the *English Journal* affirmed the importance of a new volume published by the Committee on International Relations of the National Council of Teachers of English: *War and Peace: An Anthology* (1937), edited by Ida T. Jacobs. (John J. DeBoer was one of the members of the editorial committee.) The *English Journal*, somewhat hopefully, suggested that the book "comes in response to a nation wide interest in the peace movement—an interest reflected in thousands of high-school English classes." Certainly it gave voice to that movement and affirmed its centrality to the mission of the educator. It reprinted short pieces meant to be used in classrooms, authored by, among others, Harry Emerson Fosdick, Jane Addams, Charles Lindbergh, Hendrik V. Van Loon, President Franklin Roosevelt, J. B. Priestley, Carl Van Doren, James Norman Hall, and Ernest Hemingway—all of whom argued that America must remain at peace. The arguments were exhortative—such as Roosevelt's. The arguments came in the form of proposals—such as Ernest Wilkins's "A Peace Plan Suggestion." The arguments were developed aesthetically—as in the "Funeral March of Youth." The arguments worked through shocking imagery—as in Laurence Housman's "An Incident at Verdun," in which regimental bands played loudly to cover the groans and screams of the dying between the trenches. The arguments were ironic—as in B. Franklin Hunter's "The New Star Spangled Banner": "Oh, say, will you hope for the dawn of the day / When the War-lust has fled from the hearts of a Nation?" In short, the book was a compendium of materials to be invested into a curriculum that took seriously the object of peace education.[3]

But by 1939 these voices were changing. In late 1939 Kenneth M. Gould was writing in *Horn Book* of the role of children's books in preparing for a possible entry into the European conflict, announcing that "the age of Ferdinand is dying": "We who write for boys and girls have an inescapable obligation. . . . We pray that [American children] may escape the evil fates of war, and fascism, and revolution. But if they are to become whole men and women, emotionally mature, mentally alert, and socially progressive yet stable, we must build simple, stimulating, satisfying and inexpensive literature that brings home to them the living principles of democracy and makes them spiritual citizens of a brave new world. Only such men and women can make poverty unnecessary and war impossible." There is still here DeBoer's notion of books that can contribute to a sense of international citizenship, but there is also the note of preparation for a very different role: American children may not escape the evils of war and fascism and revolution, and so children had better be prepared for war—and books may work toward that preparation.

In October 1940 Harriet Long, an instructor in the School of Library Service at Western Reserve University, argued along slightly different lines: children's books should not necessarily be trundled into peace education curricula, she wrote; instead, they might be a means to affirm "the American way of life" and "our history, our traditions, and the meaning of America," which Long set against "what is going on in Europe and Asia." Long principally cited biography and historical fiction: C. Walter Hodges's *Columbus Sails* (1939), the story told through multiple narrative perspectives; Julia Davis's *Peter Hale* (1939), a novel set in early Jamestown; Lois Lenski's *Ocean-Born Mary* (1939), an imagined biography set in eighteenth-century Portsmouth and stressing the seeds of colonial resistance; Marguerite de Angeli's *Skippack School: Being the Story of Eli Shrawder and of One Christopher Dock, Schoolmaster, about the Year 1750* (1939)—a thinly plotted though strikingly illustrated story of a Mennonite family's immigration; Maribelle Cormack and William P. Alexander's *Land for My Sons: A Frontier Tale of the American Revolution* (1939), set in Revolutionary War Pennsylvania and emphasizing the promise of western expansion; Eleanor Weakley Nolen's *A Job for Jeremiah* (1940); Robert Lawson's historical fantasy *Ben and Me* (1939), in which Franklin emerges as the "democratic being we've always known him to be"; James Daugherty's *Daniel Boone* (1939); Margaret Ann Hubbard's *Little Whirlwind* (1940), a novel of Scottish pioneers in nineteenth-century Canada; and Howard Pease's *Long Wharf: A Story of Young San Francisco* (1939), about adventures in that city during the mid-nineteenth century.

Long's choices are meant to define a national American spirit. Child readers "will sense the unconquerable spirit of those Americans of earlier times who met the challenge of this new land and who had the courage, resourcefulness, and hardihood to win out." Specifically, Long hopes that historical literature will do what historical literature sometimes does very well: speak to the present in terms of the past. Thus contemporary books for children, she argues, should speak less of the details of colonial life and more of the reasons why the colonists left Europe: "to escape tyranny, economic oppression, wars, religious persecution; evils as prevalent now as then. In the light of present conditions overseas children may be better able to appreciate something of the despair and likewise the hopefulness with which the early colonists came to a new country where they might begin life anew." Here is a very different use for a children's book: not to call for peace and world community but to highlight what Long sees as differences between Europe and America and to help children to realize that Americans may soon be required to fight to preserve those distinctions: "We are trying to keep before the young those essential ideals for which our ancestors fought, stressing the necessity for constant vigilance, both to protect those ideals and to perfect our ways of expressing them. Thus our boys and girls are presented with a challenge."

A few months later, in the spring of 1941, Kathryn L. Reynolds, a children's librarian in Grand Forks, North Dakota, wrote to the *Library Journal* to agree with Long's vision. In "Defending America in the Children's Room," she argued that children needed to know the strengths and the weaknesses of their country if they were to be prepared for what was coming. "Today, as never before, our young patrons have a right to know what our American heritage is. They have a NEED to know that other peoples in other times have thought our freedom and our democracy worth defending." She cited books in several categories. "Great Americans" included Ingri and Edgar Parin D'Aulaire's *George Washington* (1936) and *Abraham Lincoln* (1939); James Daugherty's

Daniel Boone (1939); and Paul Laurence Dunbar's *Little Brown Baby* (1940). "America Today" included Doris Gates's *Blue Willow* (1940) and Florence Crannell Means's *Shuttered Windows* (1938). "America's Neighbors" included Hazel Boswell's *French Canada* (1938) and Rose Brown's *Two Children of Brazil* (1940). For "America Growing," Reynolds cited Robert Lawson's *They Were Strong and Good* (1940); Carol Ryrie Brink's *Caddie Woodlawn* (1935); and Leo Huberman's *We, the People* (1932). For "America's Workers," Reynolds noted John Joseph Floherty's *Men without Fear* (1940), describing some of America's dangerous occupations; and Burr Leyson's *Fighting Fire* (1939). And for "America's Friends," Reynolds suggested books on "whatever our newspapers and State Department may be telling us now"—with no hint of irony. It is a short list of mostly familiar titles but chosen for their ability to act as descriptors of the democracy that Americans would soon be called to defend: "Let us make that right book mean one that will teach [children] the real meaning of tolerance and justice, freedom and democracy. If we can give them a true knowledge and love of their country . . . we shall be defending America in the Children's Room against whatever time may bring."

As America entered the war, teachers, librarians, publishers, and writers began to craft books that encouraged children to contribute to the war effort by teaching and modeling the role of the citizen in a democracy. Thus, Marion Sheridan, the head of New Haven High School, argued in December 1942 that the study of language and literature developed in each citizen an understanding of the privilege of living in a democracy: "In a war-torn world pupils must have a feeling of security that comes from the ability to use language and to interpret it. They must have understanding that comes from an emotional as well as an intellectual study of human beings as revealed by literature." The English teacher's role is to equip children to "balance tolerance, sympathy, and courage" through a facility with language acquired through reading. Frances R. Horwich's piece in the spring of 1943 for the *English Elementary Review*—"Young Children Learn the Ways of Democracy"—argued for a more narrow understanding of the role of children's books. In the middle of a war, she wrote, books can answer children's questions about the nature of democracy. She cited one school that used informational books to study the hardships of the Revolutionary War and to recognize that the road to freedom was a long road.

In the faces of these children the teacher was able to see their understanding of the relationship between the Revolutionary War and this second World War. These children understand clearly the problem of rationing. They realize the value of freedom and genuinely want to help preserve it. Time was given to the struggle and sadness and some might question whether eight-year-old children should be subjected to such information. But 1942 was a year of struggle as will be 1943 and 1944. Children are aware of it and can more easily face it when they have the information which enables them to analyze and then understand.

But which were the books to do that? Horwich's stress on "information" suggested that this education was best done through nonfiction. And Eloise Rue, writing a few months later in the same journal, agreed. In "Children's Reading and the War," she suggested with Edward Schofield that though numerous novels and aviation books centered on the war, fiction by itself was inadequate. "Should it not be a challenge to us then to take advantage of [children's] interests and introduce them to books picturing the home life and war efforts of our democratic allies and to those emphasizing the democratic principles for which we are all striving? These will help give them understanding and tolerance of the people and problems of our post-war world."[4]

Rue's and Schofield's position was widely accepted, and early lists of wartime reading were heavily—sometimes almost completely—made up of nonfiction. Leo Lerman, writing for the *Saturday Review of Literature* in the summer of 1942, acknowledged that there are "many excellent story and picture books" for wartime reading, but of the 150 books listed as "timely books on how and why we fight," only a handful are novels—familiar titles such as Florence Crannell Means's *Shuttered Windows* and Doris Gates's *Blue Willow*, as well as 1942's Newbery-winning *The Matchlock Gun* (1941) by Walter D. Edmonds. The remaining texts are all focused on American democracy; the fact that there were so many on this subject in just a single year of publication suggests the public's interest.

Sarah Allen Beard, who had organized the Young People's Division of the central public library in Brooklyn, showed this same belief in the power of nonfiction to encourage children's understanding of and participation in the war when she compiled "Books and Freedom," a selection of recommended works for teens published in the *Library Journal* in 1943. Almost all of the books were meant "to keep freedom flying in the stream of youth's consciousness"—a wonderfully mixed metaphor that suggests Beard's purposes. Almost all are nonfiction. Beard begins with books focusing on the air war, such as *Thirty Seconds over Tokyo* by Capt. Ted W. Lawson (1943), a participant in the Doolittle raid; and *Malta Spitfire: The Story of a Fighter Pilot* (1943) by Flying Officer George F. Beurling, a Canadian who fought with the Royal Air Force. Beard then recommends titles chronicling the battles in the South Pacific and land battles in the European theater, such as Ernie Pyle's journalistic and anecdotal *Here Is Your War* (1943) and the playwright Boris Voyetekhov's history of the Russian front, *The Last Days of Sevastopol* (1943), detailing the defense of that city. Beard then redefines "fiction" to mean "authentic war fiction"—really nonfiction war narratives—and includes James Saxon Childers's *War Eagles: The Story of the Eagle Squadron* (1943), an anecdotal history of American boys in the RAF beginning in the summer of 1940; *"Stand By—Mark!": The Career Story of a Naval Officer* (1943) by Lt. Cdr. Frederic Merrick Gardiner, written as a narrative to give a sense of naval life during peace and war, culminating in the Battle of Midway; and Fairfax Downey's popular *Dog of War* (1943)—it would have five printings during the war years—about Chinook, a dog who becomes part of an American battery and is eventually awarded a Silver Star. Beard includes strictly informational books (William Winter's *War Planes of All Nations* [1943], which, she writes, is "obviously useful"), group biographies (Kensil Bell's *"Always Ready!": The Story of the United States Coast Guard* [1943] and Kendall Banning's *Our Army Today* [1943], a lengthy, detailed, yet engagingly written narrative), and even humor (*Angel of the Navy: The Story of a WAVE* [1943] by Joan Angel, who begins the book with her reason for joining the navy during wartime: "And while we can't actually fight [although we'd like to, by glory!] we *can* release fighting men from desk and shore jobs so they can get out there and smash the Japs and Nazis!" (3–4). Beard includes long lists of books about military careers, "since many young people will be going into one of the services," and about life on the civilian front, since "with readjusted curriculum in wartime, young people have to decide what their immediate jobs in the working world will be"; these books include Boone T. Guyton's *This Exciting Air: The Experiences of a Test Pilot* (1943), a dramatic narrative of the author's flight training with emphasis on the need for pilots during the war, and Williams Haynes's *The Chemical Front* (1943), which gloats chillingly that "the straightforward record of our chemical war effort cannot make cheerful reading in the Axis countries" (v). In her final category, "Aiming to Invent a Better Game," Beard includes Wendell Wilkie's *One World* (1943) and James Dyett's *From Sea to Shining Sea* (1943), which Beard calls "an inspired collection depicting America as she is today." The approach here is quite apparent: librarians should be choosing books that disseminate knowledge about the war, about the services that were fighting in the war, about America, and about America's role in the international community.[5]

Beard does allow fiction "for relaxation," though even here there is a sense of the war's presence and the need for each citizen's participation: Erick Berry's *There Is the Land* is interesting, writes Beard, and the year's Newbery winner, Esther Forbes's *Johnny Tremain* (1943), is "a brave, vivid tale of what it was like for Teen-age boys in Boston's Tea Party days" and gives "the reader a sense of kinship with those who had difficulties to face in earlier days." But Beard remained suspicious about the place of fiction in the war effort and relegated such "relaxation" to "younger boys and girls," though, she claimed, "even some of them join in the cry for true reporting of the struggle."

However, not all agreed that fiction was inadequate in its contribution to the war effort. While nonfiction would provide necessary information, to ignore books of the imagination was to lose not only an important part of childhood but a vivid vehicle for suggesting why America was involved in the war at all. Bertha Mahony, writing in *Horn Book* in early 1942, argued that children's books can be a vehicle for using the imagination to support an understanding of the war: "For children it is most important that they be given a sense of the high significance of these days; that their imaginations be stirred by the struggle.... They need to know that the idea of freedom and independence is animating the struggle throughout the world." Others argued that it would be at least as important, and perhaps more important, to provide children not with more about the war in their childhood reading but with books that speak to what has always appealed to children and thus provide a level of normalcy in an abnormal time. Jean Gardiner Smith, writing an article that immediately preceded that of Eloise Rue in the *English Elementary Review*, spoke to this approach: "What types of reading ought we to give to children? There has been within recent months an almost frantic and at times hysterical attempt on the part of educators to justify their work in terms of the war effort.... If there is any hope for the future, the children of the present must have the heritage of the past"—by which Smith meant books of joy and laughter, books of the imagination. "The best that we adults can offer them in these days of stress is the haven and the security of as normal a childhood as possible. They are cognizant enough of the war.... But if they are to take their place in the post-war world, they must have had all the best that the pre-war world could have given them." She ended with a note almost of contempt for those who would ignore such books because of the war: "And whatever else we relinquish, it must not be the realm of the imagination. Children will enter it in spite of us, though why anyone should wish to stay their feet is difficult to understand." Margaret C. Scoggin, writing in *Horn Book* in late 1943, agreed. It might be good for children to read of the war, she wrote, but they also need to understand, through books, that the struggle in which America was engaged echoes the struggles of all humanity. Thus, children should be encouraged to read, "along with the practical books of the times—the great books and the good books of humor, beauty, imagination, and courage. So shall we help them recognize enduring values which transcend momentary crises; so shall we give them stability."

This mindset was reflected in the year-end review of children's books in the *New Yorker* of December 12, 1942—almost exactly a year after America's entry into World War II. Though entitled "Children's Books in Wartime," the listing had few texts that dealt with the war even obliquely, suggesting that while it is right that books reflect the experience of the war, they may become too obviously "inspirational or opportunist." Instead, Katherine S. White argued, "the best wartime reading for young people does not necessarily deal with war themes and is, as it always has been, books so well written that they re-create real life or set free the juices of the imagination or increase the flow of blood to the heart." Though she creates categories that mirror those of Leo Lerman, the chosen books are quite different. Thus she includes "Stories from the American Past" and cites Lois Maloy's *Swift Thunder of the Prairie* (1942), a story of a conflict between Native Americans and the railroad; Arna Bontemps and Jack Conroy's *The Fast Sooner Hound* (1942), about a dog that could outrun the railroads in the West; and Howard Fast's *The Tall Hunter* (1942), set in early pioneering days. "Foreign Children, Foreign Lands" includes Pearl Buck's *The Chinese Children Next Door* (1942); Eleanor Frances Lattimore's *The Questions of Lifu* (1942); and Sigrid Undset's *Happy Times in Norway* (1942), describing the country before the German invasion. "Stories of America Today" include Marguerite de Angeli's *Up the Hill* (1942), a story of Polish American children in a Pennsylvania mining town; Eleanor Estes's *The Middle Moffat* (1942); Elizabeth Enright's *The Four-Story Mistake* (1942); and John R. Tunis's *All-American* (1942). These categories are filled with novels—and though some do reflect America's wartime condition, White's final category is quite distinct from Lerman's world: "Fanciful Tales, Stories of Adventure," which includes works such as C. S. Forester's *Poo-Poo and the Dragons* (1942) and Walter de la Mare's *Mr. Bumps and His Monkey* (1942). White does conclude with books that focus on the war experience, citing, for example, Ingri and Edgar Parin D'Aulaire's *The Star-Spangled Banner* (1942) and Munro Leaf's *A War-Time Handbook for Young Americans* (1942), as well as several reference books about the war's planes and geography. But the force of her listing is all on fiction as depicting the world around us—and as being utterly appropriate for wartime reading.

In November 1942—almost a year before Sarah Allen Beard's list of wartime reading—May Hill Arbuthnot published one of the most thoughtful responses to the question of what children should be reading during the war, trying to balance the roles of fiction and nonfiction. She affirmed the notion that childhood reading should, on one level, be about the real world during wartime. Children, she argued, need to know the truth about the world insofar as they can understand such truth; protection, especially during wartime, is maintaining a false innocence: "Now in England and China they are saying that our children must be toughened if they are to survive. This does not mean that they are to be made ruthless but that they must be trained to face reality no matter how grim, to have the strength to stand up to tragedy and to survive." These tragedies, Arbuthnot claims, are not represented in "the pretty, modern picture books for young children. Should not literature help to bridge this gap? It should and it can." The question that she poses is, How?

She does not agree that the answer to this question is a diet of books about the war. Instead, Arbuthnot suggests that books during wartime should deal with the war by not focusing on the actual war itself. Instead, books should focus on what she calls "the universal truths of human relationships." She cited, for example, books by Elizabeth Enright, Wanda Gág, and Marjorie Flack as books and authors that dealt with "real life" and books by Laura Richards, A. A. Milne, Mother Goose, Marie Hall Ets, and Dr. Seuss's *The 500 Hats of Bartholomew Cubbins* (1938) as books and authors that worked as comedies. "Undoubtedly we must indoctrinate our children, not with hysterical hate, but with a passionate belief in and love for democratic principles," she writes, and she cites books about foreign countries in which American children "can learn to understand and love . . . the book-children of many countries." Here she cited Eleanor Frances Lattimore's *Little Pear, the Story of a Little Chinese Boy* (1931) as a Chinese tale, Margery Clark's *The Poppy Seed Cakes* (1924) as a Russian story, Kate Seredy's *The Good Master* (1935) as a Hungarian story, and Johanna Spyri's *Heidi* as a Swiss adventure. She also cited some works that spoke directly to the American cause, such as Robert Trumbull's *The Raft* (1942), in which the three shipwrecked protagonists "were so proud of being Americans that when they finally landed on an unknown island they summoned their last remaining ounce of strength to stand upright lest a possible enemy see an American soldier crawling! Such biographical episodes can fire even our young children with pride in this American heritage of ours."[6]

But Arbuthnot's point is that the focus is on patriotic pride, not on war. (It was not an uncommon argument; *Life* magazine would not publish a photograph of a dead American soldier for two more years.) It is the larger, universal truth and quality that helps the child to grow stronger as he or she encounters the particulars of this war, Arbuthnot insisted: "So, then, during war times we might well drop from our book lists for children those books that are so trivial that they have little or no significance. In their places let us provide stories and poetry that give children some insight into life as it really is. Through their literature even little children should be able to discern life's perils and penalties as well as its affections, loyalties, fun and triumphs." And this task carries with it a spiritual dimension, Arbuthnot points out. During wartime "children should find in their reading certain moral and spiritual reinforcement that they do not find in their activities or in human relationships in understandable form. . . . The passionate belief that right will ultimately triumph over wrong is not learned accidentally but is the result of encountering examples of it and in having those examples clearly labeled. Literature can help in this process of labeling and interpreting life's experiences for the child."

Helen L. Butler struck a very similar balance between fiction and nonfiction in "Children's Reading in Wartime," published in *Childhood Education* in February 1944. While there was a need for books that spoke directly to the war—here she also cited Munro Leaf's *A War-Time Handbook for Young Americans* and Robert Trumbull's *The Raft*—children needed books that focused on everyday situations: "Overweighing the balance of war books is a host of other books depicting the normalcies of life which teachers and librarians agree are just as important now in war as they were in peace." Like Arbuthnot, she chose books that depicted values that she felt children could discern and that would equip them for understanding the war: Armstrong Sperry's *Call It Courage* (1940), the story of young Mafatu's growth into self-confidence; Josephine Blackstock's *Wings for Nikias, a Story of the Greece of Today* (1942), in which Nikias overcomes fear to warn Greek soldiers of an invasion; and Frederic Arnold Kummer's *The Torch of Liberty* (1941), in which the torch takes on allegorical import, becoming the spirit of Democracy as it was manifested in ancient Greece and Rome, in Venice and Florence, in Holland, at Valley Forge and in the American colonies, in Argentina and South America, and finally in the European struggle: "Guard well my temple, O free men of today, lest, like the Parthenon of old, it too may lie in ruins beneath a Conqueror's cruel flag" (301).

There was an optimism in these suggestions for wartime reading, a belief that such reading was capable of equipping a child for understanding the war, for participating on the home front, for developing the larger values and beliefs that would fortify against the horrors of the war; and there was a belief, too, that such reading would also contribute to the period after the war, when America would take its place as a democratic nation, espousing its values to war-torn nations. There was particularly a sense that books about other nations could well contribute to the international community that must eventually coalesce as global understanding and empathy formed. Paul R. Hanna, writing less than a year into the war, argued for education that contributed to the conditions out of which such an international community could grow: "After our generation has won on the battlefield the right once again to determine democratically how we shall live, then those children who are to pass through our schools during the next two decades will have to take the leadership at the peace conferences throughout the century in establishing a world community organization. These future citizens of the world community are under our guidance in the schools today and what we do to and with them now will ultimately have its effect on the quality of the society they will build tomorrow." Lillian Smith affirmed Hanna's position in "Today's Children and Tomorrow's World," published, as Hanna's piece was, in *Childhood Education*: "What are we doing, what can we do, to break down the barriers of ignorance and prejudice that now separate West from East, white from yellow from black? What can be done about the color-phobia that afflicts so vast a portion of the white race? Surely the great need today is not to give our children commando drills stretching their muscles, hardening their hearts, but to give them ideas on which to stretch their imaginations, exercises in strengthening their identifications with other peoples."

❊ ❊ ❊

Such identification was the ideal, and it was not always carried out, given wartime tensions. One of the books that Marie Nelson Taylor had affirmed as an important contribution toward helping American children understand their own potential roles in the war effort was Elizabeth Foreman Lewis's *When the Typhoon Blows* (1942), which focused on the Japanese invasion of China before the American entrance into the war. Ten years earlier Lewis had won the Newbery Award for *Young Fu of the Upper Yangtze* (1932); *When the Typhoon Blows* was her sixth book chronicling the history of China's last twelve years, leading up to the Japanese invasion. Though the novel is ostensibly about young Li and his failed attempt to keep his grandfather safe during the invasion, the book is more about the hardship caused by the Japanese invaders—and Lewis's anger is palpable. Early on, Japanese warplanes drop bombs on harmless fishing vessels, a pattern that Lewis uses again and again as the Japanese drop bombs on fishing villages, on Red Cross vehicles, on hospitals. During the invasion, the pattern is repeated by the land troops, so that for Li, "all that had lent boyhood meaning was now ruthlessly destroyed" (22). The Japanese are stereotypically described throughout, and though the stereotypes emerge from the characters' points of view and not from the narrator, the repetition of them penetrates the narrative. The Japanese are described as short-legged and stocky (38), brutal and enslaving (41, 57), an "evil thing" (40), "barbarians" (53), soldiers whose "mouths do queer things when they speak" (54) (a trait that later enables Li to identify a Japanese spy), "dwarfs" (57), thieves who loot the villages they have burned (93), "marauders" (93), and "the Devil King's own sons" (57). When one villager dares to question the Japanese soldiers who enslave him, he is bayoneted mercilessly; when he does not die quickly enough, "they set him against a wall and each of the five others did what the first had done" (57). None of these descriptors is ever questioned or mitigated. His horror, instead, leads Li to resolve to become a part of the new movement toward national unity, seen repeatedly in the novel as China's sole hope, a brotherhood that warms Li's heart (180) and that is meant by Lewis to speak to the people of America, urging unity in their own war effort and identification with those suffering at the hands of America's enemies.

This same stance toward the enemy was true of much of the pulp fiction for children written during the war, which extolled American values and spirit while vilifying the enemy through exaggerated stereotypes and a highlighted malice of the Axis armies and cultures. Of these series, the most popular were R. Sidney Bowen's eight-volume Air Combat series, starring Red Randall, and the sixteen-volume War Adventure series, written at a pace of ten thousand words a day with,

Bowen claimed, no revision. The Air Combat series sold two hundred thousand books in its first year (1944); by the end of the war, the War Adventure series had sold over two million copies. The War Adventure series novels featured the American pilot Dave Dawson and his British pal Freddy Farmer carrying out missions against the enemy with skill, daring, and American know-how, rushing to the very places in current headlines. In *Dave Dawson with the R.A.F.* (1941), the two—because they look so young—are recruited to pose as Belgian youths in order to meet an Allied spy who has the secrets of Hitler's planned invasion of Britain, which they discover and bring successfully back across the Channel, leading to the destruction of the invasion bases. In *Dave Dawson with the Pacific Fleet* (1942), Dave and Freddy ferret out a spy who has hidden aboard a carrier and hopes to give away American attack plans to the Japanese navy. And in *Dave Dawson on Guadalcanal* (1943), Dave and Freddy, having located the Japanese fleet, must escape their vile Japanese captors to bring back the critical information to the American intelligence officers before the invasion of the Solomon Islands. The adventures are quickly paced, improbable, death-defying, and utterly dependent on the cliff-hanger ending that made and still makes much of pulp fiction so successful.[7]

Beneath the spine-tingling adventures lies a strong foundation of how Bowen wanted young Americans to perceive the war effort. In *Dave Dawson with the R.A.F.*—written before America's entry into the war—Dave Dawson affirms that though he is an American, he feels a part of England now (11–14). Soon afterward, the narrator suggests what this means:

> Death had come to strike at London, and was now gone. Behind, it had left more wrecked buildings, more smouldering ruins, and more dead and dying. But it had also left behind something that Adolf Hitler and all of his followers would never be able to understand, and never be able to defeat. That was British courage, the superb fighting courage of the high and the low who were now fighting on a common ground shoulder to shoulder. London had once again been hurt, and she was bleeding. But London would never die, just as England would never die. (65)

The Churchill echoes are intentional, and this novel in particular is filled with Bowen's narrator's affirmation of what the war meant: "If the world and civilization went down under Hitler's heel, then life would not be worth the living," Dave Dawson muses (93). Later, when Dave Dawson is briefly imprisoned before he makes contact with the Allied spy, he looks around at the dispirited prisoners, "the silent mass of broken men," and resolves "to give his very all, if necessary, to rid the world once and forever of such a system of living as Adolf Hitler and his crackbrained cohorts were striving to force upon all mankind. . . . [H]e would fight on to undo all the evil wrought and make the world a better place for the millions yet unborn" (159–60). To do so, he escapes from the prison by battering through a door "like an All-American halfback" (163). The sentiments are high-minded and noble, and they do carry the day in these novels. The bad guys are outsmarted and out-flown and outmaneuvered by those determined to bring hope to the millions. And the bad guys do seem easy prey. According to M. Paul Holsinger, by one count, 2,500 enemy deaths can be attributed to Dave Dawson and Freddy Farmer; the pulp heroes Red Randall and Jimmy Joyce are less prolific, yet they average an astounding 150 enemy deaths per volume.

Bowen's narrator and characters refer to the enemy in the angry diction of the time. In *Dave Dawson on Guadalcanal* alone, the Japanese are referred to as "a mess of slant-eyed devils" (14), "slant-eyed killer" (84), "the Japs" (18), "ten cent Jap" (144), "rats" (110), "Jap rats" (46), "dirty, low-down rat" (109), "rotten Jap rats" (162), "slant-eyed rats" (201), "little brown rat" (127), "this slant-eyed, pint-sized rat" (136), "killers" (112), "dirty killers" (111), "dirty blighters" (111), "Tojo" used as a synecdoche for the Japanese (21), "slobs" (84), "baby killers" (84), a "rotten race . . . [that] struck their blow under false colors" (109), "double-crossing Jap" (136), "little brown pals" (121), "the so-called Son of Heaven's follower" (136), "Son of Nippon" (142), "the Nippon killer" (179), "sons of heathens" who enjoy tying "up two white men" and so "went about their tasks with savage glee" (152–53), "short, overfed, ban-dy-legged and squint-eyed, the whole lot of them" (171), "the flat-faced Jap" who does not laugh because "the Japanese people do not possess . . . a sense of humor" (176), and "the devils from the Land of the Rising Sun" (230). The Japanese soldiers leer, hiss, and swarm like ants; they are consistently associated with demonic and animalistic imagery. When Dave Dawson sees them "swarming all over the place," his "ha-tred for them mounted to white fury" (120). And his hatred extends as well to the German officer, who, when he emerges from the submarine out of which the Japanese are swarming, "eyed them as though he'd never seen a couple of white men in his life before. Which, of course, was quite possible, in view of the fact he was of German birth" (122)—a startling act of ethnocentrism.

✳ ✳ ✳

Still, during the war—and in its wartime garb—American children's literature generally remained progressive not only in its call to identify with other nations but also in its evaluations of America's racial stances. Thus, for example, Gregor Felsen's *Navy Diver* (1942) and *Submarine Sailor* (1943) were both written with sympathetic Japanese American characters, both published with the sanction of the United States Navy, and both clear that the Japanese American community was American first and hated the militaristic government of Japan. In *Navy Diver*, the midwestern boy Jeff Drake is befriended by Taro, the American-born son of Japanese migrant workers. When asked by Jeff what might happen if war broke out, Taro responds immediately, "I'd fight for this country, of course" (25), though he acknowledges that it would be hard to fight other Japanese, comparing it to a civil war. Later, after Jeff has entered the navy, he rescues men from a sinking civilian tanker and finds that Taro is among them. This seems to be evidence of Taro's commitment to the war effort: he does what he can, shipping out on a civilian tanker rather than a navy ship because of his ethnicity. But when Jeff still wonders about his loyalty because of the internments, Taro assures him that he is a loyal American: "Whatever the authorities think best. I just want them to know that America is my country too, even if I cannot fight for her" (123). This is later put to the test when a Japanese officer is caught and Taro is the only one able to translate the papers he carries. Though suspicious, Jeff's captain abides by Taro's translation and in doing so averts an attack on the American coast. Then, when Jeff's ship is attacked during this episode, it is Taro who takes over a gun after Jeff is wounded, shooting down a Japanese zero and thus saving the day. The response is a new understanding on the part of the ship's officers: "Won't hurt any of us to find out you can't tell a good American by the color of his skin," one acknowledges (194).[8]

If Felsen celebrated democratic inclusiveness through his plotlines, Jack Bechdolt suggested the potential for disaster on the home front by showing the crumbling of such unity. At the beginning of his *Junior Air Raid Wardens* (1942)—the book that Marie Nelson Taylor had described as "devoured by young patriots"—the principal plot complication comes from a spy who sends signals at night to an off-shore Nazi submarine. But that complication is lost in the narrative when the problem is switched to the "Fifth Column" presence that is stirring up ethnic hatred in the community. In a town meeting, Cyrus Benjamin—who will eventually be revealed as the Nazi instigator—harangues the citizens of Harmony about its wartime situation: "The danger is among you. Watch your neighbors, the hyphenated Americans—German, Italian, Japanese. I say to you mistrust every man and woman whose name and antecedents bear the stamp of foreign birth. Drive out your foreign born!" (38). This is vigorously disputed by Tony Parocchi, whose parents are Italian and who claims that such charges are not only lies but problematic for the war effort: "It makes good people sore at their neighbors. It divides Americans when Americans must stick together and show the whole world, that we will fight for our country!" (40). The protagonists, Ben and Greg, wonder if this is "Fifth Column talk" (42); it is, and the junior wardens face the situation of a secret force undermining American unity by encouraging racial and religious division. Eventually, Tony, who tries to enlist in the American army but cannot due to a hip problem, is suspected of blowing up a tool plant, and Cyrus Benjamin, still unknown as the Nazi instigator, stirs up a group of citizens: "Decent people in this town ought to clear out the whole mess of 'em and the F.B.I. ought to put them in an internment camp" (102)—a slanted criticism of the American policy of internment, since this suggestion comes at the encouragement of a Nazi spy. Tony disappears, seeming to confirm his guilt, but in fact he has enlisted on a Norwegian ship carrying war supplies for the Allies—a fact revealed melodramatically on the night when a crowd comes to force Mrs. Parocchi's family out of their house. When Tony's patriotism is revealed, when Mrs. Parocchi's courage plays out as she faces the mob, and when Cyrus Benjamin's connections to Berlin are demonstrated, the hatred that once engulfed the town dissipates, and as Tony heads off to a new ship, Ben and Greg are grateful that they, too, can contribute to the war effort; otherwise they would feel themselves to be "a fine pair of slackers" (175), an overt message to readers.

American children's books would be critical of the hypocrisy of conducting a war for democracy while interning thousands of Japanese citizens—children among them. Here, *Horn Book* would lead the way. In 1943 Bertha Mahony lashed out at this hypocrisy in her editorial, "The World Republic of Childhood": "America is now fighting a terrible war against injustice and at the same time within our own boundaries American citizens are persecuting helpless minorities in the evil fashion of our enemies. Our treatment of our citizens—and the greater number of these minorities are citizens—of whatever race or color is a matter of the greatest importance to the future of the United States." That same issue included an article by Clara E. Breed, pleading for recognition of the necessity of libraries within the internment camps. A year and a half later—a month after the order was issued to allow Japanese Americans to return to their homes—*Horn Book* would privilege a review of Florence Crannell Means's *The Moved-Outers* (1945) by placing the editorial review as the opening article for its 1945 volume. The author of the review, Howard Pease—himself a writer of adventure books for young adults—argued for the significance of Means's work in its lessons of racial acceptance and as a test for how the culture would value the role of its books for children: "It explains and interprets, it enlarges our sympathy and understanding, and it makes plain that the story of Sue and Jiro has implications far more important than what happens to one family or to one minority group. Possibly it is already late for us to decide that from now on we must be more forthright in our treatment of controversial subjects in our books for young people. Let us hope it is not too late." Clara Breed, writing in that same January–February 1945 issue, agreed: "That this book can be published while the war in the Pacific is still going on shows a certain amount of courage on the part of the publishers, but their faith will surely be justified. The book is a human document, one that belongs to our picture of democracy in the United States, the democracy which is not finished but still in the making." A year later, *Horn Book* published an assessment of Means by Siri Andrews, calling her "the leader in a new kind of writing for young people which will become increasingly important in a more mature post-war world."

Florence Crannell Means had established her position a decade earlier with her novel *Rainbow Bridge* (1934), which chronicles the first months of a Japanese family's new life in America. Six years later, her *Horn Book* article "Mosaic" established her principal purpose, and she sounded much like Lois Lenski, though with a different focus: "Quite as vivid as the past . . . is the present with its varicolored racial groups, aboriginal and imported; and, shifting kaleidoscopically across the pattern of brights and darks, the continual trek of our migrant workers. It's since I've grown acquainted with the children of one after another of these groups that I've begun to harbor a deep desire: to fix this mosaic of American youth between booklids, one motif at a time." Suzanne Rahn chronicles Means's cultural experiences in Denver, in the American Southwest, and in South Carolina, noting that they contributed to the "painstaking authenticity" they created—again, sounding like Lois Lenski—and concludes that Means meant to be "the interpreter of one group to another, not of the group to itself"—yet again, like Lois Lenski. This is the role she would play in *The Moved-Outers*.

The disparity between the ideal and the practical is at the center of Means's *The Moved-Outers* (1945), the story of the internment of the Ohara family. The novel's central question is the gap between America's professed democratic principles and its treatment of Japanese American families. Means makes much of the American Japanese families' belief that the government of Japan has become warmongering: "You're an American citizen," the protagonist, Sue Ohara, tells her friend Tomi. "You can't help what those horrid Japanese war lords do" (14). And Means insists on the American heritage of these families, many of whom have lived in California for several generations. But when the FBI men come, Sue finds her situation in America ambiguous: "Here were she and Kim, American-born; as American as baseball—ice-cream cones—swing music. No, as American as the Stars and Stripes. Here they were, American from their hearts out to their skins. But their skins were not American. Their skins were opaque, their hair densely black, their eyes were ever so little slanted" (14).[9]

Sue Ohara remains the focus, and her response to the internment is muted. She even shows some sympathy for the displacement: it is wartime. Still, she needs to find a way to grapple with this breach of democratic principles, and so she mythologizes the experience to link it to the sufferings of soldiers during the American Revolution: "All this would be dignified, made bearable, if we could remember to think of it . . . as suffering for our country. For America" (58). Later she tries to connect the experience to the sufferings of the Pilgrims and then the pioneers: "This is helping to make America" (93). The anger and bitterness at the experience are displaced to her brother Kim, who, when asked to recite the Pledge of Allegiance at the camp, finishes the line "with liberty and justice for all" with "all but us"; the narrator describes the spoken tone as "with a corroding bitterness" (61).

But Means will not allow even Kim to attack explicitly the nation itself: "A democracy can't function so democratically when it's got a war on its hands" (87), Kim uncharacteristically admits, and he points out that if they had been in the hands of the Japanese rather than in the hands of American soldiers during their internment, things would have been much worse (97). His father will even admit that during a war, it is "necessary to make thorough investigation of those who had continued to show interest in Japan" (130). Means displaces the harshest criticisms to a friend, Ike: "It shows how much democracy's worth, when it can haul off and paste its citizens like this" (87). Means will not allow such direct criticism to come from her protagonists, who will in fact reject Ike's position.

In the end, Sue understands that there is injustice even in free lands: "Thinking of the dark millions who had so often, throughout the years, been subject to such dangers in this land of the free. Thinking of the

Jews, and of the pogroms that had killed so many of them in other countries" (115). Her understanding leads not to a bitter rejection of America but to an embrace of the nation with its faults. When Sue and her brothers volunteer—the boys to head to war—thus serving the country that has imprisoned them, Sue defines Japanese Americans as "new pioneers": "We, the evacuees, the moved-outers. We're American patriots, loving our country with our hearts broken" (145–46). The book ends with an affirmation: *"Let us prove that we are Americans"* (154), spoken, it seems, by Sue but italicized so as to make the words seem to be spoken by the entire Japanese American community. In the end, democracy is affirmed, though the book makes a powerful plea for understanding and tolerance even given wartime exigencies.

Several anthologies of children's stories published during the war stressed the same unity in diversity of the American democratic experience by collecting stories that consciously focused on diverse cultural groups within the American experience. Wilhelmina Harper's *Uncle Sam's Story Book* (1944) did this tamely and not expertly, given the easy stereotypes into which the stories often fall. Nonetheless, *Uncle Sam's Story Book* does bring together two stories of (quite stereotyped) African American characters, one of Native Americans, several of young girls of European origin (German, Swedish, English), stories set in New England and Appalachia and Texas and the West and Oregon and California, and one obliquely about a Chinese American woman. Implicitly, the collection extolled the wide cultural quality of the American experience. A year later, Macmillan published the much more explicit *Told under the Stars and Stripes*, twenty-seven stories about "All of America's Children"—a book developed by the Literature Committee of the Association for Childhood Education, which had already published a series of "Umbrella" anthologies for children. The purpose was clear and direct: to develop "a collection of stories concerning American boys and girls with varying national, racial, and religious backgrounds" in hopes of generating a large understanding of America's diversities.

> *Told Under the Stars and Stripes* is a collection of stories brought together in the hope of helping interpret our America more understandingly to her own boys and girls through stories of each other. It is of the boy next door, the boy or girl in school, perhaps new there, with different clothes or habits and customs, that a story concerns itself. It may deal with the customs and cultures ingrained in one's own family unlike those of other boys and girls. The rich, sturdy life of our America is what it is because of what has been brought to her from all over the world. To understand such is to understand her. (339)

Thus there are stories by Elizabeth Orton Jones of a young Bohemian girl's Nativity dream, a poetic narrative by Ann Nolan Clark of a young Native American boy whose driving desire is to know things, Doris Gates's tale of cotton pickers, and Marguerite de Angeli's story of a young Polish girl bringing her traditions to school. And there is also Florence Crannell Means's story of clashing traditions in a Japanese American family and Nan Gilbert's story of German immigrants to Iowa, which concludes with Johann's teacher's affirmation that most Americans come from across the sea: "Isn't that what America is, a gathering place for everybody with the courage to cross the sea and find it? Why, that's why our country is big and strong, Joe, because it takes big, strong people to leave all that's dear and familiar behind them, and to strike out to find a new world" (170). These stories by Means and Gilbert were included quite purposefully, for, the editors suggested, "the second World War has evoked intense antagonisms even in connection with loyal German and Japanese Americans. Yet each has made a contribution to our America" (340–41). The sense was that even in the highly emotional context of the war, children's books could contribute to and foster understanding and acceptance, overcome even easy prejudices that might be encouraged in other sectors of society given the social crisis, and point toward a more tolerant society and world.

In the winter of 1942, nine years after Rosemary and Stephen Vincent Benét had published *A Book of Americans*, the Office of War Information asked Stephen Vincent Benét to craft "a short, interpretive history of the United States for translation into many languages." It was published in 1944—the last book that he would write, drafted not in the poetry of *A Book of Americans* but in spare prose. He called it, simply, *America*, and in it he argued passionately for the notion of inclusive democracy that so ordered American children's literature during the war. "There is a country of hope, there is a country of freedom," he began. "There is a country where all sorts of different people, drawn from every nation in the world, get along together under the same big sky." He is careful to qualify this opening: "[This country] has not solved every problem of how men and women should live. It has made mistakes in its own affairs, mistakes in the affairs of the world. But it looks to the future always." Its ability to look to the future emerges from its dependence upon its people. "And 'the people,' in America, does not mean a class, a caste, or a specially appointed set of men. It means you and me and the man next door—the butcher, the baker, the farmer, the workman, the lawyer, the doctor, the woman who keeps her house. It means everybody." This meaning, he argues, is at the heart of "the American spirit, the American idea" and is behind every soldier—"tall and short, dark and fair, talkative and silent"—now fighting for freedom in Europe (4–5). Benét's book, which was advertised in *Publishers Weekly* on May 6, 1944, as being "for all Americans, young or old, natives or newcomers," could hardly have given a more succinct evocation of the meanings to which children's literature had turned in adapting to the exigencies of World War II.

Ingri and Edgar Parin D'Aulaire

In the middle of World War II, Ingri and Edgar Parin D'Aulaire crafted *Wings for Per* (1944), based on the experiences of Ingri's oldest nephew. In this picture book, Per is a Norwegian boy who lives on a farm set high in steep mountains. The farm had been built there to avoid plundering enemies and to keep the inhabitants of the country as safe as eagles in their mountain nests. But ironically, it is from the air that the German invasion comes, and Per finds that his freedom—and the opportunity to use everything in him to its fullest extent—is gone. So Per becomes part of the resistance, eventually escaping from Norway with the resolve to return like an eagle. But the D'Aulaires do not have him head to England, historically the likely country for Per's growth. Instead, the woman harboring the three refugees suggests another place for him to prepare himself for a return: "But yonder, on the other side of the ocean . . . there is another country which the enemy hasn't reached yet. It is a still bigger country, and there they have plenty of everything. There you can learn to fly." So Per heads to "the land of the free," and the full-page illustration depicts him coming into New York harbor, the Statue of Liberty centered and standing at a distance, the skyline of the city aglow.

The description the D'Aulaires give of this land is meant to contrast sharply with Per's experience in Europe.

> The country was so big that the sun shone in the east while the moon still shone in the west, and roses bloomed in the south while the snow lay deep in the north. Lush fields rolled on to the edge of the sky, and there was plenty of everything. . . . Per looked at the well-fed and well-dressed children playing in the sun. He could see in their smiling eyes that they had never known hunger or fear.
>
> "And these children will never have to know it either," thought Per. "Their freedom will be defended."
>
> But behind these happy boys and girls Per seemed to see a long row of

hungry and ragged children. They all held their heads high, but it was as though they said: "Hurry, Per, we also should have been like these."

So Per learns to fly, and as he travels back to fight in Norway, he imagines the meaning of his mission, which the D'Aulaires paint in a series of final full-page illustrations: he will shoot at the enemy, he will break the enemy's strength, he will free his country, out of his bomber will come food for children, he will see "how a new spring erases hunger and mistrust from their thin faces," and he will fly over his eagle farm and his mother will look up and say, "Look, Per has wings."

In 1944, the same year that *Wings for Per* was published, Lynd Ward called in *Horn Book* for a "vigilant awareness" to protect "the economic and spiritual conditions for cultural growth." To "cultural growth" the D'Aulaires would have added the growth of the individual—the very center of their image of America. For those coming from countries where individual growth was not protected, they argued, there was nothing more powerful about the American dream. This vision of America—that every individual can grow wings—dominates the work of the D'Aulaires. And Per works as a paradigm when he recognizes that peace, plenty, and freedom are the qualities in America that allow the individual to become most fully himself or herself. It is what brings Per—and any immigrant—to this land.

This specific understanding of America was shaped strongly by the D'Aulaires' own immigrant experience. Their books reflect their enthusiastic embrace of their adopted country, as well as their vision of what America is about, even during wartime.

Theirs was a most cosmopolitan background. Ingri Mortenson was born in Norway in 1904, into an artistic family. (Her uncle, a clergyman and poet, had translated the Icelandic *Eddas* into Norwegian, and his poetry had been set to music by Grieg.) From early on Ingri was determined to be an artist, and at age fifteen she received the support of Harriet Backer, a prominent Norwegian painter, who urged her to study—but not to marry. Ingri went to Christiania (later renamed Oslo) for a year to do this study and then on to the Hoffman School in Munich, where she met Edgar.

Edgar Parin (D'Aulaire was his mother's name) was born in 1898 in Switzerland to an American mother and an Italian father. They separated when he was six years old, and afterward Edgar spent time with each, traveling around Europe with his father, who was a prominent portrait painter. His father urged Edgar to study architecture, which he did for a time. But he then pursued art studies in Paris, Florence, and

Munich, where he, too, studied in the Hoffman School under Henri Matisse. Using these skills, he began to illustrate books that were published between 1922 and 1926 in Germany and Paris.

Edgar's first visit to Ingri's Norwegian home suggested to him the pleasures of a rooted family—something he had never had—and in 1925 they married. They made Paris their home but traveled extensively, painting in France, Italy, Germany, Scandinavia, the Netherlands, Dalmatia, Greece, and the coast of North Africa and Tunis. However, eventually the D'Aulaires decided to immigrate to America; they sensed that the energy and size of the country was itself something that held potential for their art—an impulse with which James Daugherty chimed. "We didn't seek shelter here because we had to flee from what till then had been ours," Edgar later wrote, "but because this enormous continent with all its possibilities and grandeur appealed to us and caught our imagination . . . ; this is the country where everything we had in us could be used to its full extent"—a line used in *Wings for Per*, and a line that represented the central vision of their children's books published in America.[1]

They immigrated in 1929 and came to New York City for their art. They resolved to maintain separate careers, and Edgar continued to illustrate a number of books for both children and adults. When Anne Carroll Moore suggested that they might try to work collaboratively on picture books for children, they agreed, and, taken up by May Massee at Doubleday, they published *The Magic Rug* in the fall of 1931 (coming out of their visits to North Africa) and *Ola* the next year, the story of a boy during a Norwegian winter. In the late 1930s Per Ola was born; Edgar was naturalized; they moved to a farm in Wilton, Connecticut, to raise a family; and they began work on *Abraham Lincoln* (1939), the first in their line of American biographies, which dominated the rest of their long careers. In their studio they built a Norwegian farm fireplace, and they decorated the walls with paintings of the Norwegian landscape. Later, they purchased a second home—a small Vermont farmhouse—which became a retreat. With each move—moves made possible because they had used their artistic skills to the fullest extent—they moved farther and farther into the archetypal American rural scene: "Together with our son, Per Ola, we live on Lia Farm. . . . When we first met we used to roam the world, but now we have become domesticated. When we don't paint and draw and write, we till the soil and train animals and children, and our only complaint is that the days are too short."[2] The vision of America painted in the pages of their books became their reality.

Their acceptance speeches for the Caldecott Award they received for *Abraham Lincoln* speak to their purposes and vision. Ingri D'Aulaire wrote that they were receiving the award with "half the world in flames and everything that we have been taught to stand up for as right and just in danger of extermination." In this context, the historical figure of Abraham Lincoln became for both artists "the shining symbol of democracy, fairness and tolerance," a man "necessary for our present life." In his quality of inclusiveness, Lincoln became mythic, a symbol of America itself—which is again something that James Daugherty would have affirmed. In his speech Edgar D'Aulaire spoke of the entire American experience in mythic terms. They came to America, he wrote, to enact for themselves what Abraham Lincoln had done: "This is the country where . . . we could fulfill our full measures as human beings and help in building up the world." That is the line that describes all of the figures that the D'Aulaires would write of in the ensuing years: figures for whom the context of the American experience provided the means by which they might become their fullest selves and so influence and change the world around them.

Edgar D'Aulaire's vision is that of the visual artist, filled with the images that he had imagined and seen. His early imaginings of America came from the stories of his grandfather, whom he never met, and reflect a merger of cultures.

> I imagined the vast American prairies where brilliant flowers stood as tall as the head of a man on horseback, where the hooves of horses were tinted red from strawberries, where sudden fires swept across as far as the eye could reach, with burning grass tufts shooting like rockets into the sky, where lonely farms with their small fields stood as tiny specks in the immense expanse of a yellow ocean, where the first crop of corn stood fifteen feet high. Gigantic electric storms would sweep over the country, the huge yellow rivers that cut across the prairie would swell up and carry with them everything that came in their way. It was the most perfect dreamland for a boy, living in a European metropolis.

Later, when the D'Aulaires came to America, the mythic vision seemed to come literally true for them: "But as I stood on the Brooklyn Bridge and watched the sunset behind the Statue of Liberty where the flaming red sky melted into the flat horizon of New Jersey, my childhood's stories woke up again in me." And when the D'Aulaires left New York to research Lincoln's prairie world, traveling with a large tent, the myth seemed to come literally true again: "I felt America . . . as the pioneer country."

Every night our tent was pitched in a different place, sometimes under a clump of trees, sometimes at the brink of a fast-flowing river, sometimes right in the open prairie. Every morning we were awakened by the overwhelming chorus of singing birds, as the first slanting rays of the sun struck the roof of our tent, just as you read it in the early descriptions of the prairie. . . . A thunderstorm at night in a tent on the flat prairie is something one doesn't forget.

This is the world of America that the D'Aulaires imagined. Its context is mythic, larger than life—certainly larger than a European metropolis—a context that could be the crucible for the growth of the soul to its fullest extent. It is little wonder, then, that the D'Aulaires couched all of their biographies solidly in the physical setting of America, and that the stories of these figures are stories made possible only by that large, mythic America.[3]

It is this large, mythic America that World War II was being fought to preserve, the D'Aulaires believed, and the child reader of the 1940s needed to understand what the war meant. They argued this explicitly in their celebratory *The Star Spangled Banner* (1942). Crafted at the beginning of the war, many of the spreads contain military images. There is the bombardment of Fort Henry, which was the occasion of the song. There is an image of a sinking ship, followed by another spread of a raft on which the survivors cling. Later, an enormous tank fires across a spread. Over that tank hovers an image of George Washington leading a cavalry charge: even as Washington fought to gain freedom, so, too, do the tanks of World War II fight to preserve freedom.

But to evoke the American scene during the war, the D'Aulaires frame the military images with images of domestic harmony. Often the viewpoint is that of two children; the bombardment of Fort Henry seems to emerge, for example, right out of their imaginations. Similarly, the two children later see a vast army on the march—in the shape of an eagle. On the next page, they sit beneath the Statue of Liberty, reading, as the dictators of the war fade into obscurity behind them. In another image, the children peer out from behind a soldier and sailor, covered by the flowing American flag. All of this comes to a strong conclusion in the penultimate image of the book, in which the children greet their soldier father upon his return: dog and cat wait patiently, mother hands baby to father, children hold their arms up in joy, townspeople gather behind them. It is an illustration that shows clearly what the D'Aulaires believed the war was meant to do: to preserve America for the opportunity of individual growth.

The opening double-page spread of the book shows the rewards of a culture that preserves the opportunity for individual growth by setting early America beside modern America. On the left side, a young family is building a log cabin as the mother cooks over an unfinished hearth, and the young daughter proudly holds a harvested pumpkin up to the reader. On the right, in the illustration in which the reader is introduced to the two children who take up the rest of the book, we are in exactly the same place geographically, but much has changed. In the foreground, a mother points out toward the sunset. Closest to the children, an American flag flies in the very center of the illustration (matching the more abstract flag in the skies of the first illustration). Beyond the flag, gardens are growing, fields are being planted, houses that dot the distant hills are all flying flags, and a church with its steeple is standing prominently above them all. The frontier of the first illustration has clearly been subdued and domesticated, and the prosperity and security of American citizens has been ensured.

To frame the end of *The Star Spangled Banner*, the D'Aulaires set a more urbanized scene. Some years have gone by—the baby of the earlier illustrations is now a young child—and the family has come to the town commons. Flags fly and fireworks explode. On the commons, children of all races dance together in a circle. On the edges of the commons, strolling families wave to each other as they pass the bank, and post office, and town hall, and school, and church. All is peace and prosperity and security. The military images of the interior of the book have all aimed at securing this scene of joy and freedom and peace.

Soon after the war, when the freedom and peace promised in *The Star Spangled Banner* had seemingly been secured, the D'Aulaires continued to explore the meaning of the immigrant experience in America, now focusing not on a contrast to Europe—as in *Wings for Per*—but instead examining the ways in which the large American space—both literal and metaphoric—was able to welcome new experiences and to enlarge the capabilities of those who came to American soil. To do this, they turned to the experience of their son, Per Ola, the model for *Nils* (1948).

The opening image of this picture book seems to promise an archetypal, even clichéd American experience: The young boy stands against his pony, wearing cowboy boots, a neckerchief, and a cowboy hat; a toy six-shooter is in the holster by his hip. His dog and cat sit beneath the pony. He is the American boy at play—despite a name that is typically Norwegian. When the page is turned, one sees what still seems to be a very American scene. Nils's parents watch him from inside, looking through the window past a small flock of chickens. The farmhouse stands by a barn with a substantial weathervane, and beyond, past a small river, is a small town with the expected white-steepled church. The clear sense here is that the D'Aulaires are about to present a very American story indeed.

But, in fact, the D'Aulaires intend to complicate this American scene. The dreamlike motifs on the wall of the farmhouse suggest the myths of Norway, not those of America. The trunk by which Nils's parents stand is decorated with Norwegian motifs. His parents have old tales from Norway that Nils wants to learn so that he can tell them to other cowboys around a bonfire. And the huge boulder that broods outside over the farmhouse seems out of place, as though it were ever so much older than the farmhouse below it, and more substantial. In *Nils* the D'Aulaires do want to present the American scene, but not, strictly speaking, the one of farmhouse and cowboy dreams. They set out to show instead that the American experience is more archetypally the immigrant experience and that it is an experience that places those who live it within the tension of two conflicting worlds: that of the old world, with its traditions grasped by the older generation, and that of the new world, which demands accommodation on the part of the newer generation. It is in negotiating that accommodation, the D'Aulaires suggest, that the American child finds the context within which to grow and develop—that is the true identity and gift of American experience. America is the place where growth and change and development into the full person entail both negotiation with and fervent allegiance to the culture of the new world.

The child Nils is at first unaware of the tension of cultures. He wants to take the curious Norwegian tales and put them into the cowboy experience; he will tell them by the campfire. When he plays up by the gray boulder, he imagines lassoing either an Indian or a troll; he does not imagine that those two mythologies could compete when he conceives "an Indian troll." When his mother calls him Peer Gynt to chide him for his boasting, he immediately consolidates the antics of the Norwegian hero with the skills he might need on the western frontier. "For Peer Gynt had also been keen and bold and the noblest lad in the valley. When he danced he could turn cartwheels and kick his heels at the ceiling. That would be a fine stunt for a cowboy to know."

The locus of the wisdom in the story is not Nils's parents, as might be expected, but the troll-like boulder, whose observations over the years since it was carried to its spot by a glacier (it, too, is an immigrant) have taught it the lessons of accepting differences to allow for full growth. "And it would have told about the children who had been born and grown up in Nils's home through the centuries—children who had not all spoken English, for their parents had come from many parts of the world. But they all had played around the rock and loved their home on the hill-side just as Nils did now." This is the wisdom of age and experience, and it is the wisdom of the immigrant perspective that the D'Aulaires wish to show as part of the nature of the American experience: that a recognition of difference and commonality is part of American life.

When Nils receives long stockings from his grandmother in Norway —stockings decorated with elaborate Norwegian designs—he is at first overjoyed. "They are the most beautiful stockings in the world," he declares—though the D'Aulaires hint at a coming problem: the sheep reject the smell of the wool because it is so different from their own. "But they were only sheep," the narrator concludes, suggesting the contempt the narrator feels for the rejection of something only because it differs from one's own experience. When Nils wears the stockings to school, he specifically uses them to connect himself to his Norwegian heritage: "You can't wear Norwegian stockings, for you are not Norwegian," he tells a friend. But at the school, Nils experiences for the first time the conflicts of the old and new culture: his stockings are rejected because they make him look different. And though Nils fights back physically, he quickly comes to accept the new culture's definition: "Then he noticed his stockings. They were not beautiful any longer, only different. Who had ever seen a cowboy with Norwegian stockings?" The next spread—one of the few double-page spreads of the book—lays out his dream of the cowboy life: the rodeo antics, the dress, the guitar and song by the fire, the roping, breaking broncos. But he stands outside of that experience now, and even the cowboys in his dream seem confused by his odd attire. And so Nils rejects the stockings and leaves them on the boulder, rejecting the old world in favor of the new and, in fact, using part of his old tradition to make that tradition look foolish: he places the stockings on small trees atop the boulder, making them look like silly antennae. "I can make you look different, too," he declares. His father does not understand this rejection of the old: "I wore the same kind when I was a boy." Nils's response—"your friends wore the same kind"—is exactly right but draws no subsequent response from his father.

The dream that comes to Nils that night is the dream of the immigrant experience that Ingri and Edgar Parin D'Aulaire want to capture.

Nils sits up in bed and hears the voices of those that came before him, whom the boulder had evoked earlier; their images hover in the air behind him:

"An English boy helped his father build this house," the house timbers creaked.

"A Dutch boy helped his father build me," the dutch oven murmured.

The dry leaves on the grape arbor rustled as if to say: "An Italian boy planted us."

"One for all and all for one," crowed the weathercock on top of the barn roof. "Those boys were regular fellows though they wore buckskin breeches, long stockings, and wood shoes, and they helped to make this country great."

Ashamed, Nils retrieves his stockings from the boulder, seeing them now as still different but beautiful again—thus once more uniting the experience of the two cultures in which he lives. And so he frolics on top of the great stone, recalling that Peer Gynt had once ridden a reindeer, and certainly he could ride a wild horse as a cowboy. Later, when cold weather comes, he puts on his cowboy jeans and boots—but also his stockings—and goes to school warm and cozy because of this union of cultures—and no one teases him. "Who cares if I am different," he cries—a bit idealistically but in keeping with the drive of the narrative action. He had brought the two cultures together, accommodating himself to the new—and so growing as an individual.

The book works on the small scale: this is the story of the boy who wants to fit into the larger culture of his school and finds a way to accommodate that culture while remaining linked to his parents' world. But on the larger scale, it is an affirmation that this country is a union of immigrant traditions. The frontier that the D'Aulaires present is much more complex than that of James Daugherty, for while Daugherty pushes westward along one plain, the D'Aulaires suggest that life is lived along two frontiers that sometimes meet and that sometimes remain apart, and in that meeting lies the creative tension for the child and the opportunity for growth that the American context presents. If it seems like a difficult tension in which to live, the D'Aulaires assert nothing but confidence. Their archetypal America is a land in which immigrants hold onto the old and accommodate to the new, and that accommodation represents a chance for the full growth of the individual.

In short, America provides the stage upon which the individual works out his or her relationships to the larger cultural forces that govern him or her, and it is the promise of America, in the D'Aulaires' vision, that the individual will not be subsumed under those forces but be strengthened and supported as an individual in the tension: "'Who cares if I am different!' He pulled up his blue jeans so everybody could see his beautiful warm stockings with black stars and white stars and black roses and white roses." The concluding image of *Nils* is one of a boy stronger and more confident—and larger—than he had been at the opening of the narrative.

In his Caldecott acceptance speech, Edgar D'Aulaire claimed that their immigrant identity was one of their assets as they approached their American biographies. "We counted as our biggest asset just the fact that our conceptions of our American themes had never been shaped into school clichés, which later, through experience, must be overcome." Instead, he wrote, they "had to approach the subjects as children, studying from the beginning, not hampered by standard conceptions." If Edgar meant by this that they wished to create a child's perspective, as if their readers were to look through the perceptions of a very young child, then he speaks accurately, particularly in terms of how they crafted their illustrations. But if Edgar is speaking of their presentation of America, then this is not a particularly apt metaphor for their work. It may be the case that the D'Aulaires, like a child reader, might have come to their subjects without prior historical knowledge, but the D'Aulaires did come to their subjects with a strong sense of how their figures contributed to the American culture; and this sense comes directly out of their immigrant belief in America as a land of opportunity—truly a "standard conception," even a clichéd conception. Throughout their biographies, America is consistently pictured through the immigrant's lens. It is a land of opportunity, a land of peace and prosperity, a land where anyone with wits and gumption will succeed. It is the land of the European immigrant's dream, where new cultures could contribute to the larger whole, and individuals could thrive in the creative tension that would ensue.

It is this immigrant lens that makes the D'Aulaires' work so very different from the pioneer vision of James Daugherty. In their *George Washington* (1936), the wilderness is as present as in a James Daugherty book, but it is not a place that evokes for the reader the richness of America, or the frontier, or the pioneer spirit. The wilderness is the place to be overcome, and so Washington's forays into it are mostly to survey and thus organize the land, or to subdue the Indians and thus make the land safe for settlement. In fact, much of the book is about the notion of making a place one's own. That same theme is echoed in *Buffalo Bill* (1952), where once again the frontier is evoked. But here, too, it is to be made secure from Indians and buffalo and outlaws, and Buffalo Bill's exploits are celebrations of his work with the railroad, and with the Pony Express, and with huntsmen who set out to make the frontier their own. And even when the D'Aulaires do not evoke the frontier, as in *Benjamin Franklin* (1950), there is still the sense that in this world, we need to be about the business of making a place our own—in *Benjamin Franklin*, through thrift, hard work, wit, and insight.

Thus the pleasures and lessons of the frontier and the pioneer experience that Daugherty makes so prominent in his vision of America are heartily domesticated by the D'Aulaires. The true meaning of the American experience is not the gaining of certain values and insights through grappling with the difficulties and richness of the American frontier. It is about the kind of life that is made possible once the subduing has been completed. The subduing does not provide the context for the growth of the individual American; the completion of that subduing provides the context for the individual to grow to his or her fullest extent within the subsequent crucible of peace and prosperity. Thus in the work of the D'Aulaires, though aggression and violence may at times be necessary, they are not the experiences that lead to growth; they are the experiences that lead to a world in which nurturing by the true American scene may come about.

Framed as they are by the immigrant experience of the D'Aulaires, the biographies set out to suggest the ways in which individuals have contributed to this secure American scene and to suggest the ways in which the American scene allows for, even calls forth, such contributions through the encouragement of individual growth. That is, each biography works as positing a series of principles about the kinds of contributions that each individual might make in the civilized world that is America, recalling Edgar's assertion that America "is the country where everything we had in us could be used to its full extent, and where we could fulfill our full measures as human beings and help in building up the world."

This is a principle that works particularly well with the story of Abraham Lincoln; indeed, it is central to his mythic story of a young boy in the backwoods of Kentucky rising to the presidency. For the endpapers of this biography, the D'Aulaires place the boy Lincoln—barefoot, in ragged clothes, an axe in his right hand—looking toward the map of the Midwest that covers the spread; it traces his journey from Kentucky, to Illinois, and to Washington, this last symbolized by a speeding locomotive. It is as if all of America is set before the young Lincoln—as, in the D'Aulaires' vision, it is. To show the power of this possibility, the D'Aulaires move from the spaciousness of the endpapers to an image of the Lincoln cabin surrounded by darkness and tall trees leaning in; the cabin is precariously tiny and vulnerable. It is also very enclosed. The concluding image of the book, by contrast, is mythically large. Lincoln sits on his rocking chair, his young son Tad by his side. (Lincoln is not assassinated in this retelling; the biography ends with his successful defense of the Union.) Past the rocking chair, a curtain is pulled back to reveal not the wall of the White House but an open vista that looks out to the countryside. Past the flowers are two concentric rings of children, dancing around a flagpole, the American flag flying straight out. The sky is golden, suggesting a new dawn. Here, everything is open and possible. There is plenty for all.

In fact, this principle dominates the entire telling of Lincoln's life—and is at the heart of the decision not to include any mention of the assassination. Virtually every element of the biography is aimed at suggesting that Lincoln's life is the story of possibilities. So he is born into a cabin that "wasn't much of a house." He works as a child with his father, "but the soil on the farm was meager, and the father grew tired of toiling with it." He goes to school to learn to read, but after he becomes six years old "he didn't go much to school." The family's first shelter in Indiana has only three sides and an open hearth for the fourth. "Day and night they had to keep the fire burning. In a corner they put up a bed for the parents. On the ground they spread bear skins over piles of dried leaves for Abe and Sally to sleep on." When their mother dies, "the woods seemed gloomy and dark, and the days grew long for Sally and Abe."

But the tone of the text shifts as the D'Aulaires suggest that these hardships enable Abe to become strong, quick, and powerful. His drive to read enables him to gain a quick wit, making him a likeable leader in Little Pigeon Creek. His work ethic leads him to go into business, which in turn leads him to witness the horrors of a slave market. The qualities that had marked the hardships of his youth particularly are those that enable him to enter into the political world: "Everywhere people began to wonder if Lincoln wasn't the man to keep the United States together. From the big towns in the East important men traveled to see him and asked if he would be willing to let the people vote for him as President. Abraham Lincoln thought it over for a long time.

It was so friendly and peaceful on the prairie in Illinois." And so the story progresses, charting Abe's increasing influence as a leader in the business world, in politics, and eventually in war.

Margery Fisher has complained that this treatment of Lincoln presents him as a fairy tale figure—the Cinderella of the backwoods, who emerges from obscurity and hardship to become the prince. In fact, she argues, the prettily colored pictures disarm the meaning of the harsher episodes: "What is offered of truth in the text is annulled." So, for example, though the text suggests that Abe's childhood was hard, the spread depicting the family at Pigeon Creek shows an idyllic setting: "Here in a smooth forest enclave the child Abe chops at a tree in the foreground, father ploughs in the background, mother tends the fire in front of the half-faced camp; horse, cow and calf are neatly aligned in a lean-to, and Sally is glimpsed on her way to the spring with a yoke and buckets—all placed like figures in a toy village set." Fisher concludes that the picture book form itself "constrains serious material" and so trivializes the facts of Lincoln's biography.[4] Hugh Crago has argued alternately that instead of writing in the fairy-tale mode, the D'Aulaires are working in "a heroic view" and explains the Pigeon Creek spread as "a deliberate attempt to make the homely tales of Lincoln's childhood accessible to preschool readers who might be left behind later in the book."

The D'Aulaires might have answered the criticism of the illustrations —which truly are, in Fisher's words, prettily fashioned—by arguing that they were crafting the illustrations to mirror the perspectives and understandings of very young children. Their point was to accommodate the way in which a child would understand and organize "serious material." So in writing about the full-page illustration in *George Washington* when the general takes command of the Continental Army, for example, Bertha Mahony and Marguerite Mitchell wrote as if they anticipated Margery Fisher's criticism: "This is such a scene as a child might set up with his toy soldiers, toy buildings and trees. This is exactly what the artists had in mind as they drew." The point here is not only to present a life but to present a life as the D'Aulaires believed a very young child might understand it, given the child's limited ability to contextualize.[5]

What both Fisher and Crago miss, however, is that while the fairy-tale and heroic views both play a part in the retelling of Lincoln's life, they play supportive roles. Lincoln lives out the dream that is uniquely American, argue the D'Aulaires. Like Per, like the D'Aulaires themselves, like all immigrants, Lincoln hopes to find in this country the space and freedom to become most fully himself. And if Lincoln can succeed, then why should not an immigrant child like Per? Or any child? Everything is open and possible.

And yet, that optimism is itself tempered, for the D'Aulaires' idealism falters in the recognition, added only implicitly, that in the end not everyone is invited to be a part of the open and possible; the possible is still defined by race and class. The D'Aulaires have been criticized for not being more overt on this point. Bettye I. Latimer, for example, vehemently attacks *Abraham Lincoln* as caricaturing Lincoln's life and his struggle to find his own positions in the national political debate about race.

> This book does a disservice to Lincoln and his involvement with Black and Indian people. Both groups are depicted in the illustrations as the "white man's burden." After the Emancipation Proclamation is issued, Blacks are shown kneeling at Lincoln's feet while he maintains a detached, uncaring, arrogant posture. Earlier, Lincoln is shown as a strong man who protects what is illustrated as a timid, helpless Indian chief.... The text corroborates the "white man's burden" concept. It implies that the survival of the exploited is dependent on the mercy of a god in the form of Lincoln. The incident, of course, is pure fiction and the way it is dramatized substantiates its falseness. (144)

While Latimer's interpretation is harsh, particularly when the work of the D'Aulaires is placed in the context of other works for children of the period, it is certainly fair to argue that the D'Aulaires did picture in their works a world that was principally western European. They show none of the ambivalent complexity about race relations that marks James Daugherty's work, with his sense of the worth and rights of the Native people of North America, and the tragedy of the destruction of those peoples. Here, as Latimer suggests, it is the case that African American and—for the most part—Native American peoples are sidelined. And it is undeniable that African Americans, especially when they are depicted as slaves, are very much the objects of pathos or, at best, set outside the mainstream of the idealized American experience.

A similar problem appears in *Buffalo Bill* (1952), which the D'Aulaires begin by identifying the protagonist with Native Americans; he has a childhood closely linked to that world. But soon, Buffalo Bill is out on the plains with buffalo hunters and shoots an Indian creeping upon them one night. "After that the other plainsmen treated Bill like a grown-up man." Native Americans, following this passage in the text, are always pictured as hostile, shooting poisoned arrows, ambushing Pony Express riders, but running away from the crack shots of the white plainsmen. When the tribes go to war against the encroachments of settlers, "Buffalo Bill was sorry for the Indians. But he knew that, vast as the plains were, there wasn't room for the Indians and white men both." After the wars, Buffalo Bill "rounded up some Indians," and they became part of his pantomime, mere mockeries of themselves.

It would be unfair to insist upon a sensibility that would have been somewhat anachronistic for the midcentury. And certainly Latimer may be judging too quickly, particularly if she means to disparage the body of the D'Aulaires' work, for these artists do place questions of racial inclusion in the minds even of their youngest readers. In *George Washington*, for example, one full-page black-and-white illustration has the reader looking through the windows of Mount Vernon at George and Martha, dancing formally in front of their assembled guests. Martha's two children are looking out the window at the three slave children, who are peering in—excluded. The reader, here, is given the same perspective as the slave—looking in from the outside. The next full-page illustration, this one in color, pictures the Washington family in front of their fields. Again they are formally dressed, and they seem to be posing. Meanwhile, in the fields behind them, the almost naked slaves work on the growing wheat. This accompanies a text that praises the wealth and economy of the plantation, where "George Washington was everywhere, and his hundreds of slaves and servants kept everything spick and span and in beautiful order."

The heavy discrepancy between text and illustration and the heavily emphasized distinctions between the Washington family and those held as their slaves carry a pictorial irony that does not allow for simple acceptance—even by a young reader.[6] In fact, here the D'Aulaires are refusing to accept this injustice and its evisceration of their vision of America. These illustrations anticipate the D'Aulaires' climax to *Pocahontas* (1946), in which Pocahontas refuses herself to be intimidated or defined by the English court:

> And as for Pocahontas, when she bowed before the King and saw the skinny legs that could hardly hold the fat body of the King of England, she thought of her stately father. He needed neither a crown on his head nor a scepter in his hand to show that he was a ruler.
> She held her head high as though she had been born in a snow-white palace. She was proud of being her father's daughter and of having been born in a hut of bark in the midst of the deep, dark woods of Virginia. (45)

The D'Aulaires allow Pocahontas to define herself in opposition, though they have her identify her birthplace by using a term that the English court would use, rather than her own people. But the larger sense of self that the D'Aulaires are trying to establish here is once again a representation of the immigrant's perspective—a refusal to accept European definitions and the vehement assertion that America is open to all to live to their fullest extent and so to become their truest selves.

For most of the biographies, that immigrant vision is merged into the experience of the American who grows fully into himself or herself because of the nature of America and its democracy, which allows for individual growth. But the biography that comes closest to the true immigrant experience—the physical movement from one world to another that Ingri and Edgar themselves took part in—is *Leif the Lucky* (1941), a book that Alice Jordan, reviewing it for *Horn Book*, called "a book that has lasting value for American children," though almost every character is Norwegian. The book plays out in almost mythic terms the great American Dream of moving ever westward with which James Daugherty had worked. First, Erik the Red moves from Norway to Greenland; Leif follows his father, though journeying westward all the way to North America; then, after Leif returns, his sister and her husband travel to the new land that Leif had found, and there Leif's nephew is born. Though they each will return to Greenland, the newly discovered country stands as a land of plenty, where they are not hemmed in by others, where there is richness in lumber and in furs and land.

The book ends on a Darwinian note. For many years the people of Greenland sail to this new world for timber, until long seasons of cold take their toll on this people, and they begin to diminish—literally. "The son became smaller than his father, and his son became smaller again, for they had neither porridge nor bread to eat. As they grew smaller they also lost their skill and forgot how to make sturdy, seagoing ships." Eventually the entire race seems to wither away. Thus the book serves as a cautionary tale of sorts, a story of how wealth and prosperity and strength lie in the powerful movement to the west, to America; back in old Europe lies only diminishment. It is, once again, America through immigrant eyes.

But most of the biographies deal with figures born in America. Both *George Washington* (1936) and *Benjamin Franklin* (1950) enact the story that *Abraham Lincoln* told: of one coming fully into himself because of the space and opportunities that America provides. Thus in *George Washington*, Washington begins as a child amidst wealth; his father owns several plantations, he wears beautiful suits, and he is given a pony. Washington is cared for as an infant by a slave and is taught Bible stories by "the shiny tiles of the fireplace." All seems—and is—a world of privilege. But the D'Aulaires want to show him in a country that allows him to expand to his true self, and so from these elements, they move immediately to the death of Washington's father. "Then his mother was not very rich, so he could not go to school in England as his half brothers had done. He had to learn how to provide for himself." While this is not completely true—certainly they are not living in the circumstances of Lincoln's family—that claim allows the D'Aulaires to present Washington the opportunity to show his character, which is one of determination and endurance. These are the qualities that are developed while he is out surveying land in western Virginia: "He worked hard and made maps of the land, and at night he slept on the bare ground. Often wind and rain tore the tent from over his head, but he did not mind, for he was strong as a bear." These are the qualities developed during the French and Indian War: "Hostile Indians had attacked him and he had almost drowned in an icy river. But he had come through all the dangers and returned with the French commander's answer." And these are the qualities that serve him so well during the Revolutionary War: "Washington led his soldiers through all dangers and difficulties. He retreated with his army when he saw he could not win, but whenever he had a chance he attacked." Later, at Valley Forge, "Washington did not give up, and he kept [his soldiers] together. He starved with them and froze with them, and his soldiers loved him so much that they stayed for his sake." The suggestion here is that the opportunities into which Washington had to grow early on prepared him for greatness later on, and that opportunity came about not due to inherited position but through the crucible of America.

It is for this reason that *George Washington* seems to end so very oddly, with an abrupt conclusion that ignores so much of what Washington did following the Revolutionary War. His entire presidency is summed up in a single sentence, on the last page of the text: "For eight years he was President and led his countrymen wisely and justly, and the country grew strong and rich." The significance of his administration, the unification of the country, the movement to the Constitution, the huge moment of the president laying down his power—all these are left out, principally because of the enormous singularity that interests the D'Aulaires: the honing of Washington's character within the context of the American experiment. The book concludes, "The little boy from the lone Virginia plantation had become the Father of His Country." It is the immigrant dream enacted in mythic dimensions.

Benjamin Franklin tells a similar tale. Franklin is first pictured as the youngest son of seventeen children, and the greatest hope that his father has is that he will grow up to be a good tradesman. But this is a story of growing into one's fullest self. So by the second spread, the D'Aulaires assure the reader that "he was different from his brothers. He was only knee-high to a grasshopper when he first learned to read and he wondered and asked questions from morning till night." Those questions show that Franklin is not only inquisitive but inventive and clever—qualities that do not sit well when his father forces him into a trade. Eventually his cleverness is what rescues him from the boredom of the printer's shop, and it is also what leads him to the recognition that he must go off on his own. So he leaves his brother, and "it was not long before the people in Philadelphia were telling one another how lucky it was that such a good printer and fine young fellow had settled in their town." Even the poverty that Franklin is faced with turns out to be a blessing, for from it he learns thriftiness and humility: "He was merry and happy and, though he was a master printer now, he did not hold himself too grand for any work. His fellow townsmen saw him pushing his papers through the streets on a wheelbarrow. 'He will go far,' one neighbor said to the other. 'We see him at work when we get up. He is still working when we go to bed.'" This thriftiness and work ethic are combined with natural good sense throughout the biography, and the D'Aulaires accentuate these virtues by the medallions they place at the bottom of all pages except for full-page illustrations, in which Poor Richard's pithy proverbs are printed.

Having developed these virtues, once again, the space of America allows Franklin to use them to their fullest extent: "Soon it came to pass that, if anything was to be done for the welfare of the town, people came to ask his advice." The biblical language of this statement suggests the proportions that Franklin is given, as he becomes a huge supporter of Philadelphia, of the sciences, of the colony of Pennsylvania, and finally of the American colonies. The D'Aulaires constantly point to his full development. Thus, even when his ambassadorial duties were finished in France, "rest was not yet for him. Once more his country called him to work"—meaning his work on the drafting of the Constitution. The last scene the D'Aulaires give the reader of Franklin's life is the one that they imply is there for Abraham Lincoln, though it is not: "He retired to the quiet of his library, where now he could read his beloved books in peace." The tone and placement of this line are meant to suggest how very remarkable this is, as he withdraws from the commitments to which he had given his life.

Barbara Bader has written of the D'Aulaires' sense that they came to America without the standard conceptions of what the American story was. In their works and for them personally, America "was as much a picturebook place as . . . Norway was to Americans" (45). The sense here is that their work is a canvas on which they lay out the first impressions of a country in the same way that a young child first coming to know these tales would see them. Certainly the D'Aulaires would acknowledge this element of their work; in his Caldecott acceptance speech, Edgar had insisted that they both came to these stories "as children." But the stories that the D'Aulaires tell, though seen ostensibly from a child's eye, are told from within the context of the adult vision of America that the D'Aulaires embraced. This is a new world, where everyone is free to grow to his or her fullest extent. It is the world of the immigrant's hope and dream. It is the world that World War II was fought, in part, to preserve.

PART FOUR

Positioning the American Democracy Globally

1945 — 1960

7 Globalizing American Democracy

Exporting the American Heritage

In 1949 James Cloyd Bowman, a folklorist who had been adapting American folklore for children for two decades, spoke to the American Library Association about his work. It was a rambling talk; he was light, though earnest—until the conclusion, when Bowman suddenly shifted his tone and spoke very seriously about what he discerned as the role of children's literature in the postwar years: "My belief is that our American Folklore can be made to offer [children] at least a temporary retreat from the biting winds of adversity. It can carry them into a joyous young world where cynicism and hatred are nowhere to be found." The implication, of course, is that children after the war now live in a joyless old world, where cynicism and hatred abound; it is a world from which children should be protected. Bowman's argument about the role of children's literature in America after the war is similar to the argument advanced by those who suggested during World War II that children should read books that had nothing to do with the war. But those earlier arguments had advocated reading as a way of growing stronger and more mature, so that children would later be enabled to handle the realities of wartime. For Bowman, children's literature is not necessarily something that strengthens; it is something that protects, a "retreat," a movement away from the world's stern reality that should not be the lot of innocent, immature readers.

But if Bowman was trying to describe the direction of children's literature in the post–World War II years, he was quite wrong. Jean Van Evera, a reviewer for *Parents' Magazine*, came closer in her 1946 article, "They're Not What They Used to Be." "The Never Never Land of children's books is a different place from what it was in your young days," she began. Instead of the violet-hued stories of the past, books written for children today were works of "realism." "These are not the escape books of your yesteryear in which life for the hero or heroine is only one joyous series of adventures of summer camping, motor car and boat-

175

ing trips and boarding school events. Modern literature for children is concerned with the problems of today." It is the war itself, Evera claims, that has made such violet hues impossible. "The momentous events of the six terrible years which stretched between 1939 and 1945 have brought the outside world to the doorstep of the nurseries." Thus, she asserts, it is children's books that "emphasize the need to have evil and barbarity fought and defeated wherever they are found, but do not associate these qualities with any particular race or country." Contemporary children's books address racial prejudice, present "the Negro without caricaturing him," reveal "the stupidity of anti-Semitism," attack "snobbish class consciousness." Children's books, she hopes, "will lead children to a better understanding of each other, will help to encourage mutual respect for each other's rights which in turn points the way to the goal everyone is seeking: permanent peace and security." And to do this, children's books will push beyond the acknowledgment of "quaint customs of other countries"; instead, "there must be a common denominator of love of freedom and democracy as the underlying force." In the end, what books help children discover, Evera claims, is that what is thrilling is "the society of all of their fellow humans."

Evera's description of children's literature after World War II would be prophetic; it would not be a literature of escapism but a literature of engagement. In fact, some claimed that children's literature could play an important role in the culture by focusing young minds. The question was, what to focus on. In *American Childhood* Anne Scott MacLeod suggests that children's literature of the 1950s deflected young readers from the real world around them, arguing that "postwar fiction seems detached from its surroundings. With only a few exceptions, the stories said nothing about the political and social realities that remade a world or, for that matter, about those reshaping the society at home. Material prosperity, the cold war, the nuclear threat, world power, McCarthyism, civil rights, suburbanism, TV—all are hard to find in the literature as a whole" (50). She concludes that literature for young readers was marked by silence about those issues most likely to produce anxiety in a young reader, yet those issues surely affected a young reader; she cites "war, both potential and actual; juvenile delinquency and rebellion; changing social mores." In the end, she writes, "the adolescent mind revealed in teen fiction [of the 1950s] is not just nonideological, it is ideologically untouched—like a child's, in fact" (62). Citing MacLeod, Gail Schmunk Murray, in *American Children's Literature and the Construction of Childhood*, would agree, arguing that the authors of

Cold War books for children worked to turn attention to the nuclear family and its securities in an uncertain world: "If children's literature was to play its traditional role of reiterating acceptable social mores and teaching traditional values, it would have to emphasize the protected aura of childhood and address adults' fears about the threats of the external environment" (176).

It would seem at first that MacLeod's assessment echoes Steven Mintz's description of the Cold War years as promoting "conformity, sociability, patriotism, and religiosity" (*Huck's Raft*, 282–83) not only through the family but also through extrafamily institutions: the Boy Scouts and Girl Scouts, summer camps, Sunday schools, prime-time television shows promoting very specific gender roles—all of which were booming in the 1950s. Perhaps MacLeod would note that children's books would affirm the values that Mintz lists, and, at the same time, the publishing, education, and library institutions would criticize the works that seemed to undercut those values, defining them as unhealthy distractions of childhood—distractions, say, like comic books. Why, for example, should children read the Bobbs-Merrill Childhood of Famous Americans series when there was a world of comics and new, more exotic media? The publisher supplied the answer: "Because these books compete successfully with distracting influences less helpful to your child. Children don't have to be coaxed to read them. They always ask for more. . . . Child readers put themselves readily into the places of the characters and enjoy experiences from the past—thrilling, amusing, instructive in the American values—as if it were all happening to them." (The publisher's response appears on the inside jacket of Katherine E. Wilkie's book *Mary Todd Lincoln: Girl of the Bluegrass*.) This claim by the Bobbs-Merrill company was partially a defensive position, an argument that assumed that children's literature had to justify itself as a cultural force—and that justification seemed to be a conservative, almost reactionary response to other cultural "distractions." But in these Cold War years, there was simultaneously a position that asserted that children's literature could work a proactive progressive purpose by addressing important social issues and contributing to young readers' new awareness of their place in a postwar America. "Books which portray the Negro as religious, good-hearted and good-natured, but inferior because of his superstitions, irresponsibility, and laziness contribute nothing toward the building of a better world," Dorothy Shepard Manley warned in "Improving Racial Attitudes through Children's Books." "On the contrary, they retard its development by perpetuating false ideas." Children's books, she argued, should take on the task of building a better world—not a better nation but a better world. Hardly a conservative, reactionary position at all.

Two years after James Cloyd Bowman's talk, in 1951, the American Library Association announced its sober seventy-fifth anniversary theme: "Our American Heritage in Times of Crisis." The answer for any crisis, the ALA affirmed, was a regard for those elements in America's past that had made it both strong and independent. To further this regard, the ALA commissioned three books: one from Henry Steele Commager, a historian of American culture and political and constitutional heritage then teaching at Columbia University and ardently opposing McCarthyism; a second from Gerald W. Johnson, a prominent cultural critic who was similarly anti-McCarthyist; and the last from Genevieve Foster, author of historical information books for child readers such as *Abraham Lincoln's World* (1944) and *George Washington's World* (1941). The ALA asked each of these three to write books that restated the American belief in democracy. Commager published *Living Ideas in America* (1951), aimed at a high school and adult audience, expressing, as one North Carolina librarian wrote, "how our traditions and our country's experiences in the past are reflected in our present problems with possible solutions." Gerald W. Johnson wrote *This American People* (1951), also aimed at an adult audience, focusing on the question, "Is the American Idea still valid?" With chapters on the freedoms of speech, conscience, enterprise, inquiry, association, and opportunity, his book argued powerfully that to be an American is to be willing to take risks for freedom and that all Americans must challenge all governments—including their own—that might take steps to limit the precepts of liberty. And Genevieve Foster wrote the two slim volumes of *Birthdays of Freedom* (1952, 1957) for a child audience, culminating all human advances in freedom with the Declaration of Independence. In the first volume, she posed these questions to her young readers: "We enjoy the freedom which they won. What does that mean? Freedom? Was it really worth fighting for? Would it be worth weeping over if we should wake one day to find it gone? How can we know, we, in this country, who have never known what it is to be without it? How could this freedom of ours to go where we will, and do and say what we think best, ever be lost?" The second volume opens similarly: "What, in short, was the heritage of freedom which caused those forefathers to cut themselves off from the old world and start a new nation dedicated to keeping that heritage alive?" Both books chart the successes and failures of freedom, lauding advances in understanding, individual growth, the arts, and communal prosperity and warning against tyranny and enthusiasm.

Cora Paul Bomar, a state school library advisor in North Carolina and the librarian who commented upon *Living Ideas in America*, affirmed the importance of these American Library Association texts, arguing that there needed to be children's books about the heritage of America: "We have an obligation to preserve it and share it with other people all over the world." This should be the role of children's literature in America: to preserve the American heritage for national growth and strength and to share the American heritage to promote world democracy. To this end, Bomar applauded books about "the lives of people who have influenced our way of life," such as the D'Aulaires' *George Washington* (1936); books about the US government, such as Dorothy Canfield Fisher's *Our Independence and the Constitution* (1950); books that represented America's heritage of merriment, such as Miska and Maud Petersham's *The Rooster Crows: A Book of American Rhymes and Jingles* (1945), Opal Wheeler's *Sing for America* (1944), and Sydney Taylor's *All-of-a-Kind Family* (1951); and "books about social adjustment," such as Laura Ingalls Wilder's *Farmer Boy* (1953). Bomar saw in all of these books "a picture of our American life." But there is more than applause here; her article conveys an urgency about the preservation of the American heritage and a sense that there was a need for an active effort to this end; children's literature, she argued, was one essential means to accomplish that preservation as part of its task in creating informed, participatory citizens who look to the country's future and to the global need for democracy.

As America turned from a declared war to an undeclared Cold War, the argument that children's books should affirm the American heritage was echoed and re-echoed as a call toward an informed national and international citizenry. Max J. Herzberg, writing in the *Elementary English Review* at the end of World War II, argued that the "Good Society is for us . . . above all American" and that teachers needed to stress American works to identify and preserve that Good Society: "Since literature is an interpretation of experience, since literature is the emotional and artistic expression of certain ideals, since literature often necessarily has regional values inexplicable to the stranger, it is important that we stress American literature whenever it serves us better than other literatures—and that we do so, of course, with no trace of chauvinism"—a tall order. In 1956 Jane Stewart published "Why Literature for Children and Youth?" in the *Reading Teacher*; she answered her own titular question with an answer that spoke to individual growth and a maturing in democratic values: "In the expanding world of the adolescent, the opportunities and responsibilities of citizenship are often forcibly brought to their attention. An ever-widening acquaintance with literature—books, newspapers, magazines—can deepen this awareness, develop understandings, interpret the role of the adult in the society in which they are growing up." In 1959 Paul P. Rogers wrote in agreement in the *Journal of Teacher Education* as he dismissed the success of Sputnik and rejected the lockstep nature of Soviet education: "American education must continue to be education for democracy. The American school must not produce technical robots and political nonentities." Instead, Rogers argued, the American heritage of "rational compromise" and "intelligent voluntary coordination of the diverse elements of our society" must be promoted as central to American democracy.[1]

John J. DeBoer, with his usual heightened sense, urged a more international vision. He wrote in 1958 in "Reading and the Social Scene" that the launching of Sputnik did not pose, as many supposed, a technological problem for America; what it really posed was an educational problem. He stressed the need for "funds for more and larger and better libraries in school and community, more and better trained teachers, smaller classes, and more adequate instructional equipment, all of which would contribute to a wide understanding of the choices which Sputnik imposes upon mankind." Reading, he argued, allowed children to contextualize "the raw product of the day's news reporting." In addition, he suggested, reading helps children understand the peculiar position of America: a land of plenty in a world of poverty. "If our reading does not include more than a glimpse of this contrast, it will fail to qualify us as competent observers of the current social scene. . . . Never in history have such fateful consequences hung on the success or failure of the school in creating a population that not only can read but does read and reads worthwhile material," which DeBoer principally defined as nonfiction. Leland B. Jacobs, then a professor of education at Teachers College, Columbia University, agreed. Children, he wrote in *Elementary English* in 1955, "have unquenchable curiosities concerning the world which is about and within them. . . . They must do the best that they can to comprehend this world of self and family and friends and neighbors; this world of their own country and other lands; this world of past, present, and future; this world of their planet and a vast, mysterious universe. . . . In other words, children are natural explorers who venture into areas of human experience little known to them, who investigate their physical-social world, who quest for meanings in living and being." The place for which they look for answers, Jacobs asserted, was literature.

In general, Jane Stewart, Paul Rogers, John J. DeBoer, and Leland B. Jacobs all stressed the role of nonfiction in children's reading in terms of the preservation of American culture. At the end of the 1950s, Joan Blos—two decades away from her Newbery Award–winning novel—argued similarly in the *Saturday Review* as she sought to combat the kind of cynicism that James Cloyd Bowman had identified. One role that children's books could play, she argued, was to preserve the culture by affirming it through nonfiction.

> In these times of national doubt there is a tendency to deprecate the American tradition and to regard as naïve or chauvinistic any attempt to recognize its value and its vitality. Sophistication substitutes for sentiment and adults smile at the plasticine log cabins and cherry trees of construction paper which form the February décor for countless elementary school classrooms. Yet there is nothing wrong with the symbols *per se*, and the honesty and patriotism for which they stand have a place in our national life. For young children the feeling that this is essentially a nation of "good guys" is personally strengthening and of potential social value. The realization that all has not been for the very best and that much remains to be done can come later. When it does come, it is important that the new awareness bring a feeling of challenge (not of disillusionment) and that it be combined with a sense of historical balance.

This strengthening in the American heritage would come through books, Blos argued, and the ones she chose to take up this task were very much in line with those that Cora Paul Bomar might have chosen if she were writing in 1960: books such as Arna Bontemps's *Frederick Douglass: Slave, Fighter, Freeman* (1959); Ruth Painter Randall's *I Mary: A Biography of the Girl Who Married Abraham Lincoln* (1959); Lynn Montross's *Washington and the Revolution* (1959); Catherine Owens Peare's *The Helen Keller Story* (1959); Fred Reinfeld's *The Great Dissenters: Guardians of Their Country's Laws and Liberties* (1959); Dorothy Canfield Fisher's *And Long Remember: Some Great Americans Who Have Helped Me* (1959), on the courage of American forces; Genevieve Foster's *The World of Captain John Smith* (1959); and Gerald W. Johnson's *America Is Born: A History for Peter* (1959). All are nonfiction, which, Blos argued, was effective in associating the events of the past and their meanings within the present. She acknowledged that the imagination must play a role as well, but only to "supplement information."

In her listing, however, she showed little regard for that supplement. She mentioned only two novels: Jeanne Williams's *Mission in Mexico* (1959), about a southern boy's search for his father in Maximilian's Mexico, and William O. Steele's *The Far Frontier* (1959), following a boy's growing respect for a naturalist exploring the Indian territories of Tennessee. If fiction was to play a role, it seemed from the proportions of the article that it was to play a small one in the evocation of the American heritage.

Thus the split that had divided critics of children's literature during World War II—preparing for the war by reading nonfiction about it versus growing and maturing through reading fiction that nourished the child—was in evidence during the decade of the 1950s as well.

There were those who disagreed with Cora Paul Bomar's argument that children needed to read books that focused on the American heritage. In "The Literary Heritage of Childhood," written for the *Wilson Library Bulletin* in the spring of 1959, Annis Duff, an editor at Viking Press, looked for balance. She argued that thinking of books in terms of "heritage" was problematic in that it suggested a kind of collective consciousness, whereas reading—which could indeed represent participating in a shared experience—was also individual. "The value of every book he reads is special to him," she noted of the child reader. In fact, that individual experience, that engagement of the individual imagination, was the particular value of children's books.

> We desperately need just now to possess the world; and that can be accomplished only by people who possess their own souls. Through these past few years, when the fate of humanity has been held in such precarious balance, I have been almost obsessed with the conviction that only a tragic want of imagination could have brought us so close to the brink of our own destruction—imagination being in my own definition intelligence of the spirit. . . . [A]ssociation with great books can indeed help children to possess the world by giving them a sense of how its people have lived and thought and dreamed in all times and places; can help them, too, to possess their own souls by freeing and feeding their imagination.

Thus, though Duff affirmed the value of the books that Bomar suggested, agreeing that child readers could indeed imbibe social culture from the books, she also argued that it is the task of the writer to present stories with fully rounded characters who are vital and real, responding to their own worlds, all conveyed in a finely told narrative: "Through a responding enjoyment the reader accepts and fulfills the demands made by every good book on imagination, emotion, sympathy, and understanding, and so he strengthens his understanding of himself as a moral being, and of his relationship with the people around him." Though there is a balance, Duff clearly leaned toward the power of the imagination in the cultivation of the individual young American citizen.

And there were books that worked hard at just this. Elizabeth Coatsworth's *The Sod House* (1954), for example, is built around specific social issues and deals with a moment in the American heritage—the battle over Kansas's entry into the Union—that was important for children to know. But as Duff articulated, Coatsworth was not interested in a nonfiction portrayal; she looked for an engagement of imagination and emotion. So in this short novel for young children, Friedrich Traubel, his wife, Maria, and his children, Ilse and Hans, come to America from Germany "because they were no longer free to say what they thought" (5). "I would cross ten oceans if freedom lay on the other side!" cries Friedrich, and so they arrive in Boston. It seems that Coatsworth's novel will be a clichéd affirmation of America as a land of freedom, but the novel is more complex. After a time, Friedrich is troubled by the persistence of slavery in the nation: "Sometimes here in Boston, I feel my own freedom turn bitter, thinking about other men who are not free" (8). He resolves to travel to Kansas so that he can contribute to making that state a free state and thus tip the balance of free states in Congress. When they arrive on their land, they perform a ritual:

> But before they ate, Papa suggested that they should sing "The Star-Spangled Banner." They stood side by side in the twilight, Papa's big voice leading, and Mama's voice with Ilse's soaring up into the sky, like birds, Ilse thought.
> There were red bars of sunset in the west and some long white clouds trailed above them. Far up in the soft blue sky the evening star shone,
> "O'er the land of the free
> And the home of the brave."
> It was as if a great banner hung over them all. (28–29)

Papa builds the house and prepares the land for plowing—careful not to disturb three mounds that, he thinks, might be Indian graves. But it is a difficult beginning. They are the lone New Englanders in their area, the only ones who are against slavery. Neighbors ride out to intimidate them and seem, at one point, to threaten a lynching. Their horses are poisoned. A prairie fire is set to destroy the farm. But they hang on, protected, at one point, by seven Indians who are grateful for their sensitivity regarding the graves.

It is a compelling story, with compelling characters. In the end, the family's persistence and bravery are rewarded when other families arrive and a new community is established, and the novel ends with a hope for peace. "We have come to a good land. And some day we shall have friends all about us," her father tells Ilse (62). And when she asks if those who had harassed them might also someday be friends, he affirms, "Some day they will be friends, too" (62)—a well-rounded and hopeful ending in a novel for a very young reader. The book deals with immigration and the search for freedom, with the nature of America as an immigrant country, with issues of mutual tolerance and acceptance between ethnicities, with the rights of minorities and the responsibilities of majorities, and with America as an experiment in democracy—all weighty subjects that are at the center of America's heritage. But for none of these does Coatsworth stop the plotline to preach; she follows, instead, Duff's invitation to first tell the fine story and let the narrative bear the larger meanings.

Preserving America, sharing America, cultivating America—the tasks must have seemed daunting, particularly when children's literature was asked to take on another burden as well following the war, and it was a task particularly suited to an American children's literature that had so often shown a progressive vision. America during the 1950s was a culture in which organizations such as the National Council for American Education were campaigning for the institution of a very conservative, right-wing brand of "Americanism" in schools as a response to the threat of Communism. America during the 1950s was a culture in which a book such as *How Red Are the Schools? And How You Can Eradicate Socialism and Communism from the Schools and Colleges of America* (1950) was being published and distributed. In the fall of 1952 the *Boston Post* attacked the Boston Public Library for collecting *Pravda* and *Izvestia*. In 1954 Anne Smart brought a list of "subversive" books and authors from the stacks of the Tamalpais Union High School of Marin County, California, to a grand jury, as well as to the press; in 1955 she appeared with her list on Edward R. Murrow's *See It Now*, baffling and cowing those who disagreed with her by her composure and sure style. Yet in such a culture, children's literature would be one place where ideas judged to be dangerously leftist might still be explored; in other words, children's literature was being called upon to be daring.[2]

In November 1950 Pierre Van Paassen—a crusading journalist and Unitarian minister—spoke to the Wisconsin Education Association, questioning whether the country was unified in its understanding of the nature of democracy. Democracy, he argued, means "one thing to an American sharecropper and another thing to an American banker; one thing to an American streetcar conductor and another thing to the president of an oil trust or a chain of newspapers. Yet all men say they want democracy. All are operating under the slogans of democracy. It is obvious everybody's ideas of democracy cannot be realized." Whatever democracy is, he suggested, the only way to advance democracy and peace in the world "is to restore freedom of expression in our own country." And here, at the center of his speech, as McCarthyism was ratcheting up its fearful power, Van Paassen defined what he meant by freedom of expression: "I think that democracy is to be found where the citizen may freely give expression to what his conscience gives him to think or say. Democracy is where a man without fear or without experiencing intimidation or secret pressure, may give utterance, orally or in writing, to his innermost convictions, be they ever so unorthodox or at variance with the generally held opinions on economic, social, scientific or religious matters." Speaking to Wisconsin teachers and librarians, Van Paassen expressed what children's literature would affirm again and again during the great silences of the Cold War and McCarthyism: the freedom to dissent.[3]

Certainly this was a time when children's books pictured a sweet, often pastoral American world where a genial happiness pervades, where animals—both wild and domestic—and people seem to live gleefully together: Ruth Krauss's *The Happy Day* (1949), illustrated by Marc Simont; Janice May Udry's *A Tree Is Nice* (1956), also illustrated by Marc Simont; Eleanor Frances Lattimore's *Holly in the Snow* (1954); and Robert Lawson's *The Tough Winter* (1954) all picture a rural world where there is a close, easy, happy unity set within a particular American landscape. Don Freeman's *Fly High, Fly Low* (1957) does the same thing in the urban setting of San Francisco. Of Berta and Elmer Hader's *The Big Snow* (1948), also uniting animals and humans in a pastoral setting, Anne Carroll Moore would write in the May–June 1949 *Horn Book*, "I think it peculiarly fitting that the Caldecott award comes to the Haders for a book that is so true an expression of life in America as they live it in the happy companionship of birds and animals and human beings."

Children's literature could also affirm and parade a grandiose American heritage. Robert Lawson's wartime book, *Watchwords of Liberty: A Pageant of American Quotations* (1943, 1957), would be reprinted in Cold War America, a book that celebrated, preserved, and shared the heritage that Max Herzberg and Jane Stewart and Joan Blos had called children's literature to preserve by quoting and contextualizing famous American quotations: "Taxation without representation is tyranny" (5); "There is Jackson, standing like a stone-wall" (55); "Mr. Watson, come here; I want you" (81); and "Sighted sub—sank same" (110), with the final quotation, Lawson suggested, showing "typical American matter-of-factness."

But in addition, children's literature could also dissent from the sentimental pastoral vision, or it could dissent from grandiose patriotic vision. It could, in fact, celebrate dissent as essential to an understanding of the American democracy. So Gerald W. Johnson could write in his *America Is Born: A History for Peter* (1959)—one of the books that Joan Blos had recommended on her reading list—that being an American means "being part of a continued story that goes back from you to George Washington, and beyond him to Captain John Smith, and beyond John Smith to Christopher Columbus. Part of the story is very fine, and other parts are very bad; but they all belong to it, and if you leave out the bad parts you will never understand it at all. Yet you must understand it if you are to make your part one of the fine parts" (viii–ix). (*America Is Born* was followed a year later by Johnson's *America Grows Up: A History for Peter.*) And in *The Great Dissenters: Guardians of the Country's Laws and Liberties* (1959), Fred Reinfeld could define the greatest Americans as those who refused to go along with the majority and who, in so doing, preserved freedom for all individual Americans. "Our own age," he wrote, "is not the only one that has had a powerful surge toward uniformity: the age of Emerson had its equivalent of Organization Men and men in gray flannel suits. Yet these great dissenters are recognized today as great Americans precisely because they dared to be themselves."

John J. DeBoer was sharp in this insistence on the possibility of dissent in children's literature: reading, he argued, was a means of the preservation of freedom in America. Writing in the spring of 1951, DeBoer recognized the dangers that a loud, vocal, powerful, and manipulative force might present in a society. He also recognized that such a cultural force might quickly attack the freedom of the writer—and so he stressed once more the importance of the teacher in preserving democracy and freedom.

> Teaching the meaning of democracy to youth in 1950 is not without its dangers. First is the danger that the school will impose upon youth its own particular vision of the meaning of democracy, instead of letting the youth discover its meaning for themselves. And a second, perhaps greater, danger is the reaction of a hysterical community to the real implications of democracy for America today. Now, as in every other period of American history, the defense of democracy requires courage.
>
> Only an undaunted, united profession can succeed in keeping the av-

enues of communication open. The nation-wide attack on free education, on the radio, in newspaper columns, and elsewhere, is in part designed to impede the free study of the emanating of democracy. Teachers of English, custodians of our magnificent language, should be in the forefront of those who, at great risk to themselves, are defending democracy by defending the freedom of communication.

Yet again, teachers are given the huge burden of conveying to the young those messages that would preserve American democracy.

And what were those messages?

The end of World War II brought with it new calls from teachers and librarians for an awareness that education and children's books were necessary parts of the work of educating children and young adults to an awareness of their place in an international order marked by democracy. In November 1945 Constance M. McCullough delivered a speech to the National Council of Teachers of English arguing that the act of reading held an essential cooperative quality that could contribute to, even model, relationships in the postwar world:

> Whether we are on the brink of a greater chaos than the world has ever known or greater harmony than the optimists have ever dreamed, it is important that our youth be given the tools with which to build a better life. If they must compete with others, we want them to be the best equipped. If, on the contrary, they are to be permitted to co-operate with others in the pursuit of a common future, it is to the benefit of us all that their skills be developed to the fullest capacity. The skill of reading, which is the key to all book knowledge, should be perfected.

The next summer, M. R. Trabue, dean of the School of Education at Pennsylvania State College, similarly asserted at that college's 1946 reading conference that reading itself was linked with democracy, and it was language arts teachers who faced the huge challenge and burden of inculcating reading and language skills in their students so that the ideals of democracy could advance. "Teachers of reading and the other language arts, in common with all other teachers in 1946, must strive above all else to develop in their pupils the desire to live and work together cooperatively for constructive ends. . . . No other group of teachers has ever carried a heavier responsibility. The future existence and happiness of the human race depends in large measure upon how well we do our task." Five years later, at the beginning of the Korean War, Harold Van Dorn, a professor of political science at Kent State University, wrote of the responsibility of teachers to embody democracy in their classroom praxis. He used language identical to that which had been used in the 1930s to make the same point:

"As members of a profession entrusted with the training of youth there rests on teachers a special obligation to implement the ideas embodied in democratic philosophy by classroom practices which are consonant with the fundamental tenets of democracy. . . . If these concepts become an integral part of our thinking and living in the school they will permeate our whole social fabric and enable us to meet the challenge of the present and of the future." In short, McCullough, Trabue, and Van Dorn were placing huge bets that the success of American democracy and international cooperation in the postwar world would come about only through the capable and intentional work of American teachers—particularly reading teachers.

But how, precisely, was this to be done?

In the spring of 1948 Bette Banner Preer, a librarian in the Boston Public Library, urged in the *Wilson Library Bulletin* that majority children be brought to encounters with minority cultures through meeting their representations in fiction: "Liberal-minded educators and students of reading, who are interested, have been right in refusing to ignore, in their studies and discussions, the fact that the child's reading greatly influences his general attitudes about people and places." Preer expressed some disdain for 1930s works that had dealt with African Americans, suggesting that they had been based on little information and might actually support stereotypes: "The child whose reading has established or strengthened his prejudices against people of another race has as serious a reading problem as the child who is unable to read and understand the written word." She argued that the postwar culture recognized the need for a truer, more realistic approach to racial encounters in works written for children: "The realization that the peace of the world is nurtured on a sharing of the responsibilities of life, on the recognition and safeguarding of the human rights of every individual and of all races more than just mock tolerance of one group by another, has gripped many postwar authors, and given readers a flood of writings on racism"—"racism" here defined as a quality that appears in a work dealing with exploring racial issues.

Preer described a trend toward books that were moving away from "type characterization" and toward "the ambitious, intelligent, educated, serious-minded, healthy, normally happy individual." Plots now deal with "real obstacles" faced by minority groups: "It is well for these obstacles to be realized by both races, for only then can real problems be analyzed and solved." And, perhaps most importantly, contemporary fiction dealing with minorities does not affirm a minority class that lives out a life content with a lower lot; instead, "the more recent books bring out cooperative living of both races and the desire on the part of both to share in all life activities, not one race seeking to undermine the other." She cited particularly books such as Jerrold and Lorraine Beim's *Two Is a Team* (1945); Jesse Jackson's *Call Me Charley* (1945); Marguerite de Angeli's *Bright April* (1946); Georgene Faulkner and John Becker's *Melindy's Medal* (1946); Eleanor Frances Lattimore's *Bayou Boy* (1946); Florence Crannell Means's *Great Day in the Morning* (1946); Ellen Tarry and Marie Hall Ets's *My Dog Rinty* (1946); Margaret Taylor Burroughs's *Jasper, the Drummin' Boy* (1947); and Phyllis A. Whitney's *Willow Hill* (1947). These books contribute to progress in race relations, Preer concludes, erasing prejudice by linking lives across cultural boundaries. "Stories are read and enjoyed and remembered because they enable us to associate the characters' experiences with our own," she wrote.

This is very much the aim of Phyllis A. Whitney's *Willow Hill*, a novel about the education in race relations of Val, the protagonist. (It is also a novel that recalls Jesse Jackson's *Call Me Charley* in its plot situation, though this novel is aimed at an older audience.) Val is a senior who had anticipated becoming editor of the school newspaper; but Mary Evans, an African American character who has shown better skills and a stronger work ethic, is chosen instead. The choice by the principal has been complicated by the presence of a new housing development for factory workers who will almost all be African American; their children will attend Val's high school. At first angry, Val refuses to work on the paper at all, but she relents when she recognizes that in America there should be equal opportunity for all; it should be "a country where every man could stand beside every other man and be judged on his own merits—not by his religion or the color of his skin" (65). Val is particularly troubled when she sees prejudice infect her schoolmates and many of the townspeople—especially the more powerful ones—who do not want the new development or the presence of a new population to, as they believe, undermine their way of life. "If this housing project is allowed to open right on the edge of town, it's going to affect all of us unpleasantly," says Val's mother in one of the more gentle expressions of race hatred (2). "Why don't they go back to Africa where they came from?," Tony later asks in a more vivid display of hatred (28).

Val finds it difficult to decide where she stands—with her mother and the vocal element of the town who worry about property values, or with her principal, and her friend Judy, and Stephen Reid (a new friend now living with them for a year while his parents are abroad), or with her father, who wonders, "I think America gets a bit mixed up sometimes. Maybe this will be a good chance for some of us to get our thinking straight and find out a couple of things" (39). But as she gets to know Mary Evans and recognizes how repelled she is by the disguised hatred that is taking over, and as she recognizes that Mary's "careful and guarded and vaguely hostile" quality is justified (35), she becomes an ardent champion of the new housing project and of the opportunity for communal living it presents. The rest of the novel plays out the campaign to bring their peers and the townspeople to their position, a campaign that climaxes in the first school basketball game, where Jeff Evans, the only African American player, is accused of throwing the game.

If the plot sounds like a John Tunis novel, it does, in fact, owe much to that writer's handling of minority issues. But now, after the war, there is a new inflection to that handling. Miss Kay is the principal of Val's high school, and during an assembly she sets out the problem: "In the coming weeks Willow High School is going to be faced with a problem in Americanism. How we rise to the challenge, how we meet it, how we solve it, will show just what kind of people we are—not just what kind of Americans, but what kind of world citizens—and that is even more important than being an American" (67). Here, cooperative communal living between people of different cultures is defined as "Americanism"; Americanism, in addition, is defined as a smaller version of world citizenship, where, again, people are called to cooperative communal living. In a novel written only two years after World War II, the author calls for a radical international vision that will affect strongly how America will see its global position: here is affirmed a vision of cooperating cultures where internationalism (not, as during the war, nationalism) comes first.

In the basketball game, Tony, who has been struggling with the competing interests of his father, who is against the housing project, and his own sense that Jeff Evans is a good guy and a good basketball player, causes the loss not because of his own lack of skill or even due to a lack of trying but because of his failure to cooperate. Earlier their coach had predicted, "If we win we'll be showing what the combination of a boy with a brown skin and a boy with a white skin *working together* can accomplish" (196). Tony's failure affects his entire team, especially Jeff, who loses confidence in his own abilities. Once Tony comes to recognize this, he is able to break away from his father's prejudice and move toward an active sense of cooperation. His last words to Jeff are telling: "We didn't do so good today. . . . But I guess that was mostly my fault. I think maybe we're going to climb all over 'em in the next game" (235). The plural pronouns suggest his new orientation and at least begins his reeducation in racial awareness.

The novel is heavily didactic; hardly a page goes by without its sententious moment. Not even the Pledge of Allegiance is allowed to stand without Judy's pointed commentary: "I think this is one time when we ought to stay awake while we say the Pledge to the Flag. Of course that means that some of you may choke on those words if you say them wide-awake. So I think that anybody who doesn't believe in liberty and justice for the other fellow as well as for himself ought to sit down while the rest of us give the Pledge" (203). Still, Whitney would argue that this is exactly what she is about: using a work for young readers to show that race relations in America are a model of what our international citizenship must be. And it is children who will lead the way: "Grown-ups are hopeless," says Judy, "you can't do anything with 'em. But you *can* do something with people our age" (119). Val later agrees: "It's our generation that has to work this out. . . . And it seems as if the only way to do it is by getting together. But we can't get together unless we trust each other" (170). Clearly this is heavy-handed narrative stuff, but it is a serious attempt to work out exactly what Preer had hoped for: a realistic situation with realistic characters trying to come to grips with what America means and is to become, a meaning that is caught up fully with its vision of its international role, a role reflected in its own strong or weak intercultural cooperation.

This was the urgency of children's books after the war: to move toward inclusion by acting as a bridge between cultures within the nation and by creating understanding between cultures in a global sense. It was a call to which American writers, librarians, and publishing markets responded.[4]

Thus, for example, from 1948 to 1955 the John C. Winston publishing company in Philadelphia published its Land of the Free series, aimed broadly at children from nine to fifteen. The series of sixteen books reflected the histories of immigrant groups, particularly the ways in which those groups added to the cultural mix of America, a mission articulated on the back flap: "Each book in this series is an exciting story about a distinct national group that came from another country to find freedom in the new land. Today, America is what those people of many nationalities have made it and are still making it. Each group has brought its own important contribution to the building of a new and vigorous nation." The series editor, Erick Berry, wrote her own *Seven Beaver Skins: A Story of the Dutch in New Amsterdam* (1948) for the series, while well-known authors were recruited as well: Arna Bontemps wrote *Chariot in the Sky: A Story of the Jubilee Singers* (1951); Elizabeth Jane Coatsworth crafted two for the series: *Door to the North: A Saga of Fourteenth Century America* (1950) and *The Last Fort: A Story of the French Voyageurs* (1952); and Florence Crannell Means and Carl Means wrote *The Silver Fleece: A Story of the Spanish in New Mexico* (1950). There were novels of Italians and Japanese in California, of Bohemian glassmakers and Basque sheep herders in Ohio, of Swedes in Minnesota, of the Welsh in Pennsylvania, of Norwegians in Wisconsin, of the Swiss in Oregon, of the Greek sponge fishers of Florida, of the Chinese working the Pacific railways and the Irish working the Erie Canal, of Native Americans, of Scottish fur traders, and of Cornish fishermen in Maine.

Elsie Singmaster's *I Heard of a River: A Story of the Pennsylvania Germans* is typical of the series. Hannes, a Lutheran young man, lives in an exhausted province of Germany; plagued by constant wars, the country can barely support Hannes's family, and the novel opens with his inability to find even a single rabbit that might feed his aging parents. He is described on the first page as "excessively thin, as a boy would be when he had not eaten a full meal for a long time" (1), and he, with the others in his small village, live in hiding from French marauders, who have stolen everything. The only hope is clearly America, which promises freedom and abundance.

Hannes travels to Philadelphia and, along with a group of Mennonites, settles in Pennsylvania near the Susquehanna River. The plot is thin, but Singmaster is not as interested in plot as much as what Hannes's journey means for America. She interrupts the narrative at times to stress this. After Hannes flees, she pictures a discussion between the wealthy despots of Europe and their messengers, who inform them that their people are emigrating. "The noble rulers were presently alarmed. Some had a whip within reach. 'Get after them! Tell them to come back at once!'" (49). But finally the wealthy and powerful are thwarted by those seeking freedom: "'Come along!' they shouted. 'Come with us! We're going to Paradise! Across the sea! Across the sea!'" (54). And, having arrived, the immigrants are given a communal voice: "We are here. We are free. We shall have land. Henceforth we labor for ourselves and our children" (81). The novel ends with an affirmation of the heritage that this immigrant group offers to America: theirs would be the rifles that settled the wilderness, that secured freedom for Protestant worshippers, that contributed to the winning of the Revolution.

Still less could they foresee that German garden would join German garden, and German farm touch German farm until only here and there you would see forests. They could not imagine immense harvests of wheat and oats, of corn and potatoes, carried to Philadelphia and Baltimore in canvas-covered wains, drawn by four or six horses whose collars were hung with chiming bells. It was too soon to dream of millions of pounds of butter or tobacco. They could not know that for decades the crops of no county in the Commonwealth of Pennsylvania, or in the new nation, as yet unthought of, would equal the crops of their county in value. (207)

The novel is an affirmation of the principle that America was a land founded by and composed of an immigrant population—a critical fact for the child reader to encounter as he or she grew into a citizen of the American democracy.

But children's books could also give the child reader an awareness of being a citizen of one world—precisely the call of Wendell Wilkie's enormously popular *One World* (1943), which sold half a million copies in its first month of publication.[5] Wilkie's ardent call was to international unification through the principle of mutual understanding and tolerance—and this call was taken up by the educational establishment. In October 1949 Elizabeth G. Taylor, the principal of Beauvoir School in Washington, DC, opened her article "Toward World Mindedness" with words that affirmed the notion of a single world: "Civilization is in such peril today that but one hope looms upon the horizon—prompt acceptance of the idea that all mankind must unite." In fact, she argued, "the primary function of education in the present crisis is to develop world mindedness . . . through broadening sympathies and sensitivities which come with increased knowledge and through emphasis on similarities among men despite apparent differences." The words are bold, and though she did not cite literature (outside of drama) as a means to accomplish this broadening, others would.

A few months later the NCTE Committee on Intercultural Relations published a series of short articles in the *English Journal*. Each article was entitled "Toward Better Human Relations," and each was designed to suggest a single text that would contribute to internationalism. In January 1950 the committee recommended a book by Eva Knox Evans—whose novels in the 1930s had worked hard at portraying the lives of African American children realistically—entitled *All about Us* (1947): "Here in simple but accurate form is the story of human existence in this world of ours. [Your reader] will chuckle for sure, but he will also be absorbing worth-while attitudes toward human beings." And indeed, the narrator's light tone addresses issues of racial prejudice by dismissing them as "silly." As a human being, the reader has common ancestry with all other people on earth, so Evans asks us, What allows someone to be "snooty," given this common heritage? And as Americans, we dwell in a country that has been formed by a rich inheritance from all nations: "If you ever feel like saying that you hate any of the kinds of people who have come to America, then you must remember that you are saying that you hate America itself. For it would be very queer to like our buildings or our trains, our radios or our books, our movies or our games, the food we eat, the way we dress, while we hate any of the Americans who gave them to us" (89–90). In April the committee suggested Devere Allen's *Above All Nations* (1949). "The book is wholly a picture of many human relationships," the committee wrote somewhat vaguely; it is actually an American version of a British compendium of stories from World War II that show enemies acting humanely toward each other. "Long before the living symbol and evil genius of nazism faced annihilation in the bunkers of Berlin," the foreword to the American edition argued, "still longer before the atom bomb fell on Hiroshima and the conscience of mankind, a group of British writers decided to compile a record of compassionate deeds in the very midst of war—acts frequently by soldiers on the firing line, sometimes by civilians who rose above the battle" (8–9). The overall meaning of the more than two hundred anecdotes is that cultures can live together amicably, even in times of the most acute crisis. And in June, the committee recommended Phyllis Whitney's *Willow Hill* (1947), "about the girls and boys of a high school who achieve a blending of races and nationalities into a fine and complete whole." Each of these books—and their recommendation in the *English Journal*—affirmed Elizabeth G. Taylor's argument that children should be steered toward internationalism as the great hope for the future of America—and, indeed, civilization itself. The NCTE committee believed firmly that this steering could be done with children's books. In the spring of 1950 Marion Belden Cook, an amateur librarian who focused on regional stories, wrote confidently that this was in fact happening: "Today, school children in many nations are being made internationally conscious. . . . Regional stories for boys and girls act as Ambassadors of Goodwill. Through such fiction, children are meeting their contemporaries in other lands, and all are learning that they are young citizens of 'One World.' "

Perhaps, writing during the early 1950s, the writer who best and most succinctly caught the purposes of reading for children during the Cold War years was Ellen Lewis Buell, the children's book review editor of the *New York Times Book Review*. Buell saw that reading could inform about both the nation and the larger world and that it could speak to the development of the sense of democracy in a child—but it also held another purpose:

> The aim of reading is twofold. We hope that children read for their own understanding—understanding of people and the world about them, understanding of their own problems. We hope that they will learn to read with enjoyment so that they will find the enrichment of life which books offer. We also want them to read well so that as they grow up and assume responsibility they can analyze what is going on in the world. In short, they must be able to read in order to vote intelligently, to be good citizens, to govern themselves. We have seen what has happened in countries where books have been banned and burned; we have seen the effects of brainwashing. We must keep alive children's interest in books so that they can acquire a true pleasure in reading for its own sake and in reading intelligently for the sake of the good life.

Reading, Buell insists, affords both understanding and pleasure—which are themselves part of the "good life" that a country that does not ban books can offer. Perhaps it is no small coincidence that the theme for National Children's Book Week for 1952 and 1953 was "Reading Is Fun."[6]

Virginia Lee Burton and Robert McCloskey

The Caldecott Medal for 1943 was awarded to Virginia Lee Burton's *The Little House* (1942). Since travel restrictions on civilians were in place, the American Library Association canceled its annual convention and offered the awards instead at the Hotel Roosevelt in New York City on Flag Day, June 14. There, Anne Carroll Moore called *The Little House* "an honest-to-goodness American picture book," presumably suggesting that there was something distinctly American in either its themes or their portrayal. In her acceptance that night, Burton asserted that the medium of the picture book "is without doubt one of the best possible ways of giving children a true conception of the world they live in," but it was only later that she seemed to articulate what the "true conception" might be. Asked if the theme of the book was our dependence upon the natural world and the simple life for real happiness, Burton replied that she was "quite willing to let this be its message."[1]

Certainly this myth of the rural world is a distinctly American message. Since James Fenimore Cooper's *The Last of the Mohicans* and Nathaniel Hawthorne's *The Scarlet Letter*, American writers have found this a compelling theme, picturing the city as a world of conformity, duress, and debilitation of the soul and body and the world of the forest as that of freedom, individuality, and true and unfettered expression. James Daugherty had used the same themes. But Burton's equivocal reply—not that this elevation of the pastoral was the book's theme but that she was "quite willing to let this be its message"—suggests some complexity, or at least hesitation, about her own sense of the role of the natural world and the simple, happy life in America. It is certainly the case that the urban, complex, fast-paced world of the city in *The Little House* is pictured as dingy and overbearing, blotting out the stars, stultifying and destructive in its effects upon the Little House; the natural world, on the other hand, is pictured as light, happy, filled with play and leisured chores rather than the frenetic and seemingly pointless energy of the city. But it is not the case that Burton wanted in this book to make a statement about the urbanization of America, and if Anne Carroll Moore meant that Burton was crafting a book that participated in the American tradition of distinguishing city and country—to the detriment of the first and elevation of the second—she was wrong, at least in terms of understanding the larger thematic interest that Burton showed in the body of her works. There she did not condemn the progress of new technology; rather, she examined the adaptability of American culture and society in the face of extraordinarily rapid technological progress.[2]

✳ ✳ ✳

For Robert McCloskey, screwing up one's courage to confront societal issues was not the stuff of children's books. Just the opposite. All of his work suggests a refusal to see children's books as dealing explicitly with the immediate contemporary world in the sense that the literature must somehow critique that immediate world—or confront a child with its larger cultural tensions. McCloskey's books are always celebratory of childhood, and celebratory, implicitly, of the nation that allowed children the freedom and space and creativity to play, to wonder, to have childhood adventures while secure in the safety of the family. He would take on neither the Cold War nor the social questions confronting American society in the 1950s. He would instead narrow his perspective to the family by isolating it on islands and in small, supportive communities, suggesting by that isolation its vast strengths; and that would be his answer to the question of the role of children's literature during times of crisis. If James Daugherty wanted to be the poet of the frontiersman, Robert McCloskey would be the poet of the settled family. If Robert Lawson wanted to acclaim American freedom with high historical drama, Robert McCloskey would evoke small, peaceful towns, seemingly apart from social ills, without reference to war. These are the kinds of books (and *Make Way for Ducklings* is a good example), he argued implicitly, that responded to the needs of children.

Together, these two writers and illustrators would create their own small Edens, often bounded and so set apart from the larger society, and ultimately secure—or, at least, mostly secure. But even their insecurities are hints more than stern realities, and if a child reader might wonder if the city will once again come upon the Little House, or if Centerville might one day succumb to the pressures of a commercial America, the optimistic tonalities of the texts assured the reader that somehow the Little House and Homer Price would be fine. They had made it through once; they would again.

✳ ✳ ✳

Even a cursory look at Burton's corpus would support the observation that Burton's principal theme is the elevation of American pastoralism, though the issues of urbanization and its dehumanizing effects are present. *The Little House* does pit the city against the country, with the countryside coming out as the more pleasing of the two in terms of providing happiness. The ending is ambiguous, though: the lights of the city have not been vanquished; they have simply been put in the same position they held at the beginning of the book. But in *Mike Mulligan and His Steam Shovel* (1939) the city is dynamic, filled with tall buildings, which are themselves exciting to watch being built. Mike Mulligan leaves because of new technological progress, not because he disdains the city; and he finds happiness not in the pastoral countryside but in a small town. In *Choo Choo: The Story of a Little Engine Who Ran Away* (1937), the runaway train leaves the comfort and security of his home in the big city for a romp. But the countryside through which he passes—depicted in endpapers that use the same rounded forms as *The Little House*—is represented only as something to go through, not as a site that beckons. And as Choo Choo rushes through the city, and through the suburbs, and finally does come to that countryside, the natural world becomes threatening and forbidding, a place from which he needs to be rescued. When he returns, "back through the big city and back into the train yard where Oley and Archibald were waiting," he resolves not to head out again into the open countryside, choosing instead to remain on his track between the big city and the little town. In *Katy and the Big Snow* (1943) Katy is a snowplow whose purpose and delight is to protect the city of Geoppolis. Much of the pleasure of the book lies in following Katy as she rescues policemen and doctors and postmen and technicians throughout the city, which is pictured geometrically in a large, two-page spread as the penultimate illustration of the book. And in *Maybelle the Cable Car* (1952), Burton celebrates the delights of the city of San Francisco, the book's images of the city clashing strongly with those of *The Little House* both in their lighter tones and in their strong sense of stillness.[3]

While Burton certainly played thematically with American pastoralism, she did not commit to a simple version of that theme, as if to reject the urban for the rural or to equate the rural with the simple and good life. Instead, she pictured an America that was complex, industrial, rapidly changing—a mix of urban and rural. She suggested this even in the endpapers to *The Little House*, where the Little House is pictured half a dozen times on each of three tiers, always on the same small hill. The man on horseback in the first illustration gives way to a man and woman in a carriage, then to a coach and four, then to complex bicycles, then a horseless carriage, then cars and cable cars and trucks and pickups and sleek aerodynamic passenger cars, and finally to another truck, which is carrying a horse. (The progression is not un-interrupted; in one illustration, a car is being towed by a horse because it has broken down, and another car has a flat tire.) The trees between the Little House on the top tier give way to telegraph poles on the second tier, then to electric poles, and then finally, on the bottom, to streetlights. And the landscape behind the house grows crowded first with other houses, then a development, then an apartment building, and finally high-rises. Even the figures change; individuals who had been standing vertically are, by the end, angled to show their newly rapid movement. Through these rapid changes on the endpapers, the Little House remains constant in both expression and appearance; but in the interior illustrations for the narrative, this constancy is not maintained, as the Little House becomes dilapidated and virtually un-recognizable. The tension between these two responses to change sug-gests that American progress and its expressions in technology and ur-ban life are not inherently bad or to be rejected entirely. The question is, How should Americans adapt to this rapid progress and the changes in the American landscape as society moves from a rural world of farms and small towns to a much more urban and industrial society?[4]

In *Suspended Animation*, Nathalie op de Beeck connects Virginia Lee Burton's work to New Deal murals "calling attention to alienated labor and warning of a threat to American community values" (169). More specifically, op de Beeck notes, Burton's books were "trumpeting the concerns of proletarian literature and American ambivalence about the labor economy" (170), an economy that was not hospitable to those who were unable to adapt to changing technologies. Though her books are fascinated with the machine, op de Beeck argues, they simultaneously "urge extreme caution in inventing technology and altering the land-scape too fast" (170). Thus Choo Choo's boredom with a dreary life per-forming the same mindless activities day after day, and Mike Mulligan's horror over the easy dismissal of technologies—and their "de-skilled" (169) operators—that had served faithfully and well in the past, and the Little's House's dilemma when it is overtaken by an urbanization that does not value the landscape or its heritage. Op de Beeck concludes that "Burton's texts attest to a creeping disillusionment in the United States that prior children's books refused at the level of content" (182); like regional murals, they "politicized labor and small-town life" and "sympathetically addressed national ideology and pressing personal concerns" (180). In this, they were commenting upon public life like public art, though, op de Beeck notes, they themselves were "privately held commodities" (180).

Though it is tempting to see Burton's answer to the question of how Americans might adapt to change in the retreat of *The Little House* or the simple and comfortable conclusion to *Mike Mulligan and His Steam Shovel*, Burton does not allow any simple or comfortable answer. *Mike Mulligan and His Steam Shovel* opens with a problem: advances in technology have made the steam shovel Mary Anne obsolete, though Mike and Mary Anne together have worked hard to cut canals and passes through mountains and to straighten curves for highways and to smooth fields for airports and to dig cellars for high buildings. But "Progress" is not empathetic, and when new technologies come along, steam shovels are junked. When Mike Mulligan and Mary Anne choose to leave the city for Popperville, they are not rejecting the pace and excitement of the urban world—they had been enriched and empowered by both the everyday pace of business and the larger pace of technological progress. Instead, they are adapting to changes in that world by looking for a new place and way to use Mary Anne's technology. They choose the sedate life of the small, anachronistic rural town, pictured in one spread as diametrically opposed to the city that stands on the extreme left side of the spread—with canals and highways and airports and tall buildings. In Popperville there are old cars, farm wagons, and horse-drawn carriages coexisting with that other city world yet far removed from it. In this welter, Mike and Mary Anne choose to adapt and thus become one more element from the past that is preserved for its value and goodness—perhaps for its humanity, more than anything else.

So once the contest is over and Mary Anne has indeed dug the cellar, and once the decision is made to make Mike Mulligan the town hall janitor and Mary Anne its furnace, there is a general air of contentment: "So it was decided, and everybody was happy." Mike Mulligan and Mary Anne have found a new place—just like the Little House—and Popperville willingly accepts the entrance of Mary Anne's technological prowess. But Mary Anne and Mike Mulligan are now sedentary—quite different from their old life. The ending is at least a bit melancholy and even incomplete, as in *The Little House*. As op de Beeck notes, "Burton's conclusions do not provide absolute closure, even if they provide their sympathetic heroes with temporary contentment" (40). Though it may seem that in this ending Burton has elevated the small town over the city and the old-fashioned over the technically progressive, there is no active rejection of the city because it is a city; neither does Burton condemn progress itself—to which Mike Mulligan and Mary Anne had themselves contributed. This is a book about an acceptance of the value of the past and a recognition of its usefulness and pleasures, not about rejecting technology or progress, and that acceptance may represent the most closure the story will give.

In fact, Burton takes great pleasure in technology. In *Mike Mulligan and His Steam Shovel*, she devotes the endpapers to labeling the individual parts of Mary Anne so that a child reader can see the technical aspects of her makeup. In *Katy and the Big Snow* Burton circles the first image of Katy with small images of the machine's prowess, including not only her varied accoutrements—the snowplow, the bulldozer, the hydraulic lift, the diesel engine, and the multiple speeds at which she can travel forward and backward—but also fifty-five horses to suggest her capabilities and strength. Two pages later, Burton employs the same technique to show all the many machines that the Highway Department of Geoppolis uses to build and service its roads. Nowhere is it suggested that the machines or the progress that produced them is problematic.[5]

In fact, *Katy and the Big Snow* might be said to be a hymn of praise to the machine. The first three spreads are profiles of Katy wearing different implements—a bulldozer and snowplow. This then leads into her role in the Geoppolis Highway Department, where she is by far the strongest of the trucks—once even pulling the steamroller out of a pond. The largest part of the book focuses on the Big Snow, in which Katy must deal with snow that has reached the second stories of houses —here, when the text announces that everything has stopped, Katy is pictured against an entirely white background, and the text for the page in which she appears bears only her name. She plows out the entire city, rescuing the chief of police, the postmaster, the telephone workers, the Water Department workers, the doctor, the fire chief, and even a plane signaling for help. In the end, Katy leads a parade of those she has rescued through the high snow, and the text follows the trail as it goes back and forth across the page: "Then after she had found the broken down truck plows she started home. The Fire Department had put out the fire. The doctor had saved his patient. The Water Department had repaired the main. The telephone and electricity were on. The mail could go through. And the police could protect the city. Thanks to what Katy did." Here is technology at the service of humanity, triumphing over the elements; nowhere does Burton suggest that we go back to horses and rolling the roads. This is progress in its best manifestation.

And yet, the presence of change itself certainly poses problems in Burton's books. In *Mike Mulligan and His Steam Shovel* the progression of technology causes Mary Anne's loss of the city. In *Maybelle the Cable Car* the new buses threaten to displace the cable cars. And in *The Little House* the growth of the city envelops the little house and cuts her off from the natural world she loves. There is no promise of constancy. The characters must adapt to change and new circumstances.

In the biographical article written to accompany the publication of Burton's Caldecott Award acceptance speech, her editor, Grace Allen Hogarth, wrote that when Burton began to wonder if her work was appropriate during a war, given that it did not seem to contribute to the war effort, Hogarth noted that her book "reaffirm[s] the realities, the peace and security of a little child's world"—but it actually does not do that at all, especially if it is compared to the works of Robert McCloskey. In *The Little House* the permanence, stability, and security of the Little House's world are completely undone, and there is no sense at the end that that undoing might not happen all over again sometime; in fact, since the book is about the passage of time, the ending seems to suggest that the story will indeed happen all over again. The reassurance comes only with the previous experience of survival.

The thematic element here is change itself—which was the state of midcentury America and is the state of childhood as well, despite any desire for permanence. Change is something that is both desirable and frightening, and Burton recognized the dual impulses in children; she placed them in an American scene that was undergoing them as well. What happens when society and culture shift? What happens when the nation shifts from a rural to an urban culture? What happens when technological progress is remarkably rapid? What happens when the old-fashioned can simply be discarded? How does the child—and the country—handle change?

Here again, it is the ending to *Mike Mulligan and His Steam Shovel* that tempts with an easy answer: in the face of change, one simply adapts. Mike Mulligan takes Mary Anne out of the city to find new work—and Mike Mulligan does so, though in that process he must adjust to new needs and new patterns. Mary Anne becomes a furnace rather than a steam shovel, and the pleasures of work in faraway roads and canals are given over in favor of the sedentary pleasures of stories and pies in a small town. There is stress, followed by adaptation and survival.

But this answer and vision of *Mike Mulligan and His Steam Shovel* seems coldly Darwinian and misses entirely one of the central responses to change in Burton's books: that the growth and adaptation that are necessitated through change can be mitigated—though not denied—through an empathetic valuing of the past. That is, Burton's vision of America is not that of a country that rejects progress, it is that of a country that couples progress with a firm, even tenacious grip on that which is good and lovely and honorable in its history. Mike Mulligan could have done to Mary Anne what all the other drivers had done to their steam shovels: thrown her into the dump and chosen a newer, stronger machine. But he doesn't, because he cannot bear doing so. In the illustration for this scene, Mary Anne looks at the discarded machines with horror, for this might be her fate. But Mike Mulligan covers his eyes in sorrow over their fate and holds out his arm to show that this will never be Mary Anne's end. His instinctive response to the change in the world is one of keeping hold of what has served him so long and so lovingly. They will go together to find a new place, and they will grow into it together. Here, in looking at the dual worlds of childhood and the changing nation, Burton found common ground.

In *Maybelle the Cable Car* Burton included a foreword—the only one that she wrote for her picture books about machines—in which she chronicled the birth and development of the cable car companies. Following the earthquake and fire of 1906, she wrote, San Francisco changed, eliminating many of its cable cars for streetcars and gasoline buses. This was called "Progress," the quotation marks being hers, suggesting that she did not share in the understanding that change necessarily meant progress, if progress was to be understood in terms larger than mere technology. Burton begins the story with an emphasis on stability: "Born in San Francisco long ago / they had watched their City change and grow, / the new come in and the old go out / while they remained the same." The cable cars remember the past, "when the City was small / when everyone knew everyone else / and nobody hurried and nobody worried." But they also recognize the changes that have come upon them: "Now the streets were crowded with traffic / and everyone hurried and seemed to be worried. / Electric trolleys and gasoline buses had / replaced almost all of the old family lines." In short, Maybelle faces precisely the same situation that Mary Anne faces: she is becoming technologically obsolete.

However, Maybelle has more than just a single character that refuses to see her junked. Burton's own description of the book was a "history of the cable car and how the people of San Francisco prevented its demise," and here the emphasis is on the culture's responsibility for the preservation of its past.[6] So while Big Bill the bus taunts Maybelle that "you're too old and out of date / much too slow and can't be safe," the people of San Francisco recognize another quality in Maybelle that makes her more valuable: she is the most recognizable symbol of the city. That is, her historical presence is more important than her current economic or technological status. The City Fathers first reject this notion as "just sentimental talk," but the citizens of the city vote against them—even as Big Bill himself comes to recognize that, in the end, the cable car is more effective at negotiating the steep hills of San Francisco than he is.

Maybelle the Cable Car is the last of Burton's machine-oriented picture books and in some ways her least effective; she seems hard-pressed to decide if she wants to craft a nonfiction book about the cable cars of San Francisco or a tale of an individual car that bravely struggles against forces much larger than herself—as Mike Mulligan and Mary Anne struggle against unremitting "Progress." But the book brings together themes that Burton had used in all of her machine-oriented picture books. When the news comes that the cable cars are to be discontinued, the people of San Francisco mourn. "Some people said, 'Too bad . . . / Hate to see them go . . . Progress, I suppose.' / Others sighed and said, 'We'll miss them . . . What a pity / for our City to lose her cable cars . . . We'll be like any other city.'" Must a cable car succumb to such progress? Must a Little House succumb to the progression of the city? Must Mary Anne give way to the newer, more powerful diesel shovels? What can be cherished and kept?

Burton rejects a notion of progress that necessitates the oblivion of the past. Mary Anne will find her new place providing a new function in a new world. The Little House will find a new hill, though she will still live within sight of the city lights. (Burton actually drew the story about her own house, once set on a quiet road that became a noisy highway; the house was then moved back from the road to a small hill in an apple orchard.) And Maybelle the cable car will find her place alongside Big Bill the bus, doing work appropriate to her and representing the city's distinctive past. Here, what has gone before is incorporated into the new.

And certainly this is the strongest message of *The Little House*: the past need not be discarded in the face of present progress, particular-

All the other steam shovels were being sold for junk,
or left out in old gravel pits to rust and fall apart.
Mike loved Mary Anne.   He couldn't do that to her.

Illustration from *Mike Mulligan and His Steam Shovel* by Virginia Lee Burton.

ly when that progress is not nearly so benign as it is in *Katy and the Big Snow*. The Little House begins with curiosity: "The Little House was curious about the city and wondered what it would be like to live there." The accompanying illustration shows a benign pastoral world, with rounded hills and rounded trees and a barn and a round pond—scenes that are repeated for several spreads. But the comfortable roundness of those images is disturbed by the straight lines of the road that barges directly through them, a straightness that is accentuated by the angular suburban houses and, later, by the very strongly vertical lines of the tenements and high-rises. By this time, the reader recognizes that the place in which the Little House had first been set has disappeared and that her presence there represents a disjunction. "No one noticed the Little House any more. They hurried by without a glance."

When the strong verticals threaten to entirely subdue the Little House—and when the natural world, the sky, the seasons that had surrounded her and marked the passage of time are virtually, from her point of view, obliterated—she is finally found again by a descendant of her builder: "That Little House looks just like the Little House that my grandmother lived in when she was a little girl, only *that* Little House was way out in the county on a hill covered with daisies and apple trees growing around." The descendant does not condemn the encroaching city but recognizes the appropriateness of place. So, on the next spread, all the pace and business of the city are stilled as the Little House is removed from the strong verticals and then reinstated within the same curving landscape in which she had been built. What is good from the past has been preserved and given its rightful place—just as Maybelle and Mary Anne had found their appropriate places.

Burton's Caldecott acceptance speech for *The Little House* deals principally with elements of design, and indeed her conclusion is a plea for more beautifully designed books within the education market. But she opens that conclusion with an affirmation that reflects her interest in progress. For children, she writes, "books are important means of advancing to a better world, for the future lies to some extent in the hands of the children of today. Tomorrow their ideas and their tastes will be the ones that count." Progress is not to be feared, she seems to say, but it is to be placed in context and understood. Her books are attempts to understand how the present might come to live amicably with the rapidly changing world. There can be no denial that there will be change. There is certainly the possibility that there will be loss with change. But the real hope of Burton's books is that there can be growth and adaptation with change and a valuing of the past.

✳ ✳ ✳

As Anne Carroll Moore had seen Burton's work as archetypally American, so James Daugherty saw Robert McCloskey's work as distinctly American as well. Commenting in *Horn Book* on the publication of *Homer Price* in 1943, Daugherty welcomed Homer to "Tom Sawyer's gang, that immortal and formidable band of boys of American fiction." The book represented "American comic genius in its top form," and the stories were so "woven into the daily life of the Mid-Western small town as to seem as honest-to-goodness true as the front page of the *Westport Town Crier*." In fact, Daugherty suggested, McCloskey's work should be distinctly identified with the equalities that democracy brings: "It is the true comedy of democracy in the great American tradition.... It is America laughing at itself with a broad and genial humanity, without bitterness or sourness or sophistication." He concluded that to read *Homer Price* is to feel in the end that "the salt and character, the humanities and individualism of Our Town remain triumphant and that democracy will keep her rendezvous with destiny, musical mousetraps, and all."

Daugherty sees in McCloskey's work the equalizing, democratizing effects of comedy. That is the world of Robert McCloskey. Though the 1940s and 1950s were troubled with the Cold War and with deep splits in the national understanding of how America would handle questions of differences determined by race and ethnicity and gender and economics, McCloskey maintained his "comedy of democracy," comedy understood as Daugherty defined it, in the sense of being humorous and denting the high hat, but also comedy in the more classical sense, of moving toward a happy and fulfilled communal ending. To move toward that ending, McCloskey implicitly argued that childhood needed to start in a place of safety and security so that children could be nourished by the love of home and community.

Though McCloskey was unwilling to take on explicitly the most dangerous and divisive issues of the 1940s and 1950s, and though his picture books presented a world innocent of those issues, with plotlines that seem whimsical and nostalgic to a contemporary reader, he did raise questions about the 1950s world he saw around him, but the questions that he raised were aesthetic, not political. In his stories about Homer Price and his hometown of Centerburg—the name itself suggestive of McCloskey's vision of what lay at the center of American strength and character—McCloskey elevated the world of Centerburg into an almost mythic vision of contemporary small-town America, as safe and secure as any island would be in his picture books. But in *Homer Price* and *Centerburg Tales*, texts for older readers, McCloskey also satirized, though very gently, social forces that threatened the world of Centerburg with their callousness and vanity and empowerment of economic necessity over individual experience. What McCloskey saw as a threat to the American experience of Centerburg was not the atomic bomb but tendencies in the American character itself.

✳ ✳ ✳

The America of Robert McCloskey is not the dangerous frontier; it is the settled lowlands, where families are well housed and well fed and where children are nourished by the affirmations of their parents and the adult communities around them. It is an America that is secure and confident. It is a world that can hardly imagine real trouble or danger on the horizon. This was true whether McCloskey placed his story on an isolated hillside—as in *Blueberries for Sal* (1948)—or on an off-shore island—as in *One Morning in Maine* (1952) and *Time of Wonder* (1957)— or in a small town—as in *Lentil* (1940) and his later collections of stories, *Homer Price* (1943) and *Centerburg Tales* (1951). In McCloskey's work the family life, as depicted in an isolated and purposefully narrowed world apart from the urban rush, is at the very center of life in America. The world of his books is a world set apart from the public experience. (Aside from Lentil, none of his child characters are pictured in school.) Even his *Make Way for Ducklings* (1941), though set in the city of Boston, is really about family life on two small islands, in which the ducklings are secure from the bicycles and cars that are the threatening elements of the narrative. In McCloskey's America, parents are present, and they keep their promises: Mr. Mallard meets his ducklings "just as he had promised." There may be storms, but Father is there to prepare the island, pull closed the door, and keep out the wind and salt spray, while Mother is there to sing and to hold. Nothing really terrible happens—Sal might lose a tooth, but Father is there to occupy her with the routines of the day. There may be cranky adults who threaten the peace and tranquility of the small midwestern town, but there is the young boy whose music restores, literally, the town's harmony, so that even the town crank is brought into a general glee and sense of community. Childhood in McCloskey's world is indeed a time of wonder, and it is secure, for "one pair of eyes is watching over all." In terms of the life of the child, the rural and small-town world of America is Edenic, full of potentiality and beauty, ideal for the growing child. As Seth Lerer expresses it, "Robert McCloskey's books illuminate the ways in which style is shaped and governed by the love of family" (301).

Robert McCloskey's first picture book, *Lentil*, opens and closes with endpapers that picture the small town of Alto, Ohio. The picture is dominated by a large church in the foreground. There are only three dozen or so houses in the entire town, a few stores, a park with the Soldiers and Sailors Monument, and two or three larger brick buildings to suggest municipal centers. There is still a working farm at the town's outskirts. But what is remarkable about the town—and foreshadows McCloskey's later material—is its isolation. The endpapers picture the town as more than half surrounded by a bending river, and though there is a railroad bridge in the distance, the only way to get to the other side of the river is a covered bridge, anachronistic even in 1940. Alto is virtually an island—and certainly, as it was first published in May 1940, it is an island of cohesion and peace and calm in a world at war, insulated from shifting cultural pressures.

The title character of *Lentil* leads a small-town, Tom Sawyerish life, though he is a character who is much tamer than Tom Sawyer ever thought of being. His only real problem is that he cannot sing—and this is solved early in the book with his purchase of a harmonica. Once Lentil has learned how to play—by practicing while sitting in his antique bathtub—McCloskey starts him on a virtual tour of the town, as, playing, Lentil walks down Vine Street past Colonel Carter's house (in one spread), past the drugstore and barbershop and library (a second spread), through the Carter Memorial Park (a third spread), and down a long and wide alley to school (a fourth spread). The tour that McCloskey sets for the reader is designed to make a spectacle of an idyllic mid-American town, where boys still go to school barefoot, and dogs roam the streets, and everyone knows everyone, and parades honor the town's most important citizen.

Though Lentil's family is never shown, life here is as secure as it will be on the islands of *One Morning in Maine* and *Time of Wonder*. Even the principal narrative crisis is a small one: Old Sneep, jealous of the attention paid to the returning Colonel Carter, climbs up on the railroad station roof and sucks on a lemon to prevent the band members from playing their instruments at the welcoming ceremony. (Old Sneep knows that when the musicians look up and see him puckering his lips, they'll pucker too and be unable to blow into their instruments.) Homer, of course, saves the day because he can play his harmonica, and the anger of Colonel Carter at what he initially sees as a poor reception and the ill will of the jealous Sneep dissolves in a general sense of celebration: "They marched to the colonel's house and paraded through the gate and onto the front lawn. The mayor's committee served ice cream cones to all the citizens and Colonel Carter made a speech saying how happy he was about such a fine welcome and how happy he was to be home again. When he said that he was going to build a new hospital for the town of Alto, everybody was happy—even Old Sneep!" Celebration overwhelms bitterness, and irritation gives way to generosity, all in the context of the American small-town experience.

Despite the fact that the book caricatures Colonel Carter as the stereotypical Wall Street tycoon, with striped pants, top hat, formal suit coat, bald head, and large belly, McCloskey is not interested in questions of economic power or privilege in *Lentil*. Colonel Carter is not skewered for his flaunted wealth any more than the mayor is skewered for his fawning, or Old Sneep is skewered for his grouchiness. McCloskey is instead interested in portraying a world preserved for children, a world preserved from the seemingly unsolvable global affairs of war. The last spread, which pictures Lentil standing in front of the construction site for the promised hospital, has a hopeful text: "So you never can tell what will happen when you learn to play the harmonica." Lentil has provided a simple, easy, and boyish solution for a simple, easy problem that arose out of small and petty feelings. It is a crisis and solution that fit the size of this isolated and idyllic American town. And that, suggests McCloskey, is about as far as a children's book should go.

In his second picture book, *Make Way for Ducklings* (1941), Robert McCloskey set out more fully and pointedly the largest theme of his picture books: security in the context of the family life. *Lentil* had pictured security within the community of the small town, but each of McCloskey's books beginning in 1941 focused on the secure life of the child within the family. In *Make Way for Ducklings*, McCloskey began to explore what that family life was like, and though he would vary the settings of this theme, the life that he would picture in a family of mallards would remain essentially unchanged through his last book to deal with a family, *Time of Wonder* (1957).

Make Way for Ducklings opens with the two mallard parents searching for the right place to build a nest; the opening spread shows them flying over a landscape and small town that look not unlike the Ohio landscape of *Lentil*. Still, this landscape is rejected, since "every time Mr. Mallard saw what looked like a nice place, Mrs. Mallard said it was no good. There were sure to be foxes in the woods or turtles in the water, and she was not going to raise a family where there might be foxes or turtles. So they flew on and on." Eventually they come to Boston, a landscape quite different from that of *Lentil*, and here they find an island in the Public Garden, establishing fixedly the secure island motif that McCloskey would use again and again. There are no foxes or turtles here, but there is a problem with bicycles, and so off they go to search again. They fly over the State House (in a spread that shows the very same perspective that a short time later would lead Massachusetts to paint the bright golden dome of that building black to confuse German bombers should they ever approach the city), over Louisburg Square, and over the Charles River. They finally settle on an island in that river that is secure from the bicycles but close enough to the Public Garden to benefit from the peanuts that are tossed to them from the swan boats. There they build their nest and sometimes swim across to meet Michael the policeman, who also feeds them peanuts.

McCloskey has spent almost half of his picture book to get to this point, which may seem an inordinate amount of space. But McCloskey is working to establish the nature of these two parents, who use great care and foresight to find exactly the right context for their ducklings—a place that is secure, and a place with adequate food. Those concerns—and the familial relationships that McCloskey works hard to establish—dominate the story once the ducklings are hatched. In the first spread that shows them all, Mr. and Mrs. Mallard tower atop their eight ducklings. Two of the ducklings seem aware of the reader's presence, looking directly out from the page. Of those, one is behind a clump of higher grass near Mr. Mallard; the other is beneath Mrs. Mallard. It is as though the mallards can provide security even from the intrusive presence of the reader.

When Mr. Mallard leaves, he promises to meet them back in the Public Garden, and Mrs. Mallard goes about the business of teaching her ducklings the obedience and skills necessary for survival. She teaches them to swim. (Again, in this spread, the one duckling that is aware of the reader hides behind Mrs. Mallard.) "She taught them to walk in a line, to come when they were called, and to keep a safe distance from bikes and scooters and other things with wheels." So when they head to the Public Garden at the appointed time, they are well trained. But even well-trained ducklings find it hard to cross Massachusetts Avenue, and here the friendships that the parent mallards had established earlier come into play, as Michael and four other policemen clear the way for the ducklings to make their way to the Public Garden.

The actions of these policemen, and the way in which the community responds to the needs of the ducklings, recalls the safe community of Alto, Ohio, that McCloskey had pictured in *Lentil*.

When the ducklings do reach the Public Garden, they move to the climax of the book and to a line that is suggestive of McCloskey's vision of the secure world of the family that he wants to depict: "When they reached the pond and swam across to the little island, there was Mr. Mallard waiting for them, just as he had promised." This is a line that could be repeated in most of McCloskey's books, where parents keep promises. In *Make Way for Ducklings*, McCloskey is not interested in critiquing gender roles, or in asking why Mr. Mallard left the children to the care of their mother, or in inquiring what Mr. Mallard was doing in his river exploration. He is interested in creating an image of the family that is concerned about its children and utterly dependable. In fact, in the next spread, McCloskey switches his tense to suggest the perennial care that the parents will provide: "The ducklings liked the new island so much that they decided to live there. All day long they follow the swan boats and eat peanuts. And when night falls they swim to their little island and go to sleep." In both of the spreads showing the ducklings heading to their island, McCloskey pictures the children following their mother up on to the shore, where the father waits for them. In the spread showing the ducklings following the swan boats, McCloskey shows one parent in the midst of the ducklings and the other swimming along behind them all, gathering up stragglers.

The Maine books, written and illustrated soon after World War II had ended, continue to evoke a world of enormous security and hominess, a world where it is almost impossible to imagine anything bad happening—this at a time when the adult world, in the midst of the Cold War, was not finding it hard at all to imagine something quite bad happening. In *Blueberries for Sal*, for example, the first of the Maine books, McCloskey creates a narrative situation that would seem, on a bald summary of it, to be quite threatening: a young girl out picking blueberries gets separated from her mother and encounters a bear searching for her own lost cub. It is not hard to imagine a situation in which Little Sal gets, well, mauled. But in the secure world of Robert McCloskey, this possibility never comes to mind, and he works hard to keep it at bay—not least by beginning and closing the book with the same endpapers, showing Little Sal and her mother already in the kitchen, canning the berries that, in the narrative, they have not yet picked.

Though McCloskey does not use the image of a secure island in *Blueberries for Sal*, as he had seven years earlier in *Make Way for Ducklings*, he does create a secure and isolated world in the kitchen of the endpapers. McCloskey pictures a world that in 1948 was already anachronistic, as he had in the endpapers of *Lentil*. The wonderfully elaborate coal stove on which the berries are being canned is from an earlier generation (actually from McCloskey's mother-in-law, Ruth Sawyer); in fact, the entire practice of canning fruit would seem old-fashioned to a post-war generation coming back to the expanding world of the suburban supermarket. But here the world of Sal and her mother seems wonderfully isolated and resourceful. Outside the windows—geraniums on the sills—the hills roll gently to tall pines, and only two houses show way off in the distance. Inside there is a sense of self-sufficiency and independence as well as the fecundity of a well-stocked kitchen. The two kittens looking up at Sal, who is playing more than helping in the canning business, add to a scene of domestic fullness and security.

But even the world that McCloskey pictures outside the kitchen is secure. Blueberry Hill is not bounded by water, and yet it is still a geographical entity to itself; there is no sense that Sal will really get lost here, because she stays on the hill. The natural landscape that McCloskey pictures echoes the sense of security and comfort. The darkness of the pines is always silhouetted far in the background; Sal never wanders near them to get lost in their shadows. The slope of the hill itself, which McCloskey uses to show that Little Sal and her mother, and Little Bear and her mother, are coming from opposite sides of the hill, is soft and smooth, drawn often with open strokes and even erased by the leaves of the blueberry bushes.

The landscape keeps all of the characters close and safe. Sal can be out of sight, but once her mother starts to look for her, "she hadn't gone very far before she heard a *kuplink! kuplank! kuplunk!*" (51). Similarly, Little Bear's mother, once she begins to search for her child, "had not hunted very long before she heard a hustling sound that stopped now and then to munch and swallow. She knew just what made that kind of a noise" (52). Neither of the two child figures—Little Bear and Little Sal—is ever frightened during this narrative, though both mothers are frightened when they cannot see their children. But even here, McCloskey reassures. Once the children get separated from their parents, McCloskey changes his gaze and shows a larger perspective: he draws back and illustrates a double-page spread of the hill in which the reader can see not only landmarks from previous pages but the real closeness of all four characters as well. Little Sal truly is only a short way away from her mother. And even after the encounter with the bear, Little Sal's mother does not flee the hill; after finding her daughter, she continues to pick casually on the way to the car. Perhaps this seems an unrealistic note, yet for the reader, the bear is actually Little Bear's mother, and therefore not a threat—as the child reader readily perceives. The book ends with another double-page spread, with both sets of characters having changed sides on the hill and Sal following her mother back to the car, "picking berries all the way" (55). After this, the endpaper is repeated, with the reader (or, at least, the first-time reader) comprehending more fully what Little Sal and her mother are about and with the kitchen affirmed even more strongly as a place of isolated security.

In *One Morning in Maine* that security is even more pronounced. Here Sal, now older, and Jane walk along the coast in the high grass of their island. The illustration could be threatening and even disorienting because the viewer cannot see the shoreline. The high grass that extends above Jane's waist gives way dramatically to blue water—and water troubled by the wind that streaks strongly across it, blowing out the two girls' hair. There is no sight of the horizontal shoreline to provide the reader with stability, and it seems as if the water must be about to engulf them. But the two girls, hand in hand, are absolutely at peace; each holds flowers—which are also being blown by the wind. There is really no danger here at all; it lies only in the misperception of the reader, which is corrected by the benign expressions and stances of the two characters.

As in *Blueberries for Sal*, McCloskey's focus is on his own family, and, once again, this is a story about an isolated and safe place, about the security provided by parents, and about food. The action of the narrative is precipitated by Sal's loss of a tooth on the day that she is to go into Buck's Harbor with her father. With her mother's reassurances— "Why, Sal . . . that's nothing to worry about. That means that today you've become a big girl" (12)—she heads across the island to find her father and to help dig clams, passing, on the way, a fish hawk feeding its babies, and a loon, a seal, and seagulls, and wondering if all of these animals also lose their teeth. And when she finds her father, he is equally reassuring and affirming, echoing her mother's words: "You're growing into a big girl when you get a loose tooth!" (30). The island world here is again very secure and safe, filled with natural wonders that entrance a child who is closely watched over by benevolent parents.

When Sal drops her tooth into the pebbles and sand, she is again affirmed by her father, and, her spirits renewed, she replaces the lost tooth with a gull feather, around which she creates a story—"Maybe sea gulls put dropped-out feathers under their pillows and wish secret wishes" (42)—and she is again affirmed by her father. She brings this feather to Buck's Harbor, promising that she will take care of Jane: "I'm a big girl and I can watch so she doesn't tumble into the water" (44), echoing her parents' description of her. Having left the clams with Mother, they row into Buck's Harbor, where the community of assorted friends is equally affirming and careful of them; one Mr. Condon fixes the outboard motor, and the other Mr. Condon offers the girls ice cream cones—the small, culturally cohesive community is itself another island. They return home powered by the new engine and with groceries, and looking forward to their mother's lunch—a hope that is set in all uppercase letters: "CLAM CHOWDER FOR LUNCH!" (64).

The soft strokes that mark all of the illustrations affirm the endpapers' sense of security in this world; the narrative is really quite tame, and little action enters in at all. The largest narrative crises are the loss of Sal's tooth (which leads to the affirmation of her growing maturity) and the problem with the motor (which leads to a demonstration of their father's power and competencies as he rows across the bay into town). But these crises are, in the end, small narrative problems, easily overcome. *One Morning in Maine*, as its title suggests, is much more about an archetypal day on a Maine island with a family that is supportive of each other, a support offered through gesture and word, through food, through engagement with a supportive community, and through a purposeful connection with the natural world that the parents offer to their girls.

Which leads strongly to *Time of Wonder*, a book that elevates all of these qualities and that stands as McCloskey's finest statement of the nature of America that he presents in a picture-book mode. As in *One Morning in Maine*, McCloskey wants to develop the experience of living on a Maine island, and the images repeatedly stress childhood wonder with the natural world. The book invites the reader into that world through the manipulation of point of view, as McCloskey begins with an overhead illustration of Penobscot Bay, closes in the next spread to "your island," and moves in the third spread to "IT'S RAINING ON YOU!" (10). The use of the second person allows McCloskey's narrator to address two simultaneous audiences: the two girls of the book (who are McCloskey's own daughters, Sal and Jane again) and the reader. In fact, throughout the book, McCloskey merges these two audiences and perspectives. In the next four spreads, for example, he moves from a foggy morning at the water's edge—drawn in white and pale greens—to a slightly more distinct scene in the woods, to a yellowing of the fog, and finally to a very clear and sharp blue day, where the greens have been dispatched to a faraway horizon, and the yellow has been incorporated into the long grass. The next spread is then utterly dominated by bright blues—that of the sky and of the ocean. Here, the reader progresses through the same stages of the brightening day as the characters.

Though here more than in any other book McCloskey is setting his narrative on a secure island, it is not isolated. Friends come over to play on the split rocks of the shore. Mr. Billings flies over and dips his wings. Later, the family goes in to Buck's Harbor—again for supplies—though there is none of the familiar conversation of *One Morning in Maine*, because a storm is coming, and everyone is getting ready. After that storm has uprooted a large tree, the children find an Indian shell heap, and there "you realize that you are standing on a place where Indian children stood before the coming of white men" (56)—a community gone now but still with a sense of connection.

But all of these referenced communities are tangential to the dominant community of the family, which, as in *Make Way for Ducklings* and all of the Maine books, is at the center of the story, providing a context within which there is safety and provision. When the storm finally does hit, there has been a great deal of preparation: "Home on the island, you pull in the sailboat, chain the motorboat fast to its mooring, pull the rowboats high off the beach" (40). Later, you "stack the groceries on kitchen shelves. Bring in wood to build a fire. Fill the generator with gas. Then take one last careful look, while the calm sea pauses at dead low water" (42). The short sentences work both as directions and as narrative description of action, suggesting again the dual audience of the narrator. The accompanying illustration for these short sentences shows the family's house on the side of the spread, dark against the dark island but with a single bright yellow light on, the only bright color in the spread. This is repeated in the spread for the next page, when the storm hits—but the bright yellow light, in the same place, remains solid against the powerful horizontal lines of the water flashing across the illustration. And when the next spread shows an interior image, with those same horizontal lines pushing through the room as the storm slams open the door, McCloskey pictures Father (himself) shoving back: "Father pushes and strains to close and bolt out the storm" (46). Then, while Father stuffs dishtowels into the window sills to keep out the salt spray, Mother reads and sings with the two girls—"You are glad it is a story you have often heard before" (48)—until the storm is over, and the tide is humming peacefully and rhythmically against the rocks. The final spread in the storm sequence is further removed from the island than the earlier spreads, but, once again, it shows the dark house against the dark island, with the single bright yellow light shining. Above it, circles of moonlight shine down upon the house and its family beneficently, recalling the earlier assertion that the girls can see the reflections of the stars in the water: "In the quiet of the night one hundred pairs of eyes are watching you, while one pair of eyes is watching over all" (28). As in *Make Way for Ducklings*, parents watch over children in a world that might be dangerous outside but that, in the home, is absolutely secure, blessed by the presence of parents and the overarching one pair of eyes.

The world of McCloskey's Homer Price stories—written for older readers—is not so straightforward. On one level, the world of Centerburg is still a place where childhood is a time of wonder, where marvelous adventures come Homer's way, where he can enjoy the pleasures of the tall tale, where there is a close community of the extended family, and where the child can take up the delights of what McCloskey called "comfortable clutter" as Homer pursues mechanical hobbies and works at childhood jobs around town.[7] But the wonder here is muted; the small town provides none of the natural beauty that *One Morning in Maine* and *Time of Wonder* celebrate. And though Homer remains in a secure small-town world, the security has none of the closeness of the familial scenes that dominate the Maine books; here, Homer's parents are virtually absent, and the adults that he does encounter in Centerburg are odd and bumbling and quirky. And where McCloskey had stepped back from cultural issues that the 1940s and 1950s presented to America, in the Centerburg stories McCloskey will take on questions of cultural aesthetics and their effects upon American society.

Homer Price and *Centerburg Tales* are both about a young and observant midwestern boy who lives, literally, at the center of the country, in Centerburg. Both books were part of a grouping of popular books in the 1940s and 1950s about boys living life in an idyllic, usually rural area or small town—a world that is mostly male, almost exclusively white, very safe, and innocently adventurous. Other works that participated in this world include Keith Robertson's Henry Reed series—begun with *Henry Reed, Inc.* (1958), and illustrated by Robert McCloskey; Hazel Wilson's Herbert series—begun with *Herbert* (1942), whose title character "lived in a town in the Middle West" (4) while having adventures that are almost folkloric; and Beverly Cleary's Henry Huggins series—begun with *Henry Huggins* (1950), which opens with a title page depicting Henry and his dog, Ribsy, strolling down Klickitat Street. Taken together, these books, published during wartime and into the

Cold War period, reflect a remarkably uniform (even to the alliterative names) vision of childhood set in an America that seems secure and assured, given a world that pictured itself on the brink of atomic war. None of the series explicitly engaged the social issues of the period.[8]

In this regard, these novels competed directly with Lois Lenski's vision of childhood as presented in her regional books, in which the child character is caught up powerfully in the social and economic conditions that affect the adult world. In fact, the distinction between adult and child is blurred in Lenski's work, as children take on adult roles in their world and move quickly into adult spheres of responsibility. In these small-town boy books, the opposite occurs: the adults take on childlike roles and are unaffected by the outside world. The adults exhibit childlike qualities suggesting innocence, naïveté, and a benign immaturity. The boys, meanwhile, drive the action with their power, inventiveness, cleverness, wit, and curiosity.

✳ ✳ ✳

The very first illustration of Homer Price pictures him as a hayseed —with a stalk of hay literally coming out of his mouth. He lives outside of town and contributes to the family income by doing "odd jobs." McCloskey includes this note not to suggest an economic necessity but to suggest relationships. Homer washes car windows "to help his father" and cleans cabins "to help his mother" at the Shady Rest Tourist Camp—the site of these "odd jobs"—and though a tourist camp suggests a life of movement and change, he stands as a child who is strongly situated and stable. He lives at the camp; the characters at the camp are all transient (10).

McCloskey's text works to show Homer's normalcy.

> When Homer isn't going to school, or doing odd jobs, or playing with the other boys, he works on his hobby which is building radios. He has a workshop in one corner of his room where he works in the evenings.
> Before going to bed at night he usually goes down to the kitchen to have a glass of milk and cookies because working on radios makes him hungry. Tabby, the family cat, usually comes around for something to eat too. (*Homer Price*, 10)

The description of Homer is a gathering of purposefully clichéd images —even down to the name of the cat. Homer is archetypal: he goes to school, plays with the guys, has a neat hobby, eats milk and cookies at night. He likes to listen to the state college football game (34) and pitches horse shoes (38). He rakes leaves for his uncle and wonders if he should take his pay in cash or in doughnuts (72). Homer lives in a quiet town, where the excitement tends toward the county fair. And after the fair, "life in Centerburg eases itself back to normal. Homer and the rest of the children concentrate on arithmetic and basketball, and the grown-ups 'tend to business and running the town in a peaceful democratic way" (94). Throughout the collection, Homer maintains this stance of normalcy. The bizarre events that occur in the stories may happen to him but are not caused by him. He remains in the position of the child reader, and his responses to oddity are, McCloskey proposes, the responses of an ordinary curious and engaged boy.

But all is not quite so simple as McCloskey leads the reader to believe. The opening illustration of Homer is more complex than simply an image of a boy with a strand of hay in his mouth. He is, in fact, standing behind a bust of the Greek poet Homer, set upon a small pillar. Beneath the sign "Homer," Homer Price has inscribed his own last name. The head of the poet has come off the bust and lies on the ground, its sightless eyes looking up at the young boy who so nonchalantly has taken his place. Meanwhile, Homer the boy stands with one hand in his pocket, the other posed beside his head. It is an illustration that is virtually repeated in the opening to *Centerburg Tales,* where busts of the poet Homer and Mark Twain are set on a shelf; sightless Homer, who appears quite worried, looks away, but Twain peers over at Homer and his friend Freddy, who are holding up to their faces a broom (to mock Twain's moustache) and a mop (to mock Homer's beard). In these illustrations, McCloskey replaces Homer with Homer Price in the role of the storyteller; though he is not the narrator, the point of view is consistently his. The stories that will be told are large, mythic, exaggerated, and tall (even names will be adapted from classical sources), but the stories will be held within the confines of a normal midwestern world, as Daugherty had done with *Andy and the Lion.*

In keeping with this mock use of the poet and author, McCloskey satirizes pretension and higher education—those who might read and study *The Iliad* and *The Odyssey.* When in *Homer Price* two crooks come to town, McCloskey creates one crook who is well-spoken because he has gone to college. He wears a well-cut suit, and his eyes are closed in his condescending glance (14). Later, Homer and his pet skunk come upon the robbers, and Aroma—the skunk—settles into the suitcase with the cash. When the robbers see this problem, they are surprised, notes McCloskey. But the one robber is, once again, condescending and arrogant: "That, my dear friend, is *not* a thing. It is a Musteline Mammal (*Genus Mephitis*) commonly known as a *skunk!*" (18). Like

Homer, he has read about skunks, but where Homer's reading leads to an unpretentious handiness with the world around him, the robber's reading is used to establish a persona—and is useless in the real world. The inappropriateness of his language and response is clear, as it is again when all four robbers (five in the famously incorrect illustration [25]) squeeze into a bed, and he says, "You must admit, though, that our present condition could be described as being a trifled overcrowded" (24). McCloskey reminds the reader again that this comes from the crook with a college education. In fact, in the last speech of this character, he uses his education to try to evade responsibility for what he has done: " 'Our early environment is responsible for our actions,' said the educated robber" (27).

But Homer will have none of this, and the pretensions of this world of education are pricked, as the crooks—including the educated one—are marched to the sheriff's office in their pajamas and barefoot, guarded by a young boy and his skunk. The accompanying illustration puts the educated crook in the very front, walking toward the reader, even looking at the reader, and wearing, again, fashionable clothing—albeit pajamas (29).

Later, in perhaps the most well known of the stories in *Homer Price*, McCloskey will similarly prick pretensions, this time those based on social class. In "The Doughnuts" Homer is left in the diner owned by Uncle Ulysses to make some doughnuts. Before he begins, a wealthy woman and her chauffeur come in for a snack, and immediately she overwhelms Homer, taking charge of the doughnuts and, in fact, the diner. "'Now just *wait* till you taste these doughnuts,' said the lady. 'Do you have an apron?' she asked, as she took off her fur coat and her rings and her jewelry and rolled up her sleeves. 'Charles,' she said to the chauffeur, 'hand me that baking powder, that's right, and, young man, we'll need some nutmeg' " (54–56). This is a woman used to being in charge because of her wealth, which she wears conspicuously. She will not listen to any suggestions nor any warnings. So when Homer protests that she has made too much batter to put in the machine, she can only repeat, "Just *wait* till you taste these doughnuts!" (56), assuming that her experience will be, must be, Homer's experience. Though, in fact, the doughnuts are quite good, the visit is disastrous, in that the huge amount of batter yields thousands of doughnuts, and a piece of the lady's conspicuous wealth has fallen into the batter.

Her response when she returns is similar to her first visit: "I'll offer a reward of one hundred dollars for that bracelet! It really *must* be found! . . . it *really* must!" (65). She has no sense of the chaos she has caused for

Homer and Uncle Ulysses; all she can do is to try, once again, to order the world through the power that her wealth has given to her. And after the missing jewelry is found, McCloskey dismisses her very quickly: "The lady and her chauffeur drove off with the diamond bracelet" (67). He does not give any indication of her response—except to show that, in fact, she has ordered the world, and what *must* be found, has been found. There is no indication that anything has been learned and no apparent gratitude to those whom she has controlled. Is it possible, too, that her lack of attention to the one who found the bracelet comes out of the fact that it is Rupert Black, an African American boy, someone who is completely out of her social circles and so not worth her regard, other than as someone to fulfill his appointed place in the world as she has ordered it? Someone who wears a patched and ragged coat rather than a diamond bracelet? Someone—the only one—who speaks in dialect? McCloskey is not at all explicit in this criticism, yet the narrative certainly suggests the wide discrepancy between the two worlds and sets up the irony that the lady's world is made right only by someone who is outside of her experience. Pretentiousness in *Homer Price* is answered by unexpected reality, which tends to show the weakness and ultimate silliness of such pretence.

The lady of the doughnuts and diamond bracelet will later play a role in McCloskey's look at American suburbia. In preparing the reader for this examination of cultural aesthetics, McCloskey begins with a series of tall tales in *Homer Price*; they are tall tales principally because they depend on excess for their narrative power. At the beginning of "The Doughnuts," the narrator focuses on Homer's Uncle Ulysses, who is fascinated by modern conveniences. "Uncle Ulysses is a man with advanced ideas and a weakness for labor saving devices. He equipped the lunch room with automatic toasters, automatic coffee maker, automatic dish washer, and an automatic doughnut maker. All just the latest thing in labor saving devices" (50). However, the reader is set up to identify more with Aunt Agnes, who believes that these devices are a nuisance, since all Ulysses seems to do throughout the narrative is to waste time with the sheriff over at the barbershop. The accumulation of the machines is mere excess. The problem of excess is then confirmed through exaggeration, as the doughnut machine produces literally thousands of doughnuts, most of which seem to be useless because they cannot be sold—until the diamond bracelet becomes a factor. From here on, excess becomes a narrative device—and eventually a thematic motif—in each of the stories.

The final story of the series in *Homer Price* is McCloskey's most pointed in this collection: "Wheels of Progress." The title is meant to be ironic, as McCloskey takes on the midcentury fascination with the suburb, which McCloskey pictures as a world of artlessness where convenience and repetition are elevated over beauty and individuality. The story begins with Uncle Ulysses, already introduced as the lover of the automatic and repetitive, dreaming with Miss Enders of the possibility of applying labor-saving principles to the building of houses: "'That's the principle that Henry Ford applied to making autos. Yep. Autos are mass produced, like doughnuts; ships are built like doughnuts; airplanes and refrigerators, and now *houses*. Yessiree, the *modern* house ought to be mass produced—just like cars or ships or planes. Yessiree! Mass produced, just like that there machine makes doughnuts!' and here Uncle Ulysses snapped his fingers, snap, snap, snap, snap, and said, 'Houses, just like that!'" (129–30). The accompanying illustration, in which Homer counts out doughnuts while Miss Enders and Uncle Ulysses talk, shows that only Homer is wary of this new scheme—a scheme that looks forward to the mass production of American homes that led to Levittowns across the American landscape. The illustration is virtually repeated in a few pages, but this time set not in the diner, where the plans are developed, but on the Enders estate, where the plans come to fruition. Nature itself is subdued by the process: "The trees were chopped down and hauled away; the land was leveled by huge tractors, and streets were laid out around the old Homestead in a day or two" (133). Uncle Ulysses stands on one of the ancient stumps, holding his arm out to an admiring Miss Enders, pointing out that here is progress (132–33).

The image of the prefabricated houses that McCloskey sets against the old Enders mansion (which readers familiar with McCloskey's *Lentil* would recognize as Colonel Carter's house) clearly pits beauty against unimaginative repetition, as does his text.

> Toward the end of the week a truckload of mass produced furniture was moved into every house. Each front yard had its own climbing rose bush, two dwarf cedars, and maple trees, all planted and sodded round about. Each back yard had its mass produced ash can, bird house complete with weather vane, and revolving clothes line. In fact modern production genius had thought of everything: sheets, towels, pillow cases, and a print of Whistler's Mother for over every fireplace. The houses were *complete* and ready to be moved into. (136)

The details in this paragraph grow more and more mundane. McCloskey begins with the natural world, but even Nature can be mass produced and so debased. The passage grows more and more damning as the details move from a rosebush, to a birdhouse, to sheets and towels, to a pretense at art. The suburban landscape that McCloskey sees around him in the 1940s is one that is easy and useful—but void of any beauty or invigorating spirit.

McCloskey would denounce this lack of aesthetics in the modern suburb five years later in a rather odd place: his Caldecott Award acceptance speech for *Time of Wonder*. There he pleaded for art education: "I should like to clamor for the teaching of drawing and design to every child, right along with reading and writing. I think it is most important for everyone really to see and evaluate pictures and really to see and evaluate his surroundings." The lack of this training, he argued, has led to America changing its design inspiration from nature to the machine, with its regularity and repetition, so that now in America "we have been designing, building, making things with machines, without paying the vaguest attention to the space around what we've designed." The specific example he gives is the suburban housing development: "And how do the houses look, lined up row after row, aerial to aerial in the housing development of the unimaginative builder? They look like hell!" When *Horn Book* published McCloskey's acceptance speech, it was accompanied by the illustration of the development in *Homer Price*—though the award was for *Time of Wonder*.

This gives McCloskey the chance to satirize the development: when the only landmark is gone, there is no way for anyone to recognize his or her house: "Just as alike as one hundred and one doughnuts, and *nothing*, no *nothing* to count from to find out which was which and whose was whose. There was a mad scramble, with much shouting, with the deserving tenants trying frantically to find out which house was which" (146–47). It is a gentle satire that McCloskey employs, with much of its weight hinging on the adjective "deserving." Are the owners deserving because they are following the American Dream of owning a house? Or are they deserving of this confusion because they have bought into the soulless and bland conformity of a mass-produced suburb and lifestyle?

McCloskey lets both potential readings stand, but, pointedly, he asks whether the forces of efficiency and conformity—which are boons to economic concerns—are to be balanced or deliberately set in tension with the forces of individual expression in a democracy. Homer himself—and the child reader who empathizes with his point of view—tends toward the side of the individual, though he is hardly a rebel. However, he does have the ability to stand back from the mayhem and confusion that the adult perspective brings, and though he does not comment upon that perspective, his is an outside view that is able to at least bring questions—such as whether destroying an old estate and leveling it for a hundred mass-produced houses is a true sign of progress.

In the rush to economic success, McCloskey suggests, the country is losing something of the charm and creativity of the individual. McCloskey sees the same problem in midcentury advertising, which promises what it has no intention of delivering, which deceives the individual with aesthetic glitz but ultimately empty form. In *Homer Price* McCloskey's critique comes in "The Case of the Cosmic Comic," in which a comic book superhero makes an appearance at the movie theater. The reader may understand that he is there actually in order to encourage attendance and so earn more bucks; but from the point of view of the attending children, he is there to give his worshippers a chance to meet him. But when the Super-Duper (the name suggesting his duplicity and his duping of the children) later drives his car into a ditch and gets cut up on barbed wire, it is Homer and Freddy who are there to save the day, pulling him and his car out and recognizing that he is merely a product of advertising. They resolve at the end of the story to trade off all of their comic books, because they have seen the falsehood behind them. In fact, the falsehood that has led the Super-Duper and his moneyed team to try to blur the distinction between fiction and fact leads the boys to abandon both the fact of the fraudulent man and the fiction of the comics, damaging their relationship to story itself.

The personification of advertising in *Homer Price* and *Centerburg Tales* is Mr. Gabby (again, a telling name), who is helpful in "The Doughnuts" when he comes up with the idea of advertising the thousands of doughnuts in order to deal with the absurd supply. Homer, whose perspective is always to be trusted in these two books, affirms his proper role. "Mr. Gabby's right. We have to enlarge our market. He's an advertising sandwich man, so if we hire him, he can walk up and down in front of the theater and get the customers" (62). Mr. Gabby, pictured as a whimsical, slightly comic, and homespun character, helps to do just this. Here, advertising serves a useful purpose and advertises something that really exists and has merit—and that has a beneficial result: the finding of the bracelet.

But in *Centerburg Tales* Mr. Gabby has evolved into something quite different and not nearly so benign. He has lost the homey, familiar, comfortable qualities of his former character. He now wears a sharp pin-striped suit, and he is accompanied by a partner who is drawn as the slick huckster, dressed in a plaid suit, sporting a thin moustache, closing his eyes with a superior, worldly-wise air. He has completely accepted the validity of a position in advertising, seeming not to realize the vacuous quality of that position. Advertising, Mr. Gabby claims, is "one of the most important jobs there is! You see, when some company has got a new kind of soap, or toothpaste, or catsup, Max and me think up a classy-looking wrapper, or tube, or streamline bottle to put it in, so's people will buy it" (41). His is a world of manipulation, McCloskey wants to suggest, and so he scorns the old-fashioned method of selling from a barrel for no reason other than "nobody could write their name on a barrel top and send it in to enter a prize contest or get something free" (40–41). Mr. Gabby produces nothing himself, nor does he evaluate what he is selling. He simply accepts that the act of selling is a valid position, regardless of the product—advertising is "one of the most important jobs there is!"

So completely immersed in the world of advertising is Mr. Gabby that it affects his perceptions of story itself, as if his development and manipulation of wrappers is equivalent to the act of storytelling. When one of Grampa Hercules's stories veers into a description of a steamboat, Mr. Gabby, for whom beauty and the slow development of the storyteller are mere distractions, rebukes him: "You can skip the commercial because we don't want to buy the boat. Let's get to the part about the gold" (44). Hercules's response comes a little farther into the story, when he is describing the soap that he and a partner use: "We had mighty good soap in those days. It didn't come in a fancy box or wrapper, but, by gum, when you washed something with it, that something stayed clean!" (49). Mr. Gabby "held his peace"—he is too interested in the gold in the story to interrupt again—but Hercules here has called Mr. Gabby's entire enterprise into question. Advertising has nothing to do with reality or with the authenticity of the product. It is, in a very real sense, a fraud, McCloskey is suggesting—another kind of menace to authentic cultural aesthetics, in that it is a misuse of aesthetics.

Homer's ability to observe the antics of the world around him—particularly the adult world—link him strongly to his child readers. And this is what McCloskey was clamoring for in this Caldecott acceptance speech—the power of discerning observation so that the observer can truly understand the world around him or her. McCloskey argued, "Yes, I think every child ought to study design and drawing right along with reading, and writing, and arithmetic. I can't think of a scientist, minister, politician, bulldozer-operator or any other professional man or job-holder who would not be a better citizen for having had this training." Aesthetics matter, McCloskey claims, because they affect the way we shape and design our country, and they affect the way we live within that shape and design.

What Robert McCloskey does not take on in these books are the more serious questions of the new atomic age with which Daugherty deals, or the issues of economic and social injustice that Lenski exposes, or the issues of racial and gender equality with which the Bobbs-Merrill Childhood of Famous Americans series wrestles. *Homer Price* was written in the middle of a world war—and illustrated in part while McCloskey was in basic training. *Centerburg Tales* was written at the beginning of the Cold War; but Centerburg is a world of security and easy living and innocence, particularly among the adults. This is not at all to suggest a lack of concern for social and global issues on McCloskey's part. It is to say that for McCloskey, these concerns were not the stuff of children's literature. For him, the America of children's books is an America that is safe and secure, wonderful in its natural resources, and a supportive and cohesive communal place wherein the child and his or her surrounding family can flourish. Herein lies the vitality of the American scene.

The disturbing stuff? That remains outside McCloskey's Edens, mostly unengaged.

And yet, there is this sense of loss: How many children, reading *Make Way for Ducklings* in the early 1940s, learned that their fathers were not going to be there "just as he had promised"?

And there is this prophetic sense of what could be: In *Homer Price*, a book published in 1943, a young African American boy is seated at the lunch counter of a diner. And no one—except perhaps some of McCloskey's readers—finds this at all unusual.

Conclusion

In 1944 Frank W. Mason authored *Pilots, Man Your Planes!*, a work of pulp fiction with the requisite fast-paced action, exotic settings, flat characters who are all good or all bad, and the tough but fair commander, here named Hugh Steel. Midway through the book, Major Steel is given the task of having his squadron deliver bombs that will wipe out everything around the drop site for three miles and penetrate a thousand feet below ground. Should the target be hit, the war will be over in a matter of weeks. There can be no failure, and the squadron can't turn back—if they are downed over friendly territory with the bombs still aboard, "there'll be enough explosives in those bombs to wipe out every living thing from here to Alexandria!" (135). Major Steel's normally controlled voice has risen sharply as he says this, and it starts to crack under the strain.

He is, of course, speaking of an atomic bomb. Again, the book was published in 1944.

The target is the Brenner Pass, whose closure would mean that Mussolini would immediately beg for peace. The drop site is an area that is unoccupied, Steel is careful to explain—and then comes this rather remarkable line of dialogue: "I tell you again, it's fearfully, unbelievably powerful, that stuff. It's too inhuman to use on any enemy cities, but it's the right dope to close the Brenner Pass, if anything can" (135–36).

Here, in a pulp novel written for a young reader, is a question about American character and foreign policy during wartime. Is it "inhuman" for the Allies to drop certain kinds of ordinance on enemy cities, even during the war? Even to force the end of the war? It is exactly the question that President Truman would wrestle with a year later; he would come to an answer different from that of Major Steel—and Frank W. Mason.

The golden age of British children's literature had ended in terms of its controlling influence on American children's books. At midcentury, American writers for children had turned to their own national questions and had found their own gold. The story of American children's literature in the mid-twentieth century is the story of writers, publishers, librarians, and educators who turned to America itself as the subject of children's books. They then wrestled with how that subject should be presented to a young audience and what effects that presentation should have on that same audience. They concluded that children's books should help to define America for the new generation, should extol American virtues, should be both open and honest about America's national flaws, should promote a vision of the country that extolled its diversity and inclusiveness, and should challenge young readers to consider their role as citizens engaging in progressive solutions to current cultural crises.

But all this would soon be superseded.

By the late 1950s and early 1960s American children's literature began moving its gaze from the immense world around to the deep world within. Crockett Johnson's *Harold and the Purple Crayon* (1955), *Harold's Fairy Tale* (1956), *Harold's Trip to the Sky* (1957), and *Harold's Circus* (1959) are all movements by a young child into the interior—into his own imagined world: "One evening, after thinking it over for some time, Harold decided to go for a walk in the moonlight," begins *Harold's Purple Crayon*, and soon he is off on a road, into a forest, climbing up an apple tree, running from the dragon that guards it, crossing an ocean in a boat, finding a picnic on the other shore, climbing a mountain to look for the light of his own bedroom, and falling in a balloon to the outskirts of a city, where he is directed to his own home, which he finds by framing the moon. "And then Harold made his bed. He got in it and he drew up the covers." Despite the lengthy journey, here, as in the other Harold books, there is never a time when Harold is not deeply within an imagined landscape, searching out not national issues but the roots of individual creativity and meaning.

It was a journey within that was projected, sometimes less explicitly, in other popular works of the period. In *Charlotte's Web* (1952), though the tale is set on Zuckerman's farm, E. B. White plays with the sense that much of the action occurs in the imagination of Fern during her long hours in the barn as she watches the animals that she loves. In Dr. Seuss's *The Cat in the Hat* (1957), the two children, alone in the house during a dreary, dull day, encounter the absurd antics of the absurd Cat. Like Harold, the two children never leave the house—in fact, they never even leave the house imaginatively. And the issue they face is not a national one but a very individual one: Should they tell their mother what happened that day, or should they not? "Well," asks the narrator, "what would you do, if your mother asked you?" (61). Beginning with *The Cat in the Hat*, Dr. Seuss would go on to write four of the top ten best-selling children's books of the twentieth century, the others being *Green Eggs and Ham* (1960), *One Fish, Two Fish, Red Fish, Blue Fish* (1960), and *Hop on Pop* (1963)—all contrasting strongly with the ordered, properly behaved, and always mannered Dick and Jane, and all suggesting the huge shift in subject matter away from a socially conscious publishing endeavor to a focus on the self-referentiality of childhood.

Maurice Sendak's *Kenny's Window* (1956)—the first book Sendak both wrote and illustrated—brings together a young boy's dreams and reality in a meditative, lyrical text that is organized around Kenny's search for answers to seven dreamlike questions. The story moves freely within his imagination, so that his life in his room itself seems dreamlike: "Kenny fell asleep with his head against the window ledge. And the song became a dream about a horse. Kenny was riding on a shiny black horse. They galloped past houses, and people watched from their windows and clapped their hands. They galloped all over the world and even right up to the ocean. And on the edge of the ocean was a ship, painted white, and it had an extra room for a friend." Three years later, Sendak would illustrate Janice May Udry's *The Moon Jumpers* (1959), in which he pictures a group of four children whose powerful imaginations create a world of play and dance beneath the moon: "The warm night-wind tosses our hair. The wind chimes stir. And we all dance, barefooted. Over and over the grass!" The double-page spreads—strongly reminiscent of the more famous spreads that Sendak would use for the wild rumpus of *Where the Wild Things Are* (1963)—show children in the air, their eyes closed, their hands held up into the moonlight, fully into a world more mystical and strange and luminous than the reality that their parents inhabit. Like the younger Harold, Kenny and these four children live deeply within an imagined landscape, and only slightly, it seems, within the real world.

Margaret Wise Brown's most unfortunately named final book, *The Dead Bird* (1958), pictures a group of children not watching the moon but caught up in a confrontation with death. In the face of that huge reality, they enter into an imagined world of pomp and ceremony: "The children were very sorry the bird was dead and could never fly again. But they were glad they had found it, because now they could dig a grave in the woods and bury it. They could have a funeral and sing to it the way grown-up people did when someone died." And so they bury the bird with sweet-ferns in the bottom of the grave, they wrap the bird in grapevine leaves, they put ferns and flowers on top of it, they sing and cry, and then they put on more ferns and flowers and finally a gray stone above the grave. Their response to a reality so large is a turn to the imagination. But in their world they cannot remain in the imagination; the book ends with a return to the normalcy of childhood: "And every day, until they forgot, they went and sang to their little dead bird and put fresh flowers on his grave." It is the "until they forgot" that clues the reader to the return—this, as well as the final double spread, where the children are running bases while the grave, farther off in the woods, lies ignored.

Else Minarik and Maurice Sendak's *Little Bear* (1957), *Father Bear Comes Home* (1959), *Little Bear's Friend* (1960), and *Little Bear's Visit* (1961) all stay within a close, loving, domestic world of secure childhood. *Little Bear's Friend*, for example, begins with Little Bear up in a high tree, looking "all about him at the wide, wide world" (9). But, of course, he really isn't looking at the "wide, wide world" at all; he is looking instead at the world that lies around him, and his view ends with "He saw his own house. He saw Mother Bear" (11). It is the world of Mother and Father and close friends and the love of extended family, where the imagination can call up mermaids and goblins but always return to the secure world of the child.[1]

Syd Hoff also celebrates that secure world, though he presses its boundaries with the delightfully absurd in books such as *Sammy the Seal* (1959), *Danny and the Dinosaur* (1958), and *Julius* (1959)—again, the imagination itself is the subject. In *Sammy the Seal* Sammy wants to see the world outside his zoo—and the zookeeper, who affirms that Sammy has been a good seal, opens the gate: "Sammy walked and walked and walked. He did not know what to look at first" (23). He looks up at skyscrapers, down manholes, and through restaurant windows, and finally, desperate to find water, he jumps into a bathtub. Afterward he attends school, where he learns how to read and plays a sort of volleyball. But in the end, "Sammy was in a hurry to get back to the zoo. He had so much to tell the other seals." But what he says to them, as he takes his fish dinner, is entirely centered on his own world: "There's no place like home" (64). The absurdity of the books is always brought down to the immediate experience of the child, always narrowed, in the end, to the desire for the small, secure home—the same process that Norman Bridwell would use several years later with his *Clifford the Big Red Dog* (1963), where Emily Elizabeth's Clifford is absurdly huge but always centered on the close, immediate experience of the child: "We have fun together. We play games. . . . I can find Clifford no matter where he hides"—and he is hiding behind Emily Elizabeth's house, which he may be bigger than, but which he is always connected with.

Ezra Jack Keats's *The Snowy Day* (1962)—like *The Moon Jumpers*—pictures a child going about a real landscape but investing it with mystery and heightening it with excitement, as Peter wakes up to a new snowfall. He does what all children do—he makes footprints, creates tracks through the snow with a stick, and knocks the snow down from a tree. But after these activities, Peter walks through a white field—no text in the illustration (17)—and begins a series of more imaginative interactions, during which he invests the snowfall with huge energy and size. He takes part in a snowball fight where the snowballs seem to be as large as bowling balls. He makes a snowman that smiles, waves his arms to make snow angels, and slides down what seems to be a mountain of snow that he has heaped up, pretending to be a mountain climber. That night, he dreams that the snow has melted away, but in the morning, there is yet another snowfall, and he goes outside again, this time with a friend; the illustration shows the two of them walking through what seems to be a very sharp valley whose sides rise up precipitously around them—an illustration that Keats uses to do what he has been doing throughout the book: to show us Peter's perceptions of the snowy world more than the actuality of that world. The reader is almost always within his imagined landscape.

And there is Max, whose journey to the land of the Wild Things is entirely a journey into the imagination. In fact, it is an imaginative journey designed to erase the real world around him, with confrontations and emotions that confound the young boy. He heads through a forest, across the sea, "to the place where the wild things are," and that place is exotic, frightening, attractive, and—perhaps most important—utterly other. The world is tropical, filled with configured monsters, without restraint, and dominated by the choices of the moment. In other words, the landscape is as far from a James Daugherty text as it is possible to get. This journey to the imagined landscape of the interior is not unique to Sendak—he draws from the books that have been making that same journey—but *Where the Wild Things Are* (1963) is that journey's most adept and powerful expression.

For older child readers, the journeys also would be interior. Anne Scott MacLeod dates the change in children's literature to Louise Fitzhugh's *Harriet the Spy*, published in 1964. "Without breathing hard about it," she writes, "Louise Fitzhugh discarded several cherished children's literature taboos," including the notion that parents and adults are responsible, that they provide a credible moral compass, that they themselves follow a moral compass. The resulting protagonists, Mac-Leod argues, are both isolated and self-absorbed, unable to negotiate an adult world that is untrustworthy and not particularly attractive.[2] Certainly the notion that parents and adults are what they had been in almost every midcentury book—say, Pa in the novels of Laura Ingalls Wilder—is gone in the 1960s, replaced with parents who are incompetent, ridiculous, hostile, uncaring, irrelevant, or simply absent. Enter, very soon, J. D. Salinger, John Donovan, Paul Zindel, Barbara Wersba, Robert Cormier, M. E. Kerr, and Judy Blume—and soon S. E. Hinton, Richard Peck, Robert Lipsyte, and Cynthia Voigt.

※ ※ ※

The place where the wild things are is not in America, but neither is it in the golden age of British children's books; the journeys of the late 1950s and early 1960s were not a return to earlier paths but a new venturing. And if they were less about the world that children knew outside themselves, they were more about the world that children knew inside themselves. Perhaps it is no accident that the Children's Book Week poster that celebrated the theme for 1957—"Explore with Books"—was illustrated by the Provensons with a group of children looking into books that would take them to faraway places and times, but when that same theme was used the next year, Paul Rand chose to illustrate a child surrounded by open books and with only blackness behind him, as if to suggest that the adventures would, from now on, be interior ones.[3]

Yet if so many of the children's books from midcentury seem quaintly and naively patriotic to readers today, it is best to remember that they were from a time before the enlightenments of the civil rights movement and the women's movement, and before the disillusionments of the Vietnam War and of Watergate. They assumed America's experiment with democracy was just and honorable, that the American commitment to freedom and justice was unassailable, that citizenship was fully for all and really did carry with it specific responsibilities to be gladly taken up. Children's books were supposed not only to delight in such an America and its prosperity and its place in the world but also to call attention to the necessity of supporting America, cherishing its heritage, claiming one's own place in its national story, and exporting its freedoms.

What these books never showed was how terribly fragile all these were.

ACKNOWLEDGMENTS

A book this long in the making accrues many friends who help to guide it along. Of these, I think of many in the Department of English of Calvin College, who were, as always, encouraging at just the right moments—Hettinga, my friend, the foremost. I acknowledge too the kindness of my good college, which provided both a sabbatical and a research fellowship or two toward the completion of this project. And without Kathleen Struck, librarian extraordinaire, where would any of us be?

To Conrad Bult, I proclaim here my thanks for your early interest and encouragement, for your generous and able help in the early research, and for your love of children's books that inspires.

My thanks as well to Mary Rockcastle, of Hamline University, who as a dean has no equal. Her timely letters and constant encouragement—and example of scholarly diligence and forthrightness—have put me in her debt.

Particular thanks to Karen Nelson Hoyle, recently retired from the Kerlan Collection of the University of Minnesota, and to Suzan Alteri, curator of the Baldwin Library of Historical Children's Literature of the George A. Smathers Library at the University of Florida—a hefty title appropriate to her hefty acts of grace on my behalf. And many thanks indeed to Jacalyn Eddy, whose comments on the manuscript pointed in straight directions and whose work on the bookwomen of the early part of the twentieth century was invaluable.

To Catherine Cocks, acquisitions editor of the University of Iowa Press— indeed, to all those of this wonderful press—my great gratitude.

And to Anne, who has put up with this project for so very long and who has patiently accepted the many hours in bookstores and the arcane purchases of many tomes, my love—always and again.

INTRODUCTION

1   In his *Minders of Make-Believe*, Marcus chronicles the prominence of Lou-
    ise Seaman on pages 76–83 and that of Alice Dagliesh on pages 120–23.
    Anne MacLeod provides general background about the "strong-minded
    lot" and connects the growth of the industry to the public library move-
    ment in *American Childhood*, 122–25. The history is also usefully surveyed
    in Jagusch, *Stepping Away from Tradition*. Mahony, "The First Children's
    Book Department." Seaman's comments on her publishing list are from
    her unpublished autobiography (3:11, 7:19), in the Papers of Louise Sea-
    man Bechtel, Department of Special and Area Collections, George A.
    Smathers Libraries, University of Florida.

2   Mahony, "Other Children's Book Departments"; Dagliesh, "Improve-
    ment"; Eddy, *Bookwomen*, 3.

3   Emerson's familiar call comes from the opening of his essay "The Ameri-
    can Scholar," first delivered at Harvard University in 1837 and published
    separately that same year. Anne Scott MacLeod, "Children's Literature
    for a New Nation, 1820–1860," in her *American Childhood*, 87–98. Mac-
    Leod's essay is expanded significantly in her *A Moral Tale* and supported
    in its argument by Wishy, *The Child and the Republic*, which links the in-
    culcation of traditional morals and the creation of an American charac-
    ter that was forced to adapt those morals to new circumstances. More
    broadly, Mintz affirms the nineteenth-century role of "socialization" as
    a process of "preparing children for public roles and responsibilities by
    instructing them in the inviolability of religious and social authority," a
    process that should combine "a capacity for self-restraint and an inter-
    nalized sense of duty and obligation" (*Prison*, 21–29). Cardell, *The Happy
    Family*, 4. The history of American children's books as socializing agents
    in the nineteenth century is the focus of Elbert, *Enterprising Youth*, in
    which she examines the use of children's books to inculcate civic duties;
    Clark's *Kiddie Lit* also examines this connection, though its explorations
    extend into the twenty-first century.

4   Images of these National Children's Book Week posters appear in Marcus, *75 Years*, 10 (Walter Cole), 3 and 4 (Jessie Wilcox Smith). The description of the Cole poster as representing an "American Theme" appears in "American Theme for Book Week."

5   See Miller, "Children's Books." In his slightly misnamed "Democracy and Community in American Children's Literature," Cook argues similarly that much of British and American children's literature is about inculcating the political merits of democracy. The development of children's rooms in public libraries and the power of those rooms to civilize was a huge emphasis of Anne Carroll Moore in the New York Public Library, as Eddy documents in *Bookwomen* (15–16, 38–42). This vision of the role of the public library, the children's room in particular, and the importance of school libraries in fulfilling this civilized role was expressed not infrequently during the midcentury, as in Henne, "School Libraries." The larger history of this social role of libraries is developed in Augst, "American Libraries."

6   The concern with the author's presence in a work written for children gives rise to criticism such as Galbraith, "What Must I Give Up," in which Galbraith argues for a criticism that traces authorial childhood experiences as expressed in a writer's work; and Lowe's "'Stop! You Didn't Read.'" See also Lesnik-Oberstein, "Childhood and Textuality"; her more fully developed case for the constructivist view appears in Lesnik-Oberstein, *Children's Literature*. Cadden counters Rose's assertion that children's literature cannot exist, but he does concede that children's literature is a "contested" site, "driven by both adult and children's own desires and uses" (*Telling Children's Stories*, xix).

7   Mahony is cited in Ross, *The Spirited Life*, 200.

CHAPTER 1

1   See also Mintz and Kellogg, *Domestic Revolutions*, 133–49.

2   Anne Scott MacLeod sees in this same speech Mr. Woodlawn's insistence that Caddie is passing a boundary: "But women's work, Mr. Woodlawn makes clear without saying so, requires skills and a discipline impossible to acquire in the free life his daughter has led so far. The real burden of her father's talk is to tell Caddie that her childhood, and with it her freedom, is about to end" ("American Girlhood in the Nineteenth Century: Caddie Woodlawn's Sisters," in *American Childhood*, 4). Though MacLeod correctly goes on to challenge the depiction of sharply gendered divisions on the American frontier, here, like Murray, she distorts what Caddie's father is presenting. He hopes Caddie will become a woman who has been shaped by her pioneer freedom; that she may no longer run with the colts does not mean that she must forget she ever did.

3   Carl Sandburg did something very similar for an adult audience in his *The*

People, Yes, which focuses not on major American figures but on common citizens.

4   Some critics note that the experience of Laura, in particular, mirrors the growth and development of the American frontier, so that the Ingalls family becomes emblematic of all Americans in the westward movement. "At the social level, [the Little House books] document the transmission of community values and cultural awareness to the newly settled American West. And, at the mythic level, they memorably dramatize the motifs of westering and 'growing up with the country,' becoming at last for twentieth-century readers a moving invocation of the powerful allure of the American frontier," argues Erisman (*Laura Ingalls Wilder*, 6). Perhaps so—in the sense that this may be said of most pioneer stories. This representative quality remains implicit, rather than explicit, because of the limited third-person focus on Laura's point of view, which is almost exclusively limited to her own family, and because of the intended audience. Some have argued that domestication lies, in fact, at the center of the Little House books, suggesting that the question of domestication is applied not only to the landscape but to Laura as well. Mowder, in "Domestication of Desire," suggests that Laura is more firmly in the Native American culture as a child, which Wilder uses as a metaphor for unrestraint; she is opposed to the static and limited china shepherdess that Ma controls. However, the task of Ma is to teach Laura the kind of restraint that will lead to her understanding herself as a proper woman. "The project of American imperialism [in the West]," Mowder writes, "is interpreted within the Little House books as a distinctly feminine project, one that is enacted by women upon both the landscape and upon the children." Mowder, however, gives no space to Pa here, nor does she allow for the possibility of a mutuality in the domestication, Pa's arena being outdoors, Ma's indoors. Mowder's position is challenged by both Cummins in "Laura and the 'Lunatic Fringe'" and Maher in "Laura Ingalls and Caddie Woodlawn." Both affirm that the female character is not being acculturated into a certain view of proper womanhood; instead, the Little House books show that gender expectations are fluid in the face of frontier life. Lee, in "'It's better farther on,'" argues that though Laura does seem in the novels to align her perspective with that of Pa, "Laura's slow progress toward a sympathetic understanding of her mother parallels her own growth toward acceptance of her identity as a woman," an identity that values stability and home over freedom and mobility.

5   See Stoneley, *Consumerism*, 135–40. Romines also examines questions of materialism, particularly as they apply to *On the Banks of Plum Creek*, distinguishing between Ma's work in the preindustrial world and her children's acceptance of a more industrialized society, replete with such items as a cooking stove (*Constructing the Little House*, 97–137).

6   Wilder's skepticism of government intervention in the life of the individ-

ual American is cited, for example, in Miller, *Laura Ingalls Wilder's Little Town*, 8; Miller documents more fully Wilder's antipathy to FDR and the New Deal, which she saw as eroding the virtues of independence and self-reliance, in *Becoming Laura Ingalls Wilder*, 199–200, 233–34.

7 Harold L. Ickes's speech was delivered on the radio on October 29, 1933, and reprinted in *Childhood Education*.

8 The American Library Association's "The Library's Bill of Rights" was first published in the *American Library Association Bulletin*. It is given historical context in Robbins, *Censorship and the American Library*, 11–14.

9 The leftist leanings of Mitchell and Huberman are detailed in Mickenberg, *Learning from the Left*, 40–45 (Sprague) and 236–38 (Huberman); and Simon, "Leo Huberman."

CHAPTER 2

1 Daugherty's description of Frank Brangwyn appears in his autobiographical introduction to his *Walt Whitman's America*, 13. See also Kent, "James Daugherty."

2 Daugherty had cited this same determination to turn from European influence in his "Illustrating for Children."

3 See also "James Henry Daugherty." Daugherty's work in murals is examined and pictured in Lawton, *James Daugherty's Mural Drawings*. For Daugherty, mural work was a critical part of the American democracy itself, as he expressed in a December 26, 1938, letter to Edward Bruce, chief of the Treasury Department's Section of Fine Arts: "The new work [in the Post Office and Justice Buildings] is a fulfillment of the vision of America as voiced by Walt Whitman and Thoreau and Emerson, and is a potent sign of the rebirth of the democratic spirit in our country today" (*James Daugherty: American Modernist Works*, 3). Daugherty repeated the "pageant" description almost verbatim in a letter to Albert de Salle; it is printed in de Salle, "Pictorial Pleasantries." The connection to the American Scene painters is made in Manna, "Robert McCloskey's *Make Way for Ducklings*."

4 White's *Daniel Boone* was first published with Daugherty's illustrations in 1922. The description of the May Massee relationship appears in Kent, "James Daugherty: Buckskin Illustrator." It is repeated with some variation in Kunitz and Haycraft, *The Junior Book of Authors*, 88–90, in which Daugherty cites May Massee as handing him Stewart Edward White's book and saying, "Do what you like, have a good time, and God bless you." Daugherty's own interest in Daniel Boone is suggested by his oil painting of Boone done in this same period, showing the same forms, lines, and palette of the four color plates for *Daniel Boone: Wilderness Scout*. Pictured in Agee, *James Daugherty*.

5 For a version of the Scout Law, see *The Handbook for Boys*, 33–37. Macleod

chronicles the early attempts of the Boy Scouts at instruction and character building in *Building Character*, 248–67, in which he concludes that for "the boys, after all, social experiences mattered more than formal lessons" (267). Cohoon, in *Serialized Citizenships*, argues that books for young readers were one factor in constructing the idea of boyhood and its connections to national citizenship, though she is looking at an older period than here studied. Levander supports Cohoon's description of the nineteenth-century culture's sense that boys particularly needed to be socialized into citizenship (*Cradle of Liberty*, 87–88). The connection of books to the construction of boyhood is surveyed by Kidd in his chapter, "Bad Boys and Men of Culture," in Kidd, *Making American Boys*, 49–85.

6   In the 1926 edition of the book, the order of these plates was shifted. *The Wilderness Road*, the frontispiece of the first edition, was moved to the interior of the book (142). *Vision* became the frontispiece for this later edition.

7   In the 1926 edition, *Struggle* was moved up in the text to illustrate a chapter in which White abandoned the narrative line of the biography and set out to characterize Native Americans who are, in White's text, savages—though to be admired for their woodcraft.

8   Daugherty's comment on the "real American processional" came out of his reading of Carl Sandburg's *Abraham Lincoln: The Prairie Years*, which he was planning to illustrate. (This would be published as *Abe Lincoln Grows Up*, including the first twenty-seven chapters of Sandburg's book.) "Review of James Daugherty's *Daniel Boone*"; and Moore, "The Three Owls' Notebook," *Horn Book* 15.5.

9   Daugherty shows this artistic movement away from non-American sources in his *Andy and the Lion*, published just a year before *Daniel Boone*, in which Daugherty recasts Aesop's fable, "Androcles and the Lion," from a classical landscape into an American landscape, with the suggestion that the entire tale is mediated through Andy's very midwestern imagination.

10 The book was serialized in part as *Man of the People* in the *Classmate* 50.6–11 (February–March 1943): 6:2–3, 12–14; 7:4–5, 13; 8:4–5, 11–12; 9:4–5, 13–14; 10:4–5, 7, 13; 11:4–5, 14. Here, Daugherty was more explicit than in the Viking Press edition in his identification of Lincoln as an incarnation of a spiritual democracy, as in his conclusion to the serialization: "In the terrible detonations of world conflict we are swiftly waking from the materialistic slumbers, the gilded sleepwalking of the American dream. In this hour of destiny and peril and faith reborn, let us evoke the living image of the freedom-loving and law-abiding Lincoln as the spiritually central American in all his essences of humor, courage, and creative imagination. His is the complete and unified democratic personality fit for a world pattern and prototype of government built upon the four essential freedoms" (11:14).

11 This image is repeated almost exactly as Daugherty's concluding image

for Thornton, *Almanac for Americans,* 423, though this illustration is done in pen and ink.

12 Mickenberg (*Learning from the Left,* 111–13) links this work specifically to the war, and so the opening illustration evokes the battle against Fascism (through the image of the African American soldier) and the battle against racism (through the image of the mother and child learning to read—a symbol of the power of education).

13 Three years later, Shapiro and Daugherty would again collaborate on a tall tale, *Joe Magarac and His U.S.A. Citizenship Papers.* Here Shapiro and Daugherty want to celebrate the contributions of immigrants to American society. The narrative leads to a moment in which Joe Magarac, who has been melted into a steel girder upholding a congressional building, overhears two congressmen lamenting the intrusion of immigrants into America. This is resolved when Congress comes to recognize that all Americans other than Native Americans are in fact immigrants. The endpapers depict Joe as one of the many millions of immigrants who came to America. The president himself is dancing as he hands Joe Magarac the citizenship papers, and the American eagle beside him dances as well. Beyond him is another Daugherty procession of uncounted numbers who, like Joe Magarac, contribute to the American Dream, symbolized by the waving flags.

CHAPTER 3

1 The attitudes toward Native Americans that Wilder projects in the novels are examined in works such as John E. Miller, "American Indians in the Fiction of Laura Ingalls Wilder," *South Dakota History* 30 (2000): 303–20; Donna M. Campbell, "'Wild Men' and Dissenting Voices: Narrative Disruption in *Little House on the Prairie," Great Plains Quarterly* 20 (2000): 111–22; Philip Heldrich, "'Going to Indian Territory': Attitudes toward Native Americans in *Little House on the Prairie," Great Plains Quarterly* 20 (2000): 99–109; and, briefly, Melissa Kay Thompson, "A Sea of Good Intentions: Native Americans in Books for Children," *Lion and the Unicorn* 25 (2001): 353–74. Sharon Smulders, in "'The Only Good Indian': History, Race, and Representation in Laura Ingalls Wilders' *Little House on the Prairie," Children's Literature Association Quarterly* 27.4 (Winter 2002–3): 191–202, argues that Wilder's handling of Native Americans reflects her own guilt over her participation in the myth of American imperialism, which allowed for and encouraged the dispossession of Native Americans—and yet, Smulders asserts, this sense of guilt still does not allow her to create sympathetic and realistic representations of Native Americans. Not all analyses are critical: Miller suggests that though Laura does show some of the attitudes toward the Other prevalent in her own time, "her religious training and the precepts of fairness and benevolence

that her parents imparted to her inclined her toward a more enlightened viewpoint" (*Becoming Laura Ingalls Wilder*, 206)—though here, Miller speaks of the author, not the character. Elizabeth Segel, in "Laura Ingalls Wilder's America: An Unflinching Assessment," *Children's Literature in Education* 8.2 (Summer 1977): 63–70, argues that Wilder is conscious of her depictions and that Laura seriously questions the imperialistic myth. The books, Segel asserts, examine the "moral dimensions" of America itself during the westward immigration, and their "sober critique" suggests that "the books do not endorse all of the values of the society they depict, any more than the child Laura accepted all that was prescribed to her as proper." Perhaps the most useful analysis of Ma's attitudes toward Native Americans comes in Romines, *Constructing the Little House*, 55–79, in which Romines connects Ma's racist hatred with gendered expectations: "[Ma] is largely portrayed as calmly acquiescent," she writes, "but her one major outlet for anger, resistance, and defense of the values of feminine domestic culture on the unsettled prairie is her intense, vocal rejection of Indians and Indian cultures" (69).

2 The biographical material appears in "The Hunt Breakfast," which noted Nolen's untimely death in *Horn Book* 18.5 (September–October 1942): 290.

3 Donnarae MacCann surveys and examines the cultural assumptions dominating early American publications of children's books about African Americans in her *White Supremacy in Children's Literature: Characterizations of African Americans, 1830–1900* (New York: Garland Publishing, 1998). A fuller assessment is provided in Michelle H. Martin, *Brown Gold: Milestones of African-American Children's Picture Books, 1845–2002* (New York: Routledge, 2004)—though the huge emphasis is on the last twenty years of publications. Robin Bernstein's *Racial Innocence: Performing American Childhood from Slavery to Civil Rights* (New York: New York University, 2011), focuses on some of those milestones—particularly *Uncle Tom's Cabin*—by examining the ways in which childhood performances were expressions of political ideologies that have historically affected "racial projects"—a thesis that runs parallel with the "performances" by children's books.

4 Binnie Tate Wilkin's *African and African American Images in Newbery Award Winning Titles* (Lanham, MD: Scarecrow Press, 2009) annotates the Newbery Honor and Award–winning books that include—or even mention—African American characters.

5 Rollins's NCTE speech was published as "Some Children's Books for One World." The huge role played by Charlemae Rollins in raising consciousness about the presence of African American characters in children's books is documented in Tolson, "Making Books Available."

6 Jackson's *Call Me Charley* was followed by a sequel: *Anchor Man*, in which Charley, now in high school, struggles with old friends who reject him as one who has forgotten his racial connections. A second sequel, *Charley*

Starts from Scratch, has Charley graduated from high school and now confronting racism as an adult.

7   Shereikis explores this novel—and other Tunis novels—in his "How You Play the Game," arguing that Tunis's novels, while maintaining the excitement of vigorous sports stories, picture a world "in which the heavy shadows of commercialism, racism, and hypocrisy threaten to obliterate the action."

8   Lenski makes the same point about cultural loss in *Little Sioux Girl*. In this work for very young readers, Grandma Antelope shows Eva beadwork she did as a young girl, a tradition she was unable to pass on to her own daughter because of the insistence that her daughter attend a white school. Now, neither Eva nor her mother can do the traditional beadwork at all. "Now, a Sioux girl goes to school to a white teacher and learns how to read in a book. But the skills of her forefathers are forgotten," Grandma Antelope laments (29). When she gives Eva a doll she had made with this beadwork, she identifies it first by its Native American name—"Blaye wagca"—and then by its English name—"Prairie Rose" (30). Eva—whose own name is English—can only articulate the English name. *Little Sioux Girl*, a volume in the Roundabout America series, aimed at depicting "vivid scenes from real life, in short-story or longer form, for younger readers," as its frontispiece indicated.

9   To be fair, Lenski herself had connected her work to the "One World" theme in her "Regional Children's Literature."

10 The 1947 and 1964 reviews are both cited in Ranta, "Lois Lenski."

11 When Ione Morrison Rider reviewed Arna Bontemps's *Sad-Faced Boy* (1937) for *Horn Book*, she hinted at these purposes. She argued for the broad appeal of a children's book that, she wrote, was not limited in terms of its audience by race. "Some thought that this book would be disliked by children of one race; some by those of another. . . . Just why, we wonder, should . . . anyone else conclude that because a book is about colored children it will not be read and enjoyed by others? In our experience it is accepted as a good story that happens to be about American Negro children—a story about children for children; any children. Is it possibly adults who raise artificial barriers and create issues?"

12 The collaboration between Hughes and Bontemps and its significance in promoting nonwhite cultures within a principally white publishing establishment are chronicled in Martin, "Arna Bontemps, Langston Hughes, and the Roots."

13 In "Langston Hughes and the Children's Literary Tradition," Anatol argues that Hughes's body of work for children was designed to show children the full history of their country but that his desire to promote racial goodwill and the success of the American democracy through this work created enormous tension: "Reading many of his children's works, one witnesses Hughes's lifelong battle between a staunch patriotism and

a bitter condemnation of American injustice and hypocrisy." Certainly the latter half of that equation marks *The Dream Keeper and Other Poems*, though here the tension might more accurately be said to be between an awareness of American injustice and the assumed innocence of the child's experience. The present vision of Hughes and Bontemps and their articulation of the importance of cultural distinctiveness is influenced strongly by Smith, *Children's Literature*, 229–71, "The Aesthetics of Black Children's Literature," which in turn was influenced by Johnson's *Telling Tales*.

14 Cady's hope would come true in terms of children's books that addressed questions of race, but today, in fact, few of the books he would have known dealing with such questions are in play. In *Black History in the Pages of Children's Literature*, for example, Casement exhaustively annotates 250 books for young readers that examine racial issues; none of them is older than 1965.

CHAPTER 4

1 The question of whether a child reader can discern the distinction between a biography and a fictionalized biography is made all the murkier by Hollowell's "Series in Children's Books," a response to Adair that represents, for the most part, agreement. In praise of the Bobbs-Merrill series, she noted that the books "serve as fascinating introductions to biography and history."

2 See Hannabuss and Marcella, *Biography and Children*, 11–12, 64–68, 75.

3 The headnote to the Childhood of Famous Americans series documents the connection of *Buffalo Bill: Boy of the Plains* to the army's de-Nazification program; see Schrader, *The Hoosier House*, 117.

4 Stevenson, *George Washington: Boy Leader*; Stevenson, *Ben Franklin: Printer's Boy*; Stevenson, *Daniel Boone: Boy Hunter*.

5 The sales figures are taken from Hollowell, "Series in Children's Books." The reviewer's warning appears in Colby, "The Series of Series." See also Heriot, "Children and Biography." Others, of course, disagreed with these warnings and even sought a movement of the genre into other media; in 1959 Delta Jack, a librarian of the Oliver Wendell Holmes Elementary School in Detroit, argued that, in fact, television series depictions of western figures—patently fictional—could nonetheless stimulate interest in biographies of those same figures and thus contribute to the teaching of "love of country and democratic ideals"—which Jack seemed to suggest is the purpose of biographies of American subjects. The notion that biographies written for children could contribute to American democracy is cited, too, in Brown and Brown, "Biography in the Social Sciences"; a number of writers, they note, argue that "biography has a potential in terms of democratic values, that it facilitates understanding of democracy and improves the ability to evaluate leadership potential." The sig-

nificance of the Lincoln biography in the history of the publishing house is examined by O'Bar in "The Origins and History." These sales figures agree with an assessment in 1957 by Helen Mackintosh, then president of the NCTE, who noted that in a survey of New Jersey students, the popularity of "biographies, especially of famous Americans, and stories of pioneers and explorers when combined, outranked all other choices in grades five through eight."

6 See "Sales of Juvenile Nonfiction"; Shippen, "The Landmark Books."

7 In *Learning from the Left*, 10, Mickenberg argues that much of the work done in children's biography about African American subjects was being written by leftist writers who found in children's literature a safe venue for progressive ideas during a repressive time. In fact, she paraphrases Dorothy Sterling, who wrote *Freedom Train: The Story of Harriet Tubman*, as arguing that "any book by a white writer published before 1965 and sympathetic to African Americans was probably written by a Communist or former Communist." Mickenberg's work shows that, indeed, leftist writers would play a prominent role in the development of biographies about African Americans; this work appears both in her Oxford University Press study and in "Civil Rights, History and the Left."

CHAPTER 5

1 See also Tuttle, "America's Home Front Children," 29.

2 One finds similar connections in Eleanor Estes's series *The Moffats*, *The Middle Moffat*, and *Rufus M.*, which, though set during World War I, mirror the experiences of the current war in references to such practices as rationing and the hanging of flags with stars for soldiers currently serving. The third in the series, in fact, ends with peace being declared. In contrast, Dyson argues in "Children's Books Go to War" that the Newbery and Caldecott Award–winning books of the period skirted the presence of the war by rewarding instead historical books that affirmed the historical myths of America without acknowledging the actual day-to-day presence of the war in the lives of children.

3 Two addresses by Franklin D. Roosevelt, 26–33; Ernest Wilkins, "A Peace Plan Suggestion," 43; "Funeral March of Youth," 20–21; Laurence Housman, "An Incident at Verdun," 15–16; B. Franklin Hunter, "The New Star Spangled Banner," 62. The book was lauded in *English Journal* 26.5 (May 1937): 409.

4 Numerous articles in the book field affirmed the idea that children should be reading nonfiction to equip them for the times they were living in: nonfiction provides "reassurance in a topsy-turvy world through explanation and information . . . and these books will certainly perform a great service in giving boys and girls of all ages a knowledge of the war which is taking place all around them" (Morrow, "Children's Books in a Wartime

Year"); young readers "cannot too soon be equipped with the knowledge and tolerance and understanding so desperately needed for the difficult years ahead" (Ives, "Children's Books and the War").

5   Most of Beard's citations were works for older children, but there were similar nonfiction texts aimed at a younger audience as well, including Shenton's *An Alphabet of the Army*, also published this same year. A short book with two-toned illustrations, *An Alphabet of the Army* gathered under lettered headings random bits of mostly technical information about the war effort: "Assault Detachment" under A (9); "Half-Track" under H (30); "Quartermaster Corps" under Q (46); and "Zero Hour" under Z (64). The explanations are principally technical—and dry—though there is real earnestness: Under "Yesterday" (62–63), Shenton notes: "Our Armies have always been formed from citizen-soldiers. Today the men of the Armed Forces have been selected from all walks of life. Yet because this method truly represents our whole country, we can say that our Army is the Nation, and our Nation is an Army."

6   When *The Raft* was published, its jacket announced that the survival of these men is "proof of the military value of the democratic ideal."

7   The statistics for Bowen's pace and for the books' sales were published in a giddy article (Meeker and Meeker, "For Boys Only"). In pulp fiction published for children, these stereotypes were not unique to those works published only during the war—as noted and examined in Wood, "Footprints from the Past."

8   The sanction of the United States Navy for Felsen's work is cited in Breed, "Books That Build," and is stressed in *Navy Diver* by the reprinting of a letter from the secretary of the navy affirming the work.

9   In the January–February 1945 issue, *Horn Book* also suggested that readers look at Carey McWilliams's *Prejudice: Japanese Americans: Symbol of Racial Intolerance* (Boston: Little, Brown, 1944)—though this was an adult resource. McWilliams had established his reputation as a writer who dealt with American social prejudice in his *Factories in the Field: The Story of Migratory Farm Labor in California* (Boston: Little, Brown, 1939)—published just three months after John Steinbeck's *The Grapes of Wrath*—and the wide-ranging *Brothers under the Skin* (Boston: Little, Brown, 1943).

CHAPTER 6

1   Edgar Parin D'Aulaire's comment on moving to America is cited from his Caldecott acceptance speech in Crago, "Edgar Parin D'Aulaire." The well-documented facts of the D'Aulaires' lives appear in such sources as Mahony and Mitchell, "Ingri and Edgar Parin D'Aulaire"; "Ingri and Edgar Parin D'Aulaire," in Kunitz and Haycraft, *The Junior Book of Authors*, 12–13; and Foster, "Ingri and Edgar Parin D'Aulaire." The D'Aulaires' editor, May Massee, also wrote a whimsical biographical piece, "Ingri and Edgar

Parin D'Aulaire: A Sketch," which was followed by an equally whimsical account by the D'Aulaires of one of their many trips: "The Gentle Art of Driving Reindeer."

2 The description of their moves appears in numerous sketches, as previously noted. Especially useful here is Foster, "Ingri and Edgar Parin D'Aulaire," and Mahony, Latimer, and Tolmsbee, "Edgar Parin D'Aulaire" and "Ingri Parin D'Aulaire," in *Illustrators of Children's Books*, 297. The quotation regarding the domestication of the D'Aulaires appears in Kunitz, *Junior Book of Authors*, 12.

3 The text quotes are from Ingri and Edgar Parin D'Aulaire, "Working Together on Books for Children," in Miller and Field, *Caldecott Medal Books*, 44–54. The Caldecott acceptance speeches were originally printed as D'Aulaire and D'Aulaire, "Working Together."

4 Fisher, *Matters of Fact*, 370–72.

5 The argument here on perspective is echoed in Marcus, "Life Drawings"; Marcus points out that in suiting the first encounter with the past to a child audience, the D'Aulaires worked to create a world populated with toys that have been animated, suggesting that the process was well suited to the very young child who was their books' audience.

6 Despite the irony of the illustrations in *George Washington*, however, the D'Aulaires were still ambivalent about the way they could portray slavery and in the end would not set it as a negative aspect of Washington's life. When he returns from the Revolutionary War, "with beaming faces the slaves and servants, too, welcomed their master home." Afterward, "he walked peacefully over his fields, where the slaves were singing and working." Here, the D'Aulaires' insistence on presenting only the positive in their figures has prevented them from presenting slavery as an evil enterprise.

CHAPTER 7

1 The vision of how children's literature should relate to the Soviet Union shifted quickly as wartime alliances shifted. In the spring of 1944 Helen Sattley was lamenting the lack of reading material on the Soviet Union, since "the need for understanding between the two countries is eminent and great" ("Are You Celebrating"). Four years later, Allie Beth Martin, a librarian at the Tulsa, Oklahoma, public library, urged the use of books on the Soviet Union not to celebrate but to contextualize the growing conflicts between the United States and the Soviet Union. Children, she wrote, "sense the import of the struggle between the United States and Russia from their daily papers and the radio, from conversations at home and at school. We would give to these children basic information unbiased and truly representative of the land and the peoples so that they might learn to form their own opinions based upon accurate knowledge

and understanding" ("Children's Books"). That kind of unbiased openness would come under huge pressure in the next decade.

2 The activities of the National Council for American Education and other ways in which educators were encouraged to teach American history and literature as a direct response to Communism are explored in Lora, "Education"; Kipp, "Report from Boston"; Benemann, "Tears and Ivory Towers"; Moore, "Censorship"; "As Others See Us." Robbins documents the threats to intellectual freedom in libraries during the McCarthy period in her *Censorship and the American Library*, 69–104.

3 Pierre Van Paassen's speech to the Wisconsin Education Association, "There Is Still Time," was quoted in part in the *Wisconsin Journal of Education* (January 1950): 3–5.

4 And even, one might speculate, award committees. In a climate that stressed the importance of presenting new cultures to child readers, it is perhaps understandable that one of the elements that led to E. B. White's *Charlotte's Web* (1952) being awarded a Newbery Honor and Ann Nolan Clark's *Secret of the Andes* (1952) being awarded that year's Newbery Award might be that the latter presents the stubborn and noble persistence of the Incan culture within Spanish-conquered Peru, as Cusi resolves to hold on to the secret of his ancestors and to cherish the traditions of herding llamas, who "watched him with eyes that were ancient and wise and sad with the grief of a conquered people" (80).

5 The publication figures were printed in *Publishers Weekly*, January 15, 1944, 197–99.

6 Both of the posters for National Children's Book Week picturing the theme "Reading Is Fun" depict children reading books, the one for 1952 on a high ladder against a background of bookshelves, the one for 1953 a group of children all gathered in a very contemporary chair; they are reprinted in Marcus, *75 Years*, 30–31.

CHAPTER 8

1 The comment by Anne Carroll Moore and Virginia Lee Burton's response to the thematic meaning of *The Little House* are both cited from Elleman, *Virginia Lee Burton*, 67, 62–63. See also "Newbery-Caldecott 1943 Awards," *Library Journal*, June 15, 1943, 523; "John Newbery and Randolph Caldecott Medals Awarded at Dinner for Librarians," *Publishers Weekly*, June 19, 1943, 2295; Burton, "Making Picture Books."

2 Writing of *Mike Mulligan and His Steam Shovel*, Elleman has similarly noted "Burton's theme of survival through adjustment," though she does not note Burton's complicating of that theme in the books as a whole ("Virginia Lee Burton"). In her *Virginia Lee Burton* Elleman shifts this description to "survival results from adapting to changes in life" (40).

3 A number of articles from the midcentury celebrated these books by link-

ing them to Burton's biography. These include MacCampbell, "Virginia Lee Burton"; and Burns and Hines, "Virginia Lee Burton."

4 Stott and Krier wrestle with the pastoralism of *The Little House*, arguing that though it would seem that the book should fall into that tradition, with its expression of the tensions between urban and rural lives, instead it belongs much more to the genre of romance, since it involves a linear journey back to an idealized past ("Virginia Lee Burton's *The Little House*"). Stott comes to very similar conclusions in his "Pastoralism and Escapism," where he argues that the picture book is about "two main aspects of American social history: the fear of spreading urbanization and the yearning for a return to a simpler, rural way of life."

5 Just before her death, Burton was considering another book with a similar celebration of technology. It was to be a book about the building of a little house, and its illustrations and story were to be enhanced by border illustrations dealing with elements of carpentry and building. Cited from Kingman, "Virginia Lee Burton's Dynamic Sense."

6 Burton's description of *Maybelle the Cable Car* is cited in Elleman, *Virginia Lee Burton*, 99.

7 The description of Homer's room as one of "comfortable clutter" is McCloskey's and is cited from the film *Robert McCloskey*, dir. Morton Schindel (Weston Woods, 1964).

8 Beverly Cleary's series of books about Henry Huggins continued for many years, focusing on a variety of characters Cleary introduced. In "Keith Robertson" McGrath speaks to the experience of all of these boy characters when she writes of Keith Robertson's Henry Reed that they are "model American boys of about 1950 vintage, clean-cut, wholesome, bright young fellows who would do credit to any senior Boy Scout Troop. . . . This is the mythical middle-America upon which nostalgia for a golden past is built. Home was never like this—but how nice if it had been! . . . [These characters] leave you feeling that it isn't such a bad old world after all."

CONCLUSION

1 Minarik and Sendak also crafted a fifth book in the series several years later: *A Kiss for Little Bear*, which celebrates the same close, domestic, secure world.

2 MacLeod, *American Childhood*, 199–204.

3 See Marcus, *75 Years*, 35–36.

PRIMARY TEXTS

Albjerg, Esther Marguerite, Frederic Butterfield Knight, and Edward Jackson Woodward. *We, the Guardians of Our Liberty: An Account of the American Bill of Rights.* Chicago: Beckley-Cardy, 1940.

Allen, Devere, George Catlin, Vera Brittain, Sheila Hodges, and Gert Spindler, eds. *Above All Nations.* New York: Harper, 1949.

Angel, Joan. *Angel of the Navy: The Story of a WAVE.* New York: Hastings House, 1943.

Bacon, Peggy. *Buttons.* New York: Viking, 1938.

Bailey, Carolyn Sherwin. *Children of the Handcrafts.* New York: Viking, 1935.

———. *Tops and Whistles: True Stories of Early American Toys and Children.* New York: Viking, 1937.

Banning, Kendall. *Our Army Today.* New York: Funk and Wagnalls, 1943.

Bechdolt, Jack. *Junior Air Raid Wardens.* Philadelphia: J. B. Lippincott, 1942.

Beim, Jerrold. *Swimming Hole.* New York: William Morrow, 1950.

Beim, Lorraine, and Jerrold Beim. *Two Is a Team.* Illustrated by Ernest Crichlow. New York: Harcourt Brace, 1945.

Bell, Kensil. *"Always Ready!": The Story of the United States Coast Guard.* New York: Dodd-Mead, 1943.

Benét, Rosemary, and Stephen Vincent Benét. *A Book of Americans.* New York: Farrar and Rinehart, 1933.

Benét, Stephen Vincent. *America.* New York: Farrar and Rinehart, 1944.

Berry, Erick. *Seven Beaver Skins: A Story of the Dutch in New Amsterdam.* Land of the Free Series. Philadelphia: John C. Winston Company, 1948.

———. *There Is the Land.* New York: Oxford University Press, 1943.

Best, Herbert. *Watergate: A Story of the Irish on the Erie Canal.* Land of the Free Series. Philadelphia: John C. Winston Company, 1951.

Beurling, George F., and Leslie Roberts. *Malta Spitfire: The Story of a Fighter Pilot.* New York: Farrar and Rinehart, 1943.

Blackford, Charles Minor. *Deep Treasure: A Story of the Greek Sponge Fishers of Florida.* Land of the Free Series. Philadelphia: John C. Winston Company, 1954.

Blackstock, Josephine. *Wings for Nikias: A Story of the Greece of Today.* New York: G. Putnam, 1942.

Bliven, Bruce, Jr. *The Story of D-Day: June 6, 1944.* New York: Random House, 1956.

Blyton, Enid. *Mystery Island.* New York: Macmillan, 1945.

Boatright, Mody Coggin. *Folk Laughter on the American Frontier.* New York: Macmillan, 1949.

Bontemps, Arna. *Chariot in the Sky: A Story of the Jubilee Singers.* Land of the Free Series. Philadelphia: John C. Winston Company, 1951.

———. *Frederick Douglass: Slave, Fighter, Freeman.* New York: Knopf, 1959.

———. *Sad-Faced Boy.* Boston: Houghton Mifflin, 1937.

———. *Story of the Negro.* New York: Alfred A. Knopf, 1948.

Bontemps, Arna, and Jack Conroy. *The Fast Sooner Hound.* Boston: Houghton Mifflin, 1942.

Bontemps, Arna, and Langston Hughes. *Popo and Fifina: Children of Haiti.* New York: Macmillan, 1932.

Boswell, Hazel. *French Canada.* New York: Viking Press, 1938.

Bowen, R. Sidney. *Dave Dawson on Guadalcanal.* New York: Saalfield Publishing Company, 1943.

———. *Dave Dawson with the Pacific Fleet.* New York: Crown Publishers, 1942.

———. *Dave Dawson with the R.A.F.* New York: Saalfield Publishing Company, 1941.

Bowen, William. *The Old Tobacco Shop: A True Account of What Befell a Little Boy in Search of Adventure.* New York: Macmillan, 1921.

Bridwell, Norman. *Clifford the Big Red Dog.* New York: Scholastic, 1963.

Brink, Carol Ryrie. *Caddie Woodlawn.* New York: Macmillan, 1935.

Brooke, Leslie. *Johnny Crow's Garden.* London: Frederick Warne, 1903.

———. *The Story of the Three Bears.* London: Frederick Warne, 1904.

———. *The Story of the Three Little Pigs.* London: Frederick Warne, 1904.

Brown, Margaret Wise. *The Dead Bird.* Illustrated by Remy Charlip. New York: William R. Scott, 1958.

Brown, Rose. *Two Children of Brazil.* Philadelphia: J. B. Lippincott, 1940.

Bryant, Sara Cone. *Epaminondas and His Auntie.* Boston: Houghton Mifflin, 1938.

Buck, Pearl. *The Chinese Children Next Door.* New York: John Day, 1942.

Burnett, Constance Buel. *Lucretia Mott: Girl of Old Nantucket.* Indianapolis, IN: Bobbs-Merrill, 1951.

Burroughs, Margaret Taylor. *Jasper, the Drummin' Boy.* New York: Viking, 1947.

Burt, Olive. *The Oak's Long Shadow: A Story of the Basque Sheepherders in Ohio.* Land of the Free Series. Philadelphia: John C. Winston Company, 1952.

Burton, Virginia Lee. *Choo Choo: The Story of a Little Engine Who Ran Away.* Boston: Houghton Mifflin, 1937.

———. *Katy and the Big Snow.* Boston: Houghton Mifflin, 1943.

———. *The Little House*. Boston: Houghton Mifflin, 1942.

———. *Maybelle the Cable Car*. Boston: Houghton Mifflin, 1952.

———. *Mike Mulligan and His Steam Shovel*. Boston: Houghton Mifflin, 1939.

Calvert, James. *A Promise to Our Country*. Illustrated by James Daugherty. New York: McGraw-Hill, 1961.

Cannon, Fanny Venable. *Playing Fair*. New York: E. P. Dutton, 1940.

Carpenter, Frank G. *Around the World with Children: An Introduction to Geography*. New York: American Book Company, 1917.

Carroll, Gladys Hasty. *As the Earth Turns*. New York: Macmillan, 1933.

Carroll, Lewis. *Alice's Adventures in Wonderland*. Illustrated by Peter Newell. New York: Harper and Brothers, 1901.

———. *The Hunting of the Snark*. Illustrated by Peter Newell. New York: Harper and Brothers, 1903.

———. *Through the Looking-Glass and What Alice Found There*. Illustrated by Peter Newell. New York: Harper and Brothers, 1902.

Chandler, Anna Curtis. *Treasure Trails in Art*. Boston: Hale, Cushman & Flint, 1937.

Childers, James Saxon. *War Eagles: The Story of the Eagle Squadron*. New York: D. Appleton–Century, 1943.

Clark, Ann Nolan. *Secret of the Andes*. New York: Viking Press, 1952.

Clark, Margery. *The Poppy Seed Cake*. Garden City, NY: Doubleday, Page, 1924.

Cleary, Beverly. *Henry and Beezus*. New York: William Morrow, 1952.

———. *Henry and Ribsy*. New York: William Morrow, 1954.

———. *Henry and the Clubhouse*. New York: William Morrow, 1962.

———. *Henry and the Paper Route*. New York: William Morrow, 1957.

———. *Henry Huggins*. New York: William Morrow, 1950.

Coatsworth, Elizabeth Jane. *The Cat and the Captain*. New York: Macmillan, 1927.

———. *The Cat Who Went to Heaven*. New York: Macmillan, 1930.

———. *Door to the North: A Saga of Fourteenth Century America*. Land of the Free Series. Philadelphia: John C. Winston Company, 1950.

———. *The Last Fort: A Story of the French Voyageurs*. Land of the Free Series. Philadelphia: John C. Winston Company, 1952.

———. *The Sod House*. New York: Macmillan, 1954.

———. *The White Horse*. New York: Macmillan, 1942.

Coffin, Robert P. Tristram. *Ballads of Square-Toed Americans*. New York: Macmillan, 1933.

Colum, Padraic. *The Adventures of Odysseus and the Tale of Troy*. Illustrated by Willy Pogány. New York: Macmillan, 1918.

———. *The Children of Odin*. Illustrated by Willy Pogány. New York: Macmillan, 1920.

———. *The Golden Fleece and the Heroes Who Lived before Achilles*. Illustrated by Willy Pogány. New York: Macmillan, 1921.

Commager, Henry Steele. *Living Ideas in America*. New York: Harper, 1951.

Cormack, Maribelle, and William P. Alexander. *Land for My Sons: A Frontier Tale of the American Revolution*. New York: D. Appleton–Century, 1939.

Credle, Ellis. *Down, Down the Mountain*. New York: Thomas Nelson and Sons, 1934.

Dagliesh, Alice. *America Builds Homes: The Story of the First Colonies*. New York: C. Scribner's Sons, 1938.

———. *The Silver Pencil*. New York: Charles Scribner's Sons, 1944.

Daly, Maureen. *Seventeenth Summer*. New York: Dodd, Mead, 1942.

Daugherty, James. *Abraham Lincoln*. New York: Viking Press, 1943.

———. *Andy and the Lion*. New York: Viking, 1938.

———. *Of Courage Undaunted: Across the Continent with Lewis and Clark*. New York: Viking, 1951.

———. *Daniel Boone*. New York: Viking Press, 1939.

———. *Henry David Thoreau: A Man for Our Time*. New York: Viking, 1967.

———. *The Kingdom and the Power and the Glory*. New York: Alfred A. Knopf, 1929.

———. *The Landing of the Pilgrims*. New York: Random House, 1950.

———. *Lincoln's Gettysburg Address: A Pictorial Representation*. Chicago: Albert Whitman, 1947.

———. *Marcus and Narcissa Whitman: Pioneers of Oregon*. New York: Viking, 1953.

———. *Poor Richard*. New York: Viking Press, 1941.

———. *The Sound of Trumpets: Selections from Ralph Waldo Emerson*. New York: Viking, 1971.

———. *Trappers and Traders of the Far West*. New York: Random House, 1952.

———. *Walt Whitman's America*. Cleveland: World Publishing, 1964.

———. *West of Boston: Yankee Rhymes and Doggerel*. New York: Viking, 1956.

———. *The Wild Wild West*. Philadelphia: David McKay, 1948.

D'Aulaire, Edgar Parin, and Ingri D'Aulaire. *Abraham Lincoln*. New York: Doubleday, 1939.

———. *Benjamin Franklin*. Garden City, NY: Doubleday, 1950.

———. *Buffalo Bill*. Garden City, NY: Doubleday, 1952.

———. *The Conquest of the Atlantic*. New York: Viking, 1933.

———. *George Washington*. Garden City, NY: Doubleday, Doran, 1936.

———. *Leif the Lucky*. Garden City, NY: Doubleday, 1941.

———. *The Magic Rug*. Garden City, NY: Doubleday, 1931.

———. *Nils*. Garden City, NY: Doubleday, 1948.

———. *Ola*. Garden City, NY: Doubleday, 1932.

———. *Pocahontas*. Garden City, NY: Doubleday, 1946.

———. *The Star-Spangled Banner*. Garden City, NY: Doubleday, Doran, 1942.

———. *Wings for Per*. Garden City, NY: Doubleday, Doran, 1944.

Davis, Julia. *Peter Hale*. New York: E. P. Dutton, 1939.

Davis, Russell, and Brent Ashabranner. *Point Four Assignment*. Boston: Little, Brown, 1959.

De Angeli, Marguerite. *Bright April*. Garden City, NY: Doubleday, 1946.

———. *Skippack School; Being the Story of Eli Shrawder and of One Christopher Dock, Schoolmaster, About the Year 1750*. New York: Doubleday, 1939.

———. *Up the Hill*. Garden City, NY: Doubleday, Doran, 1942.

De Grummond, Lena Young, and Lynn de Grummond Belaune. *Babe Didrickson: Girl Athlete*. Indianapolis, IN: Bobbs-Merrill, 1963.

De la Mare, Walter. *Mr. Bumps and His Monkey*. New York: Holt, Rinehart and Winston, 1942.

Donahue, Arthur Gerald. *Tally-ho! Yankee in a Spitfire*. New York: Macmillan, 1941.

Downey, Fairfax. *Dog of War*. New York: Dodd, Mead, 1943.

Doyle, A. Conan. *The White Company*. Illustrated by James Daugherty. New York: Harper, 1928.

Dunbar, Paul Laurence. *Little Brown Baby*. New York: Dodd, Mead, 1940.

Duvoisin, Roger. *And There Was America*. New York: Alfred A. Knopf, 1938.

Dyett, James G. *From Sea to Shining Sea*. New York: Oxford University Press, 1943.

Edmonds, Walter D. *The Matchlock Gun*. New York: Dodd, Mead, 1941.

Enright, Elizabeth. *The Four-Story Mistake*. New York: Farrar and Rinehart, 1942.

———. *Kintu: A Congo Adventure*. New York: Farrar and Rinehart, 1935.

———. *The Saturdays*. New York: Farrar and Rinehart, 1941.

———. *Thimble Summer*. New York: Holt, Rinehart and Winston, 1938.

Escott-Inman, Herbert. *Wulnoth the Wanderer*. New York: Longmans, Green, 1928.

Estes, Eleanor. *The Hundred Dresses*. New York: Harcourt Brace, 1944.

———. *The Middle Moffat*. New York: Harcourt Brace, 1942.

———. *The Moffats*. New York: Harcourt Brace, 1941.

———. *Rufus M.* New York: Harcourt Brace, 1943.

Ets, Marie Hall. *Mister Penny*. New York: Viking, 1935.

Evans, Eva Knox. *All about Us*. New York: Capitol Publishing, 1947.

———. *Araminta*. New York: G. P. Putnam's Sons, 1935.

———. *Araminta's Goat*. New York: G. P. Putnam's Sons, 1938.

———. *Jerome Anthony*. New York: G. P. Putnam's Sons, 1936.

———. *Key Corner*. New York: G. P. Putnam's Sons, 1938.

Fast, Howard. *The Tall Hunter*. New York: Harper and Brothers, 1942.

Faulkner, Georgene, and John Becker. *Melindy's Medal*. New York: Julian Messner, 1945.

Felsen, Gregor. *Navy Diver*. New York: Dutton, 1942.

———. *Submarine Sailor*. New York: Dutton, 1943.

Field, Rachel. *Calico Bush*. New York: Macmillan, 1931.

——. *Hitty: Her First Hundred Years*. New York: Macmillan, 1929.

Fisher, Dorothy Canfield. *And Long Remember: Some Great Americans Who Have Helped Me*. New York: McGraw-Hill, 1959.

——. *Our Independence and the Constitution*. New York: Random House, 1950.

Fitch, Florence May. *One God: The Ways We Worship Him*. New York: Lothrop, Lee and Shepard, 1944.

Flexner, Hortense. *The Wishing Window*. New York: Frederick A. Stokes, 1942.

Floherty, John Joseph. *Men without Fear*. Philadelphia: J. B. Lippincott, 1940.

Forbes, Esther. *Johnny Tremain*. Boston: Houghton Mifflin, 1943.

Forester, C. S. *Poo-Poo and the Dragons*. Boston: Little, Brown, 1942.

Foster, Genevieve. *Abraham Lincoln's World*. New York: C. Scribner's Sons, 1944.

——. *Birthdays of Freedom: From Early Egypt to the Fall of Rome*. New York: Charles Scribner's Sons, 1952.

——. *Birthdays of Freedom: From the Fall of Rome to July 4, 1776*. New York: Charles Scribner's Sons, 1957.

——. *George Washington's World*. New York: C. Scribner's Sons, 1941.

——. *The World of Captain John Smith*. New York: Scribner, 1959.

Freeman, Don. *Fly High, Fly Low*. New York: Viking Press, 1957.

Friedman, Frieda. *A Sundae with Judy*. New York: William Morrow, 1949.

Frisbee, Lucy Post. *John F. Kennedy: Young Statesman*. Indianapolis, IN: Bobbs-Merrill, 1964.

Gage, Joseph H. *The Beckoning Hills: A Story of the Italians in California*. Land of the Free Series. Philadelphia: John C. Winston Company, 1951.

Gall, Alice Crew, and Fleming H. Crew. *Bushy Tail*. New York: Oxford University Press, 1941.

——. *Flat Tail*. New York: H. Z. Walck, 1935.

Gardiner, Frederic Merrick. *"Stand By—Mark!": The Career Story of a Naval Officer*. New York: Dodd, Mead, 1943.

Gates, Doris. *Blue Willow*. New York: Viking Press, 1940.

Gill, Richard, and Helen Hoke. *Paco Goes to the Fair*. New York: Henry Holt, 1940.

Goslin, Ryllis Clair Alexander, and Omar Panacoast Goslin. *Democracy*. New York: Harcourt Brace, 1940.

Govan, Christine Noble. *Narcissus an' de Chillun*. Boston: Houghton Mifflin, 1938.

——. *Rachel Jackson: Tennessee Girl*. Indianapolis, IN: Bobbs-Merrill, 1955.

Gray, Elizabeth Janet. *Adam of the Road*. New York: Viking, 1942.

Grey, Katherine. *Rolling Wheels*. Boston: Little, Brown, 1932.

Gronowicz, Antoni. *Bolek*. New York: Thomas Nelson and Sons, 1942.

Guyton, Boone T. *This Exciting Air: The Experiences of a Test Pilot*. New York: McGraw-Hill Book Company, 1943.

Hader, Berta, and Elmer Hader. *The Big Snow*. New York: Macmillan, 1948.

Ham, A. W., and M. B. Salter. *Doctor in the Making: The Art of Being a Medical Student*. Philadelphia: J. B. Lippincott, 1943.

The Handbook for Boys. New York: Boy Scouts of America, 1928.

Hark, Ann. *Island Treasure*. Philadelphia: J. B. Lippincott, 1938.

——. *The Phantom of the Forest*. Philadelphia: J. B. Lippincott, 1939.

——. *The Seminary's Secret*. Philadelphia: J. B. Lippincott, 1936.

Harper, Wilhelmina. *Uncle Sam's Story Book*. Philadelphia: David McKay, 1944.

Hartman, Gertrude. *These United States and How They Came to Be*. New York: Macmillan, 1932.

Havighurst, Walter, and Marion Havighurst. *Climb a Lofty Ladder: A Story of Swedish Settlement in Minnesota*. Land of the Free Series. Philadelphia: John C. Winston Company, 1952.

——. *Song of the Pines: A Story of Norwegian Lumbering in Wisconsin*. Land of the Free Series. Philadelphia: John C. Winston Company, 1949.

Haynes, Williams. *The Chemical Front*. New York: A. A. Knopf, 1943.

Henry, Joanne Landers. *Elizabeth Blackwell: Girl Doctor*. Indianapolis, IN: Bobbs-Merrill, 1961.

Higgins, Helen Boyd. *Juliette Low: Girl Scout*. Indianapolis, IN: Bobbs-Merrill, 1951.

Hine, Lewis W. *Men at Work*. New York: Macmillan, 1932.

Hodges, C. Walter. *Columbus Sails*. New York: Coward McCann, 1939.

Hoff, Syd. *Danny and the Dinosaur*. New York: Harper and Row, 1958.

——. *Julius*. New York: Harper, 1959.

——. *Sammy the Seal*. New York: Harper and Row, 1959.

Hogan, Inez. *Nicodemus and the Goose*. New York: E. P. Dutton, 1945.

——. *Nicodemus and the Little Black Pig*. New York: E. P. Dutton, 1934.

Howe, Jane Moore. *Amelia Earhart: Kansas Girl*. Indianapolis, IN: Bobbs-Merrill, 1950.

How Red Are the Schools? And How You Can Eradicate Socialism and Communism from the Schools and Colleges of America. New York: National Council for American Education, 1950.

Hubbard, Margaret Ann. *Little Whirlwind*. New York: Macmillan, 1940.

Huberman, Leo. *"We, the People."* New York: Harper and Brothers, 1932.

Hughes, Langston. *The Dream Keeper and Other Poems*. New York: Alfred A. Knopf, 1932.

——. *The First Book of Africa*. New York: Franklin Watts, 1960.

Hughes, Langston, and Milton Meltzer. *A Pictorial History of the Negro in America*. New York: Crown, 1956.

Irwin, Will, and Thomas M. Johnson. *What You Should Know about Spies and Saboteurs*. New York: W. W. Norton, 1943.

Isasi, Mirim, and Melcena Burns Denny. *White Stars of Freedom*. Chicago: Albert Whitman, 1942.

Jackson, Jesse. *Anchor Man*. New York: Harper and Row, 1947.

———. *Call Me Charley*. New York: Harper and Row, 1945.

———. *Charley Starts from Scratch*. New York: Harper, 1958.

Jacobs, Ida T., ed., for the Committee on International Relations of the National Council of Teachers of English. *War and Peace: An Anthology*. Chicago: National Council of Teachers of English, 1937.

Johnson, Crockett. *Harold and the Purple Crayon*. New York: Harper and Row, 1955.

———. *Harold's Circus*. New York: Harper and Row, 1959.

———. *Harold's Fairy Tale*. New York: Harper, 1956.

———. *Harold's Trip to the Sky*. New York: Harper, 1957.

Johnson, Gerald W. *America Grows Up: A History for Peter*. New York: William Morrow, 1960.

———. *America Is Born: A History for Peter*. New York: Morrow, 1959.

———. *This American People*. New York: Harper, 1951.

Jones, Elizabeth Orton. *Maminka's Children*. New York: Macmillan, 1940.

Keats, Ezra Jack. *The Snowy Day*. New York: Viking Press, 1962.

Kelly, Eric P. *The Trumpeter of Krakow*. New York: Macmillan, 1928.

Klinefelter, Lee M. *Electrical Occupations: Covering the Entire Field of Electrical Occupations Available to Boys When They Grow Up*. New York: E. P. Dutton, 1937.

Knox, Rose B. *Miss Jimmy Deane*. Garden City, NY: Doubleday, 1931.

Krauss, Ruth. *The Happy Day*. Illustrated by Marc Simont. New York: Harper and Row, 1949.

Kummer, Frederic Arnold. *The Torch of Liberty*. Philadelphia: John C. Winston, 1941.

Lang, Andrew, ed. *The Conquest of Montezuma's Empire*. Illustrated by James Daugherty. New York: Longmans, Green, 1928.

Lansing, Marion Florence. *Great Moments in Freedom*. Garden City, NY: Doubleday, Doran, 1930.

Lattimore, Eleanor Frances. *Bayou Boy*. New York: Morrow, 1946.

———. *Holly in the Snow*. New York: William Morrow, 1954.

———. *Little Pear: The Story of a Little Chinese Boy*. New York: Harcourt Brace and World, 1931.

———. *The Questions of Lifu: A Story of China*. New York: Harcourt Brace, 1942.

———. *Storm on the Island*. New York: Harcourt Brace, 1942.

Lawson, Marie Abrams. *Hail Columbia: The Story of the Pioneer Nation of the Western Hemisphere*. Garden City, NY: Doubleday, Doran, 1931.

Lawson, Robert. *Ben and Me*. Boston: Little, Brown, 1939.

———. *Rabbit Hill*. New York: Viking, 1944.

———. *They Were Strong and Good*. New York: Viking, 1940.

———. *The Tough Winter*. New York: Viking Press, 1954.

———. *Watchwords of Liberty: A Pageant of American Quotations*. Boston: Little, Brown, 1943, 1957.

Lawson, Ted W. *Thirty Seconds over Tokyo*. New York: Random House, 1943.

Leaf, Munro. *Fair Play*. New York: Frederick A. Stokes, 1939.

——. *Grammar Can Be Fun*. New York: Frederick A. Stokes, 1934.

——. *Manners Can Be Fun*. New York: Frederick A. Stokes, 1936.

——. *The Story of Ferdinand the Bull*. New York: Viking Press, 1936.

——. *A War-Time Handbook for Young Americans*. New York: Frederick A. Stokes, 1942.

Lenski, Lois. *Berries in the Scoop*. Philadelphia: J. B. Lippincott, 1956.

——. *Blue Ridge Billy*. Philadelphia: J. B. Lippincott, 1946.

——. *Corn-Farm Boy*. Philadelphia: J. B. Lippincott, 1954.

——. *Cotton in My Sack*. Philadelphia: J. B. Lippincott, 1949.

——. *Indian Captive: The Story of Mary Jemison*. Philadelphia: J. B. Lippincott, 1941.

——. *Judy's Journey*. Philadelphia: J. B. Lippincott, 1947.

——. *Little Sioux Girl*. Philadelphia: J. B. Lippincott, 1958.

——. *Ocean-Born Mary*. Philadelphia: J. B. Lippincott, 1939.

——. *Prairie School*. Philadelphia: J. B. Lippincott, 1951.

——. *Puritan Adventure*. Philadelphia: J. B. Lippincott, 1944.

——. *San Francisco Boy*. Philadelphia: J. B. Lippincott, 1955.

——. *Strawberry Girl*. Philadelphia: J. B. Lippincott, 1945.

——. *We Live in the Country*. Philadelphia: J. B. Lippincott, 1960.

Lewis, Elizabeth Foreman. *When the Typhoon Blows*. Philadelphia: J. C. Winston, 1942.

——. *Young Fu of the Upper Yangtze*. New York: Holt, Rinehart, 1932.

Leyson, Burr. *Fighting Fire*. New York: E. P. Dutton, 1939.

Lindsay, Maud McKnight. *Little Missy*. New York: Lothrop, Lee and Shepard, 1922.

Literature Committee of the Association for Childhood Education, ed. *Sung under the Silver Umbrella*. New York: Macmillan, 1935.

——, ed. *Told under the Blue Umbrella*. New York: Macmillan, 1933.

——, ed. *Told under the Green Umbrella*. New York: Macmillan, 1930.

——, ed. *Told under the Magic Umbrella*. New York: Macmillan, 1939.

——, ed. *Told under the Stars and Stripes*. New York: Macmillan, 1945.

Litten, Frederic Nelson. *The Kingdom of Flying Men*. Philadelphia: Westminster Press, 1946.

Lockwood, Myna. *Mystery at Lonesome End*. New York: Oxford University Press, 1946.

Lundy, Jo Evalin. *Seek the Dark Gold: A Story of the Scots Fur Traders*. Land of the Free Series. Philadelphia: John C. Winston Company, 1951.

——. *Tidewater Valley: A Story of the Swiss in Oregon*. Land of the Free Series. Philadelphia: John C. Winston Company, 1949.

Malkus, Alida. *Colt of Destiny: A Story of the California Missions*. Land of the Free Series. Philadelphia: John C. Winston Company, 1950.

Maloy, Lois. *Swift Thunder of the Prairie*. New York: Charles Scribner and Sons, 1942.

Mason, Frank. *Pilots, Man Your Planes!* Philadelphia: J. B. Lippincott, 1944.

Mason, Miriam Evangeline. *Kate Douglas Wiggin: The Little Schoolteacher.* Indianapolis, IN: Bobbs-Merrill, 1958.

——. *Mary Mapes Dodge: Jolly Girl.* Indianapolis, IN: Bobbs-Merrill, 1949.

Mathews, Mitford M. *American Words.* Cleveland: World Publishing, 1959.

McClellan, Mary Butters, and Albert Victor DeBonis, eds. *Within Our Gates.* New York: Harper and Brothers, 1940.

McCloskey, Robert. *Blueberries for Sal.* New York: Viking Press, 1948.

——. *Burt Dow: Deep-Water Man.* New York: Viking, 1963.

——. *Centerburg Tales.* New York: Viking, 1951.

——. *Homer Price.* New York: Viking, 1943.

——. *Lentil.* New York: Viking, 1940.

——. *Make Way for Ducklings.* New York: Viking, 1941.

——. *One Morning in Maine.* New York: Viking, 1952.

——. *Time of Wonder.* New York: Viking, 1957.

McNickle, D'Arcy. *Runner in the Sun: A Story of Indian Maize.* Land of the Free Series. Philadelphia: John C. Winston Company, 1954.

Meader, Stephen W. *Behind the Ridges.* New York: Harcourt Brace, 1947.

Meadowcraft, Enid LaMonte. *Aren't We Lucky!* New York: Crowell, 1939.

Means, Florence Crannell. *Great Day in the Morning.* Boston: Houghton Mifflin, 1946.

——. *The Moved-Outers.* Boston: Houghton Mifflin, 1945.

——. *Rainbow Bridge.* Illustrated by Eleanor Frances Lattimore. New York: Friendship Press, 1934.

——. *Shuttered Windows.* Boston: Houghton Mifflin, 1938.

Means, Florence Crannell, and Carl Means. *The Silver Fleece: A Story of the Spanish in New Mexico.* Land of the Free Series. Philadelphia: John C. Winston Company, 1950.

Meigs, Cornelia. *The Willow Whistle.* New York: Macmillan, 1931.

——. *Windy Hill.* New York: Macmillan, 1921.

Melin, Grace Hathaway. *Dorothea Dix: Girl Reformer.* Indianapolis, IN: Bobbs-Merrill, 1963.

——. *Maria Mitchell: Girl Astronomer.* Indianapolis, IN: Bobbs-Merrill, 1960.

Miers, Earl Schenck. *The Rainbow Book of American History.* Illustrated by James Daugherty. Cleveland: World Publishing, 1955.

Millender, Dharathula H. *Crispus Attucks: Boy of Valor.* Indianapolis, IN: Bobbs-Merrill, 1965.

——. *Louis Armstrong: Young Music Maker.* Indianapolis, IN: Bobbs-Merrill, 1972.

——. *Martin Luther King, Jr.: Boy with a Dream.* Indianapolis, IN: Bobbs-Merrill, 1969.

Miller, Oliver Beaupré, ed. *In the Nursery.* Chicago: Bookhouse for Children, 1920.

——, ed. *The Latch Key.* Chicago: Bookhouse for Children, 1921.

———, ed. *My Travelship: Little Pictures of Japan*. Chicago: Book House for Children, 1925.

———, ed. *Nursery Friends from France*. Chicago: Book House for Children, 1925.

———, ed. *Tales Told in Holland*. Chicago: Book House for Children, 1926.

———, ed. *The Tower Window*. Chicago: Bookhouse for Children, 1921.

———, ed. *Through Fairy Halls*. Chicago: Bookhouse for Children, 1920.

———, ed. *The Treasure Chest*. Chicago: Bookhouse for Children, 1920.

———, ed. *Up One Pair of Stairs*. Chicago: Bookhouse for Children, 1920.

Minarik, Else Holmelund. *Father Bear Comes Home*. Illustrated by Maurice Sendak. New York: Harper and Row, 1959.

———. *A Kiss for Little Bear*. Illustrated by Maurice Sendak. New York: Harper and Row, 1968.

———. *Little Bear*. Illustrated by Maurice Sendak. New York: Harper, 1957.

———. *Little Bear's Friend*. Illustrated by Maurice Sendak. New York: Harper and Row, 1960.

———. *Little Bear's Visit*. Illustrated by Maurice Sendak. New York: Harper and Row, 1961.

Mitchell, Lucy Sprague. *North America: The Land They Live in for the Children Who Live There*. New York: Macmillan, 1931.

Monsell, Helen Albee. *Dolly Madison: Quaker Girl*. Indianapolis, IN: Bobbs-Merrill, 1961.

———. *Susan Anthony: Girl Who Dared*. Indianapolis, IN: Bobbs-Merrill, 1954.

Montross, Lynn. *Washington and the Revolution*. Boston: Houghton Mifflin, 1959.

Morse, Mary Lincoln, et al., eds. *Told under Spacious Skies*. New York: Macmillan, 1952.

Newman, Shirlee Petkin. *Ethel Barrymore: Girl Actress*. Indianapolis, IN: Bobbs-Merrill, 1966.

———. *Liliuokalani: Young Hawaiian Queen*. Indianapolis, IN: Bobbs-Merrill, 1960.

Nolen, Eleanor Weakley. *Cherry Street House*. New York: Thomas Nelson and Sons, 1939.

———. *A Job for Jeremiah*. Illustrated by Iris Beatty Johnson. New York: Oxford University Press, 1940.

———. *Shipment for Susannah*. New York: Thomas Nelson and Sons, 1938.

North, Sterling. *Greased Lightning*. Chicago: John C. Winston, 1940.

———. *Rascal: A Memoir of a Better Era*. New York: E. P. Dutton, 1963.

Oakes, Vanya. *Desert Harvest: A Story of the Japanese in California*. Land of the Free Series. Philadelphia: John C. Winston Company, 1953.

———. *Footprints of the Dragon: A Story of the Chinese and the Pacific Railways*. Land of the Free Series. Philadelphia: John C. Winston Company, 1949.

Parkman, Francis. *The Oregon Trail*. Illustrated by James Daugherty. New York: Holt, Rinehart and Winston, 1959.

Parrish, Anne. *Floating Island*. New York: Harper, 1931.

Peare, Catherine Owens. *The Helen Keller Story*. New York: Crowell, 1959.

Pease, Howard. *Long Wharf: A Story of Young San Francisco*. New York: Dodd, Mead, 1939.

Perkins, Lucy Fitch. *The Pickaninny Twins*. Boston: Houghton Mifflin, 1931.

Petersham, Maud, and Miska Petersham. *An American ABC*. New York: Macmillan, 1941.

———. *The Rooster Crows: A Book of American Rhymes and Jingles*. New York: Macmillan, 1945.

Place, Marian T. *Lotta Crabtree: Girl of the Gold Rush*. Indianapolis, IN: Bobbs-Merrill, 1958.

Purdy, Claire Lee. *He Heard America Sing: The Story of Stephen Foster*. New York: Julian Messner, 1940.

Pyle, Ernie. *Here Is Your War*. New York: Henry Holt, 1943.

Pyne, Mable. *The Little History of the United States*. Boston: Houghton Mifflin, 1940.

Quiller-Couch, Arthur. *The Splendid Spur*. Illustrated by James Daugherty. New York: George H. Doran, 1927.

Randall, Blossom E. *Fun for Chris*. Chicago: Albert Whitman, 1956.

Randall, Ruth Painter. *I Mary: A Biography of the Girl Who Married Abraham Lincoln*. Boston: Little, Brown, 1959.

Reck, Franklin. *Romance of American Transportation*. New York: Thomas Y. Crowell, 1938.

Redding, John M., and Harold I. Leyshon. *Skyways to Berlin: With the American Flyers in England*. Indianapolis, IN: Bobbs-Merrill, 1943.

Reinfeld, Fred. *The Great Dissenters: Guardians of the Country's Laws and Liberties*. New York: Crowell, 1959.

Robertson, Keith. *Henry Reed, Inc.* Illustrated by Robert McCloskey. New York: Viking, 1958.

———. *Henry Reed's Baby-Sitting Service*. Illustrated by Robert McCloskey. New York: Viking, 1966.

———. *Henry Reed's Big Show*. Illustrated by Robert McCloskey. New York: Viking, 1970.

———. *Henry Reed's Journey*. Illustrated by Robert McCloskey. New York: Viking, 1963.

———. *Henry Reed's Think Tank*. New York: Viking, 1986.

Robinson, Gertrude. *The Sign of the Golden Fish: A Story of the Cornish Fishermen in Maine*. Land of the Free Series. Philadelphia: John C. Winston Company, 1949.

Rogers, Cameron. *Drake's Quest*. Illustrated by James Daugherty. Garden City, NY: Doubleday and Page, 1927.

Sandburg, Carl. *Abe Lincoln Grows Up*. Illustrated by James Daugherty. New York: Harcourt, 1928.

——. *The American Songbag.* New York: Harcourt Brace, 1927.

——. *The People, Yes.* New York: Harcourt Brace, 1936.

Saroyan, William. *The Human Comedy.* Illustrated by Don Freeman. New York: Harcourt Brace, 1943.

Sawyer, Ruth. *Roller Skates.* New York: Viking, 1937.

Scott, Robert L., Jr. *God Is My Co-pilot.* New York: Scribner, 1943.

Sendak, Maurice. *Kenny's Window.* New York: Harper and Row, 1956.

——. *Where the Wild Things Are.* New York: Harper and Row, 1963.

Seredy, Kate. *The Good Master.* New York: Viking Press, 1935.

——. *The Singing Tree.* New York: Viking, 1939.

Seuss, Dr. *The Cat in the Hat.* New York: Random House, 1957.

——. *The 500 Hats of Bartholomew Cubbins.* New York: Viking Press, 1938.

——. *Green Eggs and Ham.* New York: Random House, 1960.

——. *Hop on Pop.* New York: Random House, 1963.

——. *One Fish, Two Fish, Red Fish, Blue Fish.* New York: Random House, 1960.

Seymour, Flora Warren. *Pocahontas: Brave Girl.* Indianapolis, IN: Bobbs-Merrill, 1946.

——. *Sacagawea: Bird Girl.* Indianapolis, IN: Bobbs-Merrill, 1945, 1959.

Shannon, Monica. *Dobry.* New York: Viking, 1934.

Shapiro, Irwin. *Joe Magarac and His U.S.A. Citizenship Papers.* Illustrated by James Daugherty. New York: Julian Messner, 1949.

——. *John Henry and the Double-Jointed Steam Drill.* Illustrated by James Daugherty. New York: Julian Messner, 1945.

——. *Yankee Thunder: The Legendary Life of Davy Crockett.* Illustrated by James Daugherty. New York: Julian Messner, 1944.

Shenton, Edward. *An Alphabet of the Army.* Philadelphia: Macrae-Smith Company, 1943.

Sherwood, Robert E. *Abe Lincoln in Illinois.* New York: C. Scribner's Sons, 1939.

Singmaster, Elsie. *I Heard of a River: The Story of Germans in Pennsylvania.* Land of the Free Series. Philadelphia: John C. Winston Company, 1948.

Skinner, Constance Lindsay. *Adventurers of Oregon.* New Haven, CT: Yale University Press, 1920.

——. *Andy Breaks Trail.* New York: Macmillan, 1928.

——. *Beaver: Kings and Cabins.* New York: Macmillan, 1933.

——. *Becky Landers: Frontier Warrior.* New York: Macmillan, 1926.

——. *Debby Barnes: Trader.* New York: Macmillan, 1932.

——. *Pioneers of the Old Southwest.* New Haven, CT: Yale University Press, 1919.

——. *Ranch of the Golden Flowers.* New York: Macmillan, 1928.

——. *Rob Roy: The Frontier Twins.* New York: Macmillan, 1934.

——. *Silent Scot: Frontier Scout.* New York: Macmillan, 1925.

——. *The Tiger Who Walks Alone.* New York: Macmillan, 1927.

——. *The White Leader.* New York: Macmillan, 1926.

Snedeker, Caroline Dale. *The Town of the Fearless.* Garden City, NY: Doubleday, Doran, 1931.

Spalding, Charles, and Otis Carney. *Love at First Flight.* Boston: Houghton Mifflin, 1943.

Sperry, Armstrong. *Call It Courage.* New York: Macmillan, 1940.

——. *The Voyages of Christopher Columbus.* New York: Random House, 1950.

Steele, William O. *The Far Frontier.* New York: Harcourt Brace, 1959.

Sterling, Dorothy. *Freedom Train: The Story of Harriet Tubman.* Garden City, NY: Doubleday, 1954.

Sterne, Emma Gelders. *No Surrender.* New York: Dodd, Mead, 1932.

Stevens, Leonard A. *Old Peppersass: The Locomotive That Climbed Mount Washington.* New York: Dodd, Mead, 1959.

Stevens, William Oliver. *The Patriotic Thing; or, What It Means to Be an American.* New York: Dodd, Mead, 1940.

Stevenson, Augusta. *Abe Lincoln: Frontier Boy.* Indianapolis, IN: Bobbs-Merrill, 1932.

——. *Ben Franklin: Printer's Boy.* Indianapolis, IN: Bobbs-Merrill, 1941.

——. *Booker T. Washington: Ambitious Boy.* Indianapolis, IN: Bobbs-Merrill, 1950, 1960.

——. *Buffalo Bill: Boy of the Plains.* Indianapolis, IN: Bobbs-Merrill, 1948.

——. *Clara Barton: Girl Nurse.* Indianapolis, IN: Bobbs-Merrill, 1946.

——. *Daniel Boone: Boy Hunter.* Indianapolis, IN: Bobbs-Merrill, 1943.

——. *George Carver: Boy Scientist.* Indianapolis, IN: Bobbs-Merrill, 1944.

——. *George Washington: Boy Leader.* Indianapolis, IN: Bobbs-Merrill, 1942, 1953, 1959.

——. *Kit Carson: Boy Trapper.* Indianapolis, IN: Bobbs-Merrill, 1945.

——. *Molly Pitcher: Girl Patriot.* Indianapolis, IN: Bobbs-Merrill, 1952.

——. *Nancy Hanks: Kentucky Girl.* Indianapolis, IN: Bobbs-Merrill, 1954.

——. *Sitting Bull: Dakota Boy.* Indianapolis, IN: Bobbs-Merrill, 1956, 1960.

——. *U. S. Grant: Young Horseman.* Indianapolis, IN: Bobbs-Merrill, 1947.

——. *Virginia Dare: Mystery Girl.* Indianapolis, IN: Bobbs-Merrill, 1958.

Stolz, Mary. *To Tell Your Love.* New York: Harper, 1950.

Swift, Hildegarde. *North Star Shining: A Pictorial History of the American Negro.* New York: William Morrow, 1947.

Tarry, Ellen, and Marie Hall Ets. *My Dog Rinty.* New York: Viking Press, 1946.

Taylor, Sydney. *All-of-a-Kind Family.* New York: Macmillan, 1951.

Thomas, Lowell. *Stand Fast for Freedom.* Chicago: John C. Winston, 1940.

Thomas, Maude Morgan. *Sing in the Dark: A Story of the Welsh in Pennsylvania.* Land of the Free Series. Philadelphia: John C. Winston Company, 1954.

Thornton, Willis. *Almanac for Americans.* Illustrated by James Daugherty. New York: Greenberg, 1941.

Three Comedies by Shakespeare. Illustrated by James Daugherty. New York: Harcourt Brace, 1929.

Tresselt, Alvin. *White Snow, Bright Snow*. Illustrated by Roger Duvoisin. New York: Lothrop, Lee and Shepard, 1947.

Trumbull, Robert. *The Raft*. New York: Henry Holt, 1942.

Tunis, John. *All-American*. New York: Harcourt Brace, 1942.

Turner, Mina. *Town Meeting Means Me*. Boston: Houghton Mifflin, 1951.

Udry, Janice May. *The Moon Jumpers*. Illustrated by Maurice Sendak. New York: Harper and Brothers, 1959.

———. *A Tree Is Nice*. Illustrated by Marc Simont. New York: Harper and Row, 1956.

Undset, Sigrid. *Happy Times in Norway*. New York: A. A. Knopf, 1942.

Van Loon, Hendrik Willem. *The Story of Mankind*. New York: Boni and Liveright, 1921.

Van Loon, Hendrik Willem, and Grace Castagnetta. *The Songs America Sings*. New York: Simon and Schuster, 1939.

Van Riper, Guernsey, Jr. *Jim Thorpe: Indian Athlete*. Indianapolis, IN: Bobbs-Merrill, 1956.

Voyetekhov, Boris. *The Last Days of Sevastopol*. New York: A. A. Knopf, 1943.

Wagoner, Jean Brown. *Abigail Adams: A Girl of Colonial Days*. Indianapolis, IN: Bobbs-Merrill, 1949.

———. *Jane Addams: Little Lame Girl*. Indianapolis, IN: Bobbs-Merrill, 1944.

———. *Jessie Frémont: Girl of Capitol Hill*. Indianapolis, IN: Bobbs-Merrill, 1956.

———. *Julia Ward Howe: Girl of Old New York*. Indianapolis, IN: Bobbs-Merrill, 1945.

———. *Louisa Alcott: Girl of Old Boston*. Indianapolis, IN: Bobbs-Merrill, 1943.

———. *Martha Washington: Girl of Old Virginia*. Indianapolis, IN: Bobbs-Merrill, 1947.

Warner, Ann Spence. *Narcissa Whitman: Pioneer Girl*. Indianapolis, IN: Bobbs-Merrill, 1953.

Weil, Ann. *Betsy Ross: Girl of Old Philadelphia*. Indianapolis, IN: Bobbs-Merrill, 1954.

———. *Eleanor Roosevelt: Courageous Girl*. Indianapolis: Bobbs-Merrill, 1965.

Wheeler, Opal. *Sing for America*. New York: E. P. Dutton, 1944.

White, E. B. *Charlotte's Web*. New York: Harper and Brothers, 1952.

White, Eliza Orne. *Training Sylvia*. Boston: Houghton Mifflin, 1942.

White, Stewart Edward. *Daniel Boone: Wilderness Scout*. Illustrated by James Daugherty. New York: Doubleday, Page, 1922.

White, William. *They Were Expendable*. New York: Harcourt Brace, 1942.

Whitney, Elinor. *Try All Ports*. New York: Longmans, Green, 1931.

Whitney, Phyllis A. *Willow Hill*. New York: Reynal & Hitchcock, 1947.

Widdemer, Mabel Cleland. *Harriet Beecher Stowe: Connecticut Girl*. Indianapolis, IN: Bobbs-Merrill, 1962.

Wilder, Laura Ingalls. *By the Shores of Silver Lake*. New York: Harper and Row, 1939, 1953.

——. *Farmer Boy.* New York: Harper and Row, 1933, 1953.

——. *Little House in the Big Woods.* New York: Harper and Row, 1932, 1953.

——. *Little House on the Prairie.* New York: Harper and Row, 1935, 1953.

——. *Little Town on the Prairie.* New York: Harper and Row, 1941, 1953.

——. *The Long Winter.* New York: Harper and Row, 1940, 1953.

——. *On the Banks of Plum Creek.* New York: Harper and Row, 1937, 1953.

Wilkie, Katharine E. *Mary Todd Lincoln: Girl of the Bluegrass.* Indianapolis, IN: Bobbs-Merrill, 1954.

Wilkie, Wendell. *One World.* New York: Simon and Schuster, 1943.

Williams, Jay. *The Battle for the Atlantic.* New York: Random House, 1959.

Williams, Jeanne. *Mission in Mexico.* Englewood Cliffs, NJ: Prentice-Hall, 1959.

Williams, Oscar. *A Little Treasury of American Poetry.* New York: Scribner, 1952.

Wilson, Ellen. *Annie Oakley: Little Sure Shot.* Indianapolis, IN: Bobbs-Merrill, 1958.

——. *Ernie Pyle: Boy from Back Home.* Indianapolis, IN: Bobbs-Merrill, 1955, 1962.

Wilson, Hazel. *Herbert.* New York: Alfred A. Knopf, 1942.

——. *Herbert Again.* New York: Alfred A. Knopf, 1951.

——. *Herbert's Homework.* New York: Knopf, 1960.

——. *Herbert's Space Trip.* New York: Knopf, 1965.

——. *Herbert's Stilts.* New York: Knopf, 1972.

——. *More Fun with Herbert.* New York: Alfred A. Knopf, 1954.

Winter, William. *War Planes of All Nations.* New York: Thomas Y. Crowell, 1943.

Ziegler, Elsie Reif. *The Blowing Wand: A Story of Bohemian Glassmaking in Ohio.* Land of the Free Series. Philadelphia: John C. Winston Company, 1955.

CONTEMPORARY COMMENTARY

Adair, Douglass. "Parson Weems, Streamlined." *New York Times Book Review*, November 16, 1952, 4, 42.

Allee, Marjorie Hill. "Books Negro Children Like." *Horn Book* 14.2 (March–April 1938): 81–87.

"American Theme for Book Week." *Wilson Library Bulletin* 7.2 (October 1932): 116–17.

Anderson, John E. "Growth toward Independence." *Childhood Education* 16.7 (March 1940): 291.

Andrews, Siri. "Florence Crannell Means." *Horn Book* 22.1 (January–February 1946): 15–30.

Arbuthnot, May Hill. "Children's Reading during the War." *Childhood Education* 19.3 (November 1942): 125–29, 137.

———. Review of *The Long Winter. Childhood Education* 17.8 (April 1941): 379.

"As Others See Us." *Library Journal*, June 15, 1955, 1458.

Bain, Winifred E. "The Cradle of Democracy." *Childhood Education* 17.1 (September 1940): 2.

Baker, Augusta. "Reading for Democracy." *Wilson Library Quarterly* 18.2 (October 1943): 140–44.

Baker, Frank E. "Major Issues in the Education of Teachers." *Childhood Education* 14.9 (May 1938): 389–93.

Baldwin, Robert D. "Let's Stake Our Claim." *Journal of the National Education Association* 28.2 (February 1939): 38–39.

Beard, Sarah Allen. "Books and Freedom: A 1943 Selection of Books for Teens." *Library Journal*, October 15, 1943, 828–32.

Biber, Barbara. ". . . And You Call This a Free Country!" *Childhood Education* 20.1 (September 1943): 21–22.

Blos, Joan W. "Importance of the Cherry Tree." *Saturday Review*, February 20, 1960, 40–41.

Bomar, Cora Paul. "Preserving and Developing Our American Heritage through Our Children." *North Carolina Libraries* 10 (April 1952): 41–43.

Bonino, Louise. "The Landmark Story." *Publishers Weekly*, July 30, 1956, 460–63.

Bowman, James Cloyd. "American Folklore for Boys and Girls." *Top of the News* 6 (December 1949): 20–24.

Breed, Clara E. "Americans with the Wrong Ancestors." *Horn Book* 19.4 (July–August 1943): 253–61.

———. "Books That Build Better Racial Attitudes." *Horn Book* 21.1 (January–February 1945): 55–61.

Brett, George P. "The Macmillan Children's Book Department." *Horn Book* 4.3 (August 1928): 25–27.

Brink, Carol Ryrie. "Newbery Award Acceptance Speech." *Horn Book* 12.4 (July–August 1936): 248–50.

Broening, Angela M. "The Role of a Teacher of English in a Democracy." *English Journal* 30.9 (November 1941): 718–29.

Brown, Ralph A., and Marian R. Brown. "Biography in the Social Sciences: The Values of Biography." *Social Education* 18.2 (1954): 67–70.

———. "The Social Studies Teacher and American Biography." *Social Studies* 43.1 (January 1952): 10–20.

Buell, Ellen Lewis. "Reviewing Children's Books." *Wilson Library Bulletin* 28.2 (October 1953): 181–83.

———. Review of *Swimming Hole. New York Times Book Review*, March 4, 1951, 26.

Burns, Paul C., and Ruth Hines. "Virginia Lee Burton." *Elementary English* 44.4 (April 1967): 331–335.

Burton, Virginia Lee. "Making Picture Books." *Horn Book* 19.4 (July–August 1943): 228–32.

Butler, Helen L. "Children's Reading in Wartime." *Childhood Education* 20.6 (February 1944): 277–79.

Cady, Edwin H. "The Role of Literature for Young People Today." *English Journal* 44.5 (May 1955): 268–73.

Cardell, William. *The Happy Family.* 2nd ed. Philadelphia: T. T. Ash, 1828.

Carter, Nellie Page. "Pickaninny Pranks." *Horn Book* 11.1 (January–February 1935): 17–22.

Colby, Jean Poindexter. "The Series of Series in Children's Books." *Junior Reviewers* 9 (August 1951): 12.

Cook, Marion Belden. "Regional Literature Serves the School and Community." *Indian Librarian* 4 (March 1950): 128–31.

Courtis, S. A. "Of the Children, by the Children, for the Children." *Childhood Education* 14.3 (November 1937): 101–5.

Cross, E. A. "And Among These . . . : An Address to Teachers of English as America Faces a Crisis." *English Journal* 30.3 (March 1941): 186–95.

Dagliesh, Alice. "Improvement in Juvenile Books during the Last Ten Years." *Publishers Weekly,* October 25, 1930, 1970–73.

Daugherty, James. "Children's Books in a Democracy." *Horn Book* 16.4 (July–August 1940): 231–37.

——. "Homer Price." *Horn Book* 19.6 (November–December 1943): 425–26.

——. "Illustrating for Children." *Bulletin of the New York Public Library* 60.11–12 (November–December 1956): 569–72.

——. "A Letter to Leslie Brooke." *Horn Book* 17.3 (May–June 1941): 204–5.

D'Aulaire, Ingri, and Edgar Parin D'Aulaire. "Working Together on Books for Children." *Horn Book* 16.4 (July–August 1940): 247–55.

DeBoer, John J. "The Meaning of Democracy in America Today." *English Journal* 40.3 (March 1951): 149–53.

——. "A Program for Peace Education." *English Journal* 25.4 (April 1936): 286–92.

——. "Reading and the Social Scene." *Reading Teacher* 12.1 (October 1958): 10–13.

——. "The Technique of Teaching for Peace." *English Journal* 22.4 (April 1933): 325–26.

——. "They Shall Not Pass!" *English Journal* 24.9 (November 1935): 765–66.

——. "The Time for the Offensive Is Here!" *Elementary English Review* 21.3 (March 1944): 114–15.

De Bonis, Albert V. "Tolerance and Democracy: A Program for the English Class." *English Journal* 30.2 (February 1941): 123–30.

DeMeyer, John Everard. "Educating for Peace." *American Childhood* 15.5 (January 1930): 3.

De Salle, Albert. "Pictorial Pleasantries by James Daugherty." *Print Connoisseur* 9.4 (October 1929): 328–37.

Dobbins, Elsie T. "Children's Books in Many Dialects." *Publishers Weekly,* October 28, 1944, 1749–51.

Duff, Annis. "The Literary Heritage of Childhood." *Wilson Library Bulletin* 33.8 (April 1959): 563–70.

Eaton, Anne T. "Constance Skinner's Stories of America." *Horn Book* 15.4 (July–August 1939): 215–17.

———. Review of *Caddie Woodlawn*. *New York Times Book Review*, May 12, 1935, 10.

———. Review of *Little Town on the Prairie*. *New York Times Book Review*, December 28, 1941, 9.

Edmonds, Mary D. "Literature and Children." *North American Review* 244.1 (Autumn 1937): 148–61.

Egbert, Evelyn. "Consider the Negro." *Childhood Education* 13.2 (October 1936): 64–66.

Escuerdo, Maria J. "Exotic but Unfair." *Childhood Education* 28.3 (November 1951): 127–28.

Estorick, Eric. "Literature and Democracy." *Journal of Educational Sociology* 12.7 (March 1939): 425–34.

Evans, Jessie Campbell. "We the People." *Horn Book* 9.1 (February 1933): 34–39.

Fadiman, Clifton. "Party of One." *Holiday* 12.2 (August 1952): 6, 8–9.

Fenner, Phyllis. "New Books for Younger Readers." *New York Times Book Review*, August 11, 1946, 14.

Fenwick, Sara Innis. "Evaluating Mystery Stories for Children." *Elementary English* 25.8 (December 1948): 521–24.

Foster, Margaret Lesser. "Ingri and Edgar Parin D'Aulaire." *Catholic Library World* 41.6 (February 1970): 347–51.

Freeman, Rev. James. "Our Greatest Task." *Childhood Education* 12.5 (February 1936): 213–15.

Garvey, Leone. "Regional Stories." *Horn Book* 27.2 (March–April 1951): 123–30.

Goldstein, Fanny. "Reading for Democracy." *Wilson Library Bulletin* 18.6 (February 1944): 452–57, 463.

Gould, Kenneth M. "Young People's Literature Grows Up." *Horn Book* 15.6 (November–December 1939): 345–51.

Graham, Gladys Murphy. "Can Children Be Educated for Peace?" *Childhood Education* 12.2 (November 1935): 51–52.

Gray, Elizabeth Janet. "Young People and Books." *Horn Book* 17.6 (November–December 1941): 474–82.

Hanlon, Helen J., and Stanley Dimond. "What the Schools Can Do in Intercultural Education." *English Journal* 34.1 (January 1945): 32–38.

Hanna, Paul R. "Toward a World Community." *Childhood Education* 19.1 (September 1942): 3–4.

Harrington, Mildred. "Regionalism in Books for Children." *Wilson Library Bulletin* 25.5 (January 1951): 372–73.

Hartmann, George W. "The Teacher as Citizen." *Childhood Education* 15.1 (September 1938): 5–7.

Henne, Frances. "School Libraries and the Social Order." In "Current Trends in School Libraries," edited by Alice Lohrer, special issue, *Library Trends* 1.3 (January 1953): 263–70.

Heriot, Grace Miller. "Children and Biography." *Elementary English* 25.2 (February 1948): 98–102.

Herzberg, Max J. "Conflict and Progress." *Elementary English Review* 21.1 (January 1944): 1–5.

Hogarth, Grace Allen. "Virginia Lee Burton, Creative Artist." *Horn Book* 19.4 (July–August 1943): 221–27.

Hollowell, Lillian. "Series in Children's Books." *Wilson Library Bulletin* 27.9 (May 1953): 736–38.

Holsinger, M. Paul. "For Freedom and the American Way: Robert Sidney Bowen's World War II Heroes: Dave Dawson and Red Randall." *Newsboy* 32.2 (March–April 1994): 9–16.

Horwich, Frances R. "Young People Learn the Ways of Democracy." *Elementary English Review* 20.3 (March 1943): 98–102.

Hunn, Fannie C. "Books Are Legacies—Still Unclaimed?" *American Childhood* 39.3 (November 1953): 11.

Ickes, Harold L. "Speech for the National Education Association." *Childhood Education* 10.5 (February 1934): 261.

Ives, Vernon. "Children's Books and the War." *Publishers Weekly*, October 23, 1943, 1592–93.

Jack, Delta. "Guiding Children's Reading." *Wilson Library Bulletin* 33.5 (January 1959): 355–56, 358.

Jacobs, Leland B. "Children Need Literature." *Elementary English* 32.1 (January 1955): 12–16.

———. "Lois Lenski's Regional Literature." *Elementary English* 30.5 (May 1953): 261–66.

"James Henry Daugherty." In *Current Biography 1940*, edited by Maxine Block, 221–22. New York: H. W. Wilson, 1940.

Johnson, Elizabeth. "A Letter to Parents." *Childhood Education* 28.9 (May 1952): 421–24.

Johnson, Siddie Joe. "Discovering America in the Children's Room." *Library Journal*, February 1, 1941, 111–15.

Jones, Mary Alice. "Books Are Bridges." *Wilson Library Bulletin* 24.2 (October 1949): 154–57.

Jordan, Alice. "American Settings." *Horn Book* 7.4 (November 1931): 271–77.

———. "Christmas Booklist." *Horn Book* 17.6 (November–December 1941): 466.

———. Review of *Leif the Lucky*. *Horn Book* 17.6 (November–December 1941): 469.

———. Review of *These Happy Golden Years*. *Horn Book* 19.3 (May–June 1943): 174.

Kilpatrick, William H. "What Is Democracy?" *Childhood Education* 14.2 (October 1937): 51–52.

Kipp, Laurence J. "Report from Boston." *Library Journal*, November 1, 1952, 1843–46, 1887.

Kunitz, Stanley, and Howard Haycraft, eds. *The Junior Book of Authors*. 2nd ed., rev. New York: H. W. Wilson, 1951.

Lansdown, Brenda. "The Problem of Identification in Learning to Read." *Reading Teacher* 8.2 (December 1954): 113–15.

Lenski, Lois. "Creating Books." *Library Journal*, October 15, 1963, 109–12, 126.

———. *Journey into Childhood: The Autobiography of Lois Lenski*. Philadelphia: J. B. Lippincott, 1972.

———. "Let Us Give Them Books." *Childhood Education* 25.2 (October 1948): 76–81.

———. "My Purpose." In *Lois Lenski: An Appreciation*, edited by Charles M. Adams, 40–41. Durham: Friends of the Library of the Woman's College, University of North Carolina, 1963.

———. "Neglected Children—in America." *International Journal of Religious Education* 26.9 (May 1950): 4–5.

———. "Regional Children's Literature." *Wilson Library Bulletin* 21.4 (December 1946): 289–92.

———. "Seeing Others as Ourselves." *Horn Book* 22.4 (July–August 1946): 283–94.

Lerman, Leo. "Reading for Democracy." *Saturday Review of Literature*, July 18, 1942, 15–16.

"The Library's Bill of Rights." *American Library Association Bulletin*, October 15, 1939, P-60–P-61.

Lindquist, Jennie D. "A Tribute to Laura Ingalls Wilder." *Horn Book* 29.6 (December 1953): 411.

Long, Harriet G. "The American Scene in Recent Children's Books." *Wilson Library Bulletin* 15.2 (October 1940): 122–26.

MacCampbell, James C. "Virginia Lee Burton: Artist-Storyteller." *Elementary English* 33.1 (January 1956): 3–10.

Mackintosh, Helen. "Children's Interests in Literature and the Reading Program." *Reading Teacher* 10.3 (February 1957): 138–43.

MacLean, Malcolm S. "What About Our Negro Americans?" *Childhood Education* 18.8 (April 1942): 343–47.

Mahony, Bertha E. "The First Children's Book Department." *Horn Book* 4.3 (August 1928): 2–24.

———. "Integrity and Realism." *Horn Book* 19.5 (September–October 1943): 285.

———. "Other Children's Book Departments since 1918." *Horn Book* 4.3 (August 1928): 74–76.

———. "Seedbed for Heroes." *Horn Book* 18.2 (March–April 1942): 75.

———. "The World Republic of Childhood." *Horn Book* 19.4 (July–August 1943): 203.

Mahony, Bertha E., Louise Payson Latimer, and Beulah Tolmsbee. *Illustrators of Children's Books*. Boston: Horn Book, 1947.

Mahony, Bertha E., and Marguerite M. Mitchell. "Ingri and Edgar Parin D'Aulaire." *Horn Book* 16.4 (July–August 1940): 256–64.

Manley, Dorothy Shepard. "Improving Racial Attitudes through Children's Books." *Elementary English Review* 21.7 (November 1944): 267–69.

Markham, R. H. "A Common Ground." *Childhood Education* 18.2 (October 1941): 2.

Martin, Allie Beth. "Children's Books about Foreign Countries: Russia." *Elementary English* 26.4 (April 1949): 202–11.

Martin, Helen. "Nationalism in Children's Literature." *Library Quarterly* 6.4 (October 1936): 405–18.

Massee, May. "Ingri and Edgar Parin D'Aulaire: A Sketch." *Horn Book* 11.5 (September–October 1935): 265–70.

Mathews, Virginia H. "Some Notes and Suggestions for National Library Week." *Wilson Library Bulletin* 32.6 (February 1958): 409–11.

McCloskey, Robert. "Caldecott Award Acceptance." *Horn Book* 34.4 (August 1958): 245–51.

McCullough, Constance M. "Broadening Experiences through Reading in the Elementary School." *Elementary English Review* 23.3 (March 1946): 101–7.

Means, Florence Crannell. "Mosaic." *Horn Book* 16.1 (January 1940): 35–40.

Meeker, Oden, and Olivia Meeker. "For Boys Only." *Collier's*, November 24, 1945, 18, 57–58.

Melcher, Frederic G. "Editorial: To the New Generation." *Publishers Weekly*, August 26, 1944, 691.

Miller, Bertha Mahony. "Children's Books in America Today." *Horn Book* 12.4 (July–August 1936): 199–207.

———. Review of *As the Earth Turns*. *Horn Book* 9.2 (May 1933): 49.

Misner, Paul J. "Making Supervision Democratic." *Childhood Education* 14.3 (November 1937): 99–100.

Moore, Anne Carroll. *Roads to Childhood*. New York: George H. Doran, 1920.

———. "The Three Owls' Notebook." *Horn Book* 15.5 (September–October 1939): 293–95.

———. "The Three Owls' Notebook." *Horn Book* 17.6 (November–December 1941): 456–58.

———. "The Three Owls' Notebook." *Horn Book* 20.2 (March–April 1947): 97–99.

———. "The Three Owls' Notebook." *Horn Book* 25.3 (May–June 1949): 196–98.

Moore, Everett T. "Censorship—and Threats of Censorship." *California Librarian* 16 (July 1955): 226–28, 262.

Morrow, Elizabeth M. "Children's Books in a Wartime Year." *Retail Bookseller* 46.579 (August 1943): 65–67.

National Council of Teachers of English, Committee on International Relations. "Toward Better Human Relations." *English Journal* 39.1 (January 1950): 41; 39.4 (April 1950): 220; and 39.6 (June 1950): 342.

Newell, Ethel. "The Indian Stereotype Passes." *Elementary English* 31.8 (December 1954): 472–76.

Nolen, Eleanor Weakley. "The Colored Child in Contemporary Literature." *Horn Book* 18.5 (September–October 1942): 348–55.

North, Sterling. "A National Disgrace." *Childhood Education* 17.2 (October 1940): 56.

Olin, Ida. "Children's Books as a Bridge between Cultures." *Horn Book* 25.2 (March–April 1949): 150–58.

Parton, Ethel. "From Indiana to California behind Oxen." *Horn Book* 9.1 (February 1933): 17–19.

Pease, Howard. "Without Evasion." *Horn Book* 21.1 (January–February 1945): 9–17.

Pratt, Willis E. "'Going Places' in Reading." *Elementary English* 24.3 (March 1947): 151–62.

Preer, Bette Banner. "Guidance in Democratic Living through Juvenile Fiction." *Wilson Library Bulletin* 22.9 (May 1948): 679–81, 708.

Raymond, Margaret Thomsen. "Touchstones and Yardsticks for Teachers in a Democracy." *English Elementary Review* 20.4 (April 1943): 123–28.

Reeve, Margarette Willis. "The Habit of World Friendship." *Childhood Education* 9.3 (December 1932): 115–18.

Review of *By the Shores of Silver Lake*. *Horn Book* 16.1 (January–February 1940): 48–49.

Review of *By the Shores of Silver Lake*. *New Yorker*, November 25, 1939, 89.

Review of *Farmer Boy*. *New York Times Book Review*, November 26, 1933, 15.

Review of James Daugherty's *Daniel Boone*. *Horn Book* 16.1 (January–February 1940): 47.

Review of James Daugherty's *Marcus and Narcissa Whitman, Pioneers of Oregon*. *Horn Book* 19.5 (September–October 1953): 364–65.

Review of James Daugherty's *The Wild Wild West*. *Horn Book* 24.6 (November–December 1948): 465.

Review of *Little Town on the Prairie*. *New Yorker*, December 6, 1941, 143.

Review of *Little Town on the Prairie*. *Saturday Review of Literature*, December 6, 1941, 15.

Review of *The Long Winter*. *Horn Book* 17.1 (January–February 1941): 32.

Review of *On the Banks of Plum Creek*. *Horn Book* 13.6 (November–December 1937): 380–81.

Review of *The Songs America Sing*s. *New York Times Book Review*, December 17, 1939, 16.

Review of *Swimming Hole. Saturday Review of Literature*, April 21, 1951, 41.

Review of *These Happy Golden Years. New York Times Book Review*, April 4, 1943, 11.

Review of *These Happy Golden Years. Saturday Review of Literature*, September 25, 1943, 19–20.

Review of *Walt Whitman's America. Horn Book* 41.1 (January–February 1965): 62–63.

Reynolds, Kathryn L. "Defending America in the Children's Room: A Summer Reading Plan." *Library Journal*, April 15, 1941, 342–44.

Rider, Ione Morrison. "Arna Bontemps." *Horn Book* 15.1 (January–February 1939): 13–19.

Roberts, H. D. "Highways to Freedom." *English Journal* 19.4 (April 1930): 330–31.

Rogers, Paul P. "Soviet Education and American Democracy." *Journal of Teacher Education* 10.1 (March 1959): 60–64.

Rollins, Charlemae. "Children's Books on the Negro: To Help Build a Better World." *Elementary English Review* 20.6 (October 1943): 219–23.

——. "New Trends in Books about Negroes for Children and Young People." *Elementary English Review* 23.7 (November 1946): 287–89.

——. "Some Children's Books for One World." *Elementary English* 24.5 (May 1947): 286–88.

——. *We Build Together.* Chicago: National Council of Teachers of English, 1942.

Rue, Eloise. "Children's Reading and the War." *English Elementary Review* 20.6 (October 1943): 214–18.

"Sales of Juvenile Nonfiction Increase in the Bookstore." *Publishers Weekly*, October 25, 1952, 1774–76.

Sattley, Helen. "Are You Celebrating Russia Book Week? It's the Week of May 1–6." *Elementary English Review* 21.4 (April 1944): 126–29.

Sauer, Julia. "Making the World Safe for the Janey Larkins." *Library Journal*, December 15, 1941, 49–53.

Scherwitzky, Marjorie. "Children's Literature about Foreign Countries." *Wilson Library Bulletin* 32.2 (October 1957): 142–48.

Schofield, Edward T. "School Libraries in Wartime." *Wilson Library Bulletin* 17.3 (November 1942): 204–18.

Scoggin, Margaret C. "Young People in a World at War." *Horn Book* 19.6 (November–December 1943): 394–400.

Seaman, Louise. "Children's Books and the Depression." *Wilson Library Bulletin* 7.7 (March 1933): 413–17, 422.

Shapiro, Lee. "Atomic Bifocals." *Childhood Education* 23.9 (May 1947): 420–21.

Sheridan, Marion C. "The Role of the English Teacher in Wartime." *English Journal* 31.10 (December 1942): 726–29.

Shippen, Katherine B. "The Landmark Books." *Horn Book* 27.2 (March–April 1951): 95–99.

Smith, Dora V. "Through Children's Books, Regions of America Come Alive." *Childhood Education* 30.3 (November 1953): 131–38.

Smith, Irene. "Laura Ingalls Wilder and the Little House Books." *Horn Book* 19.5 (September–October 1943): 293–306.

Smith, Jean Gardiner. "On Choosing Books for Children." *Elementary English Review* 20.6 (October 1943): 209–13.

Smith, Lillian. "Today's Children and Tomorrow's World." *Childhood Education* 21.1 (September 1944): 4–5.

Stern, Celia M., and William Van Til. "Children's Literature and the Negro Stereotype." *Childhood Education* 21.6 (February 1945): 305–10.

Stewart, Jane. "Why Literature for Children and Youth?" *Reading Teacher* 9.3 (February 1956): 135–36.

Taylor, Elizabeth G. "Toward World Mindedness." *Childhood Education* 26.2 (October 1949): 60–64.

Taylor, Ethel R. "The Second Grade Illustrates Favorite Books." *American Childhood* 36.5 (January 1951): 16–17.

Taylor, Harry. "What Shall My Child Read?" *New Masses*, August 11, 1942, 22–24.

Taylor, Marie Nelson. "Facing the War with Our Young People." *Wilson Library Bulletin* 17.8 (April 1943): 656–58.

Tippett, James S. "Toward a More Democratic Citizenship." *Childhood Education* 14.2 (October 1937): 58–61.

Titzell, Josiah. "James Daugherty, American." *Publishers Weekly*, October 26, 1929, 2073–76.

Trabue, M. R. "The Language Arts in 1946." *Elementary English Review* 23.8 (December 1946): 335–43.

Turner, Floss Ann. "Unity through Children's Books." *Elementary English Review* 23.5 (May 1946): 189–92.

Tuttle, Florence Piper. "Fortifying the Child against Prejudice and Provincialism." *American Childhood* 39.8 (April 1954): 10–11.

——. Review of *Little House in the Big Woods*. *American Childhood* 40.6 (February 1955): 3, 61.

Van Dorn, Harold. "A Time of Crisis: Danger with Opportunity." *Childhood Education* 28.1 (September 1951): 8.

Van Evera, Jean. "They're Not What They Used to Be." *Parents' Magazine* 21.10 (October 1946): 28–29, 159–65.

Ward, Lynd. "The Book Artist: Yesterday and Tomorrow." *Horn Book* 20.3 (May–June 1944): 231–42.

——. "A Note on James Daugherty." *Horn Book* 16.4 (July–August 1940): 239–46.

Webb, Marian A. "Regionalism in Young People's Books." *Elementary English* 28.2 (February 1951): 76–81.

Wenzel, Evelyn. "Children's Literature and Personality Development." *Elementary English* 25.1 (January 1948): 12–31.

White, Katherine S. "Children's Books in Wartime." *New Yorker*, December 12, 1942, 105–16.

Wilder, Laura Ingalls. "My Work." In *A Little House Sampler: A Collection of Early Stories and Reminiscences*, edited by William Anderson, 174–80. Lincoln: University of Nebraska Press, 1988.

———. "Whom Will You Marry?" *McCall's* 49 (June 1919): 8, 62.

Willy, Dorothy E. "War or Peace?" *Childhood Education* 16.3 (November 1939): 100.

Wofford, Azile. "Standards for Choosing Books about Other Countries." *Elementary English* 24.7 (November 1947): 469–73, 494.

TEXTUAL CRITICISM

Abate, Michelle Ann. *Raising Your Kids Right: Children's Literature and American Political Convervatism.* New Brunswick, NJ: Rutgers University Press, 2010.

Adams, Charles M., ed. *Lois Lenski: An Appreciation.* Durham, NC: Friends of the Library of the Woman's College, University of North Carolina, 1963.

Agee, William C. *James Daugherty: Works from the Estate of the Artist.* New York: Salander-O'Reilly Galleries, 1988.

Anatol, Giselle Liza. "Langston Hughes and the Children's Literary Tradition." In *Montage of a Dream: The Art and Life of Langston Hughes*, edited by John Edgar Tidwell and Cheryl R. Ragar, 237–58. Columbia: University of Missouri Press, 2007.

Anderson, William, ed. *A Little House Sampler: A Collection of Early Stories and Reminiscences.* Lincoln: University of Nebraska Press, 1988.

Augst, Thomas. "American Libraries and Agencies of Culture." In "The Library as an Agency of Culture," edited by Thomas Augst and Wayne A. Wiegand, special issue, *American Studies* 42.3 (Fall 2001): 5–22.

Bader, Barbara. *American Picture Books from "Noah's Ark" to "The Beast Within."* New York: Macmillan, 1976.

———. "A Second Look: *The Little Family.*" *Horn Book* 61.2 (March–April 1985): 168–71.

Baxter, Kent. *The Modern Age: Turn-of-the-Century American Culture and the Invention of Adolescence.* Tuscaloosa: University of Alabama Press, 2008.

Benemann, William E. "Tears and Ivory Towers: California Libraries during the McCarthy Era." *American Libraries* 8 (June 1977): 305–8.

Berkhofer, Robert F., Jr. *The White Man's Indian: Images of the American Indian from Columbus to the Present.* New York: Alfred A. Knopf, 1978.

Bird, S. Elizabeth. "Constructing the Indian, 1830s–1990s." In *Dressing in Feathers: The Construction of the Indian in American Popular Culture*, edited by S. Elizabeth Bird, 1–12. New York: Westview Press, 1996.

Blasing, Mutlu Konuk. *The Art of Life: Studies in American Autobiographical Literature.* Austin: University of Texas Press, 1977.

Bosmajian, Hamida. "Vastness and Contraction of Space in *Little House on the Prairie*." *Children's Literature* 11 (1983): 49–63.

Cadden, Mike, ed. *Telling Children's Stories: Narrative Theory and Children's Literature*. Lincoln: University of Nebraska Press, 2010.

Campbell, Donna M. "'Wild Men' and Dissenting Voices: Narrative Disruption in *Little House on the Prairie*." *Great Plains Quarterly* 20 (2000): 111–22.

Carpenter, Cari M. *Seeing Red: Anger, Sentimentality, and American Indians*. Columbus: Ohio State University Press, 2008.

Casement, Rose. *Black History in the Pages of Children's Literature*. Lanham, MD: Scarecrow Press, 2008.

Clark, Beverly Lyon. *Kiddie Lit: The Cultural Construction of Children's Literature in America*. Baltimore, MD: Johns Hopkins University Press, 2003.

Cohoon, Lorinda B. *Serialized Citizenships: Periodicals, Books, and American Boys, 1840–1911*. Lanham, MD: Scarecrow Press, 2006.

Connelly, Mark. *The Hardy Boys Mysteries, 1917–1979: A Cultural and Literary History*. Jefferson, NC: McFarland, 2008.

Cook, Timothy E. "Democracy and Community in American Children's Literature." In *Political Mythology and Popular Fiction*, edited by Ernest J. Yanarella and Lee Sigelman, 39–59. Contributions in Political Science 197. New York: Greenwood Press, 1988.

Crago, Hugh. "Edgar Parin D'Aulaire" and "Ingri D'Aulaire." In *American Writers for Children, 1900–1960*, edited by John Cech, 102–10. Detroit: Gale Research, 1983.

Cornelius, Michael G., and Melanie E. Gregg, eds. *Nancy Drew and Her Sister Sleuths: Essays on the Fiction of Girl Detectives*. Jefferson, NC: McFarland, 2008.

Cummins, Jane. "Laura and the 'Lunatic Fringe': Gothic Encoding in Wilder's *These Happy Golden Years*." *Children's Literature Association Quarterly* 23.4 (Winter 1998–99): 187–94.

Dusinberre, Juliet. *Alice to the Lighthouse: Children's Books and Radical Experiments in Art*. New York: St. Martin's Press, 1987.

Dyson, Jon-Paul C. "Children's Books Go to War: Newbery and Caldecott Winners during World War II." In *To See the Wizard: Politics and the Literature of Childhood*, edited by Laurie Ousley, 200–218. Newcastle, UK: Cambridge Scholars Publishing, 2007.

Eddy, Jacalyn. *Bookwomen: Creating an Empire in Children's Book Publishing, 1919–1939*. Madison: University of Wisconsin Press, 2006.

Elbert, Monika ed. *Enterprising Youth: Social Values and Acculturation in Nineteenth-Century American Children's Literature*. New York: Routledge, 2008.

Elleman, Barbara. *Virginia Lee Burton: A Life in Art*. Boston: Houghton Mifflin, 2002.

———. "Virginia Lee Burton: An American Classic." *School Library Journal* 48.8 (August 2002): 48–51.

Erisman, Fred. *Laura Ingalls Wilder.* Boise State University Western Writers Series 112. Boise, ID: Boise State University Press, 1994.

———. "Regionalism in American Children's Literature." In *Society and Children's Literature*, edited by James H. Fraser, 53–75. Boston: David R. Godine, 1978.

Fisher, Margery. *Matters of Fact: Aspects of Non-fiction for Children.* New York: Thomas Y. Crowell, 1972.

Frey, Charles. "Laura and Pa: Family and Landscape in *Little House on the Prairie*." *Children's Literature Association Quarterly* 12.3 (Fall 1987): 125–28.

Galbraight, Mary. "What Must I Give Up to Grow Up? The Great War and Childhood Survival in Transatlantic Children's Books." *Lion and the Unicorn* 24.3 (2000): 337–59.

Goodenough, Elizabeth, and Andrea Immel, eds. *Under Fire: Childhood in the Shadow of War.* Detroit: Wayne State University Press, 2008.

Greenwald, Marilyn S. *The Secret of the Hardy Boys: Leslie McFarlane and the Stratemeyer Syndicate.* Athens: Ohio University Press, 2004.

Gubar, Marah. *Artful Dodgers: Reconceiving the Golden Age of Children's Literature.* New York: Oxford University Press, 2009.

Habegger, Alfred. *Gender, Fantasy and Realism in American Literature.* New York: Columbia University Press, 1982.

Hannabuss, Stuart, and Rita Marcella. *Biography and Children: A Study of Biography for Children and Childhood in Biography.* London: Library Association Publishing, 1993.

Heldrich, Philip. "'Going to Indian Territory': Attitudes toward Native Americans in *Little House on the Prairie*." *Great Plains Quarterly* 20 (2000): 99–109.

Huhndorf, Shari M. *Going Native: Indians in the American Cultural Imagination.* Ithaca, NY: Cornell University Press, 2001.

Jagusch, Sybille A., ed. *Stepping Away from Tradition: Children's Books of the Twenties and Thirties.* Washington, DC: Library of Congress, 1988.

James Daugherty: American Modernist Works on Paper from the New Deal Era. New York: Janet Marquesse Fine Arts, 1992.

Johnson, Diane. *Telling Tales: The Pedagogy and Promise of African American Literature for Youth.* New York: Greenwood, 1990.

Kent, Norman. "James Daugherty: Buckskin Illustrator." *American Artist* 9.3 (March 1945): 16–20.

Kidd, Kenneth B. *Making American Boys: Boyology and the Feral Tale.* Minneapolis: University of Minneapolis Press, 2004.

Kingman, Lee. "Virginia Lee Burton's Dynamic Sense of Design." *Horn Book* 46.5 (October 1970): 449–60.

Koplowitz, Bradford. "Lois Lenski and the Battle between Fact and Fiction." *Journal of Youth Services* 5.1 (Fall 1991): 96–103.

Latimer, Bettye I., et al. "'Bright April' and 'Abraham Lincoln' Reviewed."

In *Cultural Conformity in Books for Children: Further Readings in Racism,* 141–45. Metuchen, NJ: Scarecrow Press, 1977.

Lawton, Rebecca E. *James Daugherty's Mural Drawings from the 1930s.* Poughkeepsie, NY: Frances Lehman Loeb Art Center, 1998.

Lee, Anne Thompson. "'It's better farther on': Laura Ingalls Wilder and the Pioneer Spirit." *Lion and the Unicorn* 3.1 (Spring 1979): 74–88.

Lerer, Seth. *Children's Literature: A Reader's History, from Aesop to Harry Potter.* Chicago: University of Chicago Press, 2008.

Lesnik-Oberstein, Karín. "Childhood and Textuality: Culture, History, Literature." In *Childhood in Culture: Approaches to Childhood,* edited by Karín Lesnik-Oberstein, 1–29. New York: St. Martin's Press, 1998.

———. *Children's Literature: Criticism and the Fictional Child.* Oxford: Clarendon Press, 1994.

Levander, Caroline F. *Cradle of Liberty: Race, the Child, and National Belonging from Thomas Jefferson to W. E. B. Du Bois.* Durham, NC: Duke University Press, 2006.

Lora, Richard. "Education: Schools as Crucibles in American Education." In *Reshaping America: Society and Institution, 1945–1960,* edited by Robert H. Bremner and Gary W. Reichard, 223–60. Columbus: Ohio State University Press, 1982.

Lowe, Virginia. "'Stop! You Didn't Read Who Wrote It!': The Concept of the Author." *Children's Literature in Education* 22.2 (1991): 79–88.

MacCann, Donnarae, and Gloria Woodard, eds. *Cultural Conformity in Books for Children: Further Readings in Racism.* Metuchen, NJ: Scarecrow Press, 1977.

MacLeod, Anne Scott. *American Childhood: Essays on Children's Literature of the Nineteenth and Twentieth Centuries.* Athens: University of Georgia Press, 1994.

———. *A Moral Tale: Children's Fiction and American Culture, 1820–1860.* Hamden, CT: Archon Books, 1975.

Macleod, David I. *The Age of the Child: Children in America, 1890–1920.* New York: Twayne Publishers, 1998.

———. *Building Character in the American Boy: The Boy Scouts, YMCA, and Their Forerunners, 1870–1920.* Madison: University of Wisconsin Press, 1983.

Maher, Susan Naramore. "Laura Ingalls and Caddie Woodlawn: Daughters of a Border Space." *Lion and the Unicorn* 18.2 (1994): 130–42.

Manna, Anthony L. "Robert McCloskey's *Make Way for Ducklings*: The Art of Regional Storytelling." In *Touchstones: Reflections on the Best in Children's Literature,* vol. 3, *Picture Books,* edited by Perry Nodelman, 90–100. West Lafayette, IN: Children's Literature Association, 1989.

Marcus, Leonard S. "Life Drawings: Some Notes on Children's Picture Book Biographies." *Lion and the Unicorn* 4.1 (Summer 1980): 15–29.

———. *Minders of Make-Believe: Idealists, Entrepreneurs, and the Shaping of American Children's Literature*. Boston: Houghton Mifflin, 2008.

———. *75 Years of Children's Book Week Posters*. New York: Alfred A. Knopf, 1994.

Martin, Michelle H. "Arna Bontemps, Langston Hughes, and the Roots of African American Children's Literature." In *Embracing, Evaluating, and Examining African American Children's and Young Adult Literature*, edited by Wanda M. Brooks and Jonda C. McNair, 66–80. Lanham, MD: Scarecrow Press, 2008.

McGrath, Joan. "Keith Robertson." In *Twentieth-Century Children's Writers*, 4th ed., edited by Laura Standley Berger, 817–18. Detroit: St. James Press, 1995.

McNall, Sally Allen. "American Children's Literature, 1880–Present." In *American Childhood: A Research Guide and Historical Handbook*, edited by Joseph M. Hawes and N. Ray Hiner, 377–413. Westport, CT: Greenwood Press, 1985.

Mickenberg, Julia. "Civil Rights, History and the Left: Inventing the Juvenile Black Biography." *MELUS: Multi-ethnic Literature of the United States* 27.2 (Summer 2002): 65–93.

———. *Learning from the Left: Children's Literature, the Cold War, and Radical Politics in the United States*. New York: Oxford University Press, 2006.

Mickenberg, Julia, and Philip Nel, eds. *Tales for Little Rebels: A Collection of Radical Children's Literature*. New York: New York University Press, 2008.

Miller, Bertha Mahony, and Elinor Whitney Field, eds. *Caldecott Medal Books: 1938–1957*. Boston: Horn Book, 1957.

Miller, John E. "American Indians in the Fiction of Laura Ingalls Wilder." *South Dakota History* 30 (2000): 303–20.

———. *Becoming Laura Ingalls Wilder: The Woman behind the Legend*. Columbia: University of Missouri Press, 1998.

———. *Laura Ingalls Wilder's Little Town: Where History and Literature Meet*. Lawrence: University Press of Kansas, 1994.

Mintz, Steven. *Huck's Raft: A History of American Childhood*. Cambridge: Belknap Press of Harvard University Press, 2004.

———. *A Prison of Expectations: The Family in Victorian Culture*. New York: New York University Press, 1983.

Mintz, Steven, and Susan Kellogg. *Domestic Revolutions: A Social History of American Family Life*. New York: Free Press, 1988.

Mowder, Louise. "Domestication of Desire: Gender, Language, and Landscape in the Little House Books." *Children's Literature Association Quarterly* 17.1 (Spring 1992): 15–19.

Murray, Gail Schmunk. *American Children's Literature and the Construction of Childhood*. New York: Twayne, 1998.

Nichols, Charles H., ed. *Arna Bontemps–Langston Hughes Letters: 1925–1967*. New York: Dodd, Mead, 1980.

Nikolajeva, Maria. *Children's Literature Comes of Age: Toward a New Aesthetic*. New York: Garland Publishing, 1996.

——. *Power, Voice, and Subjectivity in Literature for Young Readers*. New York: Routledge, 2010.

O'Bar, Jack. "The Origins and History of the Bobbs-Merrill Company." *Occasional Papers: University of Illinois Graduate School of Library and Information Science* 172 (December 1985): 28–29.

Op de Beeck, Nathalie. *Suspended Animation: Children's Picture Books and the Fairy Tale of Modernity*. Minneapolis: University of Minneapolis Press, 2010.

Owens, Louis. "As if an Indian Were Really an Indian: Native American Voices and Postcolonial Theory." In *Native American Representations: First Encounters, Distorted Images, and Literary Appropriations*, edited by Gretchen M. Bataille, 11–24. Lincoln: University of Nebraska Press, 2001.

Rahn, Suzanne. *Rediscoveries in Children's Literature*. New York: Garland Publishing, 1995.

Ranta, Taimi M. "Lois Lenski." In *American Writers for Children, 1900–1960*, Dictionary of Literary Biography 22, edited by John Cech, 241–52. Detroit, MI: Bruccoli Clark, 1983.

Rehak, Melanie. *Girl Sleuth: Nancy Drew and the Women Who Created Her*. New York: Harcourt, 2005.

Robbins, Louise S. *Censorship and the American Library: The American Library Association's Response to Threats to Intellectual Freedom, 1939–1969*. Westport, CT: Greenwood Press, 1996.

Romines, Ann. *Constructing the Little House: Gender, Culture, and Laura Ingalls Wilder*. Amherst: University of Massachusetts Press, 1997.

——. "Preempting the Patriarch: The Problem of Pa's Stories in *Little House in the Big Woods*." *Children's Literature Association Quarterly* 20.1 (Spring 1995): 15–19.

Ross, Eulalie Steinmetz. *The Spirited Life: Bertha Mahony Miller and Children's Books*. Boston: Horn Book, 1973.

Russell, David. "The Pastoral Influence on American Children's Literature." *Lion and the Unicorn* 18 (1994): 121–29.

Sanders, Joe Sutcliff. *Disciplining Girls: Understanding the Origins of the Classic Orphan Girl Story*. Baltimore, MD: Johns Hopkins University Press, 2011.

Schmidt, Gary D. *Robert Lawson*. New York: Twayne Publishers, 1997.

——. *Robert McCloskey*. Boston: Twayne Publishers, 1990.

Schrader, Richard J., ed. *The Hoosier House: Bobbs-Merrill and Its Predecessors, 1850–1985: A Documentary Volume*. Dictionary of Literary Biography 291. Detroit: Bruccoli Clark Layman, 2004.

Schwebel, Sara L. *Child-Sized History: Fictions of the Past in U.S. Classrooms*. Nashville, TN: Vanderbilt University Press, 2011.

Segel, Elizabeth. "Laura Ingalls Wilder's America: An Unflinching Assessment." *Children's Literature in Education* 8.2 (Summer 1977): 63–70.

Shereikis, Richard. "How You Play the Game: The Novels of John R. Tunis." *Horn Book* 53.6 (December 1977): 642–48.

Simon, John J. "Leo Huberman: Radical Agitator, Socialist Teacher." *Monthly Review* 55.5 (October 2003): 28–31.

Smith, Katharine Capshaw. *Children's Literature of the Harlem Renaissance.* Bloomington: Indiana University Press, 2004.

———. "A Cross-Written Harlem Renaissance: Langston Hughes's *The Dream Keeper.*" In *The Oxford Handbook of Children's Literature*, edited by Julia L. Mickenberg and Lynne Vallone, 129–44. New York: Oxford University Press, 2011.

Smulders, Sharon. "'The Only Good Indian': History, Race, and Representation in Laura Ingalls Wilders' *Little House on the Prairie.*" *Children's Literature Association Quarterly* 27.4 (Winter 2002–3): 191–202.

Spaeth, Janet. *Laura Ingalls Wilder.* Boston: Twayne Publishers, 1987.

Stoneley, Peter. *Consumerism and American Girls' Literature, 1860–1940.* New York: Cambridge University Press, 2003.

Stott, Jon C. "Pastoralism and Escapism in Virginia Lee Burton's *The Little House.*" *North Dakota Quarterly* 49.1 (Winter 1981): 33–36.

Stott, Jon C., and Teresa Krier. "Virginia Lee Burton's *The Little House*: Technological Change and Fundamental Verities." In *Touchstones: Reflections on the Best in Children's Literature*, edited by Perry Nodelman, 3:28–37. West Lafayette, IN: Children's Literature Association, 1985.

Susina, Jan. "The Voices of the Prairie: The Use of Music in Laura Ingalls Wilder's *Little House on the Prairie.*" *Lion and the Unicorn* 16 (1992): 158–66.

Thompson, Melissa Kay. "A Sea of Good Intentions: Native Americans in Books for Children." *Lion and the Unicorn* 25 (2001): 353–74.

Tolson, Nancy. "Making Books Available: The Role of Early Libraries, Librarians, and Booksellers in the Promotion of African American Children's Literature." *African American Review* 32.1 (Spring 1998): 9–22.

Tuttle, William M., Jr. "America's Home Front Children in World War II." In *Children in Time and Place*, edited by Glen H. Elder, Jr., John Modell, and Ross D. Parke. New York: Cambridge University Press, 1993.

VanderGrift, Kay E. "A Feminist Perspective on Multicultural Children's Literature in the Middle Years of the Twentieth Century." *Library Trends* 41.3 (Winter 1993): 355–72.

Ward, Lynd. "A Note on James Daugherty." *Imprint: Oregon* 2.2 (Fall 1975): 3–5.

Whitaker, Muriel. "Perceiving Prairie Landscapes: The Young Person's View of a Western Frontier." *Children's Literature Association Quarterly* 8.4 (Winter 1983): 30–32.

Wilkins, Binnie Tate. *African and African American Images in Newbery Award Winning Titles.* Lanham, MD: Scarecrow Press, 2009.

Wilson, George P. "Lois Lenski's Use of Regional Speech." *North Carolina Folklore* 9 (1961): 1–3.

Wishy, Bernard. *The Child and the Republic: The Dawn of Modern American Child Nurture.* Philadelphia: University of Pennsylvania Press, 1968.

Wood, Meredith. "Footprints from the Past: Passing Racial Stereotypes in the Hardy Boys." In *Re/collecting Asian America: Essays in Cultural History*, edited by Josephine Lee, Imogene L. Lim, and Yuko Matsukawe, 238–54. Philadelphia: Temple University Press, 2002.

Xie, Shaobo. "Rethinking the Identity of Cultural Otherness: The Discourse of Difference as an Unfinished Project." In *Voices of the Other: Children's Literature and the Postcolonial Context*, edited by Roderick McGillis, 1–16. New York: Garland Publishing, 1999.